Bilingualism or Not: The Education of Minorities

Multilingual Matters

Please contact us for the latest information on recent and forthcoming books in the series.

Derrick Sharp, General Editor,
Multilingual Matters,
Bank House,
8a Hill Road
Clevedon, Avon BS21 7HH
England.

MULTILINGUAL MATTERS 7

Bilingualism or Not: The Education of Minorities

Tove Skutnabb-Kangas

Translated by Lars Malmberg
and David Crane

MULTILINGUAL
MATTERS LTD

British Library Cataloguing in Publication Data

Skutnabb-Kangas, Tove
  Bilingualism or not.–(Multilingual matters; 7)
  1. Bilingualism
  I. Title   II. Tvåspråkighet. *English*
  III. Series
  404'.2   P115

  ISBN 0-905028-18-X
  ISBN 0-905028-17-1 Pbk

Multilingual Matters Ltd,
Bank House, 8a Hill Road,
Clevedon, Avon BS21 7HH,
England.

First published under the title Tvåspråkighet.
Copyright © 1981 Tove Skutnabb-Kangas and LiberFörlag, Sweden.
Translated by Lars Malmberg and David Crane.

Production co-ordination and cover design by
MM Productions Ltd,
1 Brookside, Hertford,
Herts SG13 7LJ.

Typeset by Herts Typesetting Services, Hertford.

Printed and bound in Great Britain by
Robert Hartnoll Ltd., Bodmin, Cornwall

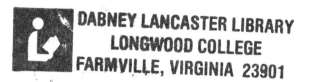
Contents

Preface

This book deals with the phenomenon of bilingualism from different angles. The literature on bilingualism outside Scandinavia is abundant. In several countries there are research and/or documentation centres wholly devoted to the study of bilingualism in some form ar another (for example, in Canada, France, the U.S.A., the Soviet Union). What one includes of all this wealth of material in a basic book on bilingualism will, of course, be determined largely by one's own personal attitudes. The way one treats the subject will be similarly determined. The list of contents describes in some detail what this book deals with, so I need not describe it here chapter by chapter. Instead, I shall say something about the principles underlying the book.

In certain areas our knowledge is secure and will not be changed by new research, only refined and elaborated. Other areas of research are newly developing, and what seems now to be the dominant view may well be proved wrong by future research. The relationship between bilingualism and the organization of the brain is a typical example of an area we know too little about. Many of the categorizations of bilingualism could just as well and as validly be formulated differently, they are thus neither "true" nor "false". It is clear that one's world view as a researcher influences the selection of material and interpretation of evidence. The only kind of objectivity one can aim for is to attempt to describe as openly as possible one's own position and the criteria one has adopted, instead of appearing to be neutral, and this I have tried to do.

The book may be said to develop in parallel fashion along three different lines. It proceeds from individual experience, general instances, description and systematization, to the more societally orientated phenomena, specific examples, and to understanding and explanation. At the beginning, I gather together the tools needed to understand and deal with the phenomenon of bilingualism: language in general, children in general, descriptions, definitions and systematizations. Towards the end I deal with specific countries and their different language policies, and try to reveal the network of causes beneath what is actually happening (and future prospects). There is, then, a development from empirical everyday concepts towards theoretical, scientific concepts.

The book has about it the marks of having been written over an extended period, not in a few days. Both the general development of the subject and my own personal development (or changes in evaluation) would now lead me to qualify what I have said in various ways.

- I would now think it important to emphasise even more strongly the societal conditions (political, economic, social, cultural) that determine bilingualism. The sections of the book I wrote last are less about language and more about what predetermines linguistic situations and what consequences flow from them for different groups.

- As to my way of writing, both the women's movement and the study of language and sex (which I see as a parallel to the study of bilingualism from the point of view of power relationships) have much affected me. The language of this book is not always as easy to read as it might be. This is particularly true of sections I wrote while still believing – a tiny bit – in the male doctrine that there is only *one* properly scientific way of writing. What I wrote later on contains more "soft data", interviews, poems, extracts from short stories, and so on. All of them may, better than more "hard data", convey to the reader, by the shock of recognition, insights arrived at by researchers. Similarly, I have used a number of images (speaking, for instance, of language bath (immersion), language drowning (submersion), language shelter, of language as being like water lilies, and so on). If the images are accurate, they will continue to grow in the readers' understanding, and they may then perhaps derive new insights from them. At their best the images may themselves convey understanding and empathy – and that is what we need, in addition to political change, if minorities and majorities are to be able to live together.

- But on the other hand I think I can see now fairly clearly the risks there are in drawing *too* sharp a distinction between a female, more personally interpretative (hermeneutic) way of approaching a problem, and other ways. Östen Dahl once pointed out to me the risks involved in "equations like these:

  male = patriarchal = capitalist = authoritarian = theoretical = BAD
  female = human = emotional = practical = socialist = GOOD"

However, it is still evident that polarization can lead to new and better syntheses. And that, too, is why (wo)man must be prepared to stand up for what is naive, emotional, irrational, which is an important part of us, rejected by the traditional male scientific ideal.

There are so many people I would like to thank, people who have introduced me both practically and theoretically to the luxury of combining work and friendship. I have learnt much from some of the pioneers in the study of bilingualism in Scandinavia and beyond – here I would like especially to thank Nils Erik Hansegård, Einar Haugen, Christina Bratt Paulston and Pertti Toukomaa. Very many members of minority groups and many minority organizations have given me insights both personal and theoretical into the strength of the ties that bind minorities together – I will mention only Mile Andric, Kristina Antoniadou, Harald Gaski, Mahmut Erdem, Sulo Huovinen, Antti Jalava, Lilja Liukka, Sunil Loona and Robert Petersen.

Some of my sources of inspiration – albeit that they are themselves members of majority groups – have been Jim Cummins, Hartmut Haberland (who has also made valuable comments on this book), Birgitte Rahbek Pedersen and Ulf Teleman. And the thousands of teachers, parents and children I have come into contact with who have convinced me that in spite of everything the effort of writing is worthwhile, too.

Skibby, in sunshine and May

Tove Skutnabb-Kangas

Translators' Note

In translating from the Swedish original we were particularly careful that the English version should be as idiomatic and as free from jargon or technicality as we could make it, so that the book would be the more easily intelligible to the general reader. Our translation, however, has been extensively adapted for the English edition by Derrick Sharp and Tove Skutnabb-Kangas, and very many modifications and additions have been made, for which we are not responsible. Some parts of the volume have not been translated by us at all, and we are conscious that in many places the style and idiom of our original version has been altered.

Lars Malmberg
David Crane

Introduction to the English edition

This book was originally published in Swedish, with a Scandinavian audience in mind. Both this and the two years between the two versions make some modifications necessary. These are of three main kinds. Some descriptions of research easily available in English have been cut if they are sufficiently well known and have been published and reviewed in many places and if the principles can be discussed without a description. For instance, Mackey's typology of bilingual education (section 6.2) and some projects about minority education (Chiapas Indians, Francophones in Manitoba, Navahos in Rock Point) are of this kind. Such Scandinavian descriptions as are of minor importance to outsiders and which would have required lengthy clarification for non-Scandinavians to make sense of have been omitted (while most of the Scandinavian examples have been retained even if the references to them are in Scandinavian languages or in Finnish). Some of the outdated parts have been replaced or omitted. I have also added a few subsections (for instance 5.2.4 and 6.5) where I have felt it necessary for the argument.

A few words about the Nordic school-system for a foreign reader. All children start school at the age of 7, which is fairly late from an international point of view. In Finland, Norway and Sweden there are state schools only (with very few exceptions), in Denmark also private schools but the state pays most of the expenses even in them. Children can leave school at 16 or after grade 9, but more than half of them continue some kind of education even after that. The length of the school day varies, and especially in the elementary school the hours spent in school are few (20–24 hours per week). Both schools and different organizations offer varied after-school activities. Summer holidays are long, especially in Finland, Norway and Sweden – we try to use the long hours of daylight. The standard of living in all Nordic countries as a group is higher than anywhere else in the world, and more homogeneously spread out.

The Nordic countries have a long joint history, with various patterns of colonization and domination where Sweden and Denmark have been the dominant countries. In order to understand the position of Finnish immigrants in Sweden it is important to know that Finland up to 1809 was part of Sweden (or colonized by Sweden, depending on whose language one talks), then until 1917 a Russian grand duchy and after that an independent republic. The attitudes of Swedes towards the Finnish mainly-working-class migrant population in Sweden may still partly reflect the joint history. There has been a free Nordic labour market since 1954, all Nordic citizens can freely settle and work in any Nordic country, and Nordic co-operation in most areas is more extensive than in other parts of the world (Nordic citizens don't, for instance, need passports in other Nordic countries). Finns are the largest immigrant group in Sweden (almost half of the immigrants come from Finland, even if some 20% of them are Swedish-speakers from the Swedish-speaking minority in Finland). Our position in Sweden can in many ways be compared to that of Chicanos in the U.S.A. or Afro-Caribbeans in Britain. In studies about the attitudes of Swedes towards different immigrant groups a decade ago (Trankell 1974) Finns and Greeks came lowest in the hierarchy (even if that may have changed somewhat now). This uniquely low position of Finns in Sweden (compared to our position as migrants in other countries, Australia, Canada, U.S.A., West Germany, etc.) is vital to remember when reading this book – otherwise the situation of Finnish children in Swedish schools may be impossible to interpret and some of the findings difficult to generalize.

A note about some of the terms used. Choice of words is also choice of perspective – mine is that of minorities and oppressed. But since that perspective is still poorly encoded in all languages, the process of naming our realities is only at the beginning, and therefore we are still using a lot of language that is not ours, often without being conscious of it. I try to use the names people use themselves about themselves and to avoid discrepancies between my words and my reality. Thus *Same*, not *Lappish*, *Inuit* not *Eskimo* or *Greenlander*, *Romanes* not *Gypsy*, etc. For migrant workers the *country of production* is not a *host country*, and calling, for instance, many Third World countries *underdeveloped* instead of *developing* brings out the agent (cf. Walter Rodney's book "How Europe underdeveloped Africa"), hopefully without romanticizing the past before colonialism. Saying *race* and meaning *colour* makes it impossible to discuss what is common in the experiences of many Finns in Sweden and Kurds from Turkey in Denmark or Chicanas and Mexicanas in California, considering that Finns are white, highly literate (we publish, buy and read more books per capita than any other country in the world most years), that Finland is highly industrialized, with a higher CNP *per capita* than for instance Britain, that the position of women is better than in most countries in the world (we were the first in Europe and second in the world to get the vote, we have more women in the parliament than other countries, women make up almost half of the work force and more than half of the university students), etc. We have to redefine racism, too. In the Swedish version of the book I made my own sex visible for instance by consistently using "she/he". When writing English I normally use s/he, but in adapting the English translation of this book we have agreed to let "woman embrace man" (as she of course does, both biologically and linguistically). I hope that the ambiguity men may feel when having to try to decide whether or not they are included when reading "she" gives them a feeling of how we women have been made to feel for centuries.

It is interesting to compare the discussion about the education of minority children in different parts of the world with our Nordic discussions. It seems to me that our discussions have been characterized by (1) a strong focus on language – probably because we Finns are the largest minority group in Scandinavia and differ from the Swedish majority mainly with regard to language (theirs is Nordic, Germanic, Indoeuropean, ours is Finno-Ugric), not so much culture, (2) few attempts at doing anything about multicultural, intercultural, multi-ethnic or anti-racist education, and almost no discussions about racism, and (3) strong participation by the minority groups themselves, well-organized and knowing what they/we want. I hope these characteristics, which are also reflected in my book, provoke a stimulating exchange of experiences. In one of my native cultures, the Finnish, all mythological fights are fought with words not arms, and we find some of the battles with swords in the Scandinavian mythology primitive and barbaric. I still believe in words as weapons. You cannot discuss with a missile – but a bilingual may be able to mediate between *both* parties *before*.

Skibby, February 1983, still sunshine, and snow and thousands of Eranthis (Winter Aconite)

T.S-K

1 Something about language

1.1 Tie and Tool

1.1.1 Language – a tie

If we are to talk about bilingualism, we must start by talking about monolingualism and LANGUAGE.

What does language mean to us? What do we use it for? What does it do for us? What would life be like without language? We shall start by thinking about this in quite concrete ways.

Let us try to consider the case of young children or of the deaf and dumb, who have no access to spoken language, in order to be able to imagine at least to some extent what it would be like to be wholly without language (we should note that the deaf and dumb person must also be unable to read and write, for reading and writing are of course forms of language).

Without language we would be very much confined to our own experience. Certainly we might be able to learn by looking at others, but if anything about their actions were unclear to us, we would not be able to ask for any explanation. Neither would we be able to ask for anything except by some such means as stretching out a hand and pointing. We should not be able to communicate with any other human being who was separated from us, whether simply by distance or in time. We should only be able to communicate with our neighbour by going to her house so that she could actually see us. Not even in the same room would we be able to say anything if the other person was not looking at us. There would be no question of speaking on the telephone: we would be obliged to go and see the person we wanted to communicate with. We would not be able to write letters. We would be able to know nothing of what people living before us had thought, since there would be no written record from the past. We would know nothing of the thought of an Aristotle, a Socrates, a Mohammed, or a Bhagavan Vjasa (rather as we know nothing now of the thought of all the great women of the past other than what emerges from the writings of men – for example, some part of what we consider to have been Socrates' thought was in fact the thought of a woman, Diotima of Mantineia). We would have to think out everything anew for ourselves without having any foundation to build on. Each and every one of us would have to re-invent things already discovered. We would not be able to communicate our emotions other than by bodily gesture: by caressing, striking, weeping, smiling, nodding. Language is what binds us together. With people living in our own time, and close enough to us to be seen or touched, language is certainly not the only means of communication, but with people far away, or even indeed simply next door, or with those who are dead, language comes to be our most important form of contact (here I disregard what is revealed by the physical objects left behind by people). Through language we receive the cultural heritage of the past, and by language we shape it anew, reworking, selecting, rejecting, recreating it together with other people. We use language, too, to pass on to a large extent this culture we have received to our own children and grandchildren, and to those of others. Language is what binds us to others, both in the historical perspective (vertically) and in the present (horizontally); the further we are removed from close physical contact with our immediate physical environment in time or space, the more exclusively dependent we are upon language to preserve between us and others any kind of tie.

1.1.2   Language – a tool

Language is a system of symbols by means of which the individual is able to describe both the external world, the reality which surrounds her, and her own internal world, her inner reality, as well as the relationship between these two. But language is not an impartial or neutral system of symbols. Such neutrality would only be possible for a system existing wholly independently of (wo)man. Language, however, is socially conditioned. Language derives its importance precisely from the fact that it is both learnt and used in association with other people. There is a dialectic relationship between language and reality (both internal and external reality): each influences the other. Language plays an important part in shaping reality, since it provides us with categories for conceptualizing it. But reality in its turn also moulds language, so that it corresponds to the need to express what people want to express. Language is in itself a world mediating between the individual and her external circumstances. By external circumstances I mean also the individual's inner world, which can be understood as that part of the "external" world which has moved within her (cf. Piaget, 1971; Vygotsky, 1973). This mediating world filters the signals which we are able to send out (or "in", to ourselves, in the process where we think in words), and it interprets the signals which come in to us from outside. As Ole Petter Opsand puts it (1976a, I):

> "Language has a function which goes far beyond the communication of verbal messages. The possession of language is prerequisite to cognitive

and conceptual development, and as a consequence to our constituting of reality which in its turn constitutes the starting point for our everyday praxis."

Language is our most important instrument for forming concepts. It is the tool the individual uses when she handles her surroundings, in order to be able to take the world to herself, to grasp it and comprehend it. The instrument must be well developed, both so that the greatest possible cognitive (intellectual) growth can take place (Cummins, 1976b, 1978a), and also to make possible the analysis of self, and of the outside world, and of the relationship between the two. Thus we need language in order to achieve the degree of awareness which will make possible the changing of reality, of that upon which the instrument of analysis focuses.

At the same time as language is our most important instrument of analysis, it is also constantly coloured and influenced by that which is to be analysed. Language is a bearer and mediator of the attitudes and values to be found in the reality (external and internal) which it has as its function to describe. Language mirrors the power structures in society at the same time as it contributes to the reproducing and perpetuating of these structures.[1] And it is above all to enable us to intervene in the process by which existing power structures are reproduced that we need knowledge about language. We must be able to analyse and master language in order not to be mastered by it (Teleman, 1979). We must have the right, both as individuals and as members of society, to define ourselves, both in relation to ourselves and to the surrounding world. We must be allowed to become an "I", an "ego", active conscious subjects, rather than being the "other", the "one acted upon", unaware objects of other people's actions.[2] Language is thus the absolutely necessary prerequisite which enables us on the one hand to become aware of the lack of agreement between our own definition of reality (of which we ourselves form a part) and other people's definition of the same reality (and so of us who form part also of their reality), and on the other hand as a consequence to try for an accommodation between these different definitions, to try to change reality.

1.2 All languages are valid for everything

Considered as tools with which to handle the world, all languages are of equal worth. Every language spoken by a group of people as a mother tongue is sufficiently developed also to be able to function as a medium of instruction. From a linguistic point of view, it is not possible to describe one language (for example, Spanish or Swedish) as "better" or "more developed" than another (for example, Guaraní or Same) – in that respect all languages are equal. Linguists have not yet been able to find a speech community with a mother tongue which could be described as conceptually or logically primitive, inadequate or deficient, according to William Labov

(1972b: 17). All languages are complex systems of rule-governed behaviour which can be analysed and described – no languages are unsystematic or irrational, according to Charles A. Ferguson (1977: 44). Nor can the structure of any language be said to represent an earlier or later stage in the evolution of human language (Fromkin & Rodman, 1974; Bolinger, 1975). Edward Sapir says (1921: 22):

> "There is no more striking general fact about language than its universality. One may argue as to whether a particular tribe engages in activities that are worthy of the name of religion or of art, but we know of no people that is not possessed of a fully developed language. The lowliest South African Bushman speaks in the forms of a rich symbolic system that is in essence perfectly comparable to the speech of the cultivated Frenchman."

Of course it must be admitted that there are differences between languages in the degree of development of a standard written norm or the elaboration of a terminology appropriate for a post-industrial society.[3] But these are technical matters, easily solved when expertise and money are available. To talk about "primitive languages" is thus completely misleading.

In addition to the fact that there are many other features common to all languages, they should all *in principle* be equally capable of functioning as instruments for cognition and communication. But we know, of course, that not all languages are equivalently used as means of communication. Kurdish should in principle be as good as Danish or Turkish when Kurdish children in Denmark are taught in school, but even so these children are taught their academic subjects through the medium of Danish, and practice in their mother tongue as school subject is practice in Turkish – the Kurdish language does not feature at school at all. This is *not* due to the fact that it would not be as good a linguistic instrument as the other two (and for Kurdish children, of course, a better instrument). Finnish is in every way as good an instrument for the expression of scientific thought as English – but even so I, for example, have to read and write considerably more in English than in Finnish in my work. More and more in the brotherhood of multinational companies business letters are tending to be written in English, even though, for instance, the Japanese language would be capable of a more subtle politeness – these are a few very dissimilar and ideologically unclear examples. The fact that in principle every language is as good as every other is thus not reflected in the pattern of use – power relations decide. One of the questions one has reason to ask oneself again as a consequence of the very dominant influence of a few "great" "world languages" is the old and much disputed one: Whose thoughts are we really thinking when we are compelled to speak a particular language?

1.3   Language and world view

The question of linguistic relativity, of the extent to which our mother tongue determines our world view, has been long debated, but it became the subject of fresh debate after some anthropologically orientated linguists (for example, Franz Boas and Edward Sapir) took up the question in connection with their work on the American Indian languages. The hypothesis of linguistic relativity has taken its name from Benjamin Lee Whorf (the Whorf hypothesis, or the Sapir-Whorf hypothesis). The "strong form" of the hypothesis was formulated by Whorf himself:

"The forms of a person's thoughts are controlled by inexorable laws or patterns of which he is unconscious. These patterns are the unperceived intricate systematizations of his own language. . . . His thinking itself is in a language. . . . And every language is a vast pattern-system, different from others, in which are culturally ordained the forms and categories by which the personality not only communicates, but also analyzes nature, notices or neglects types of relationships and phenomena, channels his reasoning, and builds the house of his consciousness." (Whorf, 1956: 252)

According to the strong hypothesis, we are more or less the slaves of our mother tongue in our thinking and our way of comprehending the world. However, a weaker form of the same hypothesis can be accepted, and we shall try to see what that might mean.

It is sometimes difficult for monolinguals to see that the particular way *their* mother tongue uses to describe and classify an extremely various and multiform reality is only *one* of many possible ways. It is often not until one begins to learn other languages and to lose one's "monolingual naivety" that one begins to realise how relative and arbitrary is the way in which one's own language describes the world. To some extent the structure of our mother tongue "selects" for us what it is necessary and less necessary for us to notice. On occasion different languages focus the attention differently. There are, for example, distinctions necessary in some languages but optional in others. Similarly, there are differences between languages in the stage at which distinctions are made, the means employed to make them, and the level at which they are made (for example, distinctions may be made morphologically, by means of endings, or lexically, by means of special words).

Some examples: both Finnish and Swedish as a rule have number distinction in the noun (we must know whether there is one or more than one of something). In Swedish the verb does not distinguish number (the verb itself will not tell you whether it is one person or many performing an action) while the verb does distinguish number in Finnish (where the verbs have endings both in the singular and plural). Both Finnish and Swedish distinguish tense: we have to mark the tense (or aspect) of a verb in every finite unreduced clause. But there are languages where this is not necessary, for example Vietnamese or certain West African languages (Hammarberg & Viberg, 1977: 21–23). Information about the time at which an event occurred may be added in these languages but does not have to be.

However, examples of this kind tell us nothing about the way in which language itself influences our thought, and we know very little about this. The fact that our language "compels" us to make a certain distinction need not necessarily mean that we are better at making such a distinction than other people whose language does not so "compel" them. Nor does it mean that people whose language does not "compel" them to make a certain distinction would not be able to do so if necessary. In Navaho the shape of an object has to be marked by adding an affix to the verb. This means, as a consequence, that all Navaho children, at a very early stage, already have to notice shape. Navaho children whose dominant language was Navaho and not English, when tested, used shape as a criterion of classification much more often than English-dominant Navaho children. But when these children were compared with different groups of English-speaking children (black children from Harlem and white middle-class children), it was found that white middle-class children used shape as a criterion of classification as often as the Navaho-dominant children (Osgood, 1966: 319). This was probably due to the fact that middle-class children, too, are trained to look at shapes. Finnish, in contrast to many other languages, has no gender, and there is, for example, only one personal pronoun in the third person singular (*hän*, which corresponds to both *she* and *he* in English), so that we Finns can talk about a person and use this pronoun for hours without having to decide to indicate whether the person is female or male. This fact, of course, does not mean that Finns are any less able to see the difference between female and male, or that we understand the world, in sexual terms, in a more egalitarian way.

How linguistic phenomena of the kind we have been describing arise is something we cannot explain – the causes are unknown. By contrast, it is easier to see the cultural reasons for at least some of the lexical differences between languages, if by no means all. Certain "lexical fields" (Ullman, 1966: 250) or "semantic fields" (Bierwisch, 1970: 170), for example the colour system, are difficult to relate to the social reality in which the users of a language live (for we can assume that most colours actually exist in most cultures). Other lexical or semantic fields, however, the terminology of kinship for example, are more readily understandable, since they are the carriers of the system of social relationships which the language users have developed. We do not know, for example, why Navaho has two words for black (one for black as darkness, the other for the colour black in objects like coal), but only one word for our "grey" and "brown" together, and similarly a common word for our "blue" and "green" (Berlin & Kay, 1969; Ullman, 1966: 251). All the same, we know that a Navaho actually sees the difference between green and blue, between forest and lake, just as well as we who have different words for the two colours. But even so, the degree to which we are bound to the classification system of our own language is great, as is shown by the many examples of misunderstanding described by ethnolinguists. A Norwegian research group investigating the situation of Pakistani immigrants reports on immigrants branded by the police as liars for insisting that someone is their brother or uncle in the absence of any blood relationship – and both the policeman and the immigrant are, of course, right in terms of the kinship classification used in their respective languages (Swetland, 1979). The many words used by Arabs for camels, and the many words for snow and ice used by Inuits are well-known examples of culturally bound vocabulary.

It is easy to see that we have words for phenomena which are important in our culture. It is often vitally important for Inuits or Indians to see the difference between snow and ice which will and will not bear their weight. But to have particular words which oblige one to pay attention to certain similarities and differences will also in its turn perhaps help one to learn to make those distinctions, to be alert to them, to remember them. We do not necessarily, however, verbalise these distinctions just because our language happens to have words for them – and we find ways (by circumlocution or inventing new words) of describing phenomena which are important to us, even if our language does not provide the words for them, or if we do not know the words.

A few examples: a Finnish immigrant child in Gothenburg who draws "fish" like this⬚ can, of course, see (or learn to see) the difference between a pike and a flounder, if someone were to show her these two kinds of fish. But if the child's only contact with fish has been with the frozen variety in packets, then she will not have learnt the words for them in spite of the fact that the words exist in her language. The speaker on the radio in Stockholm who one beautiful autumn morning commented on the attractive red and yellow colours in "those trees, you know, which have the big leaves that look like a spread-out hand" (i.e. the maple) probably could see the difference between maple, birch and spruce, but had never needed to use the words.

The world around us is made up of millions of details, and when we look at it, we "see" only some of them, the ones which contain meaning for us. And our language, its structure, vocabulary and what of it we have learned, participates in choosing which details we "see". We can literally say that each of us "sees" different things when we look at the same scene. A couple of examples of this, too:

We can think of what we get out of the world if we think of it as a fishing net: we throw out our net, haul it back in, and see what we've got. If our net has a really fine mesh we get more in, if it has a large mesh, a lot of fish (=details) escape. When we are interested in something, we learn a lot of details about that part of the world, that particular area. At the same time as we learn about details and their relationship to each other, we also learn names, words, both for specific details and for different combinations of those details. My first example is about the engine in my car. There is something wrong, and I take it to the garage, where a car mechanic looks at it. We make an experiment. Both of us are allowed the same time, a couple of minutes, to look at it. Then we have partly to describe it and partly to draw a picture of it. I know nothing about engines, and every time I have to tell somebody where the engine is in my car (back or front), I have to think in which end I put petrol – so the engine must be in the other end. The result is that my description is ridiculous, because I don't know the words (and I wouldn't, for instance, be able to see what was wrong, even if half the engine had fallen out, because I don't know what to expect to see), while the car mechanic may be able to tell what is wrong in just a couple of minutes, and will certainly be able to describe it well. The same is true with the drawings. My drawing, regardless of a certain training in observing and remembering details, is very bad, and the relations between different parts may be completely wrong. Physiologically the two of us have seen the same thing, but I haven't been able to "see" a lot of what I saw, because it doesn't make any sense to me. Learning names for details also means that you learn to attach meaning and function to those details, and knowing both the name and the function makes it easier to remember (and to describe or draw) the details, in relation to each other.

The car mechanic might say or at least think that I'm stupid and ignorant, or she might think that she of course has special knowledge that everybody cannot be expected to have: her training has produced for her a finely meshed net for that part of the reality of the world we describe as car engines; and so for each of us with our respective specialities. The relativity of shared knowledge shows often very vividly in multidisciplinary areas, where we can discuss a lot with somebody in our area, until this somebody asks "who is that?" about one of our gurus who for us is absolutely central in the field. When I have discussed paradigms in bilingual education research for a couple of days with American researchers and then get "who is that?" about Kuhn or Habermas (and that has happened), it is not only those two words (or even the content of some of their writings) that my colleagues and I don't share, but everything that has led to their thought, new ways of looking at things. The important questions arising are then not only the questions about who controls whose access to what knowledge, but especially the questions about who defines what knowledge and words we need to have in order not to be labelled as stupid or as having a poor vocabulary. Do I have a poor vocabulary when I have one single word, "jeans", for the garments for which my daughters have at least 20 words (some of them names of trade marks)? Do I need to care, when I cannot see and remember all the details about "jeans" which they "see" when we walk down the main shopping street in Copenhagen looking at what people wear, on our way to buy jeans for them. They "see" all the details (how many pockets, how they are placed, what kind of seams and waistband, flared or not) and remember them, because, in the process of finding the name for a specific combination of all those details they have "organized" that part of the world at a higher level of abstraction than I have. They have an over-riding concept, and once they have chosen that, they need to remember only one thing (the name of that concept) because they already know what it implies, while I have to remember every single detail separately (and fail) because I don't have any general name for exactly that combination of details. When we walk along Strøget, they thus "see" more of what all of us see – and language "decides", chooses what is easy (for them) or more difficult (for me) to "see" and to remember.

In all these cases it has been a question of access to words and access to experiences that these words stand for. But even if we get access to them, "language" still influences what we "see", through the perspective and value judgements words "have". Some examples:

■ If language were not discriminatory in its reference to woman and man, then the substitution of the word "man" for the word "woman" and vice versa in various expressions and idioms would change nothing except that we knew that the person referred to now is the other sex. The emotions evoked by the expression would not change. But this is not true for the majority of expressions. We ask "the man in the street" when we want to know what the ordinary person thinks, but "the woman in the street" is asked a different kind of question by some men. Do we wish to "die like a man" or "die like a woman"? Would Strindberg's life have been different if he had been *The Son of the Tjänsteman* (in Swedish, literally "service" + "man" = civil servant) rather than *The Son of the Tjänstekvinna* (= serving girl)? Why do people sometimes come up to me and say that I drive "like a man", whereas none would tell Björn Borg that he plays tennis "like a woman"? The perspective that "language favours" is the male: "men have reserved many of the positive and neutral words for themselves, for their own activities and characteristics" (Skutnabb-Kangas, 1978a: 30.3; 1978). "When the word 'man' is replaced by 'woman', the meaning often becomes negative: the connotations are of inferior status, diminished prestige, weakness, stupidity, banality, ridicule, triviality, sexual thoughts. This clearly mirrors woman's place in society" (Rekdal & Skutnabb-Kangas, 1979; Skutnabb-Kangas, 1978a: 23.2).

■ A few more words about the political perspective. What happened in Finland in 1917–18 can be called by many names, each one of which at the same time embodies a political evaluation of what happened, somebody's perspective upon it: civil disturbance, war of independence, class war, war between brothers, war of liberation. If I refer to what happened as a "war of liberation", I can immediately be classified as right wing; if I refer to it as a "class war", I am classified as left wing; if I refer to it as a "war of independence", I fall somewhere in the middle, with nationalist overtones, etc. At home each of us learns uncritically, unreflectively and naively only *one* word for each single phenomenon, and we take this word as the proper NAME for this phenomenon, as unreflectively as we accept that the "sun" is

called "sun" and not "horse" or "moon". To begin with we are quite
unaware in most cases that together with the words we also learn a way of
looking at the phenomena (Skutnabb-Kangas, 1978a: 9.2; 1978c).

The interplay between our language and our world view is difficult to
investigate but interesting. In recent years research has particularly
concentrated upon the value judgements that certain words and forms of
expression reflect, whose perspectives they reveal, whose interests they
serve. Language as an instrument of power and control is beginning to
attract ever increasing interest.

Here is an example of this as well:

The Magic of Words
In the old days the word was power
The wolf was not called "wolf" but "grey leg"
Satan was not called "Satan" but "the Evil One"
They paraphrased
and so avoided the danger
The magic of words helped people
to rule over their environment

Even these days the word is power
Even today the magic of words helps people
to rule their environment
And few of the ruled dare call the wolf
"wolf"
and Satan "Satan"

Listen carefully, but do not listen to the words!
Words are betrayed and betraying
They do not describe reality
They paraphrase

Are the "visually handicapped" less blind than before?
Has a "mental hospital" a different function from a madhouse?
Is an "internee" not still a prisoner?
Listen carefully, but do not listen to the words!

Employers call themselves "givers of work"
But still it is you who give your work to them
Some defend "freedom"
But in its name they are still prepared
to restrict the freedom of others
Some speak about our "legacy of justice"
But they only mean
our legacy of injustice
Listen carefully, but do not listen to the words!

To kill a "person" feels difficult
To kill an "enemy" already feels less difficult
To kill a "yellow monkey" begins to feel peculiarly easy
But biologically it is still the same creature
who dies
Listen carefully, but do not listen to the words!

Before the ruled can rule their own lives
they must rule the words
by which their lives are ruled
Only when we call the wolf "wolf"
and Satan "Satan"
can we take up the struggle

(Bengt Ahlfors: *Sånger – dikter* 1971, translation by Tove
Skutnabb-Kangas & Robert Phillipson)

Notes to Chapter One

1. See, for example, Londen & Skutnabb-Kangas, 1976a; Hanssen, 1979a;
   Ryen, 1976a, 1976b; Thorne & Henley, 1975; Israel, 1973; Dittmar,
   1974; Blakar, 1973; Mey, 1981; Spender, 1980.
2. See, for example, Rekdal, 1975b, 1977; Freire, 1972, 1974;
   Skutnabb-Kangas & Rekdal, 1977a, 1979; Skutnabb-Kangas & Rekdal,
   1978.
3. See, for example, Bull, 1955; Ferguson, 1968, 1977; Jernudd, 1976,
   1979; Jernudd & Das Gupta, 1971; Language Planning Newsletter,
   1975; Linell, 1978.

2　What is a mother tongue?

2.1　Definitions of a mother tongue

2.1.1.　Why is it important to define the mother tongue?

Most people in the world have no difficulty in determining what their mother tongue is, and so few people probably ever think about what criteria they use when they say of some language that it is their mother tongue. For many people, therefore, to begin to think about these criteria may seem overly theoretical, academic, hair-splitting. But even in Scandinavia this question is being discussed more and more. There are two particularly important reasons for this. Ethnic groups are often defined as belonging to a linguistic minority on the basis of their mother tongue, in particular groups not distinguishable from the majority by anything much more than by their language. The rights of linguistic minorities and society's obligation to make linguistic provision for them, for example in providing education through the medium of a minority language, are linked to the mother tongue.[1] It is symptomatic that a large proportion of the demands made by quite diverse types of minority movement (third, fourth and fifth worlds, oppressed majorities in the underdeveloped countries, migrant labour, the indigenous peoples' common front) have their origin in or aim at recognition of the mother tongue and its importance in the process of consciousness raising and integration.[2] The mother tongue has great symbolic value.

Equally symptomatic are the majority society's attempts by various means to prevent minorities from presenting these demands. The means used may be, for example, the employing of a term to describe the mother tongues of minorities different from that used to refer to the mother tongue of the majority, with the negative connotations of such a term trying to diminish the importance of minority mother tongues (for example, to refer to "training in the home language" instead of "instruction in the mother tongue" as in Sweden (see Förslag om åtgärder . . . 1975). One method is also to exclude questions about mother tongues from census forms, in spite of pressure from the minorities, and then to refer to the lack of statistical information about the size of these minority groups when they make demands based on mother tongue maintenance. Another method is to suggest that certain languages, in particular those that have no standard written form, are too "primitive", not "civilised" enough, to be used as languages of instruction or as bearers of a modern culture, and even to maintain that the use of these languages hinders the intellectual development of children (see, for example, Oestreicher (1974: 9), and as a protest at such notions, for example, Labov (1972b)).

It is sometimes maintained, too, that the kind of things that can be spoken about in minority languages, things that minority speakers handle more skilfully than majority speakers, are to do with intuition and emotions, and that it is the majorities, above all the white Anglo-Saxons, who are able to teach rational thinking, theoretically constructed and scientifically verified argument (Northrop (1946), quoted without dissent in Andersson (1977: 214–15) – a quotation which for me shows the close connection between the oppression of minorities and the oppression of women: the means used are more alike than one might at first notice . . .). There is the argument, too, that the minority languages are not analytical enough, and therefore "like other savage tongues hinder intellectual development" (Binstead (1931), about the Maori language on the Cook Islands, quoted in Benton (1978: 139)). There is also the suggestion that the culture bound up with the minority languages is not in reality a culture at all (for example, Ekstrand, 1979a).

The second reason why the question of the mother tongue is becoming more and more topical is the growing concern for the education of minority children. Many teachers and parents have to face the problem of making a choice about language of instruction with children at the nursery school stage or at the beginning of schooling proper, and sometimes they will need help to decide which is a child's mother tongue where a child speaks two languages (or a little of both, as is often the case). Sometimes there are also discussions about the child's entitlement to language instruction, in particular in cases where the child is adopted and has a mother tongue other than that of the Scandinavian parents, or in cases where the immigrant parents have switched to the majority language for use at home, but still wish their children to be given the opportunity of instruction in the language of their home country. Unfortunately, even nowadays, one finds people, researchers as well, discreetly suggesting that the majority language should perhaps after all be regarded as the mother tongue of such minority children. . . . In my view, such a suggestion can only be informed by monolingual naivety, and it reveals a total incomprehension of the importance for the individual of the mother tongue.

2.1.2 Popular criteria

Criteria used popularly to define the mother tongue are that it is:

- the language one thinks in;
- the language one dreams in;
- the language one counts in.

It is assumed that all these functions are of the kind that one only learns in one's primary language, and continues to perform in that language (for example, Rabel-Heymann, 1978: 222), even though later on other languages may become as important or more important to one. But all these are relatively poor criteria. An individual who has lived for a time in a new language which she need not even speak all that well, *can* come to be able to use that new language for these functions, even though not all speakers do (see, for example, Paulston, 1977a). It is probably different kinds of personality factor (rather than one's knowledge of the language) which decide how quickly one can go over to dreaming or thinking in a foreign language (see Vildomec, 1963).

2.1.3   Origin

The mother tongue has often, particularly in cultures where the word "mother" actually occurs in the term, been thought of as "the language which the mother speaks". This is a fairly good criterion, provided that we re-interpret the concept mother. It need not refer to a biological mother, but may be understood more approximately to refer to the person who first establishes a regular and lasting linguistic bond of communication with the child. This person, of course, will often in fact be the biological mother, since in our culture it is still usual for the mother to be the one who talks most with and to the young child. But it is not at all necessary that it should be.

We arrive at approximately the same result if we say that the mother tongue is *the language a child learns first*. In the early research into aphasia, it often emerged that the mother tongue of multilingual speakers was the last of their languages to be affected by aphasia, and the first to recover (see Jakobson, 1941). More recently, however, it has emerged that this is not always the case. Specialists in aphasia are now less inclined to assume without further question that the relationship between mother tongue and aphasia is as simple as that.[3]

2.1.4   Competence (mastery, level of proficiency)

The mother tongue can also be defined as *the language a person knows best*, a linguistic competence definition which sounds simple and unambiguous.[4] But in our ever more international and specialized age there are many who, for example, receive their education in a language other than their mother tongue. This may apply to minority children and adults, as well as to adults from linguistic majorities which in world terms are small. For a large proportion of Scandinavian linguists, for example, English is the professional language, and there are many areas within their own discipline which they command best in English (see Dahlstedt, 1975: 20, n I).[5] Many bilinguals living in a diglossic situation (see 2.2.3) with a functional differentiation between the languages will best deal with different situations in different languages, for example, Torneå Valley Finns, who are best able to discuss home, family, emotions, religion and sport in Finnish, and school, authorities, everything official best in Swedish (Jaakkola, 1969, 1973a, 1974; Koskinen, 1974).

This definition cannot give us an unambiguous notion of what is meant by a mother tongue. Nevertheless, it is most often this definition that decision makers (Andersson, 1977; Andersson & Boyer, 1970), teachers and parents use when it comes to deciding whether to place children, for example, in a Finnish or a Swedish medium class (I draw here upon conversations with different groups of teachers). "Which language does the child know best?" is the question asked. In spite of the fact that we know that having a lot of words in a language is only a small part of one's linguistic competence, the few tests for competence conducted in Sweden have almost always measured only vocabulary. This, of course, gives a very narrow picture of children's linguistic proficiency.

2.1.5   Function (use)

A more sociolinguistically orientated definition of function will describe a person's mother tongue as *the language she uses most.* But this definition will not fit the bill either, since people are often obliged, for example at work, to use a language without knowing it particularly well or without its being their primary language. Again it is most often we minorities who have no opportunity to use our mother tongue at work (see, for example, Sandlund, 1970, 1972; Allardt, 1979; Allardt, Miemois & Starck, 1979).

2.1.6   Attitudes

The mother tongue can also be defined as *the language one identifies with*, a social psychological definition, the language through which in the process of socialization one has acquired the norms and value systems of one's own group. The language passes on the cultural tradition of the group and thereby gives the individual an identity which ties her to the in-group, and at the same time sets her apart from other possible groups of reference (the language acting as a preserver of boundaries). Since this socialization process to a large extent occurs with the aid of language, language itself comes to constitute a symbolic representation of the group. Identification with a language, i.e. *internal identification*, as a consequence becomes a symbolic act.

Mikael Broo gives us a good example of this in a poem of his:

The Theft
They say
that I am a Finn
Although I am a Swede:
a Finland Swede

They do not know
that they are stealing a bit of
my identity every time
they say: Finn

(translation by Lars Malmberg)

If the social climate as regards language is a relaxed one (Skutnabb-Kangas, 1975g), so that there are no social language-related pressures or sanctions to encourage speakers to identify with a group other than their original one, then the identification criterion will probably be the most reliable. Minority languages often have a low status by comparison with majority languages. This may often lead members of minority groups to minimise or even deny their knowledge of and identification with their mother tongue, to be ashamed of their origins, and correspondingly to exaggerate their knowledge of the majority language in an effort to identify with it as quickly as possible (Skutnabb-Kangas, 1979a). The difference between bilingual competence and bilingual identification may often be great (Skutnabb-Kangas, 1975g: 15–16), although it *need* not be (see, for example, Fastbom, Koutonen-Nasiopoulos & Tsalmas, 1977). Economic or ideological factors also affect the process of identification (for economic factors, see Macnamara's example, 1969: 86, of the way in which Irish parents used to receive £10 a year per child from the government if they spoke Irish at home! Ideological factors are at work in the case of Hebrew in Israel).

The other aspect of the identification criterion has to do with the recognition of someone as a native speaker by other speakers of a language (native a..d non-native). This recognition by other speakers, i.e. *external identification*, may coincide with one's own view of oneself, or not. A differing judgement on the part of other speakers may be very frustrating, no matter whether the judgement is one way or the other. One may wish to identify oneself with some group, but may not be accepted, or on the other hand one may be identified with some group against one's will, as the following examples show:

"When Tero came to Sweden he knew only Finnish.
Today he has almost completely forgotten his mother tongue. Nobody knows that I'm a Finn, he says. But his parents are Finnish. His mother knows only Finnish. His step-father knows some Swedish. His real

father lives in Finland and knows only Finnish. ' . . . Last summer when I was in Finland they looked at me as if I was a foreigner. Apparently I don't look like a Finn. And then I've got a Swedish accent as well. Funny, because I am a Finn after all. But I'm a Swede too'." (Tero, aged 17, in *Dagens Nyheter*: 21.10.78)

"When I was teased at school I wanted to go back to Finland. But when I was on holiday there, they teased me because I was a Swede. That's stuck in my mind. I feel Finnish, but Swedish as well. I *want* to be Swedish but I can't ever. They don't accept me in Finland either really . . .

"I met some nice Finns on a trip to Russia. I like meeting Finns abroad but not in Sweden. They thought I was a Swede and that made me feel very proud.

"Somehow I've always felt like two people. The two people are always fighting with each other, the Swede and the Finn. It's a great hassle being two different people." (Pertti, aged 22, in *Dagens Nyheter*: 16.10.78)

"My Swedish mates started laughing at the other Turks. Who I'm one of.

Then I started fighting with the Swedes. . . . But all the Turks wanted was to be accepted. . . . One guy went so far even as to get rid of his own name, so as to be accepted. His name was Ahmed, but he wanted to be called Jimi Hendrix. Jimi Hendrix was accepted by the Swedes, even though he was black, because he was a big pop star. Just imagine what it's like being an underdog like that, having to do away with your own name!

". . . And then there's the problem of double roles. At school we have to be as Swedish as we can, that's the way to be accepted. At home we're Turks, we obey the Quran and our parents, and there's a very strong family feeling.

". . . Turkish parents can't help their children much with their school work. And on the other hand society and the school don't support the children's Turkish identity either. We're in between two worlds, not properly part of either." (Bülent Yilmaz, aged 19, in *Arbetet*: 17.2.79)

"How do you like your Swedish friends?"
Kiki: "I like them. But when they start talking shit about Greeks, I feel bad. 'Don't get worked up about it', they say, 'you don't count as a Greek'. But it's my own people they're talking about." (Kiki Hadjipetrou, aged 16, in *Dagens Nyheter*: 14.10.78)

In the same way as when dealing with the question of whether something constitutes two languages or one, in cases where there may be doubt, so also in my view we should allow a speaker's personal opinion, her own identification of a language as her mother tongue to prevail. At the same time we should work towards the elimination of those sanctions which, on account of the often low status of minority languages, put those who identify with them at a disadvantage, if we wish to guarantee every individual a real chance of defining themselves and of having their self-definition accepted by others.

2.1.7   Summary: one's mother tongue may change

To summarise: I have used four different criteria of definition for the mother tongue. They may all be said to represent different disciplines' ways of studying the mother tongue. All except the criterion of origin allow for the possibility that the mother tongue may change, even several times during a lifetime. This possibility of change is clearest if we use the criterion of function to define a mother tongue: the language one uses most may be a different one at different stages in one's life. What is defined as one's mother tongue may also vary even at a single point in time depending on which one of the criteria is used.

TABLE 1

Criterion	Definition of "mother tongue"	Discipline
origin	the language one learnt first (the language in which one established one's first lasting communication relationship)	sociology
competence	the language one knows best	linguistics
function	the language one uses most	sociolinguistics
attitudes	the language one identifies with (internal identification)	social psychology psychology of the individual
	the language one is identified as a native speaker of by other people (external identification)	social psychology sociology
(automacy) (world view)	(the language one counts in, thinks in, dreams in, writes a diary in, writes poetry in, etc.)	popular conceptions

I myself am a good example of this:
■ According to the criterion of origin, Swedish is my mother tongue, since both my bilingual parents spoke it to me when I was a baby, even though I heard Finnish from and spoke it to people very close to me at a very early

stage; but according to that same criterion of origin I am bilingual in Finnish and Swedish, having two mother tongues, since I have used both languages myself side by side from the very beginning.

■ According to the criterion of competence, Finnish is my mother tongue, since it is the language I feel I know best – among other things, I went to a Finnish school. But I am bilingual in Finnish and Swedish, too, according to the strictest requirements of the criterion of competence, since I have a corresponding native speaker's command of both languages, as long as Danish, which I hear every day, does not influence my Swedish too much.

■ According to the criterion of function, both Swedish and English are my mother tongues, since both privately and professionally I live in both equally in my everyday life; at present I make equal use of both. But again according to the criterion of competence, I am bilingual in Finnish and Swedish which I know how to use well enough to satisfy myself and fully to meet the demands of either linguistic community – even though at the moment I am not using this particular bilingual capacity. But again on the other hand, according to the criterion of function, I am not bilingual in Swedish and English, since neither I myself nor an English-speaking community would say that I met the demands made of a native speaker.

■ According to the criterion of attitude, I have two mother tongues, Finland Swedish and Finnish, and I am thus bilingual, since I myself identify with (parts of) both groups and cultures, and am identified by both groups as a native speaker. But the situation may look quite different in a few years' time, in respect of everything except the criterion of origin, which must of course always give the same result.

In my view one can see at what stage of development in tolerance and multiculturalism a country is by looking at the criteria used by school authorities to define a child's mother tongue. The most primitive stage uses definitions of function ("because the child is in an x-medium nursery, x must be her mother tongue, that is the language she uses all day long"). The next stage – where many countries in the Western world find themselves – uses definitions of competence. A well-known American professor writes "and these children could not even count properly in their so-called mother tongue". Because the children were not instructed in mathematics in their L1 they of course couldn't count in it. Here the failure of the school system to let children develop a thorough mastery of their mother tongue is used in order to legitimize further oppression of it. In my view the best possible situation would be one where the definition combines the criteria of origin and internal identification. It should also be a human right for every child to be given the opportunity to develop the language first learned to full native mastery, to be proud of it, and to have her own identification accepted by others. In the ideal society it should also be a human right to be able to use one's mother tongue for all purposes, both unofficial and official.

It is thus important not to regard the mother tongue (or bilingualism) as a conglomerate of stable unchanging features, but rather as a group of processes, in which continual change is possible (and often likely). These changes should be regarded as a source of enrichment rather than as a threat, as long as they are not forced upon speakers in a negative way from the outside, but reflect at least some kind of free choice on the part of the individual.

2.2   Is it possible to have two mother tongues?

The whole question of two mother tongues will be discussed from the point of view of the two code theory, that quantitative view of bilingualism which assumes that the bilingual individual has two complete linguistic systems, two codes, each of which resembles the single system of the monolingual speaker. If one believes in the possibility of complete bilingualism, the person who has two mother tongues will thus have two completely equivalent codes, two mother tongues, each of which should be comparable with the single mother tongue of a monolingual speaker. Is this possible? Let us look at the possibilities, starting with the different definitions of a mother tongue we have suggested.

2.2.1   The definition by origin

2.2.1.1 Parents with different mother tongues

If the mother tongue is defined as the language of the mother, or as the language first learnt, a child may very well have two different mother tongues. This would be the situation if the two parents each had different mother tongues, and each consistently spoke to the child in her or his native language, so that, for example, the Same mother always spoke Same and the Swedish father always Swedish, and ideally if both parents had equal contact with the child. If this child grows up with two languages, it learns both simultaneously and comes to have two mother tongues, two first languages.

Sometimes parents in bilingual families may feel that it is unnatural that they should speak different languages even to each other, particularly if before the birth of the first child they had been in the habit of speaking exclusively the language of one or the other partner. This is a common problem in Finland, where the number of mixed marriages is constantly on the increase (Forsberg, 1974; Skutnabb-Kangas, 1975g: 9–14; Mannil, 1978). More and more, people in this situation are advised to choose as their common means of communication the language which has less support in society at large, thus Finnish in a Swedish-speaking area, and Swedish in a Finnish area. However, in most cases the parents' linguistic competence determines the choice of language: it will be the language the other partner speaks best. Minority speakers are mostly more bilingual than majority speakers. According to the census of 1950, which in Finland was the last to include a question about knowledge of the two national languages, 46% of

Swedish speakers but only 8% of Finnish speakers declared that they had at least a tolerable oral command of the other language (Skutnabb-Kangas, 1975g: 14–15). Unfortunately, the majority language often comes to be the parents' common language, even though each of them may speak her or his own language to the children. In such cases one might well fear that the minority language would come to be the weaker of the two, especially where it is the language of the parent most often away from home. In many cases this will be the father. In Finland, proportionately more Finland Swedish men than women marry Finnish speakers, and in such cases the Finnish-speaking mother's language often comes to be stronger than the Swedish-speaking father's, as may also be gathered from the published population statistics. On average at the beginning of the 1950s, the children's language came to be Finnish in 60% of cases if the father was Swedish, and in 57% of cases if the mother was Swedish. Now the figures are different: in 1975, the children's main language in bilingual families came to be Finnish in 66% of the cases where the father was Swedish, and in 51% of the cases where the mother was Swedish (Mannil, 1978: 5). In 1970, about 39% of the children in mixed marriages claimed to be Swedish-speaking and 61% Finnish-speaking (Forsberg, 1974) – the figures have remained constant since the 1940s (Fougstedt, 1952, 1963; Fougstedt & Hartman, 1956, and on the latest figures Miemois, 1980). This is where the school ought to help: children should be taught through the medium of *the* language which has the weaker support. Few countries provide their minorities with their own educational facilities from nursery school to university – in this respect the Finland Swedish minority in Finland is probably in a better position than any other minority in the world. One should make the further demand, to ensure that children in bilingual families have an equivalent command of both languages, that they should also have *both* their mother tongues as school subjects (Skutnabb-Kangas, 1976b, 1978b).

If one believes that quantity is more important than quality in children's language learning, one may of course question whether the bilingual child will have enough time to be exposed to as wide a range of linguistic stimuli in her two languages as the monolingual child in her single language, for the bilingual will only have the same time to devote to her *two* languages that the monolingual has for her one. The child, of course, will not be able to experience everything at the same time in both her languages. Nevertheless, if one believes that the linguistic capacity developed by a bilingual can function as a mediating variable to further cognitive (and hence also linguistic) development in either language (Cummins, 1976a), then perhaps the purely quantitative lack in the exposure to each language is of little account and can be compensated for by the cognitive stimulation. The only remaining problem is that of avoiding functional differentiation between the languages.[6]

It will require a fairly single-minded "language policy" within the family to meet all these demands. But by and large it is possible to say that, according to the definition by origin, a child can have two mother tongues (for example see Saunders, 1982).

2.2.1.2 One language in the home – another outside

It is unclear to me, and to many others, why bilingualism should fairly seldom develop where the child hears two languages in different environments, one at home only and the other outside, for example in a day nursery. It would be extremely important to know how this kind of bilingual language development happens and why the results in these cases are so various, but there is very little empirical research (and still less theoretical) into this problem. Most of what has been done has either been based on anecdotal evidence of various kinds, or on case studies of individual children. The children studied have most often been the children of linguists, middle or upper middle class, and mostly children in situations where the second language has been chosen more or less voluntarily, where it has been encouraged by the parents, and where there has been no risk of the first language being suppressed (see McLaughlin, 1978).

The anecdotal evidence may consist of stories of the following kind: "It is a common experience in the district in Bengal in which the writer resided to hear English children three or four years old who have been born in the country conversing freely at different times with their parents in English, with their *ayahs* (nurses) in Bengali, with the garden-coolies in Santali, and with the house-servants in Hindustani, while their parents have learnt with the aid of a *munshi* (teacher) and much laborious effort just sufficient Hindustani to comprehend what the house-servants are saying (provided they do not speak too quickly) and to issue simple orders to them connected with domestic affairs. It is even not unusual to see English parents in India unable to understand what their servants are saying to them in Hindustani and being driven in consequence to bring along an English child of four or five years old, if available to act as interpreter" (Tomb, 1925: 53, quoted in Andersson, 1969: 42).

"One American missionary family in Vietnam tells this story: When they went out to Vietnam, they were three, father, mother and four-year-old daughter. Shortly after their arrival a son was born. The parents' work took them on extended trips to the interior of the country, at which times they left their children in the care of a Vietnamese housekeeper and a nursemaid. When the time came for the young son to talk, he did in fact talk, but in Vietnamese. Suddenly, the parents realized that they could not even communicate with their son except by using their daughter as an interpreter" (Andersson, 1977: 210).

There are also quite a few long-term case studies of fairly young children who have become bilingual either as a consequence of the fact that one or both parents have deliberately begun to use a language other than their mother tongue, and have tried to engage on its behalf substantial social support (see the examples in Andersson, 1979; Christian, C.C. Jr, 1977 and literature cited there and Saunders, 1982), or in cases where one language has been spoken at home and the other outside.[7]

What is important is not how quickly and how superficially fluently the children have learnt the other language, but the long-term consequences, both linguistic, cognitive, affective and social. And we have very little information about the long-term effects.

Most of the anecdotal evidence tells us nothing about the long-term consequences. Most of the evidence of this kind seems also to be derived from situations of the kind we have described above: middle class children, whose own language is not under threat, and who are much encouraged and praised by adults for learning a new one. The case study evidence, too, is often of this kind: a child of an academic family, moving to another country, with high-SES parents. In spite of the fact that it is said the child speaks the other language fluently, there are seldom reports with the empirical details which would give the reader the chance to judge whether the child's competence approached that of a native speaker. Many of the case studies do not make value judgements of this kind, but for the positive reason that the interest has been more in the study of the process of language learning itself (progression, strategies, interference, etc.) than in quantifying such features of the children's language as are generally measured by linguistic tests. However it would be valuable to know something about the end result as compared with that of monolingual children when thinking of the question put here: is it possible to have from childhood two mother tongues, absolutely genuine, comparable with the mother tongue acquired by a monolingual, as a result of any linguistic experience other than that of actually having parents each speaking a different mother tongue?

The question is particularly topical in Scandinavia where the provision of day nursery care for minority children is concerned. What difference is there for the child, it is often asked, between hearing one language from Mum and one from Dad on the one hand, and hearing one language from its parents and one from the day nursery staff on the other? The child is often with the day nursery staff for a large part of its most active waking hours during weekdays. Is not this perhaps a very good way of making young children truly bilingual, of giving them two mother tongues? Every day they will hear both languages used by native speakers who provide an excellent model for them. And since apparently an ordinary child finds it no very great burden to become bilingual within the family, why should it be any more difficult for it in a day nursery?

Even though it is rather difficult to say exactly why it should be, this type of "instruction" often seems to lead to poor results, to have unfortunate consequences for the children both linguistically and emotionally, perhaps also cognitively. Here again are some examples, both anecdotal and from case studies:

"She was four years old when she came here [i.e. to the Finnish-medium nursery school]. Both her parents were Finnish. They didn't have much time to talk to her because they worked in the evenings. As for Swedish, she only spoke this to other children in the playground. "First she was at a Swedish nursery school, and the staff there thought she was odd. She spoke both Swedish and Finnish in a disconnected way. Sometimes she used sign language. She seemed to have no contact with the world around her. No one could play with her. The psychologist diagnosed her as autistic, as entirely withdrawn into herself" (Ulla-Maija Yrjänä's account of Sirpa before she came to a Finnish nursery school, *Dagens Nyheter*: 31.10.78).

"A four-year-old Finnish boy who went to a Swedish day nursery even after a year was barely able to speak Swedish. He was like a two-year-old. He was like a little grey animal, hiding away from everybody. When he spoke Finnish his pronunciation was very defective. The Swedish staff did not understand what was the matter with him. 'At the beginning he said nothing at all', so the staff reported. 'Then he used to be sulky and nag on all the afternoon about his mother coming to fetch him.' 'Didn't you wonder why even after a year he hadn't learnt much Swedish?' This was the question asked by Ulla-Maija Yrjänä and Maija Paarma, who together had written a report on the Finnish day nursery in Akalla. 'Well, we have talked about him a bit', was the answer the staff gave, 'about him having a speech defect perhaps, or something else the matter with him.' (*Dagens Nyheter*: 31.10.78).

"At first I thought I was in charge of 15 mentally disturbed children. They were silent, or aggressive; they were thought to be autistic or retarded. They clawed and spat and kicked. Today they can express their feelings in words; they have a language" (Dorita Finell, the head of the Finnish day nursery in Husby, *Dagens Nyheter*: 31.10.78).

"I used to go round to five different places a day to try to teach the children Finnish, for two hours twice a week. . . . Every day I saw how the immigrant children were suffering in the Swedish day nurseries. They didn't speak, they were shy, frightened, aggressive, behind in their development. It was thought that some of them had brain damage. Too often the staff thought the children knew Swedish when really they didn't." (May-Lis Virtanen, immigrant assistant in Tensta-Rinkeby, retired head of the nursery school training college in Jakobstad, *Dagens Nyheter*: 8.11.78).

I have also written a longer case study of a child I myself worked with for a month. It provides an example of what could be called semi-lingualism (see Chapter 11). A summary follows:

Matti (a fictitious name) was nearly five years old. He was born in

Sweden, but his mother had emigrated from Finland. The father had never lived together with the child, but he was also Finnish. The mother knew very little Swedish, and she had been living in Sweden for many years before she went on a language course. She worked in a laundry, and her work started at 7 in the morning, which meant that Matti came to the day nursery at about 6.30 and was collected between 4.30 and 5.30 in the afternoon. Matti had been at the same day nursery (a very good Swedish one with an enlightened and interested staff) since he was eight months old. Before that he had gone to a Finnish-speaking child-minder. None of the staff at the day nursery knew any Finnish.

The mother told me that Matti had earlier been so tired when she collected him that he often fell asleep on the underground on their way home, and was put to bed as soon as they got home. This still sometimes happened. Because of this situation, mother and son had not talked to each other very much during the week when the child was very young (a fairly common situation with working parents whose children are in day care). It was at the weekends mostly that they talked. But the mother also said that she herself was often tired at the weekend, too tired to talk to the child as much as she would have liked to. They didn't meet many people at week-ends but were usually alone together. At first the mother had read stories to him, but now he couldn't concentrate any more on listening. The mother said that Matti found it fairly difficult to express himself in Finnish, his mother tongue, but she thought his Swedish was quite good, quite fluent.

The staff at the day nursery didn't think so. They thought that his command of Swedish was very poor, in spite of the fact that his pronunciation was perfect and that he sounded fluent. His vocabulary was very small, but even if he understood individual words, he sometimes didn't grasp what the words put together meant. This emerged in instances like the following:

- Six months earlier he hadn't been able to fetch things he'd been asked to get. He was very willing and went off to fetch the thing asked for, but came back with nothing or with the wrong thing. When I was there, things went a bit better.
- He wasn't able to sit and listen to stories, either when the teacher told them, or when she read them out of a book – after a few minutes he would wander off. This, the teachers said, was because he didn't understand.
- He wasn't able to watch a film either if there was too much talking in it.
- He wasn't able to recount what he had seen or heard. Nor was he able to tell coherently what he had been doing at home or anywhere else, describe what he saw in pictures, etc. On the whole the teachers said that he found it difficult to express himself in spite of the fact that he was quite clearly trying.
- He didn't join in any verbal games. He preferred games where the important thing was physical action, and where the sounds needed were not verbal but other types of sound (he liked being a car, a bus, a lion, a tiger, someone carrying a gun where the gun did the "talking" – or he liked being a

baby, who only needed to cry). Games of this kind, motor games where toys are instrumental for the game, are probably common with boys in general, by contrast with girls, whose games tend to be more verbal, more person and relationship orientated (see Rekdal & Skutnabb-Kangas, 1979; Andresen, 1978). But Matti preferred non-verbal games even more than the other boys.

His social relations with the other children were fairly good. To begin with they hadn't let him join in their games. The other children had thought of him as stupid, but this phase had passed. He was friendly and helpful, but rather wild in his games. He played mostly with children who were a year or two younger than him (with one exception). But the other children were also a bit afraid of him, because sometimes he would have terrific tantrums for no apparent reason, and kick and even bite the other children. Many of his reactions to the other children he was playing with were physical not verbal: he both hugged them and hit them. The teachers said he found it difficult to solve problems of social relationships using words. His solutions tended to be physical.

A few more details about the state of his linguistic abilities (I made rather detailed notes during the whole month): He couldn't count to more than three in either language, after that he said "paljo" (Finnish for "much") or "många" (Swedish for "many"). He didn't know the names of the colours in either language, and where he knew the name he didn't identify the colour correctly. He didn't know the names of most of the things around him, either in the day nursery or outside (I sometimes took him out for walks, and he was eager to look at everything). His vocabulary with respect to the common objects around him was not clearly diglossic. The words for some things he knew in both languages, and for others in neither (for example, most things in the kitchen – even though every day some of the children were allowed to help with the cooking, which took place in the day nursery's own kitchen, and was very well organized, so that the children learnt as they were actually and really helping. It was no merely pedagogical-therapeutic exercise). One could see that the staff had worked on his vocabulary – he could, for example, name certain animals in Swedish from the books they had. There was so much lexical interference from Swedish in his Finnish that a five-year-old monolingual Finnish child wouldn't have been able to understand what he said.

As well as simply observing I also tried to test his Finnish, but it proved to be impossible at the beginning of our month together – he wasn't able to concentrate for more than a few minutes – just as at the beginning he wasn't able either to concentrate on looking at pictures, listening to stories (either told or read out of a book), etc. After our month together I tried again, and by then his difficulties with concentrating were not so severe. It must be admitted that the tests I used (the standardized Finnish version of ITPA, Illinois Test of Psycholinguistic Abilities – see Toukomaa & Skutnabb-Kangas, 1977: 42–45 – and the Breuer-Weuffen motor sensory test, which measures a child's abilities to differentiate between linguistic sensory signals and to produce adequate motor reactions, these phonemic, optic, rhythmic, kinaesthetic and melodic motor sensory abilities being fundamentally necessary, for example, in learning to read and write) are not terribly exciting for young children, but nevertheless most of the other immigrant children I tested, even three to four year olds, were able to do the test in one forty minute session.

Matti's performance in the tests was severely sub-standard. He didn't even pass the optical test, which was something that even the three and four year olds had no difficulty with. A performance of this kind means that the prognosis for the future is very poor, unless something drastic is done. Matti's difficulties were the result of being exposed to two languages from early childhood, one at home and one in the day nursery. It perhaps should be added that there was nothing wrong with his sight or his hearing. Nor with his intelligence: at the end of our month I gave him a non-verbal intelligence test (Ravens Coloured Matrices A, Ab and B – Raven, 1965), which showed that his non-verbal intelligence was above average, near the 75th percentile.

It would of course be easy to say that Matti's Finnish could have been much better and could at the same time have been a good foundation for his Swedish, if only his mother had talked more to him. But this line of argument cannot be sustained, for two reasons at least.

The labour market, especially those sectors where immigrants often work, is so organized that people have long and tiring working hours, at the end of which they have very little energy left for doing anything else. This is true both of immigrant parents and of Swedish parents. Nor is it possible very often for such parents to make ends meet working part time, which would allow them more time for their children. To combine full-time work with looking after one's bilingual children (*after* school, mind you) is not even possible for someone with a high status job (in the opinion of Professor Jacob Mey (1978: 467), who had tried sharing with his wife Inger in alternate weeks the task of looking after the children); much less is it possible for someone with a more ordinary job. For as long as no changes are made in the circumstances of ordinary working life, to make them more human, there is nothing to be gained from "accusing" already hard-pressed parents whose "performance" is not likely to be improved by their being made to feel guilty for not having enough time and energy to talk enough to their children. Society *must* assume part of the responsibility itself.

One should perhaps also say that a single parent who tries to preserve a minority language within the family without institutional help will almost certainly fail, at least in the attempt to maintain a child's active skill in speaking the language. If the child has no chance of using her mother tongue anywhere other than at home with one parent (and perhaps sporadically and informally with friends), it is a pretty hopeless struggle. Of course the attempt *can* succeed, but only by demanding a very great deal of the parent, more than she or he could fairly be expected to cope with.

Here is an example from the experience of one of my friends:

Three children, aged 6, 7 and 9, bilingual in Danish and English, have an English father and a Danish mother. Both parents are graduates. The parents are divorced but live near one another, and the children (two living with the father and one with the mother) meet one another and both parents several times a week. The mother speaks almost nothing but Danish to the children, the father only English. The language used in nursery school, school and among the children's friends, the language they hear on the television, the language in their extended family, etc. is Danish.

All three children are bilingual, that is to say they manage fairly well in English, while their Danish is as good as that of other children of their own age. When the children are in Denmark (90% of the time) they use very little English spontaneously, which the English-speaking parent finds rather frustrating. When he speaks English to them they nearly always answer in Danish. However, the father has thought this situation preferable to precipitating any confrontation with the children ("you should answer me in . . ."). All three children can change over to English when necessary. Phonetically they all sound like native speakers of English, but their vocabulary, particularly with the two younger children, is considerably smaller than that of a comparable monolingual English child.

The following factors have been essential to the achieving of this result (that all the children are able to communicate in both languages, even if their English is considerably less good than their Danish):

■ At the beginning the home language was English. Until the youngest child was three and started at the day nursery, both the English-speaking and the Danish-speaking parent used English (it should be mentioned that both parents speak each other's language *very* well). The children spoke a great deal of English among themselves. The assumption was that Danish, which was the language of the whole environment (the family had been living in Denmark for the previous seven years), would present no problems, and it didn't.

■ The English-speaking father has *always without exception used only English* to the children, even after the Danish-speaking mother changed over to Danish. The father spends a great deal of time with the children, doing things with them.

■ The children's English has been reinforced by regular trips to England, and among other things by their staying with their English grandparents without the parents being present. Again their English has been encouraged by the fact that English has always been used in the family in situations where its use was natural: with English-speaking guests, with English *au pair* girls who spoke no Danish, in having books from England read aloud to the children, which the two older children can now read for themselves, after first learning to read Danish at school. It turned out that there was no problem in transferring to another language the reading skills acquired in Danish.

The conclusion must be that minority parents who have to choose a day nursery language for their children other than their own mother tongue will often run the risk that their children will fail to reach the level of proficiency in the minority language expected of a comparable monolingual child, and this almost irrespective of the social class of the parents and of the opportunities they have of stimulating their children linguistically. There is also the risk that the children will not learn the day nursery language as well as monolingual children. To have one language used at home, and another used outside the home and in *all* the institutions a child comes into contact with does not seem to be a particularly good way for a young child to become bilingual, especially in situations where a child's mother tongue has low status. Unfortunately we know hardly anything about the reasons for this, and there is a particular need for research in this area, for properly conducted, thorough, long-term studies which record the progress of children other than those of highly educated middle class parents or parents who have moved voluntarily from one country to another.

2.2.2   Definition by competence

If one begins with the supposition that the mother tongue is the language one knows best, then the person who has two mother tongues must know both languages equally well (*balanced bilingualism*), and know each language as well as the comparable monolingual speaker.

We can divide linguistic proficiency into four different areas, two receptive and two productive, two oral and two written. We thus have the sub-divided areas of understanding, speaking, reading and writing. I should really also like to include thinking in this breakdown, since the relationship between thought and language is still very unclear, in spite of the fact that for thousands of years this has been one of the most discussed and debated areas of the psychology of language. Especially in the case of the effect of submersion (see the section on immersion, submersion and language maintenance) on a child's language and through language on her cognitive ability, research into bilingualism seems to have something to contribute to our knowledge both of the basis of cognition (see, for example, Martin Albert and Loraine Obler's book, *The Bilingual Brain*, for neuropsychological and neurolinguistic aspects of bilingualism) and its functioning in bilingual individuals (James Cummins deals with *cognitive competence*, the ability bilinguals have to use both languages as effective instruments of cognition – see bibliography). But as long as we know as little as we do about the inter-relation of language and thought, it is perhaps just as well to try to keep them separate (for the different ways in which one might discuss language and thought in the case of bilinguals, see especially Bain, 1975a, 1976a; Bain & Yu, 1978a, and later books edited by Bain).

We can further subdivide the areas of understanding, speaking, reading and writing into different aspect levels. We then have *phonemes* (sounds), or in the case of writing *graphemes* (letters), as well as *lexemes* (words), *syntax* (sentence construction) and *semantics* (word meanings).

We can further take as a basis for subdivision different domains of life which each demand the use of a different variety of language. Let us take the most common areas: home and friends, school or work, cultural life, official situations.

This gives us a matrix of 64 squares (see the Swedish version of this book). Language proficiency matrices of this kind can be used to establish whether one can master all the different aspects of linguistic proficiency equally well in both one's languages. Is it possible, for instance, to have the vocabulary for formulating one's sentences or to have at hand all the ways conventionally necessary for addressing a written appeal to a court of law in both one's languages? Or does one know all the words with all their shades of meaning necessary for reading intricately reasoned reviews in both languages? At any rate this seems difficult. In most cases one knows certain things better in *one* language (and most bilinguals probably master some of the squares in the matrix rather poorly in both languages). The two languages are rarely mastered equally well in all the various areas, aspects and activities of life. This means, then, if we are thinking of one of the strict definitions by competence, that one can hardly at one and the same time know two mother tongues equally well – although there may be rare exceptions here – and as well as a monolingual would know her single native language. On the other hand, it *is* possible for a bilingual to know *one* of her mother tongues as well as a monolingual speaker knows her single language, and to know the other of her two languages slightly less well (or in rare instances perhaps even slightly better).

2.2.3   Definition by function and functional differentiation – diglossia

We arrive at the same result if we begin with the more sociolinguistic definition of the mother tongue: the language one uses most. Can two languages be in absolutely equal use? If one language is used as much as the other, then they should be interchangeable in all situations. One should be able to use both in all linguistic functions. Many researchers are of the view that it is an unnecessary luxury to have a double provision of the linguistic means of expression in all situations. It is their view that in such circumstances one language will gradually disappear (Fishman, 1968). According to these scholars, societal bilingualism will survive for a comparatively long time only where there is a functional differentiation between the languages. Functional differentiation, the division of labour between languages, is really a concept at the societal level. But even if at the level of the individual a speaker were to master both her languages equally well to begin with (for example, in childhood in a bilingual family), the functional differentiation in society at large between the languages would probably in the end be reflected at the individual level too. Since one would be able to use only one of the languages in certain domains, the ability to use the other language in those domains would decline, or perhaps never be "fully acquired". Then both languages would be less used and less well mastered in certain areas. In this case one would no longer be able to have recourse to two more or less complete systems, but rather to two more or less incomplete systems which complemented each other.

Different communities have different goals where the desirability of functional differentiation between languages is concerned. In the Soviet Union the official view is that functional differentiation is a necessary stage in the evolution towards a unitary national state (Lewis, 1978: 213; Bruk & Guboglo, 1981). According to Lewis, the assimilation of both small and large ethnic groups is encouraged, not only as a voluntary and spontaneous movement, but also as official centrally planned policy (Davletshin, 1967 quoted in Lewis, 1978: 218). The Russian language is taking over more and more of the linguistic functions involved in the building of a modern unitary state (administration, technology, higher education, etc.), while the other languages are becoming more and more specialized to areas of traditional culture (Lewis, 1978: 220/221 – for Soviet accounts see Bromley & Kozlov, 1981; Bruk & Guboglo, 1981; Gantskaya, 1981; Grigulevich & Kozlov, 1981b; Gurvich, 1981; Terentieva, 1981; Zhdanko, 1981).

Here we have, then, an example of *planned* functional differentiation. As a counter example one could take the strongly negative reactions provoked among Finland Swedish scholars, authors and commentators by the suggestion of Professor Bengt Loman, himself a Swede from Sweden, that some kind of functional differentiation should be encouraged for Finland Swedish.

". . . the attempt to preserve bilingualism in a country is open to certain risks if the two languages concerned may be used absolutely equivalently. If I can say everything I have to say as well in Finnish as I can in Swedish, then it becomes very likely that one of these languages, in this case Swedish, will come to be redundant. That is why a diglossic situation is something valuable. . . . The thought has sometimes occurred to me that Finland as a whole should be encouraged to develop in this direction, and that Swedish should be given a function of this kind, but I have not yet dared to venture very far in this argument" (Loman in the panel discussion, see Skutnabb-Kangas, 1977a: 221–25).

(This looks to me suspiciously like the arguments which Northrop used in 1946 – see 2.1.1. Humane extermination of a language in the name of evolution.) The reactions to Loman's suggestion in Swedish Finland were very strong (as an example of this, see Gösta Ågren, *Vasabladet* 3.10.76 – the debate raged in *Vasabladet* for quite some time). Most Finland Swedes are likely to be opposed to a policy which would have functional differentiation as its aim – this emerged clearly, for example, during the seminar debate on "Finland Swedish in the year 2000", particularly in Erik Allardt's contribution.

Particularly in Sweden, but also to some extent in the other Nordic countries, minorities are beginning more and more to demand the right to use their own languages for official purposes instead of the majority language. Certain minority groups in Sweden reply to official requests for information in their own languages, to take one example, and so an official terminology comes to be used in both languages. This is *one* way of countering functional differentiation or diglossia.

In order to have two mother tongues which are in absolutely equivalent use, used equally in all situations and absolutely interchangeable, a bilingual society would be necessary, without functional differentiation, a society in which any speaker could function in either language in all situations. Such societies are probably very difficult to find. It is possible to imagine two monolingual societies in such close proximity to each other that a bilingual individual could move freely in either. It is possible to imagine a complete micro-society functioning in *one* language in the midst of a macro-society which functioned in another language. It is possible to imagine bilingual individuals living alternately in two different monolingual societies and participating equally in the life of each. But all these possibilities are theoretical constructs remote from the ordinary experience of most bilingual speakers.

The conclusion must be that it is very uncommon to have two mother tongues, if we define these using the linguistic and sociolinguistic criteria of equal command and identical function for both languages.

2.2.4   Definition by attitude

Can an individual be identified by others as a native speaker of two different languages (external identification – see Ofstad, 1971) and can this individual also herself identify with two different languages (internal identification)? The first kind of identification is clearly possible. This emerges both from investigations using thoroughly bilingual speakers and from those using monolingual speakers with very little acquaintance with a second language. In the so called "matched guise" investigations, in which the attitudes of informants towards different national and/or linguistic groups were elicited, these informants were asked to describe their reactions to voices speaking in the two different languages. The informants were not told that the same voice occurred twice, for example once in English and once in French. In general the informants did not even notice that the same voice occurred twice on the tape, and that must surely mean that the voice was identified as being that of a native speaker in each of the languages. The developer of the "matched guise" technique, Wallace Lambert, does not suggest that he had any difficulty in finding individuals for his investigations who were sufficiently bilingual to pass as native speakers of the two languages (for example, Lambert, 1967, and several articles in Lambert,

1972). Neither have I had any difficulty in finding "complete" bilinguals for my own investigation into the possibility of complete bilingualism (see further under 2.2.5). On the other hand, Saint-Jacques (1978) justifies his use of *two* monolingual speakers, one for each language, rather than *one* speaker for both, on the grounds that perfect "guises" are very difficult to find. Even if it is sometimes difficult to find individuals who speak two languages "perfectly", it is thus possible to speak two languages so well as to be taken as a native speaker by members of each linguistic group.

Moreover, it can be questioned whether it is really necessary to speak a language perfectly to be taken as a native speaker. At least in certain limited circumstances an almost non-existent ability in a language can deceive a native speaker into thinking she hears another native speaker of her own language, as Neufeld has very elegantly demonstrated (1977).

He devised two 18-hour language training programmes, for Japanese and Chinese, and put 20 Canadian college students through both. The intention was to investigate whether adults could learn the pronunciation of a foreign language they had never heard before. He had special methods, which among other things involved preventing the students from actually trying to produce anything in the language themselves in the early stages. They were just to listen, but to do so in a concentrated way and to focus on specific features of the pronunciation in each exercise. When native speakers of the two languages assessed the students' pronunciation after 18 hours, they were told that the voices they were to assess were partly those of Japanese and Chinese who had recently arrived in Canada, and partly those of immigrants from these countries who had been in Canada for a longer or a shorter time (and who might thus show interference from English in their speech); they were also told that there might be some native English speakers in the group to make the assessment more reliable. As many as 45% of the students were judged by the native speakers to be themselves unmistakably native speakers of Japanese without any signs of linguistic interference, or they seemed to be native speakers with occasional English sounds. 40% of the students were similarly assessed when speaking Chinese. And if we also include the students who were judged to be "near native with frequent English-like sounds", the proportion rose to 75% for Japanese and 80% for Chinese.

In spite of the fact that Neufeld himself says that his experiment need not mean that the students would have achieved the same level of performance under normal language learning conditions (in this case they actually understood nothing of what they heard or repeated – in other words, they concentrated solely on the form to the exclusion of content), it remains that nearly half of them under certain specific conditions were able to deceive native speakers into thinking that they were also native speakers after only 18 hours' contact with the language. What we "hear" clearly depends to a large extent on what we listen for and what we expect to hear – something that ought to make us even more confident in relying on everybody's own notion of themselves instead of relying on the judgement of others, whether this is presented as the result of subjective assessment or of so called "objective" tests (see the discussion in Hammar, 1978 and Skutnabb-Kangas, 1979b).

If we turn now to the other side of the definition by attitude (internal identification), and ask whether an individual is able to identify with two languages and two groups, two cultures (or parts of them), the answer must be even more clearly yes. As the writer Antti Jalava says:

"People sometimes wonder which of my two languages feels most natural and most genuine, Finnish or Swedish? Finnish, of course. And Swedish. Both languages enrich and presuppose one another; to take away one would be to take away part of my life." (Jalava, 1978: 4–5)

It has emerged from a number of investigations in different parts of the world that there are a good number of individuals who identify with both their languages (and cultures) and who prefer alternatives which confirm their double identities whenever such alternatives are given. In an investigation comprising 912 persons aged 15–74 who were classified as Swedish speakers in the census in Helsinki and neighbouring districts, 17% of the total thought of themselves as bilingual or as belonging to both linguistic groups (Allardt, Miemois & Starck, 1979: 19). It is possible to differentiate even within the bilingual group, as was done by Doris Norrgård in her study of Pargas, by attempting to measure the degree of identification, whether the individual has a very strong or not so very strong sense of being bilingual ("Do you feel strongly that you are very definitely a bilingual?"). At least those who selected the strong affirmative answer can be considered to have this double identification (Norrgård, 1978).

According to both of the definitions by attitude, it is thus possible to have two mother tongues.

2.2.5   Two mother tongues = complete bilingualism – is it possible?

Let us once more look at the question of having two mother tongues from a quantitative point of view. If an individual has two mother tongues, she should be "completely" bilingual, since someone who has *one* mother tongue must reasonably be regarded as "completely" monolingual (for an account of the various problems associated with this statement, see the discussions of the different definitions of bilingualism).

This question as to whether complete bilingualism is possible may also seem a merely theoretical discussion without any kind of practical relevance. But such is not the case, above all for two reasons:

■ When certain educational aims are defined for immigrant schoolchildren, and it is said that active bilingualism is the goal, this can be understood to mean as "complete" a bilingualism as possible. There are those who say that this is an impossible educational aim, and that it should be clear to all parties that a balanced bilingualism, or native competence in two languages, cannot be achieved and the attempt at this will put an unreasonable strain upon the individual (Ekstrand, 1978a, 1978b, 1978c, 1979a). This is why it is important to establish whether and under what circumstances complete bilingualism is possible.

■ We must first establish whether it is possible to have two mother tongues and to be completely bilingual before we can clarify the very diffuse concepts around the subject of double semilingualism. There are many who think this whole concept should be abandoned, that it has done its duty as a thought-provoking slogan and that it is not possible to discuss it as a scientific concept. I do not agree completely with this view. I believe the phenomenon is a real one, but difficult to get at. I agree that we should stop using the term as a stick to beat people with, a term which is (and has been) used too lightly to brand people as semilingual. But just because I believe that the phenomenon itself exists, I think it all the more important that a clarification of the concept should be undertaken. Erling Wande's analysis of the debate about semilingualism will be an attempt at such a clarification (Wande, 1980).

If complete bilingualism is possible, and if we can establish criteria which a bilingual should satisfy in order to qualify as competently bilingual, we ought to be able to measure the linguistic proficiency and performance of any bilingual against these criteria (i.e. the monolingual norms) and to regard all deviations from this norm as deficiencies. In such a case an individual who in *both* her languages fell short of the monolingual norm could be regarded as doubly semilingual.

If, on the other hand, we are forced to accept that *complete bilingualism* is wholly *impossible*, either in practice or as a (fruitful) concept, *then we shall find it impossible to draw a distinction between bilingualism and double semilingualism*. In this case, all bilinguals would by definition be less competent in their two languages than the corresponding monolinguals, and all bilingualism would be more or less incomplete or relative. The boundary between bilingualism and double semilingualism, then, would be arbitrary.

We may begin by trying to illustrate, purely quantitatively, different possibilities (see Figure 1).

In a rough schematization, we may think of the completely bilingual individual as having two linguistic systems at her disposal, identical with the one system of the monolingual, as having an equal command of them and an ability to use them for all functions (Figure 1a). A nearly bilingual individual would then have *one* system equivalent to that of the monolingual, and a second which had not yet reached the same degree of completeness, but which would in time do so (Figure 1b). In this view of things, the person who had not yet reached the level of a monolingual speaker in either of her two languages would be a double semilingual, even if her or his command of the

FIGURE 1

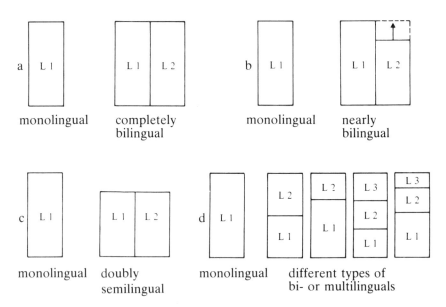

two languages taken together amounted in quantity to something much more than the monolingual's linguistic command (Figure 1c).

When the quantitative view is taken to its logical extreme, human linguistic capacity is seen as something static: the capacity does not increase, regardless of how many languages it is that "share" it. If this view is true, then it must be the case that each language spoken by a bilingual or multilingual individual will only be able to claim some fraction of the total human linguistic capacity which is available in its entirety for the single language spoken by the monolingual. The greater the number of languages sharing this capacity, the less each will be able to claim for itself (Figure 1d). This view would presuppose that different languages have nothing in common, that the individual would have to start at the beginning and make a quite new effort in learning another language, that there are no linguistic universals, that learning a second or a third language would be the same (and just as laborious) as learning one's first language. Both theoretical and applied linguistics have shown that this is not the case.[8] It is important to be able theoretically to reject this alternative, for many of the discussions of double semilingualism (for example, Nils Erik Hansegård's definition: "a semi-competent command of Swedish and a semi-competent command of the mother tongue", Hansegård, 1972: 128) may, without perhaps any conscious intention of operating with quantitative terms, start out from such static and rigid ideas of human linguistic ability, or be understood to do so.

This has been even more of a risk where the term for semilingual is quantitative in itself, as in Swedish "halvspråkig", halflingual. Hansegård, for his part, has explicitly declared, using examples, that he is not arguing in quantitative terms (Hansegård, 1977b). Arguments are often heard to the effect that it is reasonable to suppose that less in the way of linguistic capacity must be left for one language if some of it has been used already for another. Macnamara in particular has discussed this mutual balance effect. Parental love affords a good parallel: do parents love their first child less once they have a second child to love? It is just as meaningless to discuss total linguistic capacity in quantitative terms.

If we knew what "complete monolingualism", or "hololingualism" was, we would be able to decide whether complete bilingualism is possible. But such a concept does not exist. Everyone who speaks a language as her mother tongue and is monolingual speaks the language "completely", according to her needs; this is the view both of the structuralists (see, for example, Bratt Paulston, 1974) and of the generativists (for example, Chomsky, 1965). On the other hand, few people, for example, have an active command of the entire vocabulary of their mother tongue, and yet we do not call monolinguals "merolingual" (partially competent). How much of the theoretically conceivable total resource of the language a monolingual must command in order to be called "hololingual" is an impossible question. It would, of course, be possible to analyse the linguistic proficiency of a large number of different individuals, and then to derive an average level of proficiency from these results and to use it as a kind of norm, but not even this has been done for a single language. We thus lack information about what monolinguals know in their own tongue; nor do we have tests which would measure this hololingual competence in a single language (Haugen, 1964). This is why the question of complete bilingualism will not for the present be resolved with the aid of quantitative criteria. There are, however, preliminary attempts to define what it is one knows when one knows a language.

Subjective assessment has also been used to investigate the question: bilinguals have been asked whether they regard themselves as completely bilingual (Vildomec, 1963). But we should ask ourselves what we are actually measuring by asking a question like this: are we measuring the degree of bilingualism, the ability we have to compare our linguistic competence with that of other speakers, our self confidence, our degree of self criticism, or something else? The results of various investigations do in fact show that it is quite difficult to find bilinguals who would maintain that they have a complete command of two languages, or are able to use two languages equally well for all purposes.

For nearly two decades, during which I have been "professionally" interested in bilingualism, I have been going round asking people whom I thought fairly bilingual whether they thought of themselves as such and whether they thought they had an equal command of both languages. I suppose I meet more bilinguals than most people. I have found just two who thought they knew both languages equally well (one of them writes poetry in both languages – though this is not a good criterion: I do too, without thinking of myself as even remotely a complete bilingual). On the other hand, I have found many speakers who think they *get on* as well in *two* languages as monolinguals in each (see above 2.2.5).

It may be the case, perhaps, that bilinguals are more critical than monolinguals in assessing their linguistic limitations. Once one has moved away from a state of "monolingual naivety", it is likely that one will be more severe in judging one's own linguistic competence, since one will know many different ways of saying the same thing. It is, for example, easier to express certain things in one language than another, and then the bilingual speaker may well think that it is her failure that she doesn't succeed in saying something in an "easy" way in one language that she can say easily in the other. The bilingual speaker may attribute this lack of ease to an incomplete command of the language rather than to the fact that what can be easily said in one language may have no exact equivalent in the other, but will have to be expressed in a more roundabout way. In other words, it is easy to blame one's own "incomplete" linguistic competence for a difficulty attributable to the fact that the resources of the two languages are different in different areas. A bilingual individual may also be so sensitive to nuances exactly because of her bilingual experience that she is more irritated than a monolingual by the discrepancy between her experiences of a referent and her ability to put that experience into words.

Bilingual individuals are thus not reliable witnesses when it comes to deciding whether complete bilingualism is possible, since they may demand more of the idea of completeness as a consequence of their bilingualism than monolinguals do.

We are thus forced to conclude that *we cannot decide whether complete bilingualism is possible*. At the same time, however, it has also become clear that *we are equally unable to decide what complete monolingualism, or hololingualism, is*. Both monolingualism and bilingualism demonstrate great variation, which we have to accept. The variation in the repertoire of monolinguals is probably smaller in range than is the case with bilinguals, but in principle it should be possible to describe both in the same way. Where a monolingual individual has at her disposal different dialects, sociolects, sexolects and situational or stylistic varieties to communicate with, the bilingual speaker has in theory a greater possible range of variation since she has at command two different languages, each with its own spectrum of varieties. But in the same way as a monolingual speaker's choice of variant is determined by the degree of "social bilingualism" of the listener, so the bilingual speaker must also take account of the listener's linguistic knowledge, and may allow her choice of variant to be determined by other criteria, only provided that her listener is bilingual, too. A bilingual speaker's choice of variety (which may sometimes be VL1 (= a variety from within the first language), sometimes VL2 and sometimes VL1L2) should be able to be described in the same way as the monolingual speaker's intralingual choice between different varieties.

This descriptive method, however, presupposes that we reject the two code theory (see 5.2) and instead start from the assumption that the bilingual individual, like the monolingual, has one single code of competence, even if this code of competence differs from the monolingual's code in being bilingual.

In the one code theory we cannot compare the bilingual speaker's *linguistic proficiency* with that of the monolingual but only with the proficiency of other bilinguals (if even that). On the other hand, it should be possible to compare the ability of a bilingual speaker to satisfy her different communication needs with that of a monolingual, but then we are comparing the *result of communication and not the means* (see also 4.3.8). In doing this we are moving the discussion of complete bilingualism from the individual to the social plane. The important question is then not what bilingual individuals are like in comparison with monolinguals but rather what kinds of society give bilinguals the greatest chance of satisfying their communication needs.

Bilingualism is, just like other manifestations of linguistic codes, not something the individual herself has chosen, it is society's power mechanisms which are reflected in the kind of access different individuals have to different codes (for example, Teleman, 1979). Economic conditions and division of labour create the framework within which certain codes can emerge. For this reason the question of complete bilingualism must be seen in a wider perspective. We must ask ourselves what kinds of social situation produce bilinguals. What kinds of bilinguals do different societies produce? Do these societies function in such a way as to satisfy to the greatest possible degree the communication needs of bilinguals by manifesting just those linguistic codes that bilinguals have at their disposal (*that* would be complete bilingualism)? If not, what purpose do they serve? I shall return to many of these questions later in the book. I shall also return to the question of bilingualism as a realistic educational aim, and to the problem of double semilingualism.

2.3   How do we learn our mother tongue?

There are numerous good descriptions of the way a child learns its mother tongue. I am not going to repeat what has been said in these studies, but I want to take up the question of language learning from a different aspect, which I find important from the point of view of bilinguals.

As became clear from the discussion of the Whorf/Sapir hypothesis, language is not "neutral". It does not give an "objective" description of the world about us, rather it helps to organize it for us, to categorize it, to determine for us what it is important or less important to see, what it is necessary or less necessary, easier or less easy to notice, what is good and bad, right and wrong.

The language we use does not only give the listener *factual information*, information about our *state of mind*, information about our *intention*, about the desire that prompts us to speech (for example, the desire to convince, command, instruct, influence another's action), and information about the *attitude* we have *to the truth value* of what we say (we may hope, believe, doubt, question, etc.). It also gives the listener a good many indications of our particular *value judgements and perspective*. We constantly send out signals indicating our value judgements, our ideology, our philosophy, when we speak (or are silent – silence is also a speech act – see Spender, 1980) both verbally and non-verbally. We are normally more or less unaware in detail of these signals – we do not always know what we have "said". The reason we do not know has to do with the way we learn our mother tongue.

Language learning begins at a very early stage. Pregnant women have reported that the child moves rhythmically in time with the music it hears (Andersson, 1979: 44), and that it reacts to voices by relaxing. Investigations in which newly born babies, aged 12 hours to 2 weeks, were videotaped while listening to adults speaking (English and Chinese) have shown that children react rhythmically to speech by imitating the rhythm of the speech in their own movements (interactional synchrony, Condon & Sander, 1974; Condon, 1977). By contrast, they did not respond to isolated vowel sounds or knockings. The assumption has been made that such features as the intonation and rhythm of the mother tongue are imprinted so early that it is possible to discern the original mother tongue even when some individual has a complete command of a language learnt later in life, or even when the mother tongue has been supplanted by another language. It is maintained that one experiment showed that it was possible even to discern the mother tongue of immigrant grandparents in five-week-old children (Lar, 1974). It has also been found that new born babies are already predisposed towards language, just as they are predisposed to reacting to shapes that look like the human face (Söderbergh, 1979: 11). Even a very young child tries to turn its head towards human voices and to listen actively – the child seeks contact and a feeling of social togetherness right from the start. When a child begins to babble and when it utters its first words, it has already gone through a fairly long and active process of language learning in which it has not only received but has also actively tried to react to and reproduce what it has heard.

Before I proceed to describe some features of the way a child's language learning takes place, I wish to say something about the semantic theory I am using. I distinguish three different aspects of meaning in language:

1. The *expression* itself, i.e. the external form: what we say, hear and see written. Smaller units of expression may be combined into larger ones, and the meaning of the larger units of expression is connected (but not always

and not solely) with the meanings of the smaller units which form part of them.

2. A *reference* to reality, i.e. to things and circumstances: the physical reality which surrounds us and which in some sense "is there", regardless of whether we observe it or not. This does *not* mean that it appears to us in any "neutral" or "objective" form, since different observers will draw differently and unequally upon physical reality, depending upon which of its innumerable details the observer (partly by her socialization, partly for more individual and context-bound reasons) "chooses" to notice.

3. A *mental concept* of what the expression names, for example, a proposition, a statement or a notion. And in this aspect of meaning I distinguish between denotative and connotative meanings. Denotative meaning is often used merely as a synonym for referential meaning (so that the distinction between 2 and 3 disappears), and connotative meaning is often ignored and is dealt with only in discussions of the particular experiences of individuals or in analyses, for example, of ideologically charged expressions. But I wish to include them both in the mental concept which the expression awakens in the mind.

When a child learns a language, it enters a world in which those concrete objects which it sees and hears and experiences already have certain properties and relations to one another: for example, a table has the property of being hard, and the mother's breast has the property of being soft, and the breast stands in a certain relation to milk and hunger. At the same time as the child handles the things in its environment and comes to know the properties and relations which subsist in them within a context it has a total experience of (and which comes to determine the connotations the child connects with the things), it begins with the help of adults itself to attach words to things. But the words then become "labels" for the whole semantic complex, the whole mental concept. It is only later that the meanings are differentiated so that those referentially distinct meanings which may have been part of the same semantic complex are separated from one another. If bow-wow to begin with meant everything living and on four legs, the child later begins to differentiate between a cat and a horse which have "different" references in reality. The denotative meanings thus become clearer (the denotative meaning of cat is the extension of the notion cat, that is to say, of the set of all individuals that can be referred to by the word cat). The connotative meaning thus becomes the sum of all the socio-functional (in part unanalysed) semantic complexes which the child, to a large extent with the help of the environment but also as a consequence of its own experiences, has attached to the referential-concrete meanings.

I would like now to take up *one* aspect of language learning, in which the uniqueness of connotative meanings in the learning process emerges, namely the fact that such socio-functional "conglomerate notions" as one has in one's first language are no longer evident in the language learnt second, precisely because these immediate unanalysed conglomerates belong to the early stage when the child still sees the world as less structured. I shall not, however, concern myself with conceptual development – there are a number of excellent books on this subject (see, for example, the references to Luria, Piaget and Vygotsky in the bibliography).

When young children learn to speak, it is not only words they learn. At the same time as they learn the words they also come to know both the world and themselves and to place themselves in relation to the world, to find their own place in it. Since the environment helps the child to structure the world, order it, categorize it, with the aid above all of language, the child will learn together with the language a way also of looking at the world, a way of evaluating it, a perspective upon it, all suggested by its environment. Our mother tongue gives us, as it were, a pair of tinted spectacles which to begin with "determine" what we see of the world about us.

The world of a very young child is probably to begin with some kind of formless, vague undifferentiated entity, in which the child can hardly discern detail. The person taking care of the child begins little by little to point out details to the child and to give them names: mummy, daddy, flower, lamp, car, doggy. As the child sees these details often enough, perhaps touches them, tastes them, listens to the sounds they make, and at the same time hears their names (and is thus able to make use of several senses at the same time to comprehend the object), it begins to be able to recognize them and keep them separate from the undifferentiated whole, from the chaos that surrounds it: the words help to organize the world into details which it recognizes and can remember, and a remainder of reality which is still vague. We notice that the word is beginning to help the child to retain a detail drawn out of the undifferentiated vagueness when it begins to respond to the words by trying to find the object with its eyes. When, for example, we ask a baby: "Where is the lamp?", and it turns its eyes towards the lamp, we know that the organizing of the world into the known and the unknown has begun and that language is helping the child.

What characterizes the child's experiences as it begins to try to acquaint itself with the world is partly that it still has very *diffuse*, *total* and *undifferentiated* impressions in which all boundaries seem rather fluid and imprecise. This is true (1) of the boundary between *the child itself and its environment* (2) of the boundary between *the phenomenon* which the child for the moment is focusing upon *and the "environment" of that phenomenon*, i.e. both the physical environment and the situation itself in which the child is placed at that moment and (3) of the boundary between *the word* which the child learns on the one hand, *and both the phenomenon* which the word describes (its referent) *and the "environment"*, the context, on the other hand. Many observations and experiments in developmental psychology seem to provide evidence that the boundaries are rather imprecise (see, for example, Clark & Clark, 1977).

One may also assume that the child's experiences, because undifferentiated, are more strongly marked with *emotion* than those of an adult. The child will connect the words with the experiences it has had in connection with learning and using them, and with the emotions and value judgements which those situations have given rise to: the child will begin to interpret phenomena as nice, lovely, frightening, horrible, warm, secure, forbidden, agreeable, soft; all these judgements harmonizing with the situations the child has experienced and with their interpretation by the immediate environment. The words that the child can recognize and use come to be, as Anna-Greta Heyman describes the process (1976: 6):

"a steadily increasing number of identifiable fragments emerging from the chaos, and these fragments by having been given a name are fenced off from anonymity and become an interpretation of a portion of reality. These fragments become more and more numerous, the details more and more precise, and reality more and more an integral part of the child itself. The child absorbs this emotional knowledge exactly in the way that the surrounding world wishes the reality to be interpreted, and in as richly nuanced a way as the adult mediator herself is able to transmit it."

The poet Uuno Kailas conveys something of this in his old poem about words:

The words
There are lots of words –
the words are alive
and I can see them.
Some are ugly and others are beautiful.

Mother is a very sweet word – the best word.
It tastes very much like a little kiss.
Father is a nice word too,
but sometimes thunder gathers in it
and then you'd better sneak behind the door to hide.
Summer is a very warm word
and you can find it every morning
in the grass and in the pile of sand
World is a very big word
which the brain won't hold.
Birch rod is a hateful word which burns the skin.

People also have empty words.
Inconceivable words.
Like sin and death, which don't mean anything.
But you've still got to be afraid of them.

(Uuno Kailas, *Runoja*, 1932, translation Tove Skutnabb-Kangas and Martin Allwood)

The child is educated to a considerable degree through language, especially where different kinds of ethical rule are concerned, which are not derivable in a direct and purely physically observable way from the immediate situation. Sometimes rules about what the child may or may not do are easy to demonstrate physically (by preventing the child from doing something, by physical punishment, etc.). In addition the way work is organized in society, in particular the way children are expected to learn professional skills, to a large extent determines the need to put into words for the children what we want them to learn. In societies where children learn the same occupations as their parents, the process of learning is more often by imitation and observation of the behaviour of adults and older children (observation made easier by the fact that the children are commonly present as the adults are working) than by language. This model learning seems in particular to apply to traditional hunting and farming societies (for practical examples from the aboriginal population in Australia today, see Sommer, 1979). But also in cultures where adults and children are always together, and where this constant association permits non-verbal learning of ethical rules, linguistic and non-linguistic types of learning co-operate. If we examine in particular non-verbal meanings, we shall see how much we owe to language for our *ethical rules.*

The child also partly learns through language who is "one of us" and who is "one of them". The child comes to feel an affinity with those whom it can understand, those who speak in the same way as it does, those who form its own group. Language plays an important part, too, in the development of *identity.*

Denotative meanings of words are based on agreements between speakers of the same language, and for the sake of understanding therefore these meanings must be largely common to all speakers of the same language. But connotations (associations, emotional charge, and value judgements) on the other hand vary. What kind of connotation the child learns depends to a large extent on its individual experiences and on the group or groups to which it belongs. For example, words like "capitalist", "cunt", "opera" probably have different connotations for different social groups and different individuals of different sexes. One may surmise that the connotations of words show greater inter-group variation (perhaps also inter-individual variation) the more abstract the denotation of a word is (that is to say, the less the word refers to something in physical reality).

The fact that connotations are so highly charged emotionally may be deliberately misused in advertising, in political propaganda, etc. The fact that the learning of connotations occurs unconsciously, so that they are from the point of view of the learner almost an unintentional byproduct and are totally embedded in the deeper layers of the personality, makes it more difficult to analyse them and above all to free oneself from their highly emotional impact.

To give an example: A few years ago, I made a series of radio programmes for the Finnish school broadcasting service. The programmes were intended for upper secondary school. One programme dealt with female and male language. Among other things we discussed the different norms that girls and boys have in swearing, and I asked my daughter what swear words the girls in her class used. She gave me this string of words: "saatana perkele vittu jumalauta". "Vittu", cunt, the name for the female sexual organ, is one of the most common swear words in Finnish – one can hear it hundreds of times a day in the street as one goes past people. As soon as the programme had been broadcast, the then Minister of Education telephoned the Finnish Broadcasting Corporation and was very upset that a word like "vittu" had been used in a radio programme. After giving a long dressing down, the minister demanded that the word should be cut out when the programme was repeated. One would think that a minister could conceivably spend her time better than in cutting cunts out of radio programmes, but I think this example shows quite clearly that the value judgements as to what is proper or improper that a person has acquired in childhood when learning connotative meanings are so strong, that in this case, for instance, the minister reacted instinctively even though intellectually and at the denotative level she surely must have understood both the meaning of the offending word and its function in the context, i.e. that it was not being used referentially.

When the child begins to have enough experience of its environment to be able to compare different objects with the same referential meaning, more and more differentiated denotative meanings will develop. Let us take a concrete example: the word *table*. When the child first learns the word table, it may be just one particular table that it associates with the word: a red square kitchen table at which it has often eaten and thus come to know well. It has perhaps poured milk and juice on it, smeared its sticky fingers on it, gnawed at it, banged out various sounds with a spoon or with its fist or a mug on it. This is the only table the child knows and it is the table it thinks of when mummy or daddy talks about tables. Then the child gets bigger and crawls into the living room and gets to know that the low round glass object with one leg there is also called a table, in spite of the fact that it has no external characteristics in common with the object it has hitherto called a table. Then the child is taken to a neighbour's house where it sees something which is also called a table, but which is not at all like the other tables. By comparing the different tables with one another, and by trying to see what is different and what is the same, the child will gradually realize after its analysis what it is that constitutes the "tableness" of the tables: what characteristics an object must possess to be called a table (a surface used for certain purposes). When the child has reached this point, it has learnt the concept *table*.

The two kinds of meaning probably begin to develop simultaneously – or so at any rate we may surmise. But since the child needs many experiences of the same phenomenon in different forms in order to be able to compare, exclude and generalize, it probably takes longer to develop the denotative meanings. Moreover, it is possible to connect the steadily growing importance of the denotative meanings in the child's life with a developing versatility in the use of language: to begin with language is probably used more to convey emotions and expressions of the will and to make contact with other people (for example, "I want food", "I'm wet, it feels uncomfortable", "I want someone to come and pick me up"). Later it is also used to receive and convey knowledge and information, to investigate and analyse the world.

> "At the beginning, when the denotative meanings are still imprecise, the child's language learning is directed by impressions of a totality and by emotion: she is more dependent on connotation. Later the instrumental function of language as a medium for acquiring knowledge comes into greater prominence, when the child learns to use language as a tool for intellectual communication." (Londen & Skutnabb-Kangas, 1976: 2–3).

At the same time as the child learns to understand words and situations, it also learns to interpret the non-verbal messages conveyed by the environment. The child learns the kinds of intonation and pitch which are characteristic of its language. These are learnt very early. The child learns what different facial expressions and gestures mean – the cultural differences in this area are considerable. The child learns whom to look at and how, and what kinds of eye contact a woman or a man can have or not have. It learns to interpret other people's facial expressions and to react to them – and little girls quite quickly become more skilled at this than little boys (Eakins & Eakins, 1978: 155–59; Thorne & Henley, 1975) and bilinguals more skilled than monolinguals (Cummins, 1975). Similarly, the child learns what facial expressions it may have and how much it may make use of them. Women, for example, smile much more than men, just look at your photograph album and count up! The child learns how to stand, sit and walk, what movements are permissible – we know, for example, that men in all bodily positions on average take up more room in relation to their body size than do women: their legs and arms extend further from the trunk in walking and sitting. Just take a look next time you're on a bus, at a party, at a meeting, or in the street – who takes up more space? The growing child learns something about the size of its personal territory which strangers may not enter. Here, too, there are very marked cultural and sexual differences: men – and even women – allow women a much smaller personal territory than they do men; one approaches closer to a woman than to a man. The neutral speech distance also between two strangers is considerably greater between two Scandinavians or two English people than, for example, between two Arabs (about 80 cm and 30 cm respectively). Territorial differences are also seen in situations where two pedestrians have to decide who gives way to whom, or where mutual touching is concerned. Things, too, like how tightly or loosely clothes can be worn form part of the pattern of non-verbal communication. Most of the differences in non-verbal communication between speech partners signal power and submission.[9]

It is likely that the learning of non-verbal meanings is to a large extent unconscious. Often we do not know, for example, that our way of looking at other people or touching them is learnt behaviour. We often take it for granted that the way these things are done in our culture is self-evidently the only right way. Many inter-ethnic and inter-sexual misunderstandings seem due to our lack of awareness of this (see, for example, Gumperz, 1979; Eakins & Eakins, 1978; Swetland, 1979).

A good example of this has been given by Terttu Rosengren, the chief adviser for immigrant education in Gothenberg. In Turkish a quick backward jerk of the head (roughly the movement we would make to indicate agreement or affirmation) means NO (Allwood, 1979). A young Turkish immigrant girl started in a Swedish school and came into the dining room. When she had finished her helping, she was offered some more. She was full and didn't want any more, but since she couldn't speak Swedish, she resorted to gestures, and jerked her head backwards – and was given a second helping. When this non-verbal communication had been going on for a while, and the girl was being given more and more food she didn't want, her only way out was to throw the plate and the food on the floor – she couldn't make herself understood in any other way since her NO was taken in Swedish terms to mean YES.

Facial expressions, gestures and other non-verbal messages also help us to interpret verbal messages. It is important for this kind of interpretation that verbal and non-verbal messages are in harmony with one another, so that we do not, for instance, shout and look enraged when we are saying we love someone. If we send contradictory messages, the receiver will find it difficult to interpret what exactly it is we mean – this is called double bind. If contradictory messages are directed at young children for a long period of time, the consequences can sometimes be very bewildering, even dangerous (see Allwood, 1979: 18). Which of the messages gets across better, which one we actually believe and react to, if they are contradictory, seems to a large extent to depend on "what factors and what aims are most important for the individual taking part in the communication" (Allwood, 1979: 18). It is thus not possible to place verbal and non-verbal communication in any order of importance.

The three aspects of the learning process are being gradually interwoven and together constitute the learning of the mother tongue. To have mastered a language "completely" presupposes that a speaker has a complete command of it at all these levels, that she has learnt denotative and connotative as well as non-verbal meanings. This development is an inseparable part of the process by which the child familiarizes itself with the world about it, learns to know the world, and also to know itself, feels its way forward and tries to find its own place in the world. It is through this process that the child becomes a human being and develops into a unique individual.

That is why the child will find it easiest to express the results of this process, i.e. to express its own most inner personality, its strongest emotions and clearest thoughts, its own self, in the language in which this learning and development have taken place – its mother tongue.

2.4   The learning of other languages – what is different?

In the last few years, interlanguage research has shown that the learning of the mother tongue and the learning of foreign languages, both by adults and children, resemble each other in many respects. This applies above all to the progression in the acquisition of grammar and possibly also to some of the strategies used in generalizations and corrections.[10] The "mistakes" both children and adults make in syntax and morphology when they learn a foreign language largely resemble the mistakes which a young child will make when it learns the same language as its first language. But it is equally clear that, even in the growing acquisition of grammar, there are a number of mistakes *not* shared by first language learners and second language learners (for a discussion, see Canale, Mougeon & Beniak, 1978; Canale & Swain, 1979). When we look at all the case studies of children learning a foreign language, it seems convincing that there are differences between first and second language learning.[11] There are reasons for assuming that, in the area of the less easily accessible, largely unconscious processes of language learning which we have been describing for the learning of the first language, the way one acquires a second language differs from the way one acquires one's mother tongue (for example, Hansegård, 1972).

Since in most cases a child learns two languages simultaneously only in bilingual families where the parents have different languages and each consistently speaks her or his own language to the child, the more usual situation for most people is already to "know" one language fairly well when they come to learn a second. They have already gone through the process once of investigating their world, naming it, abstracting denotative meanings from their experience, comparing and excluding. They already have many concepts, many ways of classifying the world. They already "know" the world and themselves, they no longer experience the world in quite the same total, emotional and vague way as they did before they knew it. When the child (or the adult) learns another language in addition to the mother tongue, it is neither necessary nor even possible for her to go through the same process again (and in the same way). She can immediately begin to transfer concepts from her mother tongue into the new language, can immediately start with denotative meanings (even if this is not an automatic process – see Aronsson, 1978b).

Even if many denotative meanings in different languages do not necessarily entirely correspond, the references of the more concrete words still overlap to such an extent that it is possible to establish translation equivalences: for example, to say that Swedish "bord" = German "Tisch" = Latin "mensa" = Finnish "pöytä" = Spanish "mesa" = Japanese "つくえ" = Greek "$\tau\rho\acute{\alpha}\pi\epsilon\zeta\alpha$" = Turkish "masa" etc. When a Swede hears that "bord" is "pöytä" in Finnish, or "mase" in Kurdish, she need not do what she did when she originally learnt the denotative meaning of the Swedish word 'bord': she has no need to go round touching tables, putting her sticky fingers on them, gnawing at them, climbing on them or upsetting them in order time and time again as she sees another table which looks slightly different to be able to say: "Ah, this must also be a 'pöytä'," or "Ah, this must also be a 'mase'." The denotative meaning can be transferred direct.

This kind of learning of denotative meanings at the cognitive level is often all one can do in foreign language teaching in the school, even if teachers make an effort to create an "environment" for the foreign language. In most cases it is probably necessary for a learner to hear and speak a foreign language a good deal, to have a real diversity of experience in it, to live in it, so that connotative meanings can gradually begin to arise and non-verbal meanings can be absorbed (Rabel-Heyman, 1978: 224). But since the learner already "knows" the world, her experiences and the words attached to them will no longer be as emotionally charged in the new language as they are in her mother tongue. Moreover, she will also perhaps be more critical: she will be in a better position to discern what value judgements are carried by the words in the other language. At the same time, in making these comparisons, she may also become more aware of the value judgements implied in her *own* language, even if this does not necessarily mean at all that she comes to be free of them, or no longer influenced by them.

I suppose many people have had the experience I have had, that it is easier to use what for many people are "taboo words" in a foreign language than in one's own – such as swear words and sexual words. When I lived in the USA I deliberately learnt to swear in English, and I went round saying "bullshit" and "fuck your mother" quite uninhibitedly, since they had no connotation for me. Until one day my male colleagues at the university asked me in a slightly embarrassed way whether I couldn't swear a bit less – they found it awkward to be in the company of a woman who swore like a trooper. I've learnt to swear fairly easily in my mother tongues as well, but this was a difficult (and temporary) stage in my struggle for freedom. . . .

It is in second or foreign language learning no longer necessary or possible to accept everything in an unreflectingly emotional way as self-evident, holistically, naturally the only possible thing, as one did when learning one's mother tongue.

Many bilinguals testify to the fact that their second language, which they learnt later in life, feels colder, more alien, less rich in words, less subtle and on the whole poorer. It does not go as deep, it does not come as close to them, it does not affect them as strongly as the first. It feels more superficial, more "stuck on", it does not awaken the same deep layers of the personality. One is more oneself in one's mother tongue. All this seems also to be true of many bilinguals who know their second language very well, just as well, or in many cases even better, than the language they learnt first.

An exception to this seems to be connotations for words for experiences one has simply not had in one's first language. If one, for example, falls in love for the "first" time in one's life in a foreign language and not in one's mother tongue, the connotations of words connected with falling in love may well turn out to be stronger in the second language. In this case one has learnt the words in one's own language only as intellectual knowledge, without personal experience, and they are given their "real content" only in the foreign language. The same seems to be true for cultural experiences which are very different in the two languages and consequently also in the two cultures. This is something that many people describe who have moved to a foreign country just at that stage in their lives when they have begun to free themselves from the values of the home or from certain more formal social conventions typical of the older generation in their own cultures. In this case they have experienced the environment they have come into in a foreign country as something of a relief and a liberation.

The statements I have made above about the importance of the mother tongue are fairly strong, and they have also aroused much controversy. But many scholars also have tried to verify assertions of this kind empirically, either for example by using Osgood's semantic differential (Ervin-Tripp, 1973) in order to try to find out whether the connotations in the different languages come to be different, or in other ways (see, for example, Brattemo & Wande, 1980). But it is rather difficult, if not impossible, to measure the intensity and depth of experience (but see Herrell & Herrell, 1980). So far we are almost entirely dependent on what positivist-orientated scholars call "anecdotal evidence", unsystematically gathered information without any claim to be statistically representative or generalizable from. But as long as we do not even have much in the way of anecdotal evidence, let alone any other kind, to be *set against* the interpretations I have proposed above of the difference between the first language and languages learnt later in life, I think it is justified to work with them as a starting point, especially since they seem to agree well with bilingual speakers' own experiences. Let me first give some examples of different kinds of anecdotal evidence – there are very many statements of the following kind:

Theodor Kallifatides, a Greek author living in Sweden and writing in Swedish, formerly chief editor of *Bonniers Litterära Magasin* – a man who works with the Swedish language in his *professional* capacity and who very likely "knows" Swedish better than most Swedes – affirms that it is his experience that "something – sometimes a good deal – of the emotional power of words is lost when a speaker tries to express her or his emotions in a foreign language" (quoted in Heyman, 1976: 8). He also said in May, 1978

(Stedje & af Trampe, 1979) that he would be able to lie freely at any time in Swedish because his feelings of guilt and shame at lying were simply not aroused in Swedish. In Swedish it came to be no more than a matter of a certain intellectual control: he knew about it if he lied in Swedish but the knowledge did not affect him. If on the other hand he were even to try to lie in Greek, his mother tongue, all the deep seated feelings of shame and guilt which his mother had instilled in him when he was a child would be aroused within him. Kallifatides did, it is true, say this in Swedish, but what he says agrees in fact with the experience of many other bilinguals.

Let me give another similar example: Matti Lautkoski from Örebro, who is professionally engaged in the training of interpreters, and who is thus very much bilingual after nearly twenty years in Sweden, says that he can say to any Swedish woman at any time "I love you", even standing in the queue at a hot dog stall. He knows what the words mean notionally but they are simply words coming out of his mouth and he is in no way responsible for them since they arouse no feelings in him (his wife is also Finnish). But when he says the same thing in Finnish, THEN . . . every part of him feels what he says! And THESE are really strong feelings. In Finnish he can only say this to his wife – and possibly to one or two others. . . .

Matti has also said that when he hits his thumb with a hammer it doesn't help him at all to swear in Swedish. No amount of "satans djävlar" (bloody hell, literally Satan's devils) will help the pain. But as soon as he says PERRRRKELE in Finnish (perkele = devil) his finger starts to hurt less – it is then that he is able to mobilize within himself the energy he needs to cope with the pain.

The governor of Norrbotten, Sweden, Ragnar Lassinantti, who comes from a Laestadian part of the country[12] where the language of religion used to be Finnish (Jaakkola, 1973a; Hansegård, 1968, 1978), has often said that he has to confess his sins in Finnish, "otherwise it doesn't take".

Two South Same teachers I met in Snåsa, two women who spoke Norwegian "perfectly" (the South Same population of about 1000 people is obliged to be completely bilingual), told me about the way they felt when we were talking about mother tongues. One of them, who had known little Norwegian when she started school, said she felt somehow closer to herself when she spoke South Same. The other, who was married to a Norwegian and spoke Norwegian to her children, had at one stage in her life for many years lived in a place where she could not speak South Same to anyone during the winter months. She could only speak her mother tongue in the summer during the holidays when she went back to her own part of the country. She said that Norwegian worked very well in most contexts and she felt the language was natural to her. But when she was really depressed Norwegian was no real help to her. The only thing that helped then was for her to go out for a walk by herself and talk aloud to herself in South Same.

2.5   The mother tongue – our roots

When we consider the great difference between the learning of the mother tongue and the learning of any additional language, it is easier for us to understand why the mother tongue is so crucial to our personality, and why any questioning of its right to exist is inevitably not felt to be simply a questioning of the status of a *language* but is often also felt to be a questioning of the whole person, of parents and immediate environment, of the whole group the speaker comes from and identifies with. Ultimately, this may be experienced as a vote of no confidence in the speaker's whole way of life, her values and ideology. Thus when the Swedish authorities question the value of an immigrant child's mother tongue by not allowing it the same status even in the school that Swedish has, this can easily be experienced by the child as a symbolic act, a depreciation of everything the child represents. In the same way it is easier to understand why it is often difficult for us to examine our mother tongue critically and to dissociate ourselves from certain values and emotionally charged attitudes bound up with it, as we can much more easily with some other language. We often become particularly sensitive when we are away from our own country and do not hear our own language every day – I can well remember in America standing and sobbing when I heard Finnish songs which in Finland I dissociate myself from for ideological reasons, and which I treat rather ironically when I am at home and can quite easily dissect.

When we hear a child (or an adult) speak, we only hear what is on the surface, what comes out of her or his mouth. Usually when we listen to someone, we know very little about what is beneath the surface, about all the things that happened before the child came to know her language quite well, before she accomplished the feat of being able to express herself in language. We cannot see how deep the roots of language lie in the child's linguistic experience and experience of the world. We see and hear only the outward and final result.

I have often used the image of a water lily to illustrate linguistic development. When we hear the child speak, we see only what is above the surface of the water, the water lily itself (the surface flow, BICS, see 5.2.3.5). But the roots of the mother tongue lie deep beneath the surface, in the more or less unconsciously acquired connotative and non-verbal meanings. When the child learns a foreign language, that language easily becomes as it were a splendid water lily on the surface which superficially may look just as beautiful as the water lily of the mother tongue: the child certainly learns to talk fairly fluently and with an absolutely genuine accent about everyday, concrete, familiar things (see the section on optimal age, 7.3.5.4). But it is often the case that for a very long time the second language is a water lily more or less floating on the surface without roots (see Figure 2).

If at this stage we allow ourselves to be deceived by the beautiful water

FIGURE 2

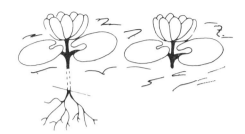

one well developed
mother tongue

interrupted development of
the mother tongue

well developed bilingualism

lily of the foreign language into thinking that the child knows this language (since she sounds exactly like a child who speaks the language as her mother tongue) well enough to be able to be educated through it, or if for other reasons the child has forced upon her education in the foreign language, the development of the flower of the mother tongue may easily be interrupted. If education in a foreign language poses a threat to the development of the mother tongue, or leads to its neglect, then the roots of the mother tongue will not be sufficiently nourished or they may gradually be cut off altogether. If the foreign language is merely a water lily floating on the surface without proper roots, a situation may gradually develop in which the child will only have two surface flowers, two languages, neither of which she commands in the way a monolingual would command her mother tongue. Thus double semilingualism. And if the roots have been cut off, nothing permanent can grow any more. The child's own language has crumbled apart, is fragile, no longer solid, and the new language is nothing more than "borrowed plumage". Sandro Key Åberg speaks about "our own language" and "the borrowed language", and his descriptions of them in these terms correspond very well with the way we actually experience our mother tongue and a foreign language:

"It is, or should be, every person's right to have her own job and her own language. It is with these tools that she makes for herself a place in the social world, formulates her sense of herself, and creates the relationships which bind her to herself, to the world, and to other people. . . . Your own language is the language you have a real relationship with . . .

"It is only by using our own language, the language we ourselves have a relationship with, that we can establish relationships in turn with the world and with reality, establish contacts with our fellow people through which the beat of another heart, the vibrations of another being can be felt. The borrowed language holds a human being apart from reality, comes between her and her world, isolates her in a world without relationships.

"The borrowed language is the one you have no relationship with, it does not grow in you, and you do not grow in it; reality comes to you ready made with it, tinned or bottled, packaged so that you cannot taste, feel, smell or see the genuine quality of reality; using it you are only a receiver not a giver. The borrowed language demands obedience, it eases you like a horse into a stall away from your freedom.

"The borrowed language is a level surface spreading out before you without depth or any savour of experience. Your own language is the country you inhabit, you can walk in it with movements that are your own, you can breathe your own breath in it, your own eyes can glitter in it, or you can see it before you with its own movements, winds blowing, water shining still or glistening in movement.

"Our own language grows in us out of our own experiences, it constantly puts out the shoots of new and green relationships, it loses old and withered ones. It offers us concourse with reality, in the course of which with both emotional and rational energies we repeatedly test, examine, assent and reject.

". . . The world and we ourselves only come really to be familiar presences to us when we speak about it and about ourselves in our own language. The images of reality in the borrowed language are no more than pictures seen through the lens of a camera, never with the eye of the senses. In the borrowed language, in the language which is not growing within us but rather settling within us like sediment, we are anonymous not only to others but also to ourselves."

(Sandro Key-Åberg, 1973)

It may sound a little pathetic to describe the mother tongue using terms and images like these: to say, for example, that the mother tongue is our skin and the foreign language is like a pair of tight jeans, which at first feel stiff and unfamiliar but after they have been worn for a time come to feel easy and comfortable, though they can still never be a substitute for the skin. Or to say the foreign language is an overcoat which we can put on or take off to put another on – we can put on a new dress (for this, read "linguistic dress") but it is still something superficial by comparison with our skin. To take away our mother tongue from us is like skinning or flaying us alive. Shakespeare knew this feeling and makes Mowbray speak of it when he is sentenced to banishment from his country and his language:

> The language I have learnt these forty years,
> My native English, now I must forgo;
> And now my tongue's use is to me no more
> Than an unstringed viol or a harp;
> Or like a cunning instrument cas'd up
> Or, being open, put into his hands
> That knows no touch to tune the harmony.
> Within my mouth you have engaol'd my tongue,
> Doubly portcullis'd with my teeth and lips;
> And dull, unfeeling, barren ignorance
> Is made my gaoler to attend on me.
> I am too old to fawn upon a nurse,
> Too far in years to be a pupil now.
> What is thy sentence, then, but speechless death,
> Which robs my tongue from breathing native breath?
>
> *(Richard II* 1.3)

Every depreciating word spoken about our mother tongue we feel as a kind of branding. This may again sound rather too poetic and romanticized, especially for positivist-orientated scholars. And this sort of language can easily be used to support different kinds of ethnocentric and reactionary movement from which I would entirely dissociate myself. It may also be difficult to understand the importance I attach to the mother tongue if one is oneself completely monolingual (with the exception of languages learnt at school), for then one has never experienced any threat to one's mother tongue and has never needed to make of one's relationship with one's mother tongue a challenging problem – monolingual naivety, as we bilinguals sometimes describe it: the somewhat naive paradisal state that allows one to take everything as self-evident and one's own way of looking at the world through the spectacles provided by one's *own* language as being by definition the only right way. But I have a fairly definite hypothesis about the importance of the mother tongue, and I believe that in this case as in so many others the evidence we can derive from creative writers confirms much of what we researchers are still unable to establish by our methods of investigation. These methods seem curiously underdeveloped even when it comes to describing, let alone measuring, the kind of phenomena we have been discussing. And so, some more quotations:

> "It is my Finnish language that is my skin, my air I breathe, my snowfall, my rage and my sorrow; it is in this language that I heal my deepest wounds, and it is here that I shape and root my deepest feelings. My Finnish language is the very source and ground of my own being."
> (Jalava, 1978: 4–5)

The Official Measure
I predict a general collection
where the goodness of the few walks in the streets
and cries unheard like the Baptist in the wilderness
I predict that every town in Sweden
will organise bazaars, funfairs, communal activities
in order to buy back the lost words for the poet
in order to return to the immigrant poets
the words they have lost
in the labyrinth of adjustment
in the sea of assimilation
Who will be able to prevent us from becoming
shadows without bodies
Who will be able to prevent us from writing
with gall instead of ink
Who will be able to prevent our songs
from urging revolt
The people without language
The people who cannot talk
gather within them gunpowder instead of words
Who would be able to prevent our songs
from lighting the fuse

(Guilem Rodrigues da Silva, 1978, translation by Lars Malmberg)

Notes to Chapter Two

1. See, for example, *Svenskt i Finland,* 1973; Schalin, 1975; *Royal Commission*, 1965; Hoffman, 1975; Allardt, Miemois & Starck, 1979; *Lagstadgade kulturella minoritetsrättigheter i Sverige*, 1978.
2. See, for example, Ralston, 1978; Elias-Olivares & Valdés-Fallis, 1978; National Indian Brotherhood, 1972; Sevilla-Casas *et al.*, 1973; Skutnabb-Kangas, 1979a, 1979b.
3. Critchley, 1974; Galloway, 1976, 1978; Langlois & West, 1978; Paradis, 1979.
4. When I use the term "competence" in this book, I intend it to have its ordinary everyday meaning of skill, proficiency, capability. I am *not* using the term in its narrow linguistic Chomskyan sense. If I mean to refer to Chomsky's concept of competence at any point, I make it clear that I am doing so.
5. The opposite may also be true: at Roskilde University Centre, where work and administration are in many ways uniquely organized, one can for example hear two Germans speaking German to each other in the car on their way to the university, introducing a few Danish words as

they get closer to the university and begin to discuss university matters, and then finally switching over to Danish fairly easily when there is a whole sequence of Danish words referring to things specific to Roskilde University Centre which make for great difficulties in German and trigger a switch to Danish. Or it may be that a German and an English teacher at the RUC who normally speak English to each other will change to Danish when discussing matters to do with the university – is Danish then their mother tongue so far as the university is concerned, since they would not be able to speak about university matters so easily in German or English? According to the definition by competence: yes of course!

6. For example, Louis Ronjat (see 7.2.2), whose linguistic development in a bilingual family has been described in detail, found it easier himself later in life to discuss technical matters in his father's language, French, which was also the language he had used at school, whereas it was easier for him to express himself in writing in his mother's language, German – West, 1926.

7. See, for example, references in articles by Yoshida, Wode, Huang & Hatch, Hakuta, Ravem and Wagner-Gough in Hatch (ed.) 1978, and McLaughlin, 1978.

8. See, for example, Greenberg, 1966; Greenberg, Osgood & Jenkins, 1966; Lyons, 1970b: 9–14; and for the experience of bilinguals, DiPietro, 1970: 13–20; Kessler, 1971: 1–25; Cummins, 1979a, 1979b.

9. There is an excellent Scandinavian systematization of non-verbal communication in Allwood, 1979; there are good bibliographies in Thorne & Henley, 1975; Key, 1977; Eakins & Eakins, 1978; and partly also in Tavris & Offir, 1977. For other systematizations or introductions, see for example Birdwhistle, 1970; Argyle, 1975 and Cooke, 1978 (with numerous examples).

10. For references, see for example Dulay & Burt, 1974; Hatch, 1977; Palmberg, 1977; Canale & Swain, 1979; and the two journals, *Interlanguage Studies Bulletin* and *Working Papers on Bilingualism.*

11. See, for example, Malmberg, 1972: 114; and references in Haugen, 1964; Vildomec, 1963; the articles in Hatch, 1978 mentioned in 2.2.1.2 or in Felix, 1979 and Pienemann, 1979a, b, and especially in McLaughlin, 1978.

12. Laestadianism is a specific Christian sect with very rigorous norms, founded by Lars Levi Laestadius.

3 Two 'Languages'

3.1   Research into bilingualism: its applicability

The study of bilingualism forms part of the field of *applied linguistics*, in contrast to (or rather complementing) *general linguistics* (and *experimental linguistics*, which approximately corresponds to phonetics and some of the more experimental parts of psycholinguistics – traditionally phonetics has been included under general linguistics, and psycholinguistics under applied linguistics).

Research into bilingualism is inter-disciplinary in character. It is impossible to understand bilingualism as a phenomenon except by crossing the traditional boundaries between disciplines. The questions to be asked in any study of bilingualism are often very complex and the results have often been contradictory. This also indicates that the problems are not of the kind that can be solved within the terms of a single discipline but that co-operation between disciplines is needed. In Scandinavia, too, many cases can be cited of complete confusion, failure to make elementary distinctions, and a surprising inability to understand the problems of bilingualism; this deplorable state of affairs can often be traced back to a narrowly psychological or linguistic approach to such problems (Skutnabb-Kangas, 1978e: 221). It is true, certainly, that within the whole subject of bilingualism specific problems inside one discipline can be concentrated on (for example, using the discipline of linguistics, we can study interference, the way one language influences another), but a specific problem cannot be placed in its proper context without a knowledge of neighbouring disciplines (for example, in studying interference, we must ask ourselves why and under what conditions interference occurs – and this is a question linguistics cannot answer). In the matter, for instance, of education for bilingualism we may without exaggeration say that the education of immigrant children is too important to be left to educational experts, and the children's linguistic development is too complicated to be left to linguists (Skutnabb-Kangas 1978e, 221).

Different researchers emphasize different things in their study of bilingualism, depending upon where they started. For example, the

following types of question have been studied (in brackets after each set of questions there is a note of what kind of researchers most often ask them):
- What happens to languages in contact with one another? What effect has bilingualism on the language system and the usage of bilinguals? What effect has bilingualism on the language of monolinguals in contact with bilinguals? (mainly linguists).
- In what way do children and adults learn two languages? Are there differences between children and adults? Are there differences between first language acquisition and second language acquisition? What do the intermediate linguistic systems look like in the process of development from monolingualism through different stages of "interlanguage" (thus Selinker, 1972 – or "approximate systems", Nemser, 1971) towards bilingualism? What can contrastive analysis, error analysis, and interlanguage studies tell us about the strategies of second language acquisition? (linguists, psychologists, educationalists).
- How do bilingual individuals function? Has bilingualism any effect on children's intellectual, linguistic and social development, and under what conditions? (psychologists, social psychologists, sociologists, educationalists, psychiatrists).
- How do bilingual individuals function in different types of society? How do bilingual societies function? What social, legal, economic and political status do bilinguals or does bilingualism have? (sociologists, anthropologists, ethnographers, lawyers, political scientists, economists, historians).
- How does one measure bilingualism at the individual and societal level? (psychologists, educationalists, linguists, demographers).

3.2   What do we mean by two different languages?

Even if most definitions of bilingualism explicitly refer to two different *languages*, not to two different varieties of the same language, few of these definitions make clear what is meant by "two different languages". The applicability of these definitions can therefore often be indefinitely widened (and the results of investigations based on such definitions can be misinterpreted and misused), depending on the kind of distance needed between two languages before one is willing to define them as separate. It is important, therefore, to be able to distinguish between what is regarded as constituting *different languages* and what is thought of as *different varieties of the same language* (regional varieties or *dialects*, social varieties or *sociolects*, sex-bound or sex-conditioned varieties or *sexolects*, situational or *stylistic varieties*). The research problems may by and large be the same no matter whether distinct languages or different varieties of the same language are being considered, but the distinction should be made clear in definitions of bilingualism.

The most common criteria we may consider in trying to decide whether or not we are dealing with two different languages are the *linguistic structure of the languages*, their *mutual intelligibility* (interintelligibility) and their *social function*.

3.2.1   Linguistic structure

The structural criteria above all focus upon the diachronic-linguistic relationships between languages. If two "languages" are not related, then they must in reality be different languages. If, on the other hand, they are related, so that we can show that they have a number of common features, sufficient to enable us to describe them as deriving from a common parent language (for example, the Germanic languages from proto-Germanic, the Nordic languages from Old Norse, although these original languages never, of course, existed as such, see Teleman, 1977b), then the structural criteria do not help us to make the distinction between two languages, for we can elaborate no quantitative criteria suggesting how much in the way of structural similarity or dissimilarity is needed before we can speak of the same language or two different languages. The closer in time the common "proto-language" is, the more difficult it is to decide whether one should speak of two different languages or merely of two different dialects of the same language. With the help of structural criteria, we can say, for example, that Finnish and Swedish are two different languages, but we cannot tell whether or not Norwegian and Swedish are.

3.2.2   Mutual intelligibility, inter-intelligibility

At first glance, mutual intelligibility would seem to be a reliable criterion: what a speaker of a certain language understands is a dialect of her language; what she does not understand is a different language (see, for example, Haugen, 1968). But this criterion is far from being unambiguous. If a speaker, A, of a language understands the neighbouring dialect, the speaker of which, B, in her turn understands the next dialect, the speaker of which, C, in her turn understands, etc. where is the boundary between language and dialect, if speaker A does not understand speaker C, and speaker B does not understand speaker D, etc? If speaker A understands speaker B but not vice versa (non-reciprocal intelligibility, Wolff, 1959), then are varieties 1 and 2 dialects of the same language for speaker A but two different languages for speaker B? Should we, in other words, insist that intelligibility be mutual (as it often is not – see Haugen, 1966a and Dahlstedt, 1970, 1975), or should we leave aside the issue of mutuality in practice, and concern ourselves theoretically only with the question of interintelligibility (see Dahlstedt, 1971, 1975)?

The relationship between Danish and the other Scandinavian languages provides a good illustration here (see Teleman, 1980 for comment on the differences). According to a number of investigations (see Maurud, 1975), the Danes are understood less well by the other Scandinavians than they themselves understand them. Is it the case, then, that Danish, Norwegian and Swedish are varieties of the same language for the Danes, whereas for both Swedes and Norwegians, Danish is a separate language? Or let us take the opposite case, which demonstrates the importance of social factors, of being accustomed to things or not. I was at the local Post Office in Skibby in Denmark. The postmistress couldn't understand my Finland Swedish at all (my Danish companion had to interpret for me), but I understood everything she said in Danish. Is Danish, then, a variety of Finland Swedish, but Finland Swedish a totally different language from Danish?

We may also ask ourselves how well speakers have to understand each other. Must communication be complete before we can speak of varieties of the same language, or is "semi-communication" enough (Haugen, 1966b: 102)? Strictly speaking, intelligibility is never complete even within one and the same language, since different connotations make the semantic experience of what is said different for different individuals (see, for example, Hansegård, 1972: 35–40). How can we decide how much it "says in the text" (Teleman, 1973), and how much of what it says can we be expected to derive from it?

Should the speaker with whose help the languages are being tested be monolingual? It is easy, for example, for a Swede who knows German, English and French to understand a little Dutch, even if she has never before heard it. Are then Dutch and Swedish dialects of the same language?

Should the primary criterion be an understanding of the spoken language, or should we also take into consideration the question of how well the written form of the language is understood? A Finn who has learnt Swedish at school for a number of years may very well be able to understand a good deal of written Danish, but will often not understand a single word of spoken Danish. Is written Danish, then, a dialect of Swedish for her, and spoken Danish a completely different language?

Should the criterion be the language as it is spoken (or read out) by a native speaker, or should we also accept the language as spoken by non-native speakers? Many of us have had the experience that a foreign language is easiest to understand when it is spoken by a fellow country(wo)man of ours (even though this is not by any means always the case – on the contrary, this may be a source of irritation that makes the language more difficult for us than when it is spoken by a native). If, for example, a Swede understands a Danish poem read by another Swede, but does not understand it when it is read by a Dane, is Danish in the first case the same language as Swedish and a foreign language in the second case?

So it is clear that the criterion of intelligibility leads to a number of inconsistencies. Different regional varieties of the same language, for example, Ostrobothnian (Swedish spoken on the Western coast of Finland)

and Scanian (Swedish spoken in Southern Sweden, bordering Denmark) may according to the criterion of intelligibility come to be classified as different languages (if their speakers do not understand each other); whereas two different languages, for example Norwegian and Swedish, may be counted as dialects of the same language (if their speakers understand each other). What for *one* speaker are dialects of the same language may for another speaker be two different languages. Tolerance of deviation from one's own linguistic usage or from one's own language variant also seems to vary greatly as between different individuals (see, for example, Teleman, 1977a). Tolerance is greatest for everyone in the case of related languages, but social factors (knowledge of languages, being used to hearing other languages, education, motivation to understand, differences in status between the languages, attitudes, etc.) also influence it. The more languages an individual knows, the more she is used to hearing other languages, the better educated she is, the better motivated she is to understand, the higher the status of the language she is listening to and the more positive her attitudes are towards it, the easier it will be for her to understand, and the more in principle she will understand. But that the principle does not always hold and that it is not applicable in an easy manner, either, I have learnt from bitter experience as an immigrant in Denmark. Even though I know several languages, and am used to hearing different languages spoken, even though I am highly educated (and my professional speciality should have given me the best kind of theoretical grasp on the problem as a whole), even though I am highly motivated, even though Danish is a high status language, even though my attitudes to Danish and the Danes are positive (I have freely chosen to move specifically to Denmark), even though for a number of years I have had a great deal of contact with Danish and the Danes, I nevertheless often found it difficult during my first two or three years in Denmark to understand Danish spoken rapidly between people who know each other well (especially when they have their mouths full – the stereotype of Denmark as a food-loving country . . .). When I asked some of my acquaintances who had lived for a long time in Denmark, and whose mother tongue was also Swedish, how long it took before they understood almost everything in Danish, they told me it took from a fortnight to a couple of months – this didn't exactly comfort me much (see Skutnabb-Kangas, 1975k on the difficulties Finns have in understanding Danish, and on the reasons for this type of answer). The problem is also that many Danes quite the reverse of me in education, experience and motivation understand my Finland Swedish very well if I speak slowly and change some words for more Danish-sounding ones. . . . And then there is the opposite case: immigrants whose command of Danish sounds "perfect" to Danes, who speak it without difficulty after many years at the Roskilde University Centre, are highly educated and well motivated, may find it *very* difficult to understand my Finland Swedish. . . . Reality is much more complicated than any theory (see also Haastrup & Teleman, 1978).

In summary, we may say that mutual intelligibility as a criterion discriminates well only in the case of unrelated languages (whose "unlikeness", too, can be demonstrated by using structural criteria only). It is less good as a criterion in the case of related languages or regional varieties, since inter-individual (between different speakers) and even intra-individual (the same speaker at different times) variation between those who make the linguistic judgements in these cases is likely to be considerable (Thelander, 1974: 23). Different individual speakers will make different judgements and the same individual will also make different judgements about the same language, depending for example upon whether her motivation and her attitudes change with the change of speaker, and upon whether she is tired or mentally alert, etc.

3.2.3 Social function

When the social function of languages is used as a criterion (Pride & Holmes, 1972: 9), then from the point of view of the social scientist it is probably most important to know what the speakers themselves think of as being different languages. What people think about their own language is the most important functional criterion (Pride, 1970: 291), because that is what influences their behaviour most.

In an investigation of Finland Swedish, the informants felt unsure when they were asked to say what they thought of these statements: "Finland Swedish is one of the dialects of the Swedish language" and "Finland Swedish is a language distinct from the Swedish spoken in Sweden" (Grönroos, 1972). According to a minority of the informants, it was doubtful whether in any sense Finland Swedish could be called a regional variant of Swedish. What these informants were probably questioning was whether the norm of the Swedish spoken in Sweden should also apply to Finland Swedish, or whether Finland Swedish should have its own linguistic norms.

The classification of the old immigrant languages may also cause us to ponder. If a Swedish American herself maintains that she speaks Swedish, should her language really be classified as Swedish, even in cases where a monolingual Swede with no English would, because of interference from English, be unable to understand what she spoke?

When we look at extra-linguistic criteria, too, we are dealing with the social function of language. National boundaries sometimes determine whether "different languages" are felt to be distinct by their speakers (for example, Swedish and Norwegian historically speaking), but national frontiers are not insurmountable obstacles, especially in cases where the frontier separates a linguistic minority from its own neighbouring linguistic community and leaves that minority as part of a country whose dominant language is relatively unrelated (for example, the Finland Swedes, the

Torneå Valley Finns). If communications continue across the border, the separated minority language need not develop into a language felt to be independent and distinct.

The criteria used by linguistics to determine what constitutes a distinct language and what only a dialect of the same language have often had to yield to cultural, ideological and political criteria, especially since the idea of the nation state has gained acceptance.[1] If group cohesion is the over-riding aim, then linguistic differences must be set aside (see, for example, Lehmann, 1975 and Ferguson & Gumperz, 1960). But a small group that wishes to urge for itself a more independent status may find it advantageous to emphasize as much as possible such linguistic differences, both in propaganda and in deed (see, for example, Hovdhaugen, 1976). In connection with language planning, especially in underdeveloped countries,[2] a great deal of work has been done to clarify the complex link between linguistic and social criteria (the complexity of the problem is very well set out, for example, in Kloss, 1969 and Ferguson, 1977). The existence or absence of a codified norm accepted by everybody seems to be decisive.[3]

The most important of all the criteria discussed above should be the various speakers' own decision as to whether the two languages are distinct or not. Here it is important that we make it as clear as possible *why* it is that speakers react to languages as they do. What tends to happen in practice, as in so many other cases, is that speakers in a position of greater power have their own way, and decide what the official view will be (see, for example, the articles in O'Barr & O'Barr, 1976).

3.3   Generalizing from research into bilingualism

There are both dangers and advantages in generalizing from the particular results of research into bilingualism.

The dangers are largely to do with the fact that inadmissible generalizations have been made from results obtained with one group to refer to another, especially about the best methods for different groups to become bilingual. It is, for example, an elementary mistake to generalize from methods used with children in bilingual families (often research into the linguistic behaviour of the children of linguists, i.e. children of highly educated and linguistically aware parents) or with children from linguistic majority groups with a high status mother tongue, and to suggest that those methods might apply with children from minority groups with a low status mother tongue, and often with little formal education. Such a mistake should not be made, but it has nevertheless often been made in the Scandinavian debate about bilingualism. The same elementary mistake can also be seen in one of the new American evaluations (Baker & de Kanter, 1981).

Many of the errors which we now see in early research into bilingualism (where bilinguals almost without exception seemed to acquit themselves less well than monolinguals, no matter what was being measured) were the consequence of mistaken generalizations and comparisons, as will become evident in the section on bilingualism and school achievement.

On the other hand, research into bilingualism may in many ways throw a clearer light on the problems that members of oppressed groups have to contend with in a linguistic community which has different norms from those obtaining in the oppressed group. The insights gained from research into bilingualism can often help us, for example, to a better understanding of the difficulties faced by dialect -speaking children or by working-class children who are confronted at school with the demand that they master middle-class language. Similarly, the study of bilingualism makes it easier to describe the experience of those women who are fighting to make a linguistic impact in a male world (see Spender, 1980). The relationship between two different languages, one dominant, the other dominated, is very similar to the relationship between the languages of the official and private sphere. What is important when we try to decide whether generalizations are legitimate or not seems to be the degree of similarity with regard to power relations, to the social prerequisites for the languages (i.e. status questions) and the speakers, and *not* the degree of similarity with regard to the varieties themselves (i.e. two different languages or two different varieties of the same language).

The study of bilingualism brings out more clearly, when two distinct languages confront each other than when simply two varieties of the same language confront each other, just what many of the factors are which decide the outcome. For example, the reasons for code shift when the situation changes emerge more clearly and can be studied more easily when the shift is from one language to another than when it is merely from one variety to another (Skutnabb-Kangas, 1972c). This is one of the reasons the study of bilingualism is important for the study of linguistics as a whole.

Notes to Chapter Three

1. Lyons, 1970b; Inglehart & Woodward, 1972: 358; Fishman, 1972c.
2. See, for example, Rubin & Jernudd, 1971; Jernudd & Das Gupta, 1971; Rubin & Shuy, 1973; Fishman, 1972c, 1974, 1978; Lewis, 1972; Lehmann, 1975; *Language Planning Newsletter*, 1975.
3. See, for example, Ray, 1970; Rubin, 1972; Haugen, 1966b, 1972c; Dahlstedt, 1975; Hovdhaugen, 1976; Weinreich, 1967; Fishman, 1966a; Fishman *et al.*, 1968; Bull, 1955; Malmberg, 1977; Jernudd, 1979.

4   What is bilingualism?

4.1   Past and present views of bilingualism

Bilingualism has often been associated with a number of negative phenomena. It has often been the weak oppressed linguistic minorities who have been forced to be bilingual, the powerless in society (and this may include numerically dominant but socially and politically oppressed sections of the population).

When two groups speaking different languages or different varieties of the same language come into contact with one another, one of the groups must often learn the language of the other, if the two are to communicate. In the case of communication between individuals, this rule can often be set aside, especially where there is an equal balance of power. But this often does not work at the group level, especially if the languages are very different from each other. Here it is very interesting to study the ways in which Scandinavians communicate with each other: who it is who modifies her language, or who it is who switches to the language of the other, and for what reasons (for in certain situations, too, it is the speaker who *changes* language who demonstrates her superiority by showing, at least at the individual level, that she can "afford" to speak the other language rather than her own).

Usually the more powerful group is able to force its language upon the less powerful. The Same, Romanies, and even Swedes, in Finland, have to learn Finnish but the Finns do not have to learn Same, Romany or even Swedish to anything like the extent that Finland Swedes learn Finnish. Tom Sandlund has shown that about half the Swedish speakers in a community in Finland will know Finnish at the point where the proportion of Finnish speakers has risen to one-third, whereas the proportion of Swedish speakers has to be two-thirds before half the Finnish speakers learn Swedish (Sandlund, 1970). The Inuit learn Danish fairly commonly, whereas the Danes in Greenland do not learn the Inuit language (Kleivan, 1976, 1977). The views of employers in Sweden about the "240 hour law" (adult immigrants in Sweden are now – February 1983 – entitled to 240 hours of instruction in Swedish during paid working hours and it is going to be increased to 600 or 700 hours this year) often display irritation at immigrants who do not sufficiently appreciate the chance to become bilingual (Nelhans, 1975), but there is no corresponding irritation felt that Swedes in their turn do not care to become bilingual, for instance, in Swedish and Turkish.

Bilingualism used to be and is still often associated with poverty, powerlessness, and subordinate social positions (see, for example, Fishman, 1970c; Mackey, 1978; Troike & Modiano, 1975). Bilingualism, then, has come to be something you "get away from" if you succeed in climbing the social ladder. It has been regarded as something negative, as a halfway house in the process of transition from *monolingualism* in a little regarded, low status minority language, via *bilingualism* in the low status mother tongue and the high status majority language, to a final *monolingualism* in the majority language. In this view, bilingualism is seen as a necessary evil, as the means by which a minority speaker may come to have some part in the power and the glory of the majority culture and language, and all the advantages associated with it.

However, this negative view has not always been the dominant one. At the beginning of our era, bilingualism was regarded as both natural and desirable. Thus we find examples of conquering nations willingly learning the language of the conquered (for instance, Romans learning Greek). Bilingualism used to be common, especially among the nobility and the clergy, but also among the bourgeoisie, particularly in and around the larger centres of trade (see Glyn Lewis' excellent survey, 1977), and attitudes to bilingualism seem to have been fairly positive until the emergence of the nation state.

At the end of the nineteenth century and the beginning of the twentieth, we find many statements and "investigations" very negative in attitude, suggesting that bilinguals are lazy, stupid, left-handed, unreliable, morally inferior and so on (see the survey in Weinreich, 1967). This disapproving view was largely dictated by the need to support the "one nation–one language" ideology as an argument for the nation state, and to justify the harsh policy of assimilation directed against both indigenous and immigrant linguistic minorities, as well as against minorities which found themselves on the "wrong" side of some national frontier as the consequence of treaties.

Without being particularly interested in the history of linguistics, one can easily find examples of this use of linguistic argument to give support to political and ideological views just by reading the titles of some of the earlier literature, for example from Germany in the early 1930s. The works of a single author, G. Schmidt-Rohr, yield the following, among a number of similar titles:

Liebe zur Muttersprache, 1931 (Love of the mother tongue); *Stille Bedrohung unseres deutschen Volkstums*, 1931 (A stealthy threat to our German nationhood); *Von der seelischen Schädigung durch Zweisprachig-*

keit, 1932 (On the psychological damage done by bilingualism); *Muttersprache im Selbsterhaltungskampf*, 1932 (The mother tongue in the struggle to preserve identity); *Rasse – Sprache – Volkstum*, 1933 (Race – language – nationhood); *Deutsche Sprache als Träger deutscher Geschichte*, 1933 (The German language as the conveyer of German history); *Volkserziehung durch Sprachpflege*, 1934 (The education of the people by the cultivation of the language); *Volkstumskampf als Kampf der Muttersprache*, 1936 (The struggle of the nationhood as the struggle for the mother tongue); *Die Stellung der Sprache im nationalen Bewusstsein der Deutschen*, 1941 (The place of the language in the national consciousness of the Germans).

(Simon (ed.) 1979: 203–204)

Comment is scarcely necessary.

We can still sometimes find traces of the "old", positive view, even though this is often so bound up with the notion of nationality and in particular with the idea of foreignness, that it is difficult to distinguish between attitudes evoked by the fact that a speaker comes from a foreign country and the fact that she is bilingual. An Italian immigrant in Sweden called Sergio, interviewed in Arne and Monika Järtelius' book *Så blev mitt liv i Sverige*, 1978 (My life in Sweden), speaks in these terms: "In Italy we always look upon foreigners as better than ourselves. Someone who comes from abroad has seen other things and learnt things I haven't."

Even though the negative view of bilingualism has changed somewhat, both in the world at large and even in Scandinavia, this kind of view can still be found, especially among monolingual speakers of majority languages. Individuals with a double linguistic and cultural identity, and the will to hold on to both languages, are still often thought of as deviant, somewhat suspect, slightly abnormal, perhaps not quite loyal (see, for example, Weinreich, 1967: 119–21; Vildomec, 1963: 49). And even though in principle what is deviant and different may be thought of as just as valuable, nevertheless "different" often comes to mean "worse", because the frame of reference is always that of the monolingual community, and what is different is always defined in relation to this norm, this monolingual, monolithic ideal of a society where bilingualism is a positive asset only when it is élite bilingualism of the kind found in the higher social groups. By contrast, the kind of bilingualism generally found among immigrants or other oppressed minorities is not accepted (Skutnabb-Kangas, 1975c: 358). These attitudes to bilingualism as something rather deplorable, something that necessarily has to be accepted but only as a passing phase, can still be discerned in the Scandinavian debate about bilingualism.

Conscious minorities wanting to hold on to their distinctiveness may sometimes also themselves see in bilingualism a threat and a danger. Members of such minority groups who become bilingual in order to have some part in the privileges of the larger majority community may stray very close to the point at which they are lost to the minority, if they are not sufficiently aware and willing to hold on to their minority identity. The minority may impose effective sanctions upon such of its members as become too much orientated towards the larger community.

In other cases, positive encouragement by the majority community of the dominant language element in the bilingual situation and an attitude towards the minority language element which ranges from seeing it as merely picturesque, to one of indifference or even hostility, may be as effective a sanction against the minority language and the possibility of bilingualism as the earlier, more openly hostile attitudes.

There has also emerged in Sweden a new kind of hostility to bilingualism, albeit that it is so well camouflaged that it is difficult at first to see in it the ghost of the twenties and thirties. It is maintained that genuine bilingualism, though greatly to be approved of, is unfortunately impossible to achieve, so that our best efforts should be reserved for the majority language. What we have here in fact, then, is a new set of motivations for the old policy of assimilation, which officially should have been abandoned.

Negative attitudes to bilingualism of this kind are all the more dangerous partly because they are presented in a way which allows one only very indirectly to perceive a latent hostility towards both immigrants and the idea of bilingualism, and partly because some of the research adduced in support of these views is good and reliable – it is only the interpretation of the research that is quite misguided.

We still need, then, a very far-reaching change in attitudes towards bilingualism and bilingual speakers before we can make the best use of the advantages that bilingualism can bring if it is allowed to develop and flourish freely.

But fortunately attitudes are changing fast. Minorities are beginning to arouse themselves, and the majorities must sooner or later wake up, too. Indigenous populations throughout the world have started to organise themselves and formulate demands (linguistic, cultural, economic, political – see Skutnabb-Kangas, 1979b). More and more of them are demanding the right to decide how and in what language their children shall be educated.[1]

Individuals, too, whose forebears were immigrants several generations back have begun to seek their roots – and, for instance, many of the students in the Scandinavian departments of American universities are of Scandinavian ancestry.

The trend is then recessive. Minority groups dominant in their own language but speaking the majority language to some extent, minorities for whom the majority language has come to be the one they command best, and individuals from minority backgrounds who either no longer know the old language or only understand a little of it without being able to speak it, all have begun to turn back towards their linguistic roots, achieving a better balance between majority and minority languages. Bilingualism is no longer seen as a passing phase, but rather as something good and permanent, something to be striven for.

How far these minorites will succeed in reversing the trend and become balanced bilinguals depends to a large extent on political and in particular educational decisions. In a world which is changing faster and faster, it has become increasingly important to have secure ethnic (see Haley, 1977) and/or linguistic roots, and the search for them has intensified (see, for example, Somby-Sandvik, 1977; Lardot, 1977; Küng, 1974).

FIGURE 3
Early view of bilingualism:

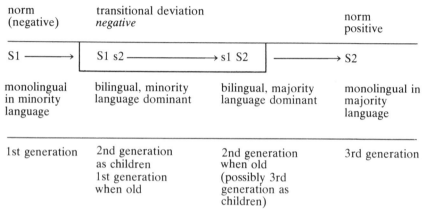

norm (negative)	transitional deviation *negative*		norm positive
S1 ⟶	S1 s2 ⟶ s1 S2	⟶ S2	
monolingual in minority language	bilingual, minority language dominant	bilingual, majority language dominant	monolingual in majority language

| 1st generation | 2nd generation as children 1st generation when old | 2nd generation when old (possibly 3rd generation as children) | 3rd generation |

Later view of bilingualism:

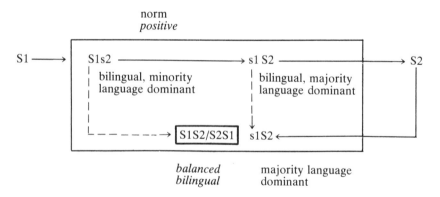

norm *positive*

S1 ⟶ | S1s2 ⟶ s1 S2 ⟶ S2

bilingual, minority language dominant

bilingual, majority language dominant

S1S2/S2S1   s1S2 ⟵

balanced bilingual   majority language dominant

4.2   Who is bilingual, and why?

4.2.1   Uni- and multilingual countries – different situations for minorities

The large majority of the countries of the world are officially unilingual. When we consider the fact that there are nearly three thousand different languages in the world[2] and fewer than two hundred states, it may easily be seen that many languages have a very restricted official status or often none at all. The number of officially bilingual countries is growing fairly rapidly. But still there are many minorities who have no chance of using their mother tongue if they want to take any part in the life of the larger community on equal terms with the linguistic majority.

Let us for a moment just consider Europe. According to Sulo Huovinen's survey (1977) which covers 36 countries (the Channel Islands are excluded but the Faroes and Greenland are counted as countries in their own right), 25 of the countries of Europe are officially unilingual. There are 7 officially bilingual countries (Belgium – where he does not take German as officially equivalent to the other two languages – the Faroes, Greenland, Ireland, Rumania, Finland, and Czechoslovakia). According to Huovinen, only Andorra and Switzerland (the position of Romansh in Switzerland is weaker than that of the other three languages) are officially trilingual. Yugoslavia is officially quadrilingual, and the Soviet Union has more than four official languages. According to Huovinen, there are 5 unilingual countries without autochthonous, indigenous minorities: Iceland, Portugal, Liechtenstein, Monaco, and San Marino. In addition to the unilingual countries, there are only 4 countries in Europe where all the languages native to the country are official: The Faroes, Greenland, Ireland, and Andorra. *In all other European countries*, there are thus minorities whose languages do not have the same rights as the official languages. According to Huovinen, discrimination is practised in 21 of these countries.

The position of minority languages is under threat throughout the world, even in countries where many of them are recognized officially or semi-officially. In India, for example, where over 400 languages are in some way or another officially recognized, there were according to the 1961 census 1652 distinct mother tongues (Pattanayak, 1976, 1970). Minority languages in the strongest position are those *officially recognized in bilingual or multilingual countries*. Seen in world terms, the legal protection enjoyed under the Finnish constitution by the Finland Swedish minority is probably the best in the world (see Kenneth McRae's books on minorities).

§ 14 of the Finnish Constitution (1919) enacts that Finnish and Swedish shall be the official languages of the republic, and that the state shall make satisfactory and equal provision for the cultural and economic needs of the Finnish and Swedish speaking population. In the Language Law (1922) which has been changed several times to improve the protection afforded to the minority, the following provisions are enacted: (in §1 and §3):

"As stipulated in this law, the official languages of the country, either Finnish or Swedish or both Finnish and Swedish, are to be used in courts of justice, other government offices, municipal and other offices in self-administration areas and corresponding communities, in accordance with the language of those concerned."

"A Finnish citizen has the right in questions which concern himself, or if he is being heard, to use his own language, Finnish or Swedish."

The Finland Swedes thus enjoy equal status with the Finnish-speaking Finns, and formally speaking do not constitute a minority (Broo, 1978: 22). Various laws elaborate regulations concerning language rights, and in Finland a considerable organizational and institutional network has been created in Swedish. Swedish-speaking children have their own educational establishments, from day nursery to university, and the Swedish medium schools are administered by a separate Swedish section of the National Board of Education. In the church, the Finland Swedes have their own dioceses, in the army their own regiment, in the broadcasting services their own programme section, etc. (Broo, 1978: 22–3).

The next strongest position is enjoyed by those *minority languages which have limited official rights*. These rights are often territorial, so that a certain part of the country is bilingual, whereas the rest is unilingual (for example, in the Netherlands with both Dutch and Frisian in Friesland; or in Italy with French and Italian in Valle d'Aosta, and German and Italian in Alto-Adige – see Anderson, 1978).

However, even a language without any official rights may derive support from the fact that it is officially used in another country. If the language receives *support from being the majority language of another country*, the speakers will find it easier to maintain cultural activities, to obtain textbooks, and so on. But this need not always be the case, even when the "mother" language is geographically very close: for example, the German language is not much used in writing (other than in purely dialect literature) by the German speaking minority in Alsace in France, although both Swiss German and standard German are close by. If the minority language situations either side of a border complement each other, as is the case with the German speakers in Denmark and the Danish speakers in Germany (or, rather the German minded and the Danish minded, as Bent Søndergaard, one of the leading experts on the border situation, prefers to call them), there may be relatively little friction. Matters are immediately more difficult if the minorities in the two countries are the products of different historical, political and economic factors: the Swedish minority in Finland, for example, is very much like the Finnish majority in its socio-economic, occupational and educational characteristics, whereas the immigrant, working-class Finnish minority in Sweden, roughly the same size, does not resemble the Swedish minority in Finland in its relationship to the Swedish majority in Sweden. The Swedish-speaking minority in Finland represents the former ruling class, while the Finnish-speaking minority in Sweden is an oppressed immigrant group – even if Finns in Sweden from a global point of view probably are the strongest, best organized migrant labour group in the world. It is only in the last few years that the minority of Finland Swedish speakers have in fact come to recognize their similarity in some sense with the immigrant minority of Finnish speakers in Sweden, and have come to feel some solidarity with them. Those Finland Swedes who have emigrated from Finland to Sweden and have had very tangible reasons for reflecting upon how little in the way of legal rights is enjoyed by the Finnish immigrants in Sweden, by contrast with the legal position of Swedish speakers in Finland, have been instrumental in arousing people to the need for solidarity:

Solidarity
We are today
in the same boat
we and the Finns
and we stand up
and shout
what the hell are you doing
here
of course you can't demand
the same rights here
as we have in Finland

We who know so well
the lot of the minority
we who have fought
for the same demands
and aspirations
where is our understanding
and sympathy
why don't we do anything
to help
our fellow countrymen
(Mikael Broo, 1980, translation by Lars Malmberg)

Where either a linguistic minority in one country is not complemented by a linguistic minority in the neighbouring country, or where two complementary minorities are very dissimilar in status, then very different situations may develop in different countries: there may be discrimination against the minority, as against the German speakers in France, neither West nor East Germany having a French-speaking minority, or there may be a fairly benevolent attitude on the part of the majority, without any discrimination, as is the case with the German-speaking minority in Belgium.

If the minority language has the *support of another official minority language in a neighbouring country*, the situation is hardly affected by comparison with the effect upon a minority language of its presence as a majority language in a neighbouring country. But if the *support* comes only from a *neighbouring unofficial minority language* (as for example with Same, Basque and Romansh), then the situation for the language may be fairly difficult. In these cases the existence of a written standard and a literature comes to be a matter of great importance. In an article about linguistic minorities (1976), Even Hovdhaugen writes:

"In our highly educated modern societies it is unrealistic to suppose that a minority language can survive without the help of a closely supportive written standard."

However not even the support of a well developed written form flourishing in several different countries is always enough. The Kurds, "the most numerous people in the world without a country of their own" (Chaliand, 1980), a population of 15 to 20 million split between five countries (Turkey, Iran, Iraq, Syria, the Soviet Union), are linguistically oppressed in all these countries except the Soviet Union. Turkey, where over half of all the Kurds live, does not even recognize their existence. They are simply called Mountain Turks. The Kurdish language has been forbidden in Turkey since 1923. It is neither taught nor used as the medium for teaching, and this in spite of the fact that there is a flourishing literature in Kurdish from the period before 1923. There are also underground publications produced in Turkey and abroad (which are forbidden in Turkey by decree no. 9 A 112511 of the Ministry for Domestic Affairs, dated 3.1.1967). Turkey also tries to prevent the use of Kurdish in other countries (see the example in 12.3.4). The existence of a codified written standard and the fact that the language is used in many countries by a very large number of people (a greater number than the populations of Norway, Denmark and Finland put together) is thus no guarantee that its speakers will be officially given any chance even to learn to read their own language.

Those linguistic groups are in a very difficult position whose only support is *from a non-standardized language* (for instance, the Romanies in a number of different countries) or *from a vernacular in another country, lacking any kind of standardized written form. Linguistic groups*, however, having no written tradition, found only in one country, and *lacking the support of speakers in another country, are the most threatened of all*. This is the case with many Amerindian languages in the United States, Canada and Latin America, as also with many small languages in Africa and Asia. Attitudes towards these languages and linguistic groups may range from attempts to equip them with alphabets, to record them, describe them (for example, Ebert, 1979) and to provide the most elementary teaching materials (for example, Vorih & Rosier, 1978; Holm, 1975; Albo & Quiroga, 1975; Hernández-Chávez, 1975) on the one hand, to attempts at total eradication on the other. As an example of the former attitude, we may instance the creation of alphabets for many languages in the Soviet Union in the 1920s (Girke & Jachnow, 1974; Lewis, 1972), or similar work in India today carried out by The Central Institute of Indian Languages (1976), (Pattanayak, 1970, 1976), as also some of the work with aboriginal groups in Australia (Rado, 1979; Malcolm, 1978; Sommer, 1979). Examples of the opposite attitude are to be found in Latin America.

Since most speakers of minority languages have to become bilingual if they wish both to retain their own culture and to have some extensive part in the life of the larger community, it is easy to understand that most bilinguals in the world are bilingual because they are *forced* to be. Most minority languages have not the same status, the same official rights as the corresponding majority languages; many of the minority languages are discriminated against and their speakers are oppressed, both politically and economically and also linguistically. Bilingualism is for them not something voluntary but is forced upon them if they are to survive in the majority community.

4.2.2   Bilingual individuals

We may divide the bilinguals of the world into three or perhaps four large groups, each group under a distinct kind of *pressure* to be bilingual, with different *prerequisites* for it, needing to pursue a different *route* (method) to achieve bilingualism, and facing quite different *consequences* if it fails.

These groups are: élite bilinguals, children from linguistic majorities, children from bilingual families, and children from linguistic minorities.

4.2.2.1 Elite bilinguals

The first group consists of so-called élite bilinguals, those who in most cases have freely decided to become bilingual, and who could have avoided it, had they wanted to, or whose parents could certainly have done so. This includes all upper- and middle-class children who travel or live abroad for a time, or who win scholarships for study abroad, the children of academics, diplomats, international civil servants, business(wo)men and so on. It also includes those children who in the past had nannies and governesses who spoke a different language, and children and young people who nowadays have foreign holiday guests to stay in the summer (very often guests who speak a high status language).

Bilingualism for these children and young people is *voluntary*; there are neither internal nor external pressures on the children, insofar as the decision itself to move to another country is made voluntarily by the parents. On the other hand, the children will usually find that they *have* to learn the language of the new country once they have settled in it if they are to have any contact with the native speakers. The pressure to learn the new language is frequently felt more acutely by the children than by the parents, since the parents can often force other people in the new country to speak their own language or some "international" language, which need not be the language of that country. Case studies in which differences between children and parents have become evident can be found in section 2.2.1.2.

The children's *prerequisites* are often of the most *favourable* kind. They will often have been encouraged to acquire a very good command of their mother tongue, or this is done during the time spent abroad, and this mother tongue is not generally in any way threatened by the foreign language (even if perhaps for a time the mother tongue is only used within the home and not outside). The children know that they will be able to use their mother tongue fully again when they go back to their own country, and their command of it is often maintained by reading, holiday trips to their own country and so on, if the stay in the foreign country is at all prolonged. Often, too, they will meet with friendliness, understanding and patience as they try to cope with the foreign language, and will be supported and encouraged in their attempts to acquire it. The *method* by which the language is learnt will often be a combination of the so-called "natural method" (where the children find themselves in situations in which they have to communicate with others in the foreign language) and teaching. Often élite bilinguals will also have some elementary knowledge of the new language before they leave their own country. In any case their social standing is often high enough to protect them, even in direct confrontation, from most of the humiliating and depressing experiences of the kind minority children often undergo. If the children fail to become bilingual, the *consequences* for them at the personal level may certainly be somewhat more serious than they would be for majority children in an immersion programme, but they will be in no sense catastrophic. These consequences may often amount to no more than being sent away to school in the home country, or having rather less contact with native speakers in the host country during their stay, or preferring the company of speakers of their own language, or the like.

The type of élite bilingualism represented by these children and young people has never resulted in problems. It has been thought of as something positive, as an enrichment at the individual level. What also characterizes this type (and distinguishes it from the foreign language learning of majority children at school) is precisely its *individual* character. It is usually individuals who make the decision to become bilingual, and they make that decision more or less alone, and not in organized groups (like classes at school and so on). The international schools (the Kennedy School in Berlin, the European Schools, and so on) are perhaps exceptions here. However, it is rather difficult to classify these: I should like to count those schools which take in children for the whole of their school career (for example, the French School in Stockholm) as schools for majority children, and those schools intended for children who will only stay for short periods (for example, the Kennedy School) as properly speaking élite bilingual establishments.

4.2.2.2 Children from linguistic majorities

This group consists largely of children who learn something of a foreign language at school, for example, Swedish children learning English or French. Another group is children in immersion programmes, children from a linguistic majority with a high status mother tongue, taught through the medium of a foreign language. For our purposes this is the important part of this group, and the part of it our discussion will chiefly focus upon. Children who merely make some acquaintance with a foreign language at school are the subject of other books.

Children from linguistic majorities may become bilingual for at least two reasons. *Firstly*, the situation may be that *social unrest among minorities may be prevented* by guaranteeing a minority language more prestige (i) by its use as a language of instruction for the *majority* and (ii) by enabling it to be more widely used for official purposes (and this is made possible only if speakers other than those drawn from the minority are given a chance to learn it). Partly (some people from) the *majority* group are given further *advantages*. This happens where the preventing of social unrest in the minority group entails acceding to some of their demands, so that the economic interests of the majority should not be threatened. These demands often involve greater privileges for bilinguals. In order for members of the majority group to be able not only to retain the privileges they already have but to have some share of the privileges guaranteed to bilinguals, they must themselves become bilingual (traditionally it has tended to be only members of the minority group who would be bilingual). It is, for example, substantially a situation of this kind which has given rise to the *linguistic immersion programmes* developed in Canada, in which English-speaking majority children are taught through the medium of French, the minority language. There is a clear connection between the emergence of immersion programmes and the language conflicts which have manifested themselves in open discussion of the possibility that Quebec might secede from the federation (see, for example, Lamy, 1978; St. Clair & Eiseman, 1978).

Secondly, majority children may become bilingual by linguistic immersion in situations in which a more prestigious minority language or a so-called world language (a language of wider communication) is taught to an (oppressed) linguistic majority in a (formerly) colonized country – as is the case, for example, in many African states.

Usually, majority children, particularly of the first category, become bilingual more or less *voluntarily*: the motivation is often simply their own and their parents' desire to take advantage of the opportunity to become bilingual. Such majority children are therefore subject neither to external societal *pressure* nor to internal family pressure to become bilingual.

The *methods* and *materials* used for teaching majority children in, and also to some extent through the medium of, a foreign language are better developed than the methods and materials designed for any of the other groups.

The *risk of failure* is small. If the children fail to become bilingual with the help of the school, the consequences will not be disastrous for them either linguistically or academically: in any event they will usually be perfectly competent monolingual speakers, and will have at their disposal a linguistic competence comparable with that of monolinguals. They can also continue to function in society using their own language, since in most cases it is in fact the official language. There is thus no pressure on such children to become bilingual, and the risks associated with failure are minimal.

4.2.2.3 Children from bilingual families

The second group consists of children from bilingual families, i.e. families in which the parents have different mother tongues. If the children come from families in which one parent speaks the majority language (for example, a Swedish–Greek family in Sweden, or a Finnish–Swedish family in Finland), they are under no external pressure from the society to become bilingual; instead society "encourages" them towards monolingualism, provided that they become monolingual in the official language and not in the language of the other parent. On the other hand, they are often subject to *family internal pressure*: it is naturally desirable that they should be able to communicate with either parent in her or his own language. The parents mostly want the children to learn their respective languages. Sometimes the situation will even arise in which the parents cannot themselves speak each other's languages, but communicate rather with the help of a third language which is neither parent's mother tongue, and which can be, though it need not be, the language of the surrounding community. In these circumstances, the child has to learn both parents' languages if she wishes to communicate with both of them, if the parents do not want to switch permanently and produce a situation where one or both will never be able to use their own language at home. A "voluntary" change of language is, of course, also possible, but I think of this as often being the result of an ignorance of the importance of the mother tongue. I have seen many cases in which this realization has come too late, and in which the parents have afterwards bitterly regretted their change of language. Such a "voluntary" change may also be the expression of a colonized consciousness, caused by great pressure to assimilate. *Prerequisites* and *methods* for these children will be further discussed in section 7.2.

There is certain *risk* that the child will fail to become "completely" bilingual in a bilingual family (owing to the very complicated factors affecting the balance between the two languages at different stages in the child's life), and instead will grow up monolingual or very dominant in one of the two languages. The *consequences* for the whole family and for the child itself may be negative, if the child does not succeed in becoming bilingual: the child may well have a less satisfactory relationship with one or both of the parents if she does not share a mother tongue with them. The child can then not communicate with one of the parents in her or his mother tongue, and as a consequence may be unable to have any share in this particular parent's cultural heritage or to acquire any very profound knowledge and understanding of it and of the parent's background. The monolingual child will also be unable to enrich and hand on that cultural heritage (other than in a picturesque and nostalgic way). The child will also lose the possibility of contact with the country from which one of the parents comes, and the possibility of living there for a longer or shorter time without serious language problems, if she should wish to do so. But at any rate, the child will at least become monolingual in the language of one of the parents and in this language will have a native speaker to learn from; and if that language is the official language of the country, there is hardly any risk that the child will not acquire native mastery. If *both* parents come from linguistic minorities, particularly from minorities whose languages have no official status in the society (rather than one of the parents speaking the language officially recognized in that community), the situation of children in bilingual families will be the same as that of children from linguistic minorities. It may often be even more difficult to have two minority languages within the family and yet a third outside, as distinct from the situation of a single minority language in the family and another language outside. But if the parents know what to do, and have time and patience, this kind of situation may function perfectly satisfactorily and the children may become very competently trilingual (see, for example, Orblin, 1980 for a case study of a family in Sweden with a Finnish mother and a French father).

4.2.2.4 *Children from linguistic minorities*

Children from linguistic minorities are subject to a *strong external pressure* to become bilingual (or at any rate to learn the language of the larger community well), since their own language usually has limited official rights, as was clear from the survey in 4.2.1. In addition to the external societal pressure, such children are often also subject to a strong *family internal pressure* to become bilingual. The parents usually want their children to learn the majority language well, especially to ensure that they have better educational and economic prospects than they themselves had. This desire seems to be universal in the minority family. However, the parents will naturally also want their children to learn their own language well. This is self-evident and embarrassing to point out. Exceptions to this rule are those fortunately few parents who for ideological reasons want to dissociate themselves from their own group (for example, some refugees), or who are under particularly strong pressure to assimilate. Such parents, ignorant of the importance of the mother tongue, will give undue priority to the majority language at the expense of their own.

The *methods* and *materials* used to help minority children to become bilingual are still very far from as well developed as one would like them to be, in spite of the considerable amount of work done in the last few years in a number of countries. The risk of failing in the attempt to become bilingual is *greater* for minority children than for the children of any of the other categories, and the *consequences* of failure may be *catastrophic*:

■ If the child becomes almost monolingual or very dominant in her own language, then most future educational opportunities will be closed to her. She will not be able to compete in the labour market with other young people from the majority. Her chances of sharing in the life of the larger community and of influencing it will be severely limited. It will also be impossible for her to try to improve the situation of her own group, together with others, to demand linguistic and other rights for her group, since such demands must be made in the majority language which she does not command well enough.

■ If the child becomes almost monolingual or very dominant in the majority language, and forgets her own language, or indeed never has the chance to learn it properly, then she comes to be excluded from contact with her parents, their origin and culture. The risk of alienation, rootlessness and problems of identity is very real, even if such children and young people may often appear outwardly to function perfectly well as majority members (see, for example, Child, 1943; Laurén, 1973). The loss or the poor command of the mother tongue may also have unfortunate consequences for the mastery of the majority language. There is also the risk that children will take over the values of the larger community together with its language, and in such a case both the cultural wealth represented by another culture and the revolutionary potential to be found in minorities with an ethnic consciousness are lost.

■ If the child does not acquire any language at close to native level, then the disadvantages of both the earlier alternatives are combined, with none of the benefits. We may caricature the situation by saying that children from linguistic minorities who become monolingual have one of these two choices:

■ to become monolingual in their parents' mother tongue, and balanced, well-integrated people, but with no chance of earning a living or of influencing their own situation (unless they choose to return to their parents' homeland and be educated there – for many this will be a political and economic impossibility) or

■ to become monolingual in the majority language, rootless marginal people with no contact with themselves, but with a job. . . .

Either alternative is, of course, impossible. Children from linguistic minorities thus bear the greatest *pressure* to become bilingual, and the *risks* of failure are gravest for them. This is a strong argument that the school as a system should feel a specially great responsibility for them. They have not chosen themselves to become bilingual: they are *forced* into something where a failure often may be a catastrophe. It is little wonder, then, that bilingualism has been often associated with various kinds of misery. Their situation ٮ further discussed in 7.1.2 and 7.4. The majority of the world's bilinguals belong to the category of those who are obliged by circumstances to become bilingual; that should be kept in mind as a starting point in every discussion of bilingualism.

4.3   Definitions of bilingualism
4.3.1

It may seem that "bilingualism" is a homogeneous and well-defined goal, which can scarcely cause confusion of any kind when encountered for example in documents setting out the aims of immigrant education.

However, this is not the case: there are almost as many definitions of bilingualism as there are scholars investigating it. Every researcher uses the kind of definition which best suits her own field of enquiry and her research aims. In this sense all definitions are arbitrary.

This has contributed to the conceptual confusion which has beset the study of bilingualism. Students of the subject have apparently at times been unaware of quite what definition they were using (see Kangas, 1972a: 86), and at other times have failed to make their definition explicit. Other writers have then made unjustifiable generalizations to quite other kinds of bilingual individuals and/or populations (see above, section 3.1 on the applicability of research into bilingualism. Some of the negative "consequences" which have previously been associated with bilingualism can be explained as precisely the result of such misunderstanding (Skutnabb-Kangas, 1975a: 84, 60; Barik & Swain, 1976). This terminological confusion can be clearly seen in some of the Scandinavian discussions about "bilingualism" or "semilingualism" among linguistic minorities, in particular immigrants.[3]

As has become clear in section 4.2, bilingualism can be discussed as characteristic of an individual or as a phenomenon in a society. But most definitions have to do with individuals. In what now follows I shall distinguish as I did with the definitions of the mother tongue, between four main types of definition, depending on which aspect of bilingualism they use as a criterion. Linguists and psychologists are often more interested in bilingual individuals. Psychologists and psycholinguists often describe children who are originally bilingual, from the very beginning (cf. Merrill Swain's PhD thesis with the title "Bilingualism as a first language"), i.e. they use *origin* as a criterion. Linguists often do this, too, but their definitions of bilingualism are more often based on the linguistic *competence of* the bilingual, the way she *masters* her two *languages*. Sociologists are more often interested in what one does with the languages, what they *are used* for or *can be* used for. They define bilingualism in terms of the *function* the languages fulfil in or for the bilingual individual or in a bilingual community. Sociologists and social psychologists (and demographers) are also interested in the way in which the speaker and the people among whom she lives *react to the two languages*. They then define bilingualism in terms of *attitudes*. Some definitions make an attempt to combine at least two aspects, often those of competence and function. All definitions can in principle also be broadened to accommodate multilingualism.

The choice of definition is thus wholly dependent upon what it is to be used for. It is important to note that there is no generally accepted definition of bilingualism applicable in all cases. In view of the plethora of definitions, I shall choose to deal only with a few typical ones – it would of course be possible to choose different definitions and classify them differently (see, for example, Takač, 1974; Johansson & Wikström, 1974).

4.3.2   Definitions based on competence

Definitions by competence are many and varied. It should in principle be possible to accommodate them at points along a continuum extending from the moment of an individual's first contact with a word in a foreign language to the state of complete bilingualism, if it exists.

The classic definition of bilingualism is by Leonard Bloomfield: "native-like control of two or more languages" (Bloomfield, 1933: 56). An equally rigorous definition is by Maximilian Braun: "active, completely equal mastery of two or more languages" (Braun, 1937: 115, quoted in Haugen, 1968). Einar Haugen, the "grand old man" in the research into bilingualism, has a rigorous definition which resembles the ones mentioned earlier: "native competence in more than one language" (Haugen "On the meaning of bilingual competence" n.d., 3). Definitions which also exclude interference fall within the same category, for example, Oestreicher's: "complete mastery of two different languages without interference between the two linguistic processes" (Oestreicher, 1974: 9). In order to distinguish this complete bilingual ability (which at the functional level also presupposes a non-diglossic use of the two languages, so that a speaker is able to use both in all the functions for which one of them can be used) from a less complete ability, Halliday and others suggest the term "ambilingual" for complete bilinguals (Halliday, McIntosh & Strevens, 1964: 141 – Lat. *ambo*, Greek αμφω = both of two).

Moving away from these very rigorous and demanding definitions at one end of the continuum, and coming more to the middle, we may take as an example Einar Haugen's much quoted definition in which he says that bilingualism begins "at the point where the speaker of one language can produce complete, meaningful utterances in the other language" (Haugen, 1953a: 7). Some scholars require no more than "at least some knowledge and control of the grammatical structure of the second language" (Hall, 1952: 14). Others want to broaden the scope of the definition to include even the initial stage of bilingualism, at which a speaker merely *understands the foreign language without being able to speak it* (Pohl, 1965: 344; Diebold, 1964: 469 – "incipient bilingualism"). Others again are prepared to reckon with less knowledge still. John Macnamara lists the four areas of linguistic ability (understand, speak, read, write) and further subdivides each area into four levels (phonemes/graphemes, lexicon, syntax and semantics). In his view a person is bilingual if she possesses at least *one* of the language skills listed above in her second language "even to a minimal degree" (Macnamara, 1969: 82). This would allow us to call a Swede bilingual if, for example, she knew some of the Russian or Greek or Arabic graphemes (letters) without being able to read or understand the words put together from them.

In the last few years scholars have begun to talk about bilingualism even when discussing the *command of different varieties of the same language* ("socially bilingual", Gumperz, 1969: 243). Of course in principle the research problems are the same – bilingual usage lends itself to the same kinds of description as linguistic variation in general (Dittmar, 1974: 211). In this view everyone comes to be seen as bilingual, since linguistic variation occurs in all socially stratified societies (see, for example, Ferguson, 1977: 46–47), and all known societies are socially stratified.

These, and more could be added, give us examples of the full range of possible definitions based on linguistic competence.

4.3.3   Discussion of definition by competence

It seems to be difficult to produce a usable definition based on competence. I shall take up some of the problems involved.

Definitions of bilingualism are needed to describe and compare bilingual individuals or different situations in which bilinguals find themselves. Mostly it would be desirable to be able to express the degree of bilingualism in operational (measurable) terms and to describe and measure it reasonably unambiguously. Competence needs to be measurable because the definitions are often needed to evaluate unambiguously the results of teaching or to distinguish individuals who can be described as sufficiently bilingual for certain purposes (language teacher, bilingual secretary, interpreter, translator, diplomat, student studying at home and abroad, immigrant counsellor) from those who do not fulfil the demands. It follows from this that a usable, measurable definition should differentiate clearly between different groups of bilingual speakers.

Definitions by competence tend either to be *too narrow*, so that hardly anybody falls within the criteria, or *too broad*, so that practically everybody becomes bilingual. And if a definition either includes or excludes everybody, it is in practice useless, since it does not discriminate adequately.

Those definitions which lie somewhere between the extremes encounter great difficulties when it comes to specifying sufficiently precisely the degree of competence in all areas. Definitions should specify what is required in the four areas of linguistic ability (understanding, speaking, reading, writing). Are receptive skills enough, or should an individual also be able to produce – to speak and/or write? Is a person bilingual if she understands what people say even though she cannot say anything herself? Is a person bilingual if she can read a language without difficulty, even though she cannot speak or write it, or even understand it when it is spoken? Is a person bilingual if she can utter a number of sentences from a tourist phrase book even though she cannot understand what is said in reply? Are primary linguistic skills enough, or should a bilingual individual also master the secondary skills (reading and writing)? As we know, most of the world's languages are *not* read and written regularly – either they have no written form at all, or they are only rarely written and by few people (Ferguson,

1977: 48). Is a young child bilingual if she speaks two languages perfectly but is too young to be able to read? And what about an adult who has the same skills as the child, without being able to read and write? Is a Finnish Romany in Sweden trilingual, for example, if he speaks Finnish, Swedish and Romanes but cannot read or write in any of the three languages? Not even the very rigorous definitions consider the problems of these subsidiary areas of language. Those definitions, for example, which talk about "a native competence" still tell us nothing about them, because both a child who cannot read and an illiterate adult (in a culture where there is no homogeneous written language or where illiteracy is common) can of course have a native competence in their mother tongue. A further area of linguistic ability has come prominently into the debate in recent years, that of cognitive competence: the ability to use a language as an effective instrument of thought (for the development of the concept of cognitive competence as it relates to bilinguals, see the work published by Cummins, 1977–83).

There is a further difficulty about definitions by competence: who is to be the basis for comparison? Who constitutes the norm when we specify the requirements a person should fulfil in order to be considered bilingual? If we have in mind the examples given above, of the child and the illiterate adult, it becomes clear that we must also specify the native speaker who is to be the norm. The differences between native speakers are great, as we know: *one* adult will only with difficulty be able to write a private letter or read a popular article in the press with any real profit, whereas *another* will quite unaided be able to compose a submission to a court of law, or write a difficult piece of scientific prose.

The most natural thing, perhaps, would be to make a comparison with a speaker who resembled the subject of the investigation in as many respects as possible (sex, age, academic ability, education, social group, language aptitude). But here, too, we encounter problems. What we would expect of an individual for her to be described as bilingual would differ from case to case. If one person with only primary education and another with a university degree had the same competence in two languages, the former would perhaps be counted bilingual whereas the latter would not, since perhaps more would be expected in the second case, and the demands would be different. It may also often be impossible to determine what should be required, because an equivalent monolingual is perhaps not to be found. Bilingualism and its attendant circumstances may make the bilingual individual quite unlike any monolingual speaker of either of the two languages. Let us, for example, think of an intelligent, middle-aged, Kurdish woman from Turkey, but living in Sweden, who went to school in Turkey (in Turkish) for one or two years only, and who is illiterate. What Swedish woman could we find to compare her Swedish with? And should what we expect of her Swedish differ from what we expect of her Turkish (should her ability to read and write, for example, be expected to be the same as that of an intelligent, middle-aged Swedish woman)?

The example of the Kurdish woman leads us to two further problems. In the first place we must ask whether monolinguals in general can be used as the norm at all against which the competence of bilinguals is measured, or whether rather bilinguals should only be compared with other bilinguals. In the second place there is the question of the relationship between the two languages, L1(= the language first learnt) and L2. It is often assumed in definitions that the bilingual individual has a "complete" command of L1, and that all that actually has to be defined is the level of command of L2. *Balanced bilingualism* is then proposed as the ideal and it is assumed that what this means is that the individual has a *good* command of both languages, which need not at all be the case. These questions were the subject of further enquiry in the section 2.2.5 on complete bilingualism and bilingualism as an educational aim for minorities. The greatest difficulties definitions by competence face are thus:

1. that they are either too broad or too narrow to be able to discriminate adequately,
2. that it is difficult to specify accurately the level of competence the definition requires in subsidiary areas of linguistic ability,
3. that they mostly do not specify whose linguistic ability the bilingual individual's competence is to be compared with, and that they do not decide whether the norm is to be the competence of monolinguals or the competence of other bilinguals, and
4. that they often define the level of linguistic command required only as it applies to L2, and take for granted a complete command of L1, or that they implicitly suggest balanced bilingualism as the ideal.

4.3.4 Definitions based on function

Early research into bilingualism, which was often based on definitions by competence, tried to provide a *purely grammatical–qualitative description* of the bilingual individual's two codes. Only later was quantification introduced. Early research was particularly interested in the "purity" of and the interference between the codes, respectively. But as early as the 1950s (Weinreich, Haugen) and at the beginning of the 1960s, scholars began to turn their attention more and more to the *function of the two languages in and for the bilingual speaker and in a bilingual society*. Interest was now moved from a description of the languages involved to their users.

The first definitions of bilingualism by function had already appeared by the early 1950s. The definitions by function vary much less than definitions by competence. The classic definition among those based upon the use made of languages is by Uriel Weinreich: "The practice of alternately using two languages will be called *bilingualism*, and the persons involved, *bilingual*" (Weinreich, 1967: 1) William F. Mackey's definition is very similar: "The alternate use of two or more languages by the same individual" (Mackey, 1970: 555). Els Oksaar's definition is along the same lines, except that she also includes the requirement that a speaker should be able to switch codes automatically. In her view, a bilingual is someone: "who in most situations can freely use two languages as means of communication and switch from one language to the other if necessary" (Oksaar, 1971: 172). Her definition, which starts from the bilingual individual rather than the social situation in which two languages are used, is an attempt to combine competence and function in the definition. Wilga Rivers makes a rather similar attempt, and suggests that we should: "consider the child bilingual as soon as he is able to understand and make himself understood within his limited linguistic and social environment (that is, as is consistent with his age and the situation in which he is expressing himself)" (Rivers, 1969: 35–36). William F. Mackey summarizes the function-orientated view of bilingualism: "Bilingualism is not a phenomenon of language; it is a characteristic of its use. It is not a feature of the code but of the message. It does not belong to the domain of *langue* but of *parole*" (Mackey, 1970: 554).

4.3.5   Discussion of the definitions by function

The definitions by function were partly needed to counterbalance the very narrow definition of linguistic competence used by theoretical linguists, particularly in the early years of the development of transformational-generative grammar. According to Noam Chomsky, linguistic theory should concern itself primarily with the investigation of a speaker's competence. Chomsky (1965: 3–4) saw competence as the speaker/hearer's knowledge of her own language, and distinguished this from performance, that is the actual use of the language in concrete situations (a distinction not unlike de Saussure's, 1959: 7–15 first published in French, 1916). Chomsky's ideal speaker/hearer was *someone who lived in a completely homogeneous speech community*, had a perfect command of its language, and was not affected by any grammatically irrelevant factors, such as limitation of memory, distraction, shift of attention or error (momentary or characteristic) (Chomsky, 1965: 3), in making practical use of her knowledge. Even in the case of monolinguals, there are reasons for objecting to a linguistic theory which leaves out of account as "irrelevant" certain factors which are necessary for comprehension (see, for example, Wold, 1978; Canale & Swain, 1979).[5] But according to Chomsky's definition of the ideal speaker/hearer, *bilinguals* when considered from the theoretical linguist's viewpoint come to be even more *peripheral* as *objects of investigation* than "non-ideal" monolinguals. They usually live in much less homogeneous linguistic communities than monolinguals, and many of the "grammatically irrelevant" factors mentioned above are precisely of the kind that, for example, trigger code shift. What distinguishes bilinguals from monolinguals will therefore in any narrow definition of competence largely belong to the domain of performance – see Mackey's description of bilingualism at the end of the previous section – and thus lie outside the area of grammar in the strict sense.

The task of formal grammatical analysis in transformational-generative grammar was after all to try to describe all the rules and principles which the native speaker/hearer instinctively commands as the consequence of her competence, her linguistic knowledge (Chomsky, 1966: 10–11). The native speaker/hearer is *both* able to decide what is or is not grammatical in her language *and also* to produce an infinite number of grammatical sentences. Transformational-generative grammar emphasises the creative aspect of language, the native speaker's ability to produce, with the help of a finite number of rules, an infinite number of sentences which she has never heard before (Chomsky, 1968, 1975).

The attempts made to redefine competence and to refine the distinction between competence and performance were partly in order to broaden the concept of competence away from a purely linguistic in a more sociolinguistic direction (*communicative competence*), and later also to give it a more psycholinguistic emphasis, language being seen as an instrument of thought (Bruner, 1975; *cognitive competence*, Cummins, 1977, 1978). It was also suggested that there were several different intermediate levels between the earlier extremes of competence and performance. In the sociolinguistic view the task of grammar is not only to describe the rules that produce grammatically correct sentences in a specific language but also to describe what is "acceptable" linguistic behaviour in different speech situations. In this view, communicative competence includes both grammatical-linguistic competence as understood by the old generativists and also a sociolinguistic competence, a familiarity with the social norms governing the use of language, a familiarity with what is and is not acceptable linguistic behaviour in different situations, and with the kind of grammatical or non-grammatical utterances appropriate or otherwise in different social situations. There is also a movement away from the simple dichotomy between competence and performance towards more refined descriptions of linguistic ability as a whole. It is impossible to describe linguistic competence or to study a language as such in a social vacuum, since language *is itself* a social phenomenon. It is coming more and more to be accepted that the study of the purely linguistic-grammatical instrument is inadequate, if that instrument is not studied in relation to its function. In a new attempt to analyse what is at the heart of the two dichotomies (competence-performance and grammatical-communicative) Michel Canale and Merrill Swain (1979) have made the distinction between grammatical competence, which describes the knowledge of grammatical rules, and sociolinguistic competence, which describes the knowledge of rules of language use. Communicative competence would thus in their view refer to the relation and interaction between grammatical and sociolinguistic competence. In all these cases, performance refers to the actual use of a speaker's competence in real situations, and communicative performance would then be the demonstration in real situations of the knowledge of both the grammatical and sociolinguistic rule systems and their interaction in practice and for authentic communicative purposes (thus not, for instance, in a foreign language class).

When students of bilingualism increasingly favour definitions by function rather than by competence, it is thus due to a greater realisation of the validity of Mackey's description. The same shift of focus from language as a thing in itself to language users and to speech communities is characteristic of all aspects of current linguistics, not just the study of bilingualism.

4.3.6   Definitions based on attitudes (identification)

As has already become clear in the discussion of the possibility of an individual having two mother tongues according to the definition by attitude, one can in the definition of bilingualism by attitude focus on the *speaker's own view* of what is her native context ("identifies herself with both languages and/or linguistic communities and/or cultures"). Strictly speaking, we should also include under definitions by attitude everything that tells us something about the speaker's own conception of how well she commands the language and how well, naturally and effortlessly she feels she can use it; in other words, the speaker's own conception of her competence and of how well she fulfils the demands for bilingualism according to the different definitions by function (see the discussion of these aspects in Malmberg, 1977: 133–36).

It is also possible to take as the starting point *other people's assessment of the speaker* ("accepted as a native speaker by both communities"). As Bertil Malmberg (*idem* 135) puts it: "The speaker must not stand out from his environment when using the other language, i.e. he must be accepted as a native speaker." However, Malmberg modifies this position somewhat by saying that the speaker must also be able to: "act in both language groups without any disturbing deviance being noticed (we are not, of course, including here regional or individual features)" (*idem*, 135). But this modification is open to the same objections as the definitions by competence: it does not specify what kind of native speaker is to be satisfied that no deviation has occurred. An absolutely "monolingual" peasant among academics, an equally "monolingual" professor in a pub among "ordinary people", or a man who is unconscious of sex roles both linguistically and politically ("a male chauvinist pig" as *they themselves* usually put it) among women aware of these issues can each of them be a more seriously disturbing presence on account of their use of language than a person with a different mother tongue or a "foreign" accent. An ideological consensus can easily bridge a linguistic divide, whereas a "common" language need not be *any* kind of guarantee that even basic communication is possible (see, for example, Spender, 1980).

4.3.7 Discussion of definitions by attitude

Even though definitions by attitude may superficially look very easy and unambiguous, since they do not usually involve the notion of degree (to what degree do you identify yourself with one/the other group? Does X sound wholly/nearly/to some extent/hardly/absolutely not like a native speaker of language Y?), but rather involve clear-cut dichotomies (identifies with/does not identify with; sounds like/ does not sound like a native), they are in reality far from unambiguous.

All the different dichotomies are in actual fact continua. When we consider a speaker's own view of her competence, the ease with which she communicates in both languages, or her identification with each of the languages, we find that we are not asking simple either/or questions, but are rather making measurements along vertical and horizontal scales: there can be every degree of competence, facility and identification, and at different times the same speaker can operate at different points in the scale depending both on internal (fatigue, motivation, etc.) and external factors (how long ago the speaker last spoke the language, what kind of subject area is being discussed, who she is speaking to, status differences between speakers, etc.). The same qualifying factors will apply to the view others take of a speaker, but in this case the interaction between the judge and the judged is liable further to weaken the reliability and validity of the judgement made.

The point at which we are to draw the line between bilingual/non-bilingual is thus bound to be a matter of dispute, especially since the inter-individual variation is so great. The same individual may easily be classified as bilingual on one occasion (or in one country) and as non-bilingual on another occasion (or in another country).

4.3.8 Synthesis: descriptive profiles instead of definitions

Firstly, I shall put side by side in summary form some of the most important definitions of the mother tongue and of bilingualism. I hope it will emerge even more clearly than before that there is no one single "correct" definition of the mother tongue or of bilingualism. The form of the definition will depend on what it is being used for. At the same time it should become clear that definitions both of the mother tongue and of bilingualism are fully possible. Difficulty of definition cannot, thus, be used as an argument to justify the omission of questions about mother tongue or bilingualism, for instance, from census forms. It is quite possible to choose a single definition and explain it in detail.

As has already become clear, each of the definitions above is notably inadequate if it is to be used *alone* for those purposes which were listed as the areas where definitions of bilingualism are needed. Some combination of the more satisfactory aspects of the various definitions can therefore perhaps be used as a general definition, for example as a basis for different kinds of measurement. This general definition will necessarily be more complicated. In my own definition I try to combine several different criteria:

"A bilingual speaker is someone who is able to function in two (or more) languages, either in monolingual or bilingual communities, in accordance with the sociocultural demands made of an individual's communicative and cognitive competence by these communities or by the individual herself, at the same level as native speakers, and who is able positively to identify with both (or all) language groups (and cultures), or parts of them" (Skutnabb-Kangas, 1980b).

It is fairly clear from my definition that I had a specific group in mind when I formulated it, namely immigrant and minority children, who I hope will be given the opportunity to become so completely bilingual that they satisfy the demands in my definition, something I think of as entirely possible. The decision, for instance, to say "at the same level as native speakers" rather than "at the same level as a native speaker equivalent to the bilingual in as many respects as possible" was a deliberate choice with both a scientific and a political background. If I had chosen the formulation "an equivalent native speaker", I would have implied even more decidedly than I do already that a precisely equivalent monolingual speaker could be found, and thus that to be bilingual represents some sort of deviation. I would have implied even more strongly that the monolingual individual and monolingualism are the norm. In the definition as it stands I try at least to ensure for the individual a measure of autonomy by referring to the demands made by the individual herself.

This is the more scientific side: to try to avoid suggesting that equivalent native speakers are to be found. The more political side of the argument involves saying that since immigrant children are largely working-class they should not be expected to achieve a linguistic proficiency better than that of equivalent monolingual working-class children, who of course are also linguistically and in other ways oppressed. This kind of expectation would involve an acceptance of the fact that both the tests and the school system are structured so as to make it inevitable that working-class children make a poorer showing than middle-class children – and of course this is a fact I am not willing to accept. Therefore I cannot say "equivalent native speaker". And I could go on like this – each definition should be analysed in detail so that the groups one has in mind are clearly identified, and the reasons for the choice of certain specific formulations are made quite evident. Many of

TABLE 2

Criterion	The mother tongue is the language	A speaker is bilingual who
Origin	first learned (the speaker has established her first lasting linguistic contacts in)	a. has learnt two languages in the family from native speakers from the beginning b. has used two languages in parallel as means of communication from the beginning
Competence level of proficiency command	best known	a. complete mastery of two languages b. native-like control of two languages c. equal mastery of two languages d. can produce complete meaningful utterances in the other language e. has at least some knowledge and control of the grammatical structure of the other language f. has come into contact with another language
Function use	most used	uses (or can use) two languages (in most situations) (in accordance with her own wishes and the demands of the community)
Attitudes identity and identification	a. identified with by self (internal identification) b. identified by others as a native speaker of (external identification)	a. identifies herself as bilingual/with two languages and/or two cultures (or parts of them) b. is identified by others as bilingual/as a native speaker of two languages

(Skutnabb-Kangas, 1980b)

these choices are made for non-linguistic reasons: for example, because of the reality which the definitions are to be used to describe. . . .

At the same time one must constantly emphasise that all definitions must be subject to change. As has already been made clear several times, both in discussing the mother tongue and bilingualism, an individual can have different mother tongues according to different definitions, and be bilingual according to one definition but not according to another (*horizontal variation*). In the same way, (i) one's mother tongue, (ii) whether or not one is bilingual, and (iii) which languages one is bilingual in, all can change many times during one's lifetime (except according to the definition by origin which allows for no such change) (*vertical variation*).

If we are to make any progress beyond the inadequacies of the definitions, it would probably be best not to make use of simple (or even indeed complicated) definitions in the assessment of bilingual speakers, but rather to use descriptive profiles to characterize bilingual speakers from various points of view (instead of, or at least in addition to, evaluating or judging them). It is here possible to *start from the speaker herself*, to enquire how well the speaker succeeds, with the help of various strategies, in satisfying her needs to communicate with the surrounding world, regardless of which language it is she is using. Again, secondly, it would be possible to *start from the demands made by society at large upon the bilingual's communicative ability*, and to try to see how well she meets these demands. A third possibility would be to try to satisfy both parties, using a profile which takes into account both the demands and attitudes of the speaker herself and those of society at large.

From the point of view of the individual, it may be less important which of her languages she uses to communicate with, so long as she achieves what she sets out to achieve. The *means* of the communication comes to be less important than the goal, the *result*. From the bilingual individual's point of view, a comparison with monolinguals is perhaps possible only so far as the *result* of the communication is concerned, not the means employed (see also 2.2.5). From the point of view of society, on the other hand, the means may well also be important, since bilinguals communicate not only with other bilinguals but probably also to a large extent with monolinguals (and at any rate on monolingual speakers' terms). The demands made of bilinguals thus come to be the same as those made of monolinguals, and this applies when the bilinguals are speaking to both monolingual groups involved. Society can thus demand a level of performance equivalent to that expected of a monolingual, and then from the point of view of society the use of a monolingual norm as a basis for comparison seems legitimate.

In a bilingual profile all aspects of the matter should, then, be taken into account. Both *competence, function and attitudes* must be included. By function we mean both internal function (function towards onself – language as the means for cognition, investigation, reflection and consciousness) and also external function (function towards others). The *demands* both of the *individual* and of *society* must be included, as also the *linguistic media* themselves (L1, L2 and various combinations of these), and the *result* of their operation.

In various attempts made to define the goals of foreign language learning, many aspects of the matter have been discussed, all of which will contribute to the elaboration of bilingual profiles. In these attempts, too, the dichotomies discussed above have been used as starting points. Certain goal analyses have taken as their basis the demands made by society, in that they have analysed *situations* which the foreign language learner is expected to cope with at a certain level (see for example, Freihoff & Takala, 1974a, 1974b; Sinclair & Coulthard, 1975; Wilkins, 1972) whereas other analyses have been based on the individual's *meaning potential*, that is the need the individual experiences to express herself and the different strategies she uses to do so (see, for example, van Ek, 1975; Canale & Swain, 1979; Haastrup & Phillipson, 1983).

The progress in the study of semantics and the attempts to incorporate the new knowledge into the framework of grammar will certainly contribute to a more precise formulation of the demands. An ideal bilingual profile would be one which, both from the individual's and society's point of view, allowed for the greatest possible degree of self-realisation and of competence as a functioning member of society. One could specify from the point of view of the various disciplines, purely linguistic, psychological, sociological, and social psychological (Ingram, 1976) demands on competence, on internal and external function, on attitudes and especially on both internal and external identification (Ofstad, 1971).

Notes to Chapter Four

1. See, for example, Roessel, 1970; National Indian Brotherhood, 1972; Gooderham, 1975; Platero, 1975; Modiano, 1975: all these deal with the American Indians' demands for education in their own languages. See also Cornejo, 1974; Sevilla-Casas and others, 1973; RSKL, 1978; Nahmad, 1975; Escobar, 1975; Elias-Olivares & Valdés-Fallis, 1978; Ralston, 1978.
2. The number depends on what we count as languages and what as dialects. Is there, for example, one Same language with three main dialects (South, North and East Same) – see Dahlstedt, 1975: 22, n. 6? Or are there in total three Same languages or perhaps even seven? See *Samerna i Sverige*, SOU, 1975: 99 and 1975: 100.
3. These discussions have often been very lively, whether arising from simply terminological differences or, what is worse, more or less complete conceptual confusion and mixing together bilinguals of different types with completely different societal prerequisites for becoming bilingual. Examples of both kinds of discussion can be found in

Stolt, 1975a, 1975b; Skutnabb-Kangas, 1975b; Hansegård, 1975, 1977a; Loman, 1975; Toukomaa, 1975a, 1975b; Wande, 1977; Skutnabb-Kangas & Toukomaa, 1977; Malmberg, 1977; the plenary discussion between Hansegård, Loman and Toukomaa in Skutnabb-Kangas, 1977a; Loona, 1977; Ekstrand, 1978a, 1978b, 1978c, 1979a. For further references, see the discussion of semilingualism.

4. See, for example, Leopold's four volumes on his daugher Hildegard's bilingual development, Leopold, 1939–50. For references to various case studies of the linguistic development of individual children, see Vildomec, 1963: 25–28; Hatch, 1977: 62–66; McLaughlin, 1978 and Saunders 1982.

5. Chomsky's concept of competence is also inadequate as it comes to define a child's language learning as falling outside the proper area for linguistic description (see, for example, Chomsky's thoughts on LAD – the Language Acquisition Device – and other thoughts on the psychological relevance of grammatical models and their development). This is because a linguistic community which includes a child beginning to learn a language is by definition not homogeneous (Bense, 1973).

5 Different aspects of bilingualism – dichotomies

5.1 Different kinds of bilingualism

5.1.1 Natural bilingualism – school bilingualism/cultural bilingualism

The term *natural bilingual* is used to refer to an individual who has learnt two languages without formal teaching in the course of her everyday life as her natural means of communication, and often learnt them relatively young. The reason this happens may be either internal, to do with the family (that the parents speak different languages), or external-societal (that the community speaks a different language from the family). Bilingual competence for such individuals is something they *must* acquire in order to manage their life properly. The opposite of natural bilingualism should strictly speaking be unnatural bilingualism, and the use of the term natural may reflect how difficult people find it to learn a language by formal tuition and how easy it seems to be by contrast to learn a language in the process of natural communication with others. The term may also derive from our experience of how "unnatural" adults sound when speaking a foreign language with an accent.

School bilingualism is, as the name indicates, the result of learning a foreign language at school by formal teaching, and it implies that the learner has not had much opportunity, or indeed any, to use the language as a natural means of communication. The language has, so to speak, remained within the four walls of the school. The knowledge of the foreign language for school bilinguals is usually not something vital, but a desirable extra, something they enjoy or find is useful in their work or when coming into contact with native speakers of the language. It may also be useful in contact with other non-native speakers of the language, whether individuals or groups, where the foreign language is the only common one (as, for instance, with a Dane and a Finn speaking English together).

Cultural bilingualism largely coincides with school bilingualism, but the term is more often used to refer to adults who learn a foreign language for reasons of work, travel, and so on. The term may also have about it something of the older ideal of "the educated person", the one who had at her command one or two of the "major" European languages, i.e. "languages of culture". To be "educated" implied a knowledge of languages, just as it implied an easy acquaintance with a large number of bourgeois rituals which were defined as "culture".

The distinction between natural bilingualism and school bilingualism has also been the background against which a number of evaluating terms have been devised. At one extreme, only natural bilinguals are regarded as bilingual, and school bilinguals (and here we must include cultural bilinguals) are described as having no more than a good command of a foreign language. Bertil Malmberg in one of his definitions puts it in this way: "A bilingual is an individual who, in addition to his mother tongue, has acquired from childhood onwards or from an early age a second language by natural means (in principle not by formal instruction), so that he has become a fully competent member of the other linguistic community within the sphere, the occupational or social group, to which he naturally belongs" (1977: 134–35). Malmberg also adds: "A knowledge of a second language laboriously acquired does not result in bilingualism. This then establishes an acceptable boundary between bilingualism and a knowledge of foreign languages" (1977: 135). In Bertil Malmberg's view, the bilingual should be able to function in both linguistic communities "naturally, and with no greater effort in the one language than in the other (with a certain exception made in the case of vocabulary, and with some allowance for differing levels of education in the two languages)" (1977: 135). According to this kind of definition, "bilingualism" coincides with "natural bilingualism" and with "complete bilingualism", and it is regarded as something very positive.

The other extreme is to regard natural bilingualism as something negative. Joshua Fishman says somewhere (I cannot locate the quotation) something about the way French/English bilingualism is regarded in the United States. If you have learnt French at university, preferably in France and even better at the Sorbonne, then bilingualism is something very positive. But if you have learnt French from your old grandmother in Maine, then bilingualism is something rather to be ashamed of. In other words, we have here a social evaluation which clearly identifies a connection between bilingualism and membership of a dominated, low status group on the one hand, and a connection between cultural bilingualism and belonging to the middle or upper levels of a dominant, majority group, on the other hand.

This brings the discussion back to the section dealing with the question of who is bilingual and why (4.2). For most naturally bilingual people bilingualism is a must, something absolutely needed if they are to manage their lives properly, since there is either internal, family pressure, or external, societal pressure upon them, or both. For school and cultural bilinguals, on the other hand, bilingualism is often more or less voluntary. A knowledge of the other language is not vital for them, but a desirable extra, something they enjoy or find useful, in their work or when coming into contact with native speakers of the language, or for their own private reading, and so on.

5.1.2   Elite bilingualism – folk bilingualism

There is an almost parallel distinction between *elite bilingualism* and *folk bilingualism*. Elite bilinguals are usually highly educated, and some part of their education has been in foreign languages, with some opportunity to use the languages naturally. Folk bilinguals, on the other hand, have usually been forced to learn the other language in practical contact with people who speak it (and who can oblige others to speak their language). Folk bilinguals often come from a linguistic minority, but sometimes also, especially in the third world, from oppressed linguistic majorities (see the discussion in 4.2.2).

Elite bilingualism has never been a problem, as Christina Bratt Paulston remarks (1977b: 35), but folk bilingualism is connected with many educational difficulties. However, it is important to make the point that folk bilingualism is not problematic in itself, but rather that educational problems arise if the teaching of children bilingual in this way is wrongly organized.

5.2   One code or two codes?

5.2.1   What does "one code or two codes" imply?

The question of what it looks like inside a bilingual's head has always fascinated both those professionally engaged in investigating it and the lay(wo)man. Is it the case that the bilingual individual has two quite distinct linguistic systems, one for each language, or is it rather that she has one single system which looks different from the monolingual system? Is it the case that the bilingual has two great storage barrels in her head, or is there just one with the two languages mixed up together in it? Is it damaging for the child that her mother sometimes speaks Kurdish and sometimes Turkish – will the child be totally confused? – or is it better that the child should hear the same person always speaking the same language? I have tried to gather together questions of this kind under the heading of the joint subtitle "one code or two codes?". Many of the issues are as yet imprecise and we know too little about this whole area. However, in the Scandinavian debate, even what we do know has not attracted much attention, and it may therefore be appropriate to provide here some kind of background for the distinctions. First of all let me try to systematize, at least to some extent, the different

ways in which the distinction between codes can be approached:
■ *from a linguistic point of view* – then one is most interested in the question as to whether the bilingual has a single integrated linguistic system, with some special rules for each of the languages, or two separate systems. The problem can be focused upon at different levels, for instance as a semantic/philosophy of language question, or as a purely syntactical or phonological one. Questions particularly canvassed from a linguistic point of view have to do with interference, both quantitative (how much) and qualitative (what type) and with the ease or difficulty of translation or interpretation, as well as with the ease or difficulty of other kinds of code switching;
■ *from a neuropsychological and neurolinguistic point of view* – then one is most interested in the way in which the bilingual brain is organized by comparison with the monolingual, and whether bilinguals differ from each other in their mental organization. Most attention so far has been devoted to the ways in which bilinguals "store" their two languages, whether they are stored together or separately: one barrel or two? The way in which the languages are stored, of course, is important for the consideration of interference and translation;
■ *from the point of view of sociology and the psychology of learning* – discussion has here centred on *methods of learning* (with or without formal instruction), on learning age (before, during or after school age), and on the *learning context* (both in the same environment, or one at home and the other outside). All these questions represent a more *macrosociological* point of view. There has also been discussion of the principle "one person – one language", as opposed to the situation where most people that the child learns the languages from speak both languages interchangeably. This is a more *microsociological* point of view. The debate has concentrated above all on the educational consequences of the various alternatives.

5.2.1.1   The development of the distinctions – compound, co-ordinate and subordinate bilingualism
     The distinction between compound and co-ordinate bilingualism was first presented by Uriel Weinreich in his classic *Languages in Contact* (1967). Weinreich's account was soon followed by Charles Osgood's and Susan Ervin-Tripp's discussion of the distinction against the background of a modified stimulus-response theory (Ervin & Osgood, 1954). Since these two accounts are fundamental to the whole of what has been on occasion a very lively ensuing discussion of this distinction which has now been going on for a quarter of a century, it may be useful to give some detailed description of them here.
     In the chapter on "The Nature of the Sign in Language Contact" (Weinreich, 1967: 9), discussing this distinction, Weinreich writes:
          "Once an interlingual identification has occurred between semantemes of two languages in contact, it becomes possible for the

bilingual to interpret two signs whose semantemes, or signifieds, he has identified as a compound sign with a single signified and two signifiers, one in each language. Instead of treating the English *book* and Russian *kníga* as two separate signs (*A*), he could regard them as a compound sign (*B*):

	"book"	"kníga"			"book"≡"kníga"
(*A*)	|	|	(*B*)		/ \
	/buk/	/'kn'iga/			/buk/ /'kn'iga/

Several writers have gone so far as to distinguish two types of bilingualism according to the two interpretations of the sign. Ščerba reports (1926) that the bilingual Sorbians have only one language with two modes of expression; in other words, they possess one set of signifieds with two signifiers each, as in *B* above. Elsewhere (1945) he classifies this as 'pure' bilingualism, reserving the term 'mixed' presumably for type *A*. Loewe (1888) calls *B* a 'two-member system of the same language'.

It would appear offhand that a person's or group's bilingualism need not be entirely of type *A* or *B,* since some signs of the languages may be compounded while others are not (pp. 9–10).

"One more interpretation of the sign by bilinguals needs to be considered, an interpretation which is likely to apply when a new language is learned with the help of another (by the so-called 'indirect method'). The referents of the signs in the language being learned may then be not actual 'things,' but 'equivalent' signs of the language already known. Thus, to an English speaker learning Russian, the signified of the form /'kn'iga/ may at first be not the object, but the English word *book,* thus:

$$(C) \left\{ \frac{\text{"book"}}{\text{/buk/}} \right\}$$
$$\text{/'kn'iga/}$$

Type *C* would seem to correspond to Roberts' 'subordinative' bilingualism (1939) while *A* would be the 'coordinative' type (p. 10)." Weinreich also seems to think that a change from type *C* to type *A* may occur, but says nothing about any change from type *C* to type *B* (Weinreich, 1967: 11).

In order to make Weinreich a little clearer I should like to interpret what he says using images for co-ordinate, compound and subordinate bilingualism first suggested by Hartmut Haberland after he had read this section in Weinreich's book. Haberland starts with Weinreich's image of an American English/Russian bilingual, and for the subordinate bilingual an American monolingual learning Russian at school. He continues with an

example of compound and co-ordinate bilingualism as between Finnish and
Greek, giving as an example of subordinate bilingualism a Finn learning
Greek at school. For the subordinate bilingual the signified in the first case is
the phonological representation of book, i.e. /buk/, rather than an image of
the Marx and Engels' book (see Figure 4).

FIGURE 4

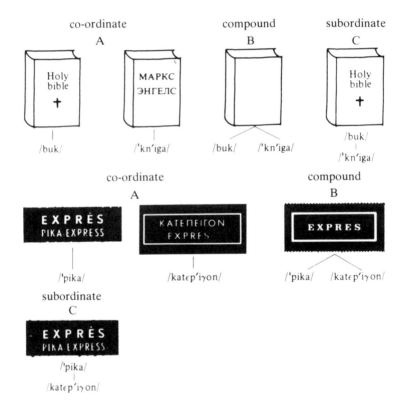

Ervin & Osgood's distinction is based on a behaviourist model of the
way in which the mediating processes linking sign and response operate. As
can be seen from Figure 5, the co-ordinate bilingual has different
mediating processes for the two languages, while the compound bilingual
has the same process for both. In Figure 5, S stands for sign (what in usual
stimulus-response theory is called the stimulus) and R stands for response; r
and s stand for "mediating processes or meanings", and A and B as well as
the numbers 1 and 2 stand for the different languages involved.

FIGURE 5   (From Ervin & Osgood 1954.)

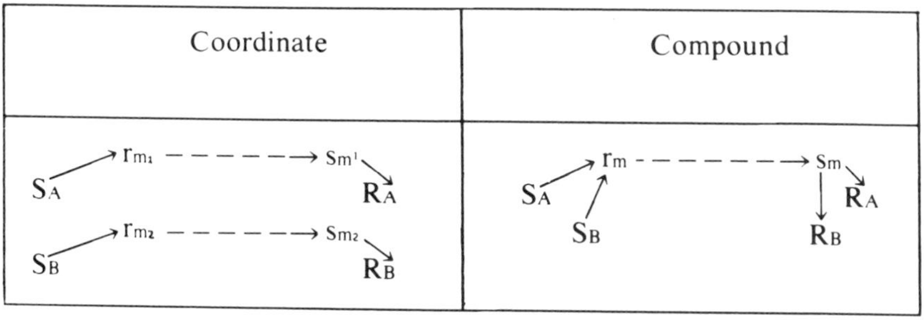

Coordinate	Compound
$S_A \rightarrow rm_1 \dashrightarrow Sm^1 \searrow R_A$ $S_B \rightarrow rm_2 \dashrightarrow Sm_2 \searrow R_B$	$S_A \rightarrow rm \dashrightarrow Sm \searrow R_A$ $S_B \qquad\qquad R_B$

Ervin & Osgood include Weinreich's type C (subordinate bilingualism) under compound bilingualism, and this has largely obscured Weinreich's clear and pedagogically useful distinction (see the critique in Paradis, 1978b: 166). The distinction has also been presented in this rather obscure way in Sweden in articles and books on pre-school education, and this has proved unfortunate because it does not allow the possibility of distinguishing between school bilinguals and natural bilinguals, and between foreign language learning and second language learning. Ervin & Osgood have also contributed in other ways to the conceptual chaos by starting to use as criteria for their types both the learning context, the method of learning, and partly also the learning age, all of them completely mixed up. In their view, then, speakers are compound bilinguals if they have either learnt one language by means of the other (as in the older kind of foreign language teaching in schools), or both languages in the same environment, for example at home. Co-ordinate or "real" bilinguals are those who have learnt two languages in different contexts, for example one at home and the other at school (probably by the direct method, as Macnamara remarks, 1970: 28) or at work. Other writers have further altered the criteria,[1] so that if one is to achieve any clarity, the distinction has to be seen from the viewpoint of many different disciplines. And the remarkable thing about this distinction is that it has been the subject of lively debate and a great deal of experimentation, even though the evidence for its existence is still very slight, and even though Weinreich himself reached the conclusion also reached in the most recent overall account, that we might most plausibly say of a bilingual speaker's languages "that the two languages are to some extent compound and to some extent co-ordinate" (Albert & Obler, 1978: 234).

5.2.1.2   From a linguistic point of view – one or two systems?
As long as bilingualism was regarded as something negative and temporary which speakers escaped from as soon as they approached the monolingual standard of proficiency in the majority language, the "normal" state of affairs from the point of view of those who established the norm was

to be monolingual. A monolingual society with monolingual individuals was the norm, and consequently the use of language by bilinguals came to be judged against this monolingual norm. Therefore it was also assumed that bilinguals had (or ought ideally to have) two separate linguistic rule systems, two codes, either one of which resembled the single monolingual system. This approach was fruitful in early research into interference, as it made possible the analysis of the bilingual's oral or written expression as belonging either to L1 or L2. The analysis could be carried out even on the phonemic level, so that certain phonemes within a morpheme could be identified as belonging to L1 and others within the same morpheme as belonging to L2.[2]

As more and more sociolinguistic investigation showed that bilingualism was a permanent phenomenon in many societies (Gumperz, 1964, 1967, 1969, 1971; Fishman, 1966a, 1968, 1972c), by contrast with the earlier view that a progression from monolingualism in L1, through bilingualism in L1 and L2 to monolingualism in L2 was the common pattern, theories were evolved suggesting that there was a single bilingual repertoire, one code. The one code theory means that bilinguals have a single linguistic system, accommodating both the substantial common ground between their two languages (see also Cummins, 1980–83, about the common underlying proficiency) and also the many special rules needed for each separate language. Gumperz describes two unrelated languages, Marathi and Kannada, whose phonetic and grammatical structures have come to be very nearly identical after several hundred years of close contact. In practice, the speakers of these languages, Gumperz claims, have one grammar and two lexicons (Gumperz, 1969: 246).

As against this, Karl Diller, trying to show that the distinction between co-ordinate and compound bilingualism is untenable, has maintained that "no two languages sufficiently resemble each other grammatically to be compounded together" (Diller, 1974), and "the same applies to the lexicon".

Nevertheless it is fairly clear that:
"learning a language after the native one, *at whatever age,* cannot demand a repetition of all the same steps. In our argument, learning a language is like learning to ride a bicycle; once one has learned the basic principles of riding a bicycle (or of using language), one never again has to achieve certain elements of knowledge" (Albert & Obler, 1978: 230).

It is less clear how much any two languages must have in common for us to be able to speak of them as forming a single compound system. At best, the categories and criteria one adopts are arbitrary. In my view, the matter of whether we treat a bilingual's linguistic equipment as forming one system or two is only of consequence when we come to discuss the psychological relevance of the different kinds of bilingualism: does the bilingual speaker herself feel that she has two different systems (which overlap, at least as far as linguistic universals are concerned)?

If the postulating of a single code helps us to understand, for example, how bilingual children learn linguistic rules in different environments (and we would be able, for instance, in teaching to leave aside certain regular features we know the child has already learnt in another language), then it would be possible to try to write a teaching grammar based on this one code theory. The assumption that there is only one code is one of the reasons why it is thought to be desirable to use contrastive grammars in foreign language teaching and in particular in second language teaching. The learning process itself should then demonstrate whether the one code theory is correct. Error analysis and interlanguage study (interlanguage is the language used by the learner in trying to approach the target language during the language learning process) should also be included in the discussion, to show to what extent they can be used to support one interpretation rather than the other.

As far as I can see, the question of one code or two is largely one of choosing *the* descriptive model which (on the basis of other criteria used in choosing any model for describing human behaviour) gives the best results in the description, relative to the goal one has when choosing to make a description in the first place. Just as with choice of definition of bilingualism, this also is a question of relative validity (take the description which fits your research goals) rather than of absolute validity.

From the educational point of view, I believe the distinction between co-ordinate, compound and subordinate can be very helpful, for example in discussions of cultural relativity and concept formation in bilingual education, especially when the importance of anchoring words in a specific cultural context is emphasized. Similarly, I believe this distinction may be very helpful when we try to illustrate the differences between mother tongue learning and second language learning in relation to connotative meanings (see the section on mother tongue learning, 2.3).

5.2.2   From a neuropsychological and neurolinguistic point of view – one or two barrels?

5.2.2.1 The nature of the question

First let me use a non-technical image to describe what the distinction between compound and co-ordinate bilingualism could be taken to mean as far as the storing of the two languages, especially the lexicon, is concerned. We may imagine that the co-ordinate bilingual has two storage barrels (I am thinking in terms of beer kegs – Kolers' (1968) original image was of water tanks), one for each language; while the compound bilingual has one large barrel with two taps (see Figure 6).

In order for the compound bilingual not to have Turkish coming out when opening the Danish tap or Danish out of the Turkish, the various words she uses must all have labels of some kind to indicate which items belong to which language; the items must be marked. And the tap has to be

FIGURE 6

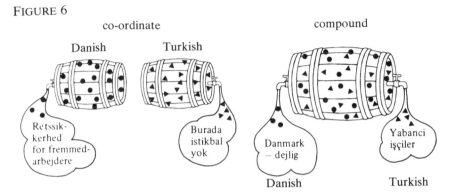

equipped with some kind of filter which allows only the correctly marked items to pass through it.

Interference could then be explained in several different ways, depending on what gives rise to it. Certain elements would either not be clearly marked, or would be unmarked or doubly marked from the beginning, perhaps because so similar that interlingual identification could occur, or perhaps because they had been learnt in a context which did not clearly identify the language they belonged to (and in an environment where interference was accepted, so that the bilingual child was not made to feel that it ought not to use items from one language when speaking the other). Some labels might also gradually come off, so that certain items would be left unmarked, and the speaker would be unclear as to which language they belonged to. And certain items might come to acquire free floating labels, either in addition to or instead of their own.

In his book on American Swedish, Nils Hasselmo has examples which can be placed in each of these different categories. Hasselmo asked his informants about the acceptability of various expressions (1974: 175) – they were asked to give an opinion about a number of recorded sentences, each containing an English or a Swedish test word (for example, "De movade till Minneapolis; Han är upstairs"). The range of possible answers suggested was: (i) yes, I would almost always say that, (ii) yes, I would sometimes say that, but might also say . . ., (iii) no, I wouldn't say that, but other people do, (iv) no, no one would say that. Hasselmo also used an identification test, where informants were asked to judge whether certain words in various recorded sentences were "proper Swedish" or "borrowed from English" (Hasselmo, 1974: 180).

Most informants gave fairly decided answers: in the acceptability test, only 4% of the answers fell into the category "sometimes", and 10% into the category "other people say it". Most of the informants thus had quite clear views about acceptability – the norm was fairly strict, regardless of how correct they were. Many speakers thought that certain English words were in fact Swedish and vice-versa, but very few were uncertain about which language they thought a word belonged to. There were thus few expressions floating about without labels, or with double labels, but a fair number with changed labels.

Before we go on with the discussion about storage and barrels, it might be as well to point out that to talk about "storing" words and items is of course to use a metaphor. It is an image we use to describe our mental picture of the way the human brain works. Words like "store" are very deceptive, however, because they invite us too easily to think that the way the brain stores and has access to information resembles the way a person stores up matter and scoops it out. The barrels thus explain by metaphor what is already a metaphor.

If we want to imagine a version of this image about barrels that would serve for monolinguals, we would think of the monolingual as having a single barrel; but even in this case not all the items in the barrel would have the same label. In the monolingual barrel there will be a number of words floating about labelled "foreign", and the history of any language is among other things a study of the way in which these "foreign" items change and come to be felt as genuinely Swedish, Danish, Norwegian and so on, rather than Greek, Latin, German or English, or whatever. Monolinguals also have a filter system, which has the effect of often making them indicate in some way, by pronunciation, pause, or some special expression ("as one might say", "as Americans say", "the so-called", etc.), that they are aware that the word they are using has a foreign label or a double label.

As for the quantity of interference, the co-ordinate bilingual would then presumably have much less of it, since the items belonging to the two separate languages are stored separately, and the chance (or risk, depending on which attitude we have towards the desirability of interference) of any mixture between the two is reduced. By contrast, compound bilinguals could be expected to show more interference.

Some investigators (for example, Sandra Ben-Zeev, see section 9.4.3) have put forward a hypothesis to explain the greater metalinguistic awareness of bilingual speakers, their greater awareness of the distinction between linguistic form and linguistic content, or the greater ability they have to discuss language as a system. The hypothesis is that the greater efforts they have to make to avoid interference and to keep their codes as "pure" as possible obliges them to pay much closer attention to the structures of their two languages and to contrast them. If this is true, compound bilinguals who have to make greater efforts to avoid interference should perform better than co-ordinate bilinguals in tests designed to measure various kinds of metalinguistic awareness.

The opposite should be the case where interpreting and translation are concerned. Since compound bilinguals would be able to choose expressions from either language with equal ease, translation and interpreting should in principle involve no greater difficulty than, for instance, the monolingual experiences in making stylistic choices within a single language. By contrast it should be more difficult for the co-ordinate bilingual to interpret and translate since this would involve moving between the two barrels rather than moving about within a single barrel.

If we take the distinction to its absurd logical extreme, the co-ordinate bilingual would not be able to explain in L1 what she has heard in L2, and she would find it difficult even within herself to communicate across the linguistic divide. The compound bilingual, on the other hand, would run the risk of not being completely understood by speakers of either L1 or L2 (Macnamara 1970, 25–32).

5.2.2.2 The brain and bilingualism

What we know about the linguistic organization of the brain derives mainly from three sources: *anatomical studies* during operations and post mortem, *experiments* of different kinds, often with rather sophisticated equipment, and the study of different kinds of *cerebral disorder,* brain damage, aphasia, and so on. It seems fairly clear that bilingualism, or indeed the learning of a second language in general, modifies the brain's linguistic organization, even if it is far from evident in detail what it is that happens, and above all how it happens.

By comparison with the brains of other animals, the human brain, and in particular the cerebrum, is highly developed and specialized. We still have only very incomplete knowledge of the way the brain deals with language. Even though certain so-called language centres can be identified in the brain, areas which are more important than others for linguistic functions (for example, Broca's area for language production and Wernicke's area for language reception, and the angular gyrus for coupling word and referent), nevertheless it seems that a large part of the brain is in some way or another involved with linguistic functions. It was earlier thought to be secure knowledge that many of the most important language functions were located in the left hemisphere of the brain in the majority of individuals. It was also thought that this localization, the so-called lateralization (*latus* = "side" in Latin) to one half of the brain, was reached by a gradual process and was completed by the age of puberty (see, for example, Lenneberg, 1967). The connection of lateralization to the preferred use of one hand (and foot) and to the general plasticity of the brain also seemed to be fairly clearly evident (the dominance of the left hemisphere was related to righthandedness, and the plasticity of the brain was assumed to diminish decisively by puberty, at the same time as the process of lateralization was assumed to have been completed). However, studies made of bilinguals have considerably complicated the picture. Some of the hypotheses advanced for which experimental evidence can be adduced are these:

■ It need not necessarily be the case that language functions are predominantly lateralized to the left hemisphere of the brain in all or even most individuals. There are lefthanded individuals (especially those who come from families where lefthandedness is common) in whom the right half of the brain is dominant. In some of them language is lateralized to the right hemisphere. In other lefthanded individuals the process of lateralization does not seem to have occurred so clearly as in many righthanded individuals, and they seem to function more bilaterally, with a more equal load on both halves of the brain. It may be the case that in general the linguistic organization of the brain is considerably more bilateral in bilinguals than in monolinguals.

■ In childhood bilinguals lateralization to the left side of the brain may happen earlier than with monolinguals.

■ Irrespective of the age at which a *second* language is learnt, the right side of the brain seems to be important in the process.

It is not clear what happens as the second language becomes more and more fluent: it is difficult to say in advance how the organization of the brain is affected. Important factors are (1) the age at which the language is learnt, (2) the way in which the language is learnt, (3) the use of and division of labour between the two languages, (4) affective factors (attitudes to the two languages), (5) the order in which the two languages are learnt (the organization of the brain may be different, depending upon which of the languages is learnt first), and (6) language-specific factors (different structural features in, for example, Hebrew, Hopi, English and French may have different qualitative effects on the brain) (Albert & Obler, 1978: 244). The learning of a second language may also affect the organization in the brain of the *first* language. The first language, even if it is already lateralized to the left side, may tend towards right side dominance, and the second language, as it becomes more thoroughly assimilated, may tend to occupy more and more of the left hemisphere, even if the right hemisphere continues to have a function. As I have already indicated, the result is impossible to predict in advance, but often the linguistic organization of the bilingual or multilingual brain tends to be more bilateral than that of the monolingual brain (Albert & Obler, 1978).

To summarize, then, it may be said:

■ that the brain is a much more plastic organ than has hitherto been thought, and that it remains capable for a long time, perhaps a lifetime, of a certain kind of internal re-organization;

■ that a bilingual may be using more of her brain capacity for her two languages than the monolingual;

■ that lateralization is not a simple, irreversible process complete by a certain point of time (or beginning at a certain point: there are hypotheses based on experiments which suggest that even new-born babies might be lateralized);

■ that the bilingual's two (or more) languages need not resemble each other in relation to the dominance patterns of the two halves of the brain *vis-à-vis* language or in the way the different aspects of the same language are localized;

▪ that the bilingual is probably more bilateral than the monolingual. Since research in this area develops extremely fast, the reader is referred to more specialized neurolinguistic literature (see also Lambert, 1981).

5.2.2.3 Labelling of languages

We can discuss the way the languages are labelled in the barrels (so that we know which language an item belongs to) from different points of view, depending on which phase of the process we wish to illuminate: the reception and storing of the input, the storing of the information, or the output.

In a study published in 1963, Paul Kolers (who has clearly since changed his mind) describes how English-speaking bilinguals with Thai, Spanish or German as their mother tongue, were asked to take a word association test involving both their languages (in such tests the subject is offered a word and asked to reply as fast as possible with the word that first comes into her mind, after having heard the test word, the trigger). The subjects replied to about a third of the triggers in both languages with a simple translation of the association they had had in the other language. This happened mostly with triggers referring to concrete objects. However, when the trigger denoted abstract entities or emotions, the replies were often very different for the two languages. Kolers' interpretation of his data was that experiences and memories are *not* stored in any supralinguistic form, but that they *are linguistically labelled*. In an article five years later he changed his view, and he now believes that semantic entities are stored simply as meanings *without linguistic labels*.

Various studies[3] show that information input is treated semantically by the brain as a single system irrespective of the language of the input. Informants are often unable to remember in which language they heard a word or sentence[4] (even if they have been instructed specifically to try to remember the language), whereas they do remember the content itself. Many bilinguals are often unable to remember, too, after the event, which language it was they had a conversation in (Doob, 1957; Heras & Nelson, 1972). I can testify to this myself: it has often happened that I have had no idea afterwards which language I was using in a conversation with someone as bilingual as I am, and with whom for various reasons I sometimes use one language, sometimes the other; and this in spite of the fact that my professional interest makes me, I believe, fairly aware of language. What the informants in the various case studies remember is the content, *not* the language in which it was expressed.

The ability to handle information semantically seems to increase with age (Champagnol, 1973; Riegel, 1968; Ianco-Worrall, 1972). It has also been found that there are correlations between type of bilingualism and methods of processing information, so that *compound bilinguals* (and here the Ervin-Osgood definition has often been used, which combines under one heading Weinreich's two categories of compound and subordinate) give a larger number of translation equivalents in word association tests (see Gekoski, 1970) and tend to *rely more heavily on the non-semantic properties* of words (that is, phonological properties, coincidence of initial letter, formal similarities, and so on). *Co-ordinate bilinguals,* on the other hand, tend to show a more varied pattern of associations in their respective languages, and to *rely more heavily on semantic properties* in handling information, both at the level of the word and of the sentence. It has been suggested, partly because of this, that compound and co-ordinate bilingualism represent earlier and later stages in a developmental continuum, and that the co-ordinate bilingual's way of dealing with information would represent a more mature and adult phase than the compound bilingual's. This hypothesis could, however, perhaps arise from the failure to distinguish between compound and subordinate bilingualism, because a scrutiny of studies that purport to demonstrate that compound bilinguals are less balanced and "mature" reveals that it can often be subordinate bilinguals that are being tested, people who are just in the process of learning a new language and who therefore, of course, rely more on translation equivalence.

5.2.2.4 What happens between input and output?

The question of one barrel or two is really part of a larger question about labelling in general, namely the part which discusses what happens between input and output. It has already been said that information is processed by some method of semantic analysis. This process also divides the information into items that can be ignored (forgotten), items for the short term memory, and items for the long term memory. It is likely that items in the short term memory of bilingual speakers are stored in the way said to be characteristic of compound bilinguals, a way more dependent on non-semantic properties. We can draw this conclusion, for instance, from studies of what is called shadowing, the almost simultaneous exact repetition of what is heard while the voice one is "shadowing" is continuing to speak, or of simultaneous translation by both amateur and professional interpreters (Treisman, 1965; Gerver, 1974; Goldman-Eisler, 1972). The more semantic handling of information then seems to occur when the information is transferred to the "real" store. Most studies seem to speak of common storing irrespective of language. There are good surveys of experiments which support the hypotheses either of separate storage for each language or of common storage, to be found in McCormack, 1974 and 1977; Paradis, 1978b; Albert & Obler, 1978. Many of the early studies, which have hitherto been taken as supporting the theory of separate storage (two barrels), prove to be interpretable as providing support for the common storage theory (single barrel) (see especially McCormack, 1977).

The distinction between the storage of information itself and the process needed to make the stored information accessible was not really made in the early research. Since the bilingual of course has to speak in *one* of her two languages at any one time (and not some common intermediate language) the information must be verbalized (given a linguistic form) at some point en route between the store and the speaking mouth or the writing hand and here the bilingual is forced to choose *one* of the two languages. It is often difficulty of access to the store and not inadequate storage which causes problems and takes time (see, for example, Tulvin & Colotla, 1970).

This may also largely explain why bilinguals often (but not always) perform less well than monolinguals in tests designed to measure speed of linguistic reaction. Speed of reaction must, of course, be culturally conditioned, in the sense that rapid response may in some cultures be regarded as desirable (quick witted), and in others as a sign of foolishness or lack of thought (quicker in words than in thought). But in other respects, too, speed is a poor criterion of degree of bilingualism. In spite of this many writers who have concluded that bilinguals are slower than monolinguals regard speed very uncritically as a good thing in itself.

In Scandinavia it is particularly Edith Mägiste (1979) who has conducted speed experiments with bilinguals, and found that bilinguals are slower than monolinguals (see also section 8.4 on speed of reaction). The bilingual must of course have a greater field of choice than the monolingual since she has the items in both her languages to choose from (and the total number of linguistic units at the disposal of the bilingual may be assumed to exceed the total at the disposal of the monolingual, even if the bilingual's lexicon in each one of her languages were thought likely to be smaller than the monolingual's in her single language – and this need not be the case). It must also take additional time, naturally, for the bilingual to make the choices since these choices are hardly ever likely to be a simple universal choice ("now I'm going to speak Finnish"); some linguistic items will for instance not always be absolutely clearly labelled, especially where the two languages are related.

It appears then that the *receptive side, the input or decoding side, might function more as a single compound system, and likewise the storage of information,* at least at the deeper levels (see, for example, Paradis' account of the various levels in different bilinguals, 1978b: 169–71), whereas the *productive side, the output or encoding side, looks more like two co-ordinate different systems.* This must be kept distinct from how successful the bilingual is in keeping her two languages clearly distinct from one another in the actual process of using them.

One might mistakenly conclude that exactly the opposite is the case, that on the receptive side there are two distinct systems, and on the productive side a single compound one, if one has in mind as examples of bilingual performance, speakers who have learnt their second language after puberty, or who are in the process of learning it. Such bilinguals can *hear* the difference very well between an L1 phoneme and the equivalent L2 phoneme, but in their own *speech* they do not succeed in producing the L2 phoneme, but use the L1 phoneme indifferently for either language (see Paradis, 1978b: 172). The distinguished linguist and phonetician of the Prague school, Roman Jakobson, was a good example of this: whether speaking English (he lived for several decades in the USA) or some other language, he seemed to use a phonemic system derived from his mother tongue, Russian, in spite of the fact that in the receptive mode he must clearly have been able to register very fine phonetic differences. This state of affairs is thus not only characteristic of subordinate bilinguals (many of these use only one phonemic system), but is not unknown among much more completely bilingual speakers. We have evidence here too, then, which supports the conclusions of neurolinguistic research, that the phonological representation in the brain can function more independently than the rest of the linguistic representations.

5.2.2.5 Surface fluency and language as an instrument of thought (BICS and CALP)
          The relative independence of the phonological representation may also help to explain one of the important reasons why a young child's ability to speak a foreign language is often thought to be better than it really is, a mistaken judgement which may often have very serious consequences, especially with immigrant children and children from linguistic minorities. Jim Cummins (1979c, 1980a) makes a distinction between two different aspects of the linguistic ability of bilinguals. The first he calls BICS ("basic interpersonal communicative skills"), those aspects of linguistic skill which are called upon when somebody speaks with another person about everyday things in a concrete, cognitively less demanding situation where contextual cues can be drawn upon to interpret meaning and where understanding of the message is not solely dependent on understanding of the verbal part of the message. This aspect of linguistic ability is measured by tests for accent, for how genuine one sounds, for oral fluency, basic vocabulary and basic syntax. This can be called *surface fluency*, because it is this aspect of a speaker's linguistic command we immediately attend to when we hear somebody speak in face-to-face interaction and have to judge a person's linguistic ability. It is here particularly that phonological representation manifests itself.
          The second aspect Cummins calls CALP ("cognitive/academic language proficiency") and this aspect shows high correlations with verbal parts of intelligence tests and with tests of vocabulary, synonyms and analogies, as well as tests of syntactic maturity (see also Oller, 1979). It is this cognitive competence which has recently come to seem important in addition to communicative competence. This aspect of language ability can be seen as a *cognitive instrument,* as the ability to use language as an instrument for thought, in problem solving.
          A survey of a number of different studies (Cummins, 1979c, 1980a, 1980b) has shown that these two aspects of linguistic ability are not

necessarily closely related to each other. That an individual can speak a foreign language fluently in concrete everyday situations says *nothing* about her ability to use language as a cognitive instrument in cognitively demanding situations where contextual cues are not of much help. All normal healthy children learn to speak their mother tongue fluently, so that they experience no linguistic difficulty in the course of their ordinary life. The great differences that have been observed between different children's linguistic performance belong to the domain of language as a *cognitive instrument*. Discussion of bilingualism and intelligence tests has revealed that tests designed to measure this aspect of linguistic proficiency are usually very unfair to bilinguals in general. But it is enough to say here that this aspect of language proficiency (regardless of the unfairness of the demand) is required from minority children even in a foreign language, and it is largely this proficiency which still determines success or failure in schools. When people make the mistake of thinking that a child "knows" a language when she shows superficial fluency, and that fluent command means secure cognitive command of the kind required at school, we are doing a gross injustice to many immigrant children. Both neurophysiological evidence and the cumulative evidence from results in many tests that point to a distinction between surface and cognitive abilities, seem to suggest that fluency and cognitive command do not necessarily correlate highly. This should be taken into account in the assessment of the languages of bilinguals, and especially where decisions have to be made as to the language of instruction for minority children. We should thus not be deceived into thinking that an immigrant child commands Swedish/Norwegian/Danish well enough to be taught in that language if all we have heard is the child speaking fluently about everyday concrete things in ordinary face-to-face

FIGURE 7

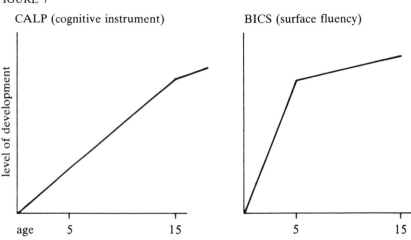

situations. In different ways we should try to measure the child's cognitive competence in the foreign language before we make the choice of placement or before we decide about the child's need for auxiliary teaching.

It is also possible to represent on a graph the development of these two aspects of language ability, as Jim Cummins does (Cummins, 1980b: 30). He assumes that these two aspects of a child's developing ability in her mother tongue are differentiated at a fairly early stage, so that the surface fluency develops rapidly and reaches a plateau at about the age of 5 or 6, whereas the development of cognitive linguistic ability tends to be more in line with the child's general intellectual development.

If we assume that there is the same type of differentiation between cognitive and surface development in the learning of a second language, especially with children and young people who are often very quick to acquire an ability to communicate in a foreign language in concrete context embedded situations, then we would have to assume that for them there is a considerable discrepancy for a long time in their second language between surface fluency and more academic ability. Investigations show that it may take from four to seven years for a child who comes to a new country more or less at pre-school age or later to develop in her new language those abilities which Cummins brings together under the CALP heading, to the level of a monolingual speaker, or to the CALP level she has in her mother tongue (see Cummins 1980a, 1980b and, for instance, Mägiste 1979 for further references).

A theoretical graph would look something like this:

FIGURE 8

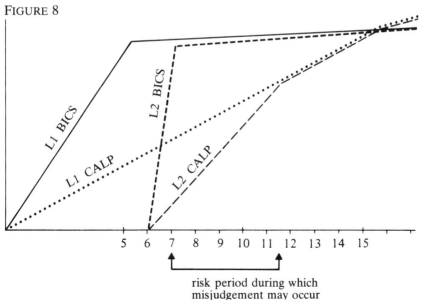

Then the period between 7 and 12, approximately, would be the period, when placing the child in an L2 learning environment, that is in a class or school functioning in a foreign language, may not give it the best opportunity for development. This would be a period of risk for a child who has begun to learn a second language around the age of 5. The risk of being misled by the child's considerable surface fluency in the second language would also be at its greatest during this period. We will come back to this when discussing the development of the "typical migrant child".

5.2.3   From the point of view of the psychology of learning, and of sociology

The distinction between compound and co-ordinate bilingualism has also been reduced to a discussion and description of different *ways of learning* the two languages (compound without formal instruction, co-ordinate – and subordinate – with the help of formal instruction), different *learning ages* (compound before school age, co-ordinate after starting school) and different *learning contexts* (compound: both languages in the same environment, by the same people who mixed and switched all the time, co-ordinate both languages in separate environments from different people). It seems to me that all these factors can be more fruitfully discussed using other points of departure than the compound–co-ordinate distinction, and this is done in other chapters. A mixture of compound and co-ordinate is probably the usual pattern for most bilingual children. From the point of view of interference and probably also a psychological sense of security *some* differentiation in the learning context seems to be desirable for the child. Practical aspects of how such a differentiation might be organized inside the family are discussed in section 7.2.4.

Instead one additional aspect of psychology of learning is discussed here, namely what the risk period introduced in 5.2.2.5 might mean in classroom situations.

5.2.4   What happens when a child is forced to function in cognitively demanding decontextualized situations through the medium of a less-well-mastered language?

In this section we will discuss in very concrete terms what happens during the risk period (see 5.2.2.5) when the child may already be able to function fluently in L2 in cognitively less demanding situations, in face-to-face interaction where contextual cues can be used, discussing concrete everyday things, but where the child still does not command L2 well enough to be able to use it on a par with native L2-speakers in cognitively demanding decontextualized situations. Do we in this situation give the child the optimal opportunities for further growth of her capacity to use language as an instrument of thought and problem solving, if the child is instructed through the medium of L2? My starting point here is that many aspects of the cognitive/academic language proficiency, CALP (see 5.2.2.5) are based on a common underlying proficiency (CUP) – (for a development of these concepts see Cummins 1979c, 1980b, 1980d, 1981a) instead of a separate one. Cummins illustrates the CUP with an image of dual icebergs:

FIGURE 9

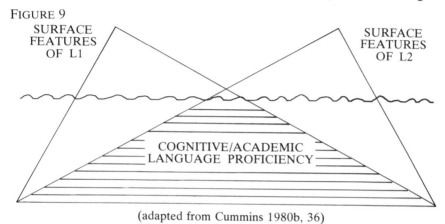

(adapted from Cummins 1980b, 36)

Another way of representing this is the following, which is a slight modification of Cummins, 1980b: 50–51:

FIGURE 10

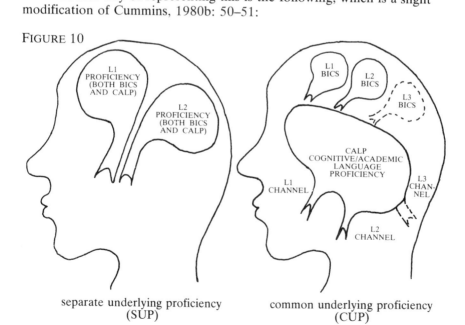

separate underlying proficiency
(SUP)

common underlying proficiency
(CUP)

According to the assumptions in a theory based on SUP (Separate Underlying Proficiency), the only way to teach a minority child L2 would be to expose the child to L2 as much as possible, i.e. to teach the child through the medium of L2, "put in" as much information and knowledge through the L2-channel as possible. Also, according to SUP-based theories, teaching the child through the medium of L1 would obviously strengthen L1-proficiency, but it would not enrich L2 (or it might rather diminish the possibilities for L2-growth, because so much time would be spent working through L1). According to a CUP-based theory, on the other hand, the child certainly needs exposure to L2 in order to develop surface fluency which has to be developed "separately" for every new language, but that can equally well or perhaps even better be done in different types of out-of-school (or at least out-of-formal-lesson) activities. One of the most important tasks for school would instead be twofold: to give the child optimal opportunities for developing the CUP which benefits both languages, and to "open up" the L2 channel. The teaching of a second language ("opening up" an L2-channel) under different circumstances is further discussed in section 9.6. Here we will discuss what happens when the child during the risk period when the L2-channel still does not function as well as the L1-channel, is forced to get information, process it and express the results of the process in L2. The starting point is the assumption that this CUP, the capacity for using language for problem solving, grows optimally when the interaction with the environment is as intensive as possible (when as much as possible flows in through one of the channels, gets processed and comes out again). The concrete situation to be discussed might be one where the "typical" minority child sits in a submersion classroom (where many of the students have L2, the language of instruction, as their mother tongue), listening to the teacher explaining something that the child is then supposed to use for problem solving.

The first result of the input or part of it being incomprehensible is that the child gets less information than a child listening to her mother tongue. Sometimes it is possible to infer or guess the meaning even if one does not understand all the words in a sentence (and Cloze-tests are a good example of this realization) (see also 7.3.5.2). But often not understanding one or two key words may mean missing whole sentences. The effect of lack of understanding is also differential: the same number of words not understood affects a poor learner and a beginner much more than it affects an advanced learner, who in turn is affected more than a native speaker.

Listening to a second or foreign language is more tiring than listening to L1. Even native speakers grow tired in classroom situations (see e.g. Cohen, 1981) and take pauses, stop listening every now and then. Listening to a foreign language demands more intensive attention (partly because there is less redundancy for a foreigner). It seems reasonable to suggest that a learner, receiving incomprehensible input and trying to understand it, has to have more frequent (and maybe longer) pauses than the native child in the same class. This also reduces the amount of input that the child gets. If we draw a curve of the native child's and the minority child's degree of concentration during one 90-minute lesson and assume that the concentration ideally should be at top level most of the time (with a programmed pause in the middle), it is easy to see how much more content the minority child misses by not being able to listen as intensively all the time as the native child in the same class:

FIGURE 11

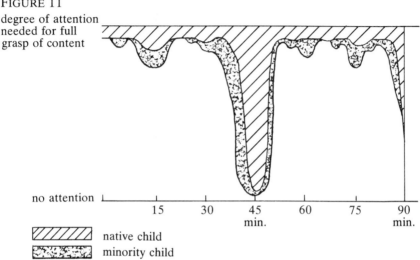

degree of attention needed for full grasp of content

no attention

| 15 | 30 | 45 min. | 60 | 75 | 90 min. |

 native child

minority child

Two defensive strategies, used by many children partly to avoid getting bored when the input is incomprehensible, partly to try to retain self-confidence, reduce the input even more. These can be discussed in relation to adults, who in the same situation have access to other strategies; children are in a much worse and more helpless and frustrating position.

If a grown-up is placed in a situation where she doesn't get much out of it because of language, she can:

■ simply walk out, i.e. *physically disappear,* either immediately or when the situation, for instance a lecture, is over (and this is what a lot of adult immigrants/guest workers have done in bad second language lessons in many countries where the drop-out rates are high);

■ try to change the situation (avoid repeating it, get extra instruction, get help from an interpreter, etc.).

If a child tries these solutions, different types of either immediate or slow indirect negative sanctions follow. In countries where the authorities try to keep all children, even immigrants, at school, progressively more sanctions can be imposed directly to oblige the child to come to school again: letters home, discussions with the child and the parents, referral to a school psychologist, social workers and even the police. Often the threat of taking the child away from home is enough to keep the child physically in school. In guest worker countries where the school in extreme cases may even try to prevent minority children from getting elementary education (as the state of Texas does with children of so-called undocumented aliens, i.e. illegal immigrants), the negative sanctions come slowly. It may be easier for the child to see the connection between the solution and the result if she is punished immediately than if she becomes unemployed later – these are two aspects of the same punishment. The strategy a child who is prevented from staying away physically can use in a frustrating situation is to *stay away psychologically* when the input is incomprehensible. The child can simply ignore the teaching, not be mentally present. Adding these lapses to the ones discussed earlier reduces the amount of input even more, by comparison with the native child in the same class.

A person who does not understand the language of instruction is bound to perform worse than the one who understands, and poor performance often leads to poor self-concept, making the affective filter high. Self-confidence is extremely important in second language learning (for a review of the evidence see Krashen, 1981b, and for evidence about misconceptions about self-confidence in minority children, Stone, 1981).

Again, if a grown-up is in a situation where she does not understand the language, she may feel frustrated but it will not necessarily affect her self-confidence, because she blames the language, not herself. An adult has experience of the same type of situation in the mother tongue. She can compare and conclude that *she* is not stupid but has simply had priorities other than learning that specific language. But a child who is forced to start school or day-care in a second language has no experience to compare with. The child's image of herself as a pupil/learner in a situation where the child, without knowing it, is at a disadvantage, is bound to be interpreted as negative by the child: I must be unusually bad and stupid. The child does not have any memories to fall back on about similar situations in L1 where she did well, unlike the adult. And that of course does not give the child a fair chance of developing a healthy self-confidence. The child inevitably blames herself. One of the possible ways of avoiding all this is not to listen at all. Then the child has "anticipated" the incomprehensible input and she can, in order to maintain her self-confidence, resort to the explanation which says that she would have understood, had she listened. The child can tell herself that the things discussed were not interesting enough and therefore she did not want to listen, and because she had *chosen* not to listen she did not understand. In this way the child does not need to blame herself for the failure – and the input is reduced even more.

A child in a submersion programme, forced to get information in school through L2 at the same time as she is supposed to be learning L2 gets both less comprehensible input and less input in general than the native child in the same class (towards whose needs the tuition usually is geared, both

linguistically and otherwise), and less than she would in a corresponding situation through the medium of her own L1, because:
▪ she does not understand every word and may miss the meaning of long sequences;
▪ she grows tired more rapidly and needs more (and longer) pauses;
▪ she opts out psychologically, does not listen, because it is impossible to skip the teaching, opt out physically;
▪ she does not listen, in an attempt to retain a normal self-confidence.

The result is less input, and less than optimal learning conditions.

When the child tries to *process* the information which has come through the medium of L2, this often proves to be much more of a strain than doing the same thing with the help of a language that the child masters. In a study by Georgios Tsiakalos in Bremen measuring physiological symptoms of stress, it was shown that students solving problems presented through the medium of L2 showed much higher levels of stress than they did when equivalent problems were presented through the medium of their L1. We know from other studies that a certain fairly low amount of stress may even be beneficial for performance (think of stage fright!), while high levels of stress have a negative impact on the level of performance (e.g. a tense examination situation, which may make the student feel that her head is absolutely empty). Tsiakalos' conclusion is that his study can be seen as strong evidence for an interpretation of the situation of minority students, forced to operate through the medium of an L2, as a situation of chronically high and excessive levels of stress. And that of course is not conducive to the type of problem-solving activities which help develop the child's language-related cognitive capacities in an optimal way, because that development requires that children solve problems which are close to the upper limits of what they can manage, both linguistically and cognitively. And since it is precisely in that type of problem-solving that the levels of stress may become too high for a minority child operating through the medium of L2, the child's problem-solving capacity may be reduced because of the stress. When the child has the additional burden of not having had as much information input as the native child in order to solve the problem, it is amazing that minority children are not doing even worse than they are.

If the child still happens to succeed in understanding the input and solving the problem against all the odds in the high-anxiety situation, she must communicate the solution to the others – reacting in some way to verbal input assures active attendance to the message. It has been shown that a long receptive period when the learner does not need to produce anything in L2 but can use all her energy for trying to understand (and is allowed to react either non-verbally or through the medium of L1) gives very good results (Terrell, 1981; Krashen, 1981; Legarreta-Marcaida, 1981). In such a situation the child can develop a more lasting *internal motivation* to use the language, because she is not forced to use L2 before she feels confident and accepted and ready for it: then the child reacts verbally in L2 because she wants to and not because of a more superficial, *external* necessity, a forced motivation. In a submersion class the child must react in L2 immediately because the teacher usually does not understand the child's L1. In an immersion programme the children's success is partly explained by the fact that the child can choose when she wants to start using L2, the child is praised for her attempts to do it, and she can always resort to the native tongue if she wants to, because the teacher understands both languages. It is obvious that it is much more difficult for the minority child in a submersion programme to communicate the solutions she has arrived at, through the medium of L2, than it is for the native child who can do it through her L1. The child is also forced to use more energy thinking about form, *how* to say it, which means that less attention can be paid to content, *what* to say. And if the child knows that she can't convey what she wants to convey, because of language difficulties, it may partly make her feel insecure, stupid and less self-confident, and partly either reluctant to speak or frustrated and aggressive – all types of behaviour which are more common among immigrant children than among native children. And again it is more difficult for a child than for a grown-up to be able to blame the language instead of blaming herself.

All this means, then, that instruction through the medium of L2 during the risk period (which may be a question of several years), does not give the minority child the same possibilities which the native child in the same class has to develop her cognitive/academic language proficiency – which is decisive for school achievement – and this seems to a certain extent to explain why even extensive exposure to L2 does not necessarily lead to a corresponding development of L2. If the child instead uses the L1-channel for cognitively demanding tasks until the L2-channel is well developed, the common underlying proficiency thus developed also benefits L2 later.

Notes to Chapter Five

1. Lambert, 1969; Lambert & Rawlings, 1969; Segalowitz & Lambert,1969; Lambert, Havelka & Crosby, 1958; Fishman, 1964; Kolers, 1963; Jakobovits, 1968; Diller, 1974, etc.
2. See Haugen, 1964: 43–68; Weinreich, 1967: 68; Hasselmo, 1969: 122–23; 1970: 180–83.
3. See, for example, Lambert, Ignatow & Krauthammer, 1968; Doob, 1957; Heras & Nelson, 1972; Kolers, 1965; Nott & Lambert, 1968; Kintsch & Kintsch, 1969; Saegert, Obermeyer & Kazarian, 1973; Hamers, 1973; Hamers & Lambert, 1972.
4. Kolers, 1968; Nott & Lambert, 1968; Evers, 1970; Lopez, Hicks & Young, 1974.

6 Planning the education of prospective bilinguals

6.1 What is and what is not bilingual education?

Bilingual education can mean many different things. The usual Anglo-American definition requires that *two languages should be used as media of instruction*. According to this definition, much of the education immigrant children and other minority children receive in different countries would not count as bilingual, since the only language of *instruction* is often the majority language. For instance, foreign language teaching for majority children, or a programme for minority children in which their mother tongue figured only as a subject (in Sweden called "home language teaching" or even "home language training") would thus not satisfy the requirements of the American definition of bilingual education and would not attract the provision for such bilingual programmes made in the Bilingual Education Act of 1968.[1] Nor is an educational system properly called bilingual which provides intensive second language instruction in the majority language for minority children (rather than putting them directly into majority language classes), not even if there are reception classes or preparatory classes solely for children from linguistic minorities who receive special instruction in the majority language. The term "bilingual education" thus relates only to *language of instruction* and requires that at least two languages should be used as means of instruction in subjects other than the languages themselves. This term is *not* intended to apply to the educational goal, but to the means.

6.2 Some typologies of bilingual education – Mackey, Fishman, Gonzáles

There are many ways of classifying bilingual education. One of the most elaborated typologies is that developed by William F. Mackey (1972). In the

Swedish version of this book I presented it at length, even if I think it has major shortcomings – understandably because it is old – because many of the aspects discussed in it have not been considered in Scandinavia and because they will become more and more important when immigrants become minorities. Since it is freely available in English, I will here only list some of the divisions it uses, with a few remarks about some of the confusing points. Then I will mention two other typologies (even if there are many others which could equally well be chosen, by Baker & de Kanter, Bratt Paulston, Spolsky, Tucker, Troike, etc. – see bibliography). Lastly I will present some of my own ways of typologizing education which I hope will complement the others.

Mackey discusses four different dimensions in his typology, and cross tabulates in the end the first three, producing 90 possibilities. I will give only the factors inside each dimension that he then combines.

When discussing *the relationship between the language(s) of the home and the school* Mackey distinguishes between learners from unilingual and bilingual homes, with the home language (one or both) used or not used as school language. In the second dimension, *curriculum,* Mackey distinguishes between (1) medium of instruction (single or dual medium), (2) pattern of development (maintenance of two or more languages or transfer from one medium of instruction to another), (3) distribution of the languages (different or equal and the same), (4) direction (towards assimilation (acculturation) into a dominant culture or towards integration into a resurgent one, i.e. irredentism), and (5) complete or gradual change from one medium to another.

Mackey's third dimension is *the linguistic character of the immediate environment as compared with the wider national environment.* Here he uses a model of four different circles, each of which takes in a larger area than the previous one. His scheme of expansion is from the *home,* to the *school,* to the *immediate environment* or *region,* and finally to the whole *country,* the *nation.* All ten of his curriculum types can be placed in the school category, and these can be set beside the nine varieties of environmental pattern he distinguishes (according to whether each circle is mono- or bilingual and whether the languages in all of them are the same or different), to give us 10×9 possible combinations.

Mackey's fourth dimension has to do with the *function* of the languages, their *status* as regional, national or international languages, and with *differences* between the languages, but since he does not use this dimension to expand the typology, they will not be dealt with here.

It is obviously difficult to try to typologize bilingual education in such a comprehensive way as Mackey has attempted. Some of the main difficulties with Mackey's typology will be listed:

■ There does not seem to be any natural hierarchy between different dimensions. This has in Mackey's case meant that the same notion may occur several times (for instance, when "transfer" in the curriculum dimension is used only to mean a mismatch between the languages of home and school as it is sometimes in Mackey's typology – and this mismatch has already been distinguished once in the first dimension).

▪ It is difficult to distinguish between a historical/present, or diacronic/synchronic or vertical/horizontal aspect, when discussing transfer and maintenance the way Mackey does.

▪ The concepts "transfer" and "maintenance" are difficult. Mackey uses them in the same dimension in several different ways, so that transfer sometimes refers to a historical, vertical change in the whole school system, where the language of instruction has been changed at some point, sometimes it refers to the individual child, either so that the language of the instruction changes at some point during the child's education or even so that it is called a transfer when the language of the school and the home are not the same, as discussed earlier. Maintenance sometimes refers to the same language or languages being used as media of instruction during the child's school career, regardless of whether it is a majority or a minority language, sometimes it means that they just figure in the curriculum, also as subjects, and sometimes it refers to trying to maintain both languages at the same level of proficiency.

▪ These examples show that it would be important to distinguish between a historical description of the school system and changes in it, and the organization of the school as a system now. Likewise it should be possible to distinguish between the school as an institution in itself, and the individual child. For instance, in the kind of school my own children have attended in Helsinki all subjects are taught in both Finnish and Swedish, but an individual child gets all her instruction in one language only, either Finnish or Swedish (in addition to the 3 or 4 foreign languages that everybody has as subjects, including Finnish and Swedish). The school policy is to allocate classrooms, halls and playgrounds in such a way that the children come into contact with the other language during every break. But the teaching environment for each individual child is still monolingual. It is as if two completely monolingual schools have been mixed together so thoroughly that a Finnish class is never next door to or sharing a hall with another Finnish class. – I will try to address some of these difficulties in my typology, which covers only a small part of the area covered by Mackey.

6.3   Fishman's typology

Joshua Fishman's typology is very concisely set out but it nevertheless takes up many of the distinctions which are important to minorities (Fishman & Lovas, 1970). It is particularly suitable for the characterizing of the different models of minority education in America. As it deals with some aspects of bilingual education which are missing from Mackey's curriculum types, I shall describe it briefly here.

Fishman's Type I, *transitional bilingualism,* envisages a scheme in which the minority language is used only during the first few years of schooling and then only in so far as it is needed to help the children to adapt to school life and/or to learn their various subjects until their knowledge of English (the majority language) is good enough to allow it to be used as the language of instruction. Type II, *monoliterate bilingualism* (the ability to read and write in only one of the languages), allows for the development of oral proficiency in both languages, but here no attempt is made to help the children learn to read and write in their own mother tongue, only in the majority language. Type III, *partial bilingualism,* attempts to develop in the child a fluent command of both languages, also in reading and writing, but with only a few subjects actually taught in the children's mother tongue. These subjects are often those of particular significance to the child's ethnic group and its cultural heritage. Type IV, finally, *complete bilingualism,* encourages the children to develop both their languages in all linguistic functions (understanding, speaking, reading, writing, thinking) in all domains, thus without any kind of diglossia. Both languages are generally used to teach all subjects (except in the teaching of the two languages themselves). This type of system has as its aim the maintaining and developing of the minority language.

Fishman's typology rests on the assumption that any particular programme is best judged by its *aim,* thus making the distinction between the organization and the aim of a programme that Mackey does not make.

6.4   Gonzáles' typology

J. M. Gonzáles uses a sliding scale in his classification of different types of bilingual educational programme. In his typology, too, the most important criterion of any scheme is its *aim,* but he assesses even more clearly than Fishman to what extent any particular programme serves the interest of the minority. Moreover, his various types of programme cover a broader area than Fishman's.

Type A. English as a foreign language/bilingual (transitional). This has a strictly compensatory/remedial orientation.

Type B. Bilingual maintaining. The child's proficiency in another language is seen as a positive characteristic, worth maintaining and developing.

Type C. Bilingual/bicultural (maintaining). Resembles Type B, but also integrates the target group's "history and culture" as an integrated part of the content and methodology of the curriculum.

Type D. Bilingual/bicultural (restoring). A serious attempt is made to give the children an opportunity to learn the language and culture of their foremothers and forefathers, knowledge of both of which may have been lost in the process of assimilation.

Type E. Culturally pluralist. The children are not subject to any restriction on account of the linguistic group to which they belong. All children take part in linguistically and culturally pluralist education.

It is probably true that Gonzáles' typology has both a historical and a utopian perspective: it exhibits a developmental trend, and Gonzáles himself makes it quite clear what kind of development he regards as positive. Thus he does not want his types of programme aimed only at certain restricted groups; rather he wants *all* schoolchildren, both minority and majority children, to become multilingual and multicultural – and *that* is an idealistic utopia.

6.5   Monolingual or bilingual – relationship between method and aim

The background of my own typology is the Scandinavian discussion about the best ways to educate minority children and some of the misconceptions about the nature of that education. Among the *misconceptions* (which Jim Cummins has discussed at length in some of his latest articles) two of the most persistent are the ones saying that *it is always best to teach a child through the medium of her mother tongue* (and, consequently, that it is harmful to teach a child through the medium of a foreign language), and that *the mother tongue must always be stabilized before instruction through the medium of another language can be started.* The danger with these claims (and others of the same kind) is that they are true under certain circumstances and false under others, and the circumstances are seldom specified. If this type of claim (which applies perfectly well to many minority groups in Scandinavia and which we have used, specifying the circumstances, in demanding mother tongue medium classes) is made to appear as if it was a general truth, it becomes easy to show that it does not always apply. If school authorities have "bought", for instance, mother tongue classes thinking that these claims are always true, regardless of the circumstances, they certainly become confused when hearing something that could be taken as counter-evidence, for instance that Turks in Bavaria, West Germany, are *not* doing well in mother tongue medium classes, or that 100,000 children in Canada are being taught through the medium of a foreign language and are doing very well indeed. When one looks at different programmes and notices that some programmes teach children through the medium of L1, some through the medium of L2, and some succeed in making the children bilingual (at least to a very large extent and to a high level) while others do not, quite regardless of whether the children have been taught through the medium of one language or two, or through the medium of L1 or L2, confusion is unavoidable, unless one tries to single out a few factors and understand some of the principles.

In my typology I distinguish between language of instruction (monolingual or bilingual) and the aim of the programme, first from a linguistic point of view (where I treat monolingualism/bilingualism as both an independent and a dependent variable, i.e. I see, for instance, monolingual education in the minority language for majority members as *causing* bilingualism). Then I proceed by trying to see what societal goals the linguistic aims serve, and here the societal goals become the independent causal variable, decisive for which language(s) is chosen as the medium of instruction (mediating variable) to produce monolingualism or bilingualism (dependent variable), which in its turn is decisive for whether or not the societal goals can be achieved. I also distinguish between the majority language and the minority language in discussing both the medium of instruction and the linguistic aim. Under "child" I indicate from whose perspective the programme is classified, the minority or the majority child's (see Table 3), whereas the linguistic makeup of the class is indicated under "type of class", where classes where all the children have the same mother tongue are classified as "same", regardless of whether this same L1 is the minority language or the majority language (that should be clear from the context). I will briefly discuss each type in the typology and give some examples. I would like to remind the reader again that I define "minority" in terms of power relationships, not numbers.

Monolingual education through the medium of the majority language the goal of which is monolingualism for majority children, type 1, is the most common way of educating majority children in most countries with a large so-called international language as the majority language, like West Germany, the United States, Great Britain, Soviet Union, France, China and Spain. Canada is here one of the most notable exceptions. It is likewise used in many smaller countries which are or pretend to be linguistically homogeneous, like all Scandinavian countries. In all these countries children often have some foreign languages in their curriculum as subjects, but they seldom approximate to anything resembling bilingual competence.

When the goal is *monolingualism in the majority language for minority children,* type 2, a submersion programme is used. It is often a situation with a very strong assimilationist goal on the societal-political level, assimilation here meaning that the minority members, in order to be accepted, have to become as much like the majority as possible and give up their special characteristics, language, culture, etc., i.e. this is a cultural, not a structural definition. Often structural incorporation of the minority is not allowed on an equal footing with the majority members, i.e. the minority members do not have equal rights in the educational, social and political fields and on the labour market (but often they *do* have the same duties, for instance as far as paying taxes is concerned – see Ekberg, 1980). The mother tongue of the minority children is not even taught as a subject for them (let alone taught to majority children) in countries where cultural pluralism is not supported, and where it is seen as a threat to the unity of the country (for a development of a discussion about stages in minority and majority views about cultural

TABLE 3

medium of instruction	child	type of class (same L1 or mixed)	programme type	societal goal	linguistic aim

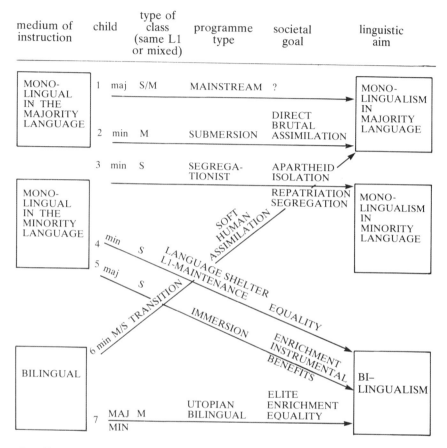

pluralism vs assimilation, and structural incorporation vs segregation see Skutnabb-Kangas & Toukomaa, 1976).

One of the more implicit goals in this type of programme is also that those minority children who succeed in the programmes at the same time are socialized into accepting those values which are connected with that part of the majority society which controls the schools. In that way those minority children who succeed are pacified: they are alienated from their own group, and they do not feel solidarity with those minority children who do *not* succeed (see e.g. Hernández-Chávez, 1978). It is the "we-made-it-and-they-can-do-it-too-if-they-work-hard-enough" syndrome. Those minority children, on the other hand, who do not succeed, are pacified by shame: they are made to feel that it is their own fault that they don't succeed – the "blame-the-victim" technique (see Chapter 12).

This is the most common model still for most minority children in the world. These programmes, which show bad results all over the world, assimilate the children at the same time as they prevent them from getting a good education. This model is used with almost all minority children in Australia and in Canada (though there are exceptions, notably the French but also, for instance, some of the Ukrainians). It was the model in the United States before the bilingual education programmes came into existence, and it is the model that the conclusions in the new "evaluation" of bilingual education research would lead to again if implemented (even if the new programmes are called "structured immersion" instead of submersion, to sell them better – Baker & de Kanter, 1981). This model is used almost exclusively in Denmark, Norway, France, Great Britain, Holland, etc. and to a great extent in Sweden (programme 1 in 11.4.3) and West Germany (programmes 1–3 in 11.4.2). These programmes educate future assembly line workers and future unemployed, future losers. One of their perhaps unintended results is also the kind of violent physical reactions which we have seen (and certainly will see more of) in uprisings in many cities during the last decade or two – and in the crisis climate now and the many racist attacks, more or less silently approved of by the establishment, in a way which would have been unthinkable ten years ago, they are going to increase very rapidly (see Chapter 12). This type of education, which Nils Erik Hansegård (1972: 119) calls "language-shift education" or "cultural genocide", corresponds to Mackey's type SAT, Single-Medium Accultural Transfer (transfer here meaning the mismatch between home and school).

Monolingual education through the medium of a minority language can be of three different kinds. If the goal is *monolingualism in the minority language for a minority,* type 3, it is often a situation with different types of segregational or apartheid programmes, for instance, the education for different African groups in different "home lands", Bantustans, in South Africa, or typically for Turkish but also for other guest worker children especially in Bavaria but also in other parts of West Germany (i.e. programme 6 and to a certain extent also 5 in 11.4.2). In this type of programme the implicit societal goal may be described as twofold, depending on the minority. With indigenous groups like the ones in South Africa, reproduction of apartheid and isolation from other subordinated groups seems to be the goal. The physical segregation helps the linguistic one – because the Africans are needed in their capacity as workers in jobs which require communication with the dominating group they cannot be "kept" completely monolingual in their own languages, but the education sees to it that they do not learn enough of the power language to be able to influence the society or, especially, to acquire a common language with the other subordinated groups, a shared medium of communication and analysis, a prerequisite for solidarity and common action. The linguistic segregation is a central part of the Bantustan-policy, both in South Africa and in Namibia – and that puts, for instance, SWAPO in a difficult situation where political unity and educational considerations to a certain extent might demand different solutions for language choice for independent Namibia (United Nations Institute for Namibia, 1981; SWAPO, 1982; Angula, 1982).

In the case of guest worker minorities where one of the goals in education is to keep the children unintegrated, ready to be sent home whenever their parents' labour is not needed any more (see Chapter 11), this type of education both prepares them for repatriation and prevents them from getting their share of the goods and services of the mainstream majority society if they (are allowed to) stay. Segregation is here a combination of physical (housing, guest worker schools) and psychological segregation (discrimination, racism). As far as I can judge this type does not figure in any of the typologies mentioned.

These programmes also educate future assembly-line workers, but these youngsters may have a better chance of uniting, developing solidarity and protesting than the youngsters coming from submersion programmes. These youngsters, or at least an élite among them, may have a constructive, articulate rage as a motive, and they may succeed in canalizing it, whereas the only motive forces many submersion students have may be shame, rootlessness, an unanalyzed destructive rage without direction and goal. This more positive perspective for segregation than submersion programmes may hold true more for indigenous than for migrant minorities, though.

Monolingual education the goal of which is bilingualism for minority children, type 4, is a maintenance or language shelter programme, where the L1 of the children is the medium of instruction for the first several years, possibly throughout the obligatory schooling, with the majority language as a second language. These programmes seem to function well (see 7.4). Good examples are the Swedish-medium schools for the Swedish-speaking indigenous minority in Finland, the mother tongue classes for immigrant children in Sweden (i.e. programme 3, 11.4.3), or the Francophone schools in English Canada. Maintenance programmes have arisen as a protest against suppression of minorities, and often their existence shows that the minority community has started a dynamic struggle to get their share of the goods and services of the majority society. A very good example of this is the programme declaration of the newly founded National Hispanic University in California, presented at the CABE (California Association for Bilingual Education) conference, January 13–16, 1982, in San Francisco. Often these programmes are a sign of revitalization, as for instance with Ukrainians in Canada. Sometimes they also reflect a situation where the minority had more power when the programmes came into existence, but even in these situations (like the one for the Swedish-speaking minority, a former power-majority) the programmes now seem to fulfil the same purpose for the children as "regular" maintenance programmes.

Monolingual education the goal of which is bilingualism for majority children, type 5, is the Canadian speciality, immersion programmes in their early grades, before the instruction through the medium of the children's mother tongue has started. These types of programme are likely to arise in situations where a linguistic majority needs to become bilingual for instrumental (not integrative) reasons, in order not to lose old privileges or in order to get new benefits or privileges, guaranteed to bilinguals. This is a situation where the minority has become strong enough to get through demands for bilingualism and benefits for bilinguals, for instance on the job market. But because previously the minority members were the ones who were bilingual, they were the ones who would get all these new benefits unless majority members now also become bilingual. These types of programme are supported by the powerful majority community and that helps the L1 of the children in its development, even if it is not the language of instruction in the early years. In Canada and the United States there are many such programmes, in French, German, Spanish, Hebrew, Ukrainian, etc. (see Lambert & Taylor, 1982; Lambert, 1983), but curiously enough they have not yet spread to Europe. From all the existing evidence we can predict that we would get very good results. Just to be a bit provocative we could, with good scientific backing, say: *not a single child* in West Germany, France, Great Britain, Holland, Sweden, Denmark and Norway needs *any* instruction in school through the medium of respectively German, French, English, Dutch, Swedish, Danish and Norwegian, during the first 6 years of education. Everybody in these countries could be taught through the medium of minority languages (which for minorities should be their own mother tongues, and for majorities any of the minority languages) (see Skutnabb-Kangas, 1983a). When we get the first European immersion programmes, it will show that some of the minorities are approaching the strength needed for making their language instrumentally attractive to majorities – and I would like to predict that Finns in Sweden will soon be able to do that: to get Sweden to guarantee the Finnish language a special official or semi-official status in Sweden.

The two models, types 4 and 5, monolingual education leading to bilingualism, seem to lead to very good results for both minority and majority children, especially in situations where there are great status differences between the minority and majority languages and groups, but even in situations with smaller differences. One of the prerequisites for the model to function is that the other language, the language which is not the language of instruction, is taught as a subject. *The main principle for leading to high levels of bilingualism in general,* namely SUPPORT VIA INSTRUCTION IN THE LANGUAGE WHICH IS OTHERWISE LESS LIKELY TO DEVELOP, also applies to these programmes. The monolingual instruction in these programmes is always conducted in *that* language which the children would otherwise be less likely to learn to an advanced level, especially in its more formal aspects, in the society outside school. And that is for both the majority children and the minority children the minority language, i.e. for the majority children it is a foreign (or second) language, but for the minority children their mother tongue. One of the most difficult differences in outcome, the one between types 3 and 4 (where in both cases minorities are taught through the medium of their L1 but with different results), is further discussed in chapter 11.

Bilingual education the goal of which is monolingualism for minority children, type 6, may sound a bit harsh, because a complete monolingualism is not the goal here either. But characteristic of this type of programme is that the goal is assimilation, too. It is said, often even officially, that the children need not be taught bilingually any more (or even have instruction in their mother tongue as a subject in many cases) when they have learned enough of the majority language to be able to follow instruction through the medium of the majority language – this is typically the case, for instance, in the United States. The criteria for when they can be transferred to majority-medium instruction are often based on loose evaluations of when the children can manage orally in simple face-to-face interaction discussing concrete everyday things, situations where contextual cues help the child to understand (i.e. when they master BICS-basic interpersonal communicative skills, superficial linguistic fluency in context-embedded cognitively less demanding situations – for concrete descriptions of this see Cummins, 1981b, Cicourel, 1982 and Skutnabb-Kangas, 1982c). Often children at this stage still do not have any chance of succeeding as well as majority children in cognitively and linguistically more demanding de-contextualized tasks (see sections 5.2.2.5, 5.2.4). The result often is that they fail miserably at school, regardless of superficial oral fluency (see Cummins, 1981a). All the transitional bilingual programmes belong to this type, i.e. programme 2 in Sweden and programme 4 in West Germany (Chapter 11).

Even if it is sometimes said officially that the goal in this type of programme is bilingualism (as is done in Sweden, for instance, especially about the compound classes – see Skutnabb-Kangas, 1982a), the most important value being stressed is that the children learn the majority language (as early as possible and as fast as possible). This has been exceedingly clear with the U.S. federally-supported bilingual education programmes, the primary goal of which must be the rapid acquisition of English, according to Secretary of Education Shirley Hufstedler (1980) in President Carter's administration – and this trend seems to have increased since then. Often no real efforts are made to give the children a fair chance of reaching native competence in their L1, even if lip service is paid to the importance of maintaining and sometimes even developing the mother tongue and the cultural ties of the minority children. This can easily be checked by looking at the measures which are taken to give equal status to both languages involved in the schools. The real attitude is often evident when we look at the degree and kind of effort made to ensure equality between the two languages. In trying to determine whether the unstated aim is monolingualism or bilingualism, we can try to establish whether both languages have *the same status as either compulsory or optional at school.* We can try to discover *what kind of obligation is involved and upon whom it falls;* for example, whether the educational authorities are (or are not) bound to make provision for instruction in or through the medium of one of the languages, and especially whether there are exceptions to the rules (and of what kind) which allow the authorities the option of not providing such teaching. We are interested, too, in the obligation the child has to attend such classes as are provided. It is also important to note whether the teaching in or through the medium of each language has *equivalent status in the curriculum,* so that the timetable gives equal weight to both, or whether there is some inequality here, so that for example teaching in one of the languages is outside normal timetabled hours (as is the case with teaching in the immigrant mother tongues in Denmark), or clashes with lessons in other important subjects which the child must consequently miss (as is the case in Sweden).

We can also examine what kind of *job security* and *working conditions* are enjoyed by *teachers of minority languages,* as well as *how well they are trained,* and whether attempts are made to ensure they have the same status as other teachers in all respects. We can compare, too, the *number of hours* allotted on the timetable to each language, in order to establish whether the language the children have less opportunity to use in a variety of social situations is (or is not) given considerably more room on the timetable. A further aspect to be examined concerns the *kind of financial resources available to each language.* We can also examine the status of each of the languages as it is reflected in the *communication* that takes place *within* the four walls of the school (the language used for signs on the walls, in schemes and diagrams, in materials provided in the classrooms and the library, for ordinary internal messages and information, for the social ritual of daily work in the school, school parties, and so on), as well as with parents, the public at large and the authorities. If such a comparison reveals several respects in which the languages have *not* been made equal (granted that the language which has a weaker status outside school should be "compensated for" inside the school), that shows that the real goal probably is closer to monolingualism than bilingualism, regardless of all the pious phrases.

The last type, 7, is *bilingual education the goal of which is bilingualism.* It is a type of education where great emphasis is placed on trying to reach high levels in *both* languages, and where a realistic evaluation is made of how much support each language needs. It should be clear here, too, that if one of the languages would not otherwise develop, it should get most of the resources and time inside school, as Wallace Lambert (1979) says. Even if the status differences are not very great, one or the other of the languages will most often need compensation inside school, often because it is less used in that particular society or in the environment where the children live. But it also seems that this type of model functions best in situations with fairly small status differences between the languages and speakers (regardless of the reasons the differences are small), and often (but not always) with children from privileged backgrounds, and often with students above the elementary level. The aforementioned types 4 and 5, monolingual education leading to bilingualism, could at a later stage, for instance after 6–9 years, develop to bilingual education leading to bilingualism (and they often do). But then the development of the minority language should receive special attention. If there are both majority and minority children in bilingual programmes, mutuality is absolutely essential. *Both groups should learn both languages* (for a good case study description of how that can be done see Jan Curtis' article in Cummins & Skutnabb-Kangas, in preparation). More time should be spent with the minority language. If the minority children are the only ones to become bilingual, and the majority children learn but a few songs and phrases of the minority language (as in Sweden in programme 2), then it is closer to the situation described earlier as bilingual education leading to monolingualism, even if it may be good for the attitudes of majority children.

The types presented could also be seen as forming a progression, where types 2, 3 and 6 (and 1) do not respond to the needs of individual children and do not give them the advantages that high levels of bilingualism can lead to – quite the opposite, they can be disastrous, at least for individual minority children – whereas 4, 5 and 7 give all children good chances. And of course, in an ideal society of equality, peace and mutual understanding, all children should be educated bilingually (see Gonzáles' type E).

One can also look at the monolingually organized programmes inside another type of framework. Here I leave out the mainstream, the transitional (because they later function in the same way as submersion programmes, even if in the beginning they are more human) and the bilingual programmes leading to bilingualism (because they are not (yet?) a realistic large-scale alternative). If we cross-tabulate the language used (IL) or not used (NIL) as the medium of instruction, with whether it is (L1) or is not (L2) the mother tongue of the children, and suppose at first that the IL always develops to a native-like level (+), we get 4 logical possibilities where we assume that the NIL either *does have* (+) a chance to develop (despite not being IL, through society support, language arts instruction, positive peer contact and the like), or that NIL *does not have* (−) this chance, i.e. does not develop, starts to deteriorate or is replaced by the IL.

TABLE 4

	1	2	3	4
IL	L2 +	L2 +	L1 +	L1 +
NIL	L1 +	L1 −	L2 −	L2 +

According to this scheme, the children in the first and last case would become bilingual, while the children in the two middle cases would become either monolingual or dominant in one of the languages, in each case the language of instruction. When we compare these four completely theoretical cases with the distinctions made earlier we can see that they correspond to them. The *first* case, where L2 is the language of instruction and where L1 does develop, is the situation in *immersion* programmes. The *second* case, where L2 is also the IL but where L1 does not develop or starts to deteriorate, is the situation in *submersion* programmes. The *third* case where L1 is the IL and where L2 does not develop, is the situation in *segregational or apartheid* programmes. And the *fourth* case, where L1 is also the IL but where L2 does develop, is the situation in *maintenance or language shelter* programmes, *mother tongue classes*.

Now if it really were the case that the IL would develop to a native-like level in all situations, we could stop screaming about minority education. We could think that it is a pity that a potential for bilingualism, biculturalism and international understanding is lost in the two middle cases, but we know that a lot of children in the world are monolingual and happy with that, and do well in school. But it is quite clearly the case, contrary to the common belief which has guided minority education, that using a language as IL does not guarantee that that language develops to a native-like level in all aspects of linguistic competence (see 10.2.3). Some programmes produce deficits in IL too, and these deficits vary both quantitatively and qualitatively. These deficits, if any, seem to be absolutely minor in immersion and maintenance programmes, and if they exist, they can be "cured" so to say inside the system, by the individual, with the help of school: better teacher training, better teaching materials, etc. (L1–IL in maintenance), by increasing peer contact in situations where there are no societal status-obstacles to increasing them (L2–IL in immersion), or where the self-confidence, pride and strength given by the school organization gives children the means to cope and increase peer contact with the other group even if there may be some discrimination against them (L2–NIL in maintenance). It also seems that any deficits produced in these programmes have to do with aspects of language which don't necessarily affect school achievement (i.e. they are BICS-related factors, which in both cases may affect the L2 of the children but can easily be coped with later with increased peer contact with speakers of the children's L2).

The isolationist segregatory apartheid programmes may sometimes show deficits in IL, even if it is the L1 of the children, especially in guest worker situations with poor teaching conditions and materials. But they show especially big deficits in the NIL, because of poor teaching (which mostly is not the teachers' fault) and lack of contact with NIL (and NIL-speakers), because of physical segregation, psychological discrimination or, mostly, a combination of both. As long as the goal of these programmes is segregation, it would be naive to think that the instruction of L2 could be improved so as to produce native competence in it, because native competence in the majority language is precisely what these programmes want to *prevent*. Here part of the solution of the problem quite clearly lies outside the school system and outside the families and individuals themselves. What is needed – in Jane Hill's words – is not language treatment but social treatment. The greatest deficits seem to be produced in the submersion programmes for minority children, both indigenous and immigrant – here they can affect both languages. The deficits in the mastery of the foreign IL often seem to manifest themselves in the more cognitive/academic aspects of language proficiency (CALP), and since this is the aspect that the instruction in the higher grades in more context-reduced situations more and more draws on, many children who in the beginning did well (because of well developed BICS) start to fail (see e.g. Cicourel's description of this, 1982 and 10.2.3). More and better L2-teaching doesn't seem to help here either – the deficit needs social rather than linguistic remedies.

To sum up, it seems that an instruction in an L2 which at the same time prevents the CALP of the L1 (which is part of the common underlying proficiency for cognitive/academic ability *across* languages – see Cummins 1981a) from developing or does not support it, produces poor results in both languages, and, accordingly, in school in general. A life (and school) situation which develops the common underlying proficiency produces good results, quite regardless of which the language of instruction is, L1 or L2. It is *not* axiomatic (as Unesco says, 1953) that L1 is always the best possible medium of instruction. The question is in which circumstances the common CALP can be developed. Going back to the earlier characterization of programmes, it seems that those programmes whose goal is bilingualism (and not monolingualism), namely immersion and maintenance, succeed in developing CALP and making the children bilingual, either now, or in some cases with the help of minor improvements which can be made inside the school system. Those programmes, on the other hand, which in the typology were characterized as monolingual programmes whose goal is monolingual-ism, seem to produce (a risk of) deficits of a major character, deficits which pertain to the more cognitive/academic decontextualized aspects of language proficiency (in one or both languages) and, accordingly, affect school achievement, and which cannot be coped with with the help of measures inside the school, quite regardless of how good, liberal and well-intentioned (see Stone, 1981) the teachers are. These programmes produce bad results because the bad results serve certain social, economic and political functions. This aspect will be further developed in Chapter 11. Some of the different types will be further discussed in relation to school achievement and cognitive development in 9.5.

Notes to Chapter Six

1. See, for example, Andersson & Boyer, 1978, 2nd edition; Andersson, 1977: 192–97; or *Bilingual Education: Current Perspectives,* Volume 3: Law.

7 How can a child become bilingual with the help of school and family?

7.1 Different methods for different groups

7.1.1 Limitations

As has emerged from the different typologies considered in the last chapter, a number of matters need to be borne in mind in any discussion of how best children become bilingual. It is certain that there are no general methods applicable to every child in any country, in all circumstances and historical periods. But in order to be able to say something useful about those situations which are at present of most immediate concern in Scandinavia, we must severely restrict the number of aspects which can be discussed. I shall therefore in what follows adopt the classification used in 4.2.2 and discuss only children from bilingual families, children from linguistic majorities (in so far as their experience throws light on the different alternatives available for the education of minorities), and children from linguistic minorities. Consideration of élite bilinguals will be omitted, since for them becoming bilingual is hardly ever a problem. Moreover, many of the factors affecting the choices for majority children can also be generalized to cover the case of élite bilinguals.

When we begin to study the various attempts at trying consciously to help children become bilingual with the help of the school, we find that the variety of method is quite amazing. Such attempts have included the most various kinds of experience under the most varied conditions. As is usual with research into bilingualism – or indeed with educational research in general – the planning and the evaluation of the research projects have included many sources of error. The Hawthorne effect can be observed in most studies: the fact that one knows that somebody is going to come and test one or test the results of one's teaching tends in itself to improve the results, whatever pedagogical methods are being used. Besides, many of the important variables have not been controlled: SES (= socio-economic status), the degree of bilingualism, initial characteristics in general, IQ, and so on. One often feels quite hopeless trying to find a way through one defective experiment after another (even though some experiments show a high degree of *technical* perfection in their psychometric and statistical treatment of the material) in the hope of arriving at important general conclusions. However, when one contemplates the many different kinds of erroneous generalization freely made by researchers and others, it gradually becomes apparent that there are certain fundamental distinctions between groups and situations which must always be made if one's research is not going to be wholly misdirected. My choice of important distinctions to be discussed here is much influenced by the rather depressing recurrence in the Scandinavian debate on bilingual education of the same old mistakes over and over again. The same types of mistake can also be seen in American research. Some of the debates which have partly arisen because of these mistakes are presented in Cummins & Skutnabb-Kangas (forthcoming).

Some of the necessary distinctions not always made are between:
- children from linguistic majorities and children from linguistic minorities, in their language learning (see also 4.2.2.2 and 4.2.2.4 for the distinctions, and 10.3.2 for some of the consequences for developmental matters),
- children for whom being taught in a foreign language poses no threat to their mother tongue, and children for whom being taught in a foreign language poses a serious threat to the development of their mother tongue,
- the learning of a foreign language and the learning of a second language spoken in the immediate environment,
- the learning of a foreign language at school (only) and the learning of one's own mother tongue.

Lars Henric Ekstrand, one of the Swedish researchers who makes all the mistakes outlined above, freely draws parallels, for example, between Swedish children who learn a little English, French or German at school, and immigrant children who learn their own language above all at home but also at school. His argumentation is that since Swedish children do not become bilingual (in the sense of achieving a native speaker's command of English, French or German), it is not worth while for immigrant children to try to achieve a native speaker's command of their own mother tongue. . . . This type of reasoning seems to be typical for assimilationist researchers who think that the majority language should be made the dominant language, indeed the mother tongue, of the minority children, and that, as far as their mother tongue, the minority language, is concerned, "for some immigrant children the optimum might well be to keep the level a bit above the risk level for complete decay" (Ekstrand, 1979b: 11).

A further distinction that has not been made by very many of the writers on this subject is that between élite bilinguals and minority children, between children of highly educated parents, often themselves linguists (either in monolingual or bilingual families) and children of working-class parents from indigenous or immigrant minorities. What has worked for élite bilinguals, is suggested for immigrant bilinguals, without any consideration given to the different socio-economic circumstances – and when it does not work, the immigrant parents are blamed.

I shall discuss some of these distinctions more closely in order to show that the preconditions for bilingualism are quite different in different circumstances and that we must therefore employ different methods for different groups.

7.1.2 Majority children and minority children

Majority children who learn a foreign language either as an ordinary school subject (for example, Swedish children learning French at school) or in immersion programmes (English-speaking children in Canada being taught in French) usually have a high-status mother tongue in no danger of being replaced by the language they are learning – an *additive* language learning situation (Lambert, 1975). In the case of *immersion programmes* the child herself and her parents have voluntarily chosen that the child should become bilingual and that this should be by being taught in a foreign language. The child has alternatives to both these choices: either not to become bilingual at all but monolingual, and to go to a school where the language of instruction is the child's mother tongue. Any failure to become bilingual entails no risk of failure in regard to other school subjects, general school achievement, to the contact with family, friends, or the group the parents represent, or to the child's own future prospects, educational, cultural, economic or political standing. The child may live her life quite happily as a monolingual; all she has to do is to move to another school. The majority child normally learns the foreign language with the help of a bilingual teacher and together with other children in the same situation (where all the children are in the process of learning the language, where none is a native speaker of it, and where the norm on which the organization of the teaching depends is *not* that of a native speaker but of a learner of the language). The process of learning takes place in a positive and supportive atmosphere where the child is praised for success, where she need not feel ashamed of her own language (which is developing well in any case) and her origins, and where as a consequence the chances of success are good.

The typical situation for a *minority child* learning a foreign language in a submersion programme is that she is actually taught through the medium of this foreign language and that she has a low-status mother tongue which is constantly in danger of being replaced by the more prestigious majority language through which she is being taught – a *subtractive* language learning situation. The child is forced to accept both the necessity of becoming bilingual and of being taught in a foreign language – there is usually no alternative. The consequences of any failure to become bilingual are catastrophic (see section 4.2.2.4). The minority child usually has a monolingual teacher who does not understand what the child says in her mother tongue. The learning takes place in a class where some of the children speak the language of instruction as their mother tongue and where the norm is a child who already knows the language, not a child learning it. The minority child is therefore defined as deviant and in need of compensatory teaching. The child is not encouraged to develop her own language. The child's mother tongue brings her no credit and is of no value at school (see Catani, 1982). The child is often made to feel ashamed of her own language, her ethnic group and her origins. The chances of success are not great.

The terms we have chosen in Swedish for immersion and submersion, are more concrete: *språkbad,* language bath, and *språkdränkning,* language drowning (implying that an active agent tries to drown the child, it is not accidental). I have elaborated these images in the Swedish version to illustrate the programmes. Since the images are vivid and quite pedagogical (not to say demagogic) I retain them here, too, even if the English terms do not have the same strong connotations.

Immersion, language bath, is something voluntary and rather enjoyable. The children can come out of the water if they begin to get cold (leave the programme and transfer to an L1-medium school if they start feeling it's difficult). All the time they have the swimming instructor to tell them what to do (the teacher who understands their L1), and water wings so that they don't need to worry about drowning (their mother tongue, which they can fall back on at any time and which is valued and encouraged). Moreover, the swimming is done with other children who are not too good at it either, and need and want lessons (the class consists only of pupils in the process of learning the new language). And the parents who already may know how to swim, come to the pool to watch and clap – the whole thing is taking place in a sheltered pool (the parents have *chosen* to send the children, they follow their progress closely and with interest and have the opportunity to discuss it with the teachers who speak their language, too).

In *submersion, language drowning, sink-or-swim,* the children are thrown into the cold water at the deep end without knowing how to swim and without an instructor (the majority teacher who does not know their language is often both unable and unqualified to help). They have no water wings (their L1 and their culture are of no value at school). Birgitte Rahbek Pedersen (1980a: 23) describes the situation by asking questions: "What is the immigrant child allowed to bring with it to school, then? Its language? – No, the teacher doesn't understand it. The other aspects of its culture? – No, it is not in accordance with reality. Its body? – Yes, but preferably differently packaged, or perhaps stripped down altogether. There's not much left of the little immigrant child then, is there?" (Birgitte Rahbek has worked mostly with the Arab culture and Muslim children). The children have no chance of getting out of the water either, they *have* to stay (there are no alternative schools or classes in their L1), however helpless or sick or cold they feel. They must either learn to swim – or they will drown. Most of the other children in the water can swim well, and little consideration is given to the fact that the minority children cannot (the norm is set by the majority children who feel at home – more or less – with everything that goes on in their language). The parents cannot help either, they cannot stay afloat in the water themselves – they can, if you like, swim very well in milk or honey, or climb trees or sail, or whatever image we want to use to convey that they are competent in their own language and culture – but exactly this special skill, swimming in water, is something that many of them do not master. Moreover, the place where their children are swimming is exposed, it is not a sheltered swimming pool, the shore is unsheltered and full of thickets, and they easily get lost (the parents often feel bewildered by the strange and complicated educational system, so unlike their own, using so strange a language). In a language shelter programme, mother tongue medium classes, a minority child would have proper water wings and would be well instructed before ever venturing into deep water.

It should be easy to see that the two situations, of the minority and the majority child, are so different that we cannot apply generalizations derived from one situation to the other. It is self-evident that some of the more psycho-physiologically determined mechanisms and strategies of language learning are the same in whatever situation the foreign or second language is learnt, but these constitute only a small part of the language learning process.

Moreover, the terms "majority" and "minority" are not simply numerical notions. They stand for a whole variety of phenomena mostly associated with majority or minority status. They should never be handled in a mechanical fashion, as, for example, Ekstrand does when he tries to argue that the distinction between them is unimportant, using the experiences of French speakers in Quebec (Billy, 1978) as an example (Ekstrand, 1979b: 23). Even if the Francophones are in a minority so far as the whole of Canada is concerned, they are *not* in a minority in the province of Quebec *numerically* (albeit that the Anglophones have the dominant economic influence in Quebec). Even if the Finland Swedes are a numerical minority in Finland, they actually control more capital than their numbers would suggest they might. By a purely mechanical approach to the concepts of majority and minority, I could argue similarly that the white population of South Africa is under a linguistic threat from the black majority. This last example demonstrates with the greatest possible clarity that an exceptional situation is not to be made the basis for any general rule. In addition, all the minorities I have mentioned now have their own schools and universities, and this clearly alters their educational situation.

The distinction between majority and minority is thus very necessary, but the two concepts should not be treated in a mechanical fashion, as if it were (only) a question of numbers. On the contrary, we must examine what "majority" and "minority" really mean in any particular context. We should above all examine those social differences that reflect differences in power between majority and minority, both at a macrosocietal level and in the school system.

7.1.3   Learning a foreign language and learning a second language

Learning a *foreign language* is learning a language not used (by the speaker or by others) in the immediate environment as a daily means of communication. It may, of course, be used in the mass media (for example, English on Finnish television – see Phillipson 1983 on the change from a foreign to close to second language), but there will be no naturally occurring daily need to use the language for purposes of communication. Learning a *second language,* on the other hand, is learning a language used daily in the speaker's own environment, perhaps not in the immediate environment, at least in early childhood, but at any rate in the larger community. As soon as one is outside one's own home, there will be a chance (or a risk of being forced) to use the language actively, or at any rate one will hear it used. Before I proceed to discuss what consequences it has from a language learning point of view, I would like to make another distinction which is important if we want to see what the most important difference is between a foreign language and a second language as far as minority children are concerned. I distinguish here between input and intake. Simply *hearing* a language (on television or in one's own environment) without anyone (even oneself) expecting that one will react linguistically or by action to what one has heard, need not necessarily result in one's learning the language. That means that input does not necessarily result in intake. This has been demonstrated both for adults (Hatch, 1979) and for children (Hatch, 1979; Aronsson, 1978a). Exposure to a language, whether extensive or not, cannot be taken to guarantee intake, so Karin Aronsson says, after many years of observing Finnish immigrant children in Sweden who hear a lot of Swedish spoken without necessarily learning very much of it. For input to become intake what is required is that it be worked on in some way, and the motivation for this often derives from the demand (made of one from the outside or purely internal) that one should in some way react to the input.

For many Scandinavian children who learn foreign languages, for instance French or German, at school, the input outside the French or German lessons is minimal. There is, it is true, sometimes a little French or German to be heard on television or in films (and some Danish children can also get German television) and sometimes the children will meet tourists, but for most children these two languages are never more than school subjects. In the case of English, the input through television, pop music, films and so on may be even greater outside school than in English lessons in school, but here too the intake is probably markedly less than the input. Generally speaking, it is probably true to say that, in spite of increasing internationalization, most of the contact with foreign languages for Scandinavian majority children still tends to be during language lessons at school (this is not to say that all the input during lessons is worked on and becomes intake). If, in these circumstances, the foreign language teaching were removed from the school, or if it were started much later than now, this would mean the children not learning these languages at all or learning them much less well. (Children in Finland and Sweden now start their first foreign language in grade 3 (as 9 year olds) and the second in grade 7, whereas the start in Norway is one year and in Denmark two years later.) It would also mean that the children, even if they experienced a great deal of linguistic input through the mass media, would not actively process it and convert it to intake to anything like the same extent as now. The children would have scarcely any contact at all with those languages which are not heard much in Scandinavia (i.e. most languages other than English) if they were not included on the school timetable.

Learning a *second language,* on the other hand, is something quite different. A child learning a second language has a number of opportunities of hearing and seeing it in the neighbourhood, in the larger community, on the radio, on television, on street signs, in newspapers, in fact everywhere (we have in mind here, of course, a minority child in Scandinavia who has the majority language as the second language). Even if some of a child's contacts with the second language, initially at least, may be of the input-without-intake variety, i.e. may derive from situations where no active linguistic or other reaction is expected, there will be, all the same, many opportunities for the child to practise speaking the second language. If, in this kind of situation, the teaching of the second language, or at least teaching by means of it, is delayed (or indeed if there is no teaching of or in the second language during the child's initial contacts with institutions such as the day nursery, kindergarten, school), the result will *not* be that the child does not learn the second language, especially those elements of it that produce surface fluency (section 5.2.3.5). The input of the second language is massive, for most immigrant children in Scandinavia anyway – it cannot be avoided. Since the immigrant languages have no official status in Scandinavia, there is fairly strong external pressure even on children (and perhaps especially on children) to process at least part of the input and turn it into intake. However, a better way of turning input into intake than that *external pressure* which now obliges many immigrant children and adults to begin to use the second language even where they feel they are not ready for it, would be an *internal pressure,* a voluntary motivation on their part to learn the second language. This is exactly what monolingual classes in the children's own language, i.e. *language shelter programmes* (or mother tongue (medium) classes as we prefer to call them), try to achieve. They help to motivate the children to *want* to learn and make active use of the second language in addition to their mother tongue. Minority children whose mother tongue is valued and put on the same footing as the majority language by being used as a language of instruction are in a better position to "integrate themselves", in Göte Hanson's phrase. They stand a good chance of achieving the degree of self-confidence and the knowledge of the second language they need, to wish and dare to begin to communicate with native speakers of it. As Göte Hanson shows in the case of Finnish-medium classes for immigrant children in Södertälje, one of the results of giving instruction in the children's own mother tongue is that they become "linguistically active", and that "they are happy to speak Swedish" and "think it is fun going to school". All these things are evidence of the fact that they have achieved the kind of self-confidence and experience, the kind of "internal pressure" which will allow the second language input to be actually learnt and assimilated. In summary we can say that:

▪ To delay or eliminate the teaching of a *foreign* language means that all or at least much of the children's contact with the language disappears, or that the contact remains minimal, at least as far as intake is concerned. The children will not learn the language and will thus not become bilingual.

▪ To delay or eliminate the teaching of a *second* language does *not* mean that the children have no contact with it. For immigrant children, the input of the second language is bound to be massive, even if formal teaching is delayed or omitted altogether. With these children, the crucial question is what kind of pedagogical (or other) measures should be taken to ensure that the input is processed and learnt. If something can be gained by delaying the teaching, and the children can be given better chances of learning and more enthusiasm for working on the second language input, there is no risk that they will fail to become bilingual.

The situations for children learning a foreign language and those learning a second language are so different, especially as regards what happens when the organization of formal teaching is changed, that they should be strictly distinguished apart.

The other distinctions will not be considered here: that between learning a foreign language at school and learning one's own mother tongue should be so clear as not to need mention – again, the two situations can be thought of as equivalent only as a result of monolingual naivety. The distinction between élite bilinguals and minority children has already been dealt with in section 4.2.2.

Since there are crucial differences between different categories of children who *are trying to become bilingual with the help of the school* (or in the family), it is fairly clear that the different groups need different methods. As I mentioned at the beginning of this chapter, I will have to impose severe limitations on my treatment of the matter: only a few of the largest and from the Scandinavian point of view most important groups will be dealt with. The reason I pay so much attention to immersion programmes is both that they elucidate the situation of minority children, and also that it is high time immersion programmes were introduced into Scandinavia – so far there have been none, even though the conditions for them are particularly favourable. This was in fact suggested in a discussion after a paper by Wallace Lambert (1983) in Stockholm, but the enthusiasm shown by Swedish school authorities was not overwhelming.

7.2   Children from bilingual families

7.2.1   Limitations of case studies

Mention has already been made of pressures towards bilingualism from within the family upon children whose parents speak different mother tongues (see 4.2.2.3). When we look at many of the studies where bilingualism has proved to have had beneficial consequences, above all for children's cognitive development (the aspect most studies have focused on), we find that many of the children who show evidence that they have benefited have either quite certainly come from bilingual families or may have done so. *Whether* they have in fact come from bilingual families in these latter cases has not been established because the criterion for their inclusion in the bilingual category has been a different one, often a high degree of bilingualism as established by testing, and not selection as bilingual as a result of background data. The investigator may sometimes have had this background information without reporting it, because a monolingual or bilingual family background has not been one of the independent variables under investigation. It has often been claimed that growing up in a bilingual family is the best (and most effortless) way of becoming bilingual.

In spite of this, remarkably few studies have been made of children from bilingual families and what studies there have been have tended to be very uniform in approach. This is partly because research into child language was relatively late to appear and partly because the study of a child's linguistic development requires much time and effort. It is much easier to do quick cross-section studies than to tape record (or observe carefully in other ways) a young child as often as is necessary in order to follow all the different stages of her linguistic development for a long enough period to yield interesting and "comprehensive" results at least in some specific area.

What we know about the linguistic development of children in bilingual families usually derives (as I said in section 2.2.1.2) both from carefully conducted case studies and from less formal anecdotal evidence. In many (but not all) cases it has been the children of linguists, thus advantaged middle-class children, who in my classification would fall into the category of élite bilinguals. There are very few case studies (= longitudinal studies) of low-SES-children's linguistic development – one exception is Tabouret-

Keller's (1962) of a French- and German-speaking child with working-class parents. The range of case studies available, then, does not allow us to generalize very securely about the more psycholinguistic, sociolinguistic, and in particular, educational consequences of bilingualism in the family. By contrast, much of the purely linguistic observation can probably be applied without difficulty to children in other social circumstances, as some cross-section studies seem to show (for example, Carrow's study (1971) of 3–10-year-old Mexican-American children).

Another drawback is that what is examined in case studies, particularly in the early and/or less detailed ones, need not necessarily include those aspects of a child's linguistic development we should like to know something about today. One exception is Leopold's great study, which is still the most comprehensive case study there is. Leopold was able to make sure by daily observation and because he was a sensitive and skilful linguistic investigator that most of the things we can think of being interested in are either already recorded or can be extracted from his scrupulously reported observations. Most other studies leave many questions unanswered. The new book by Saunders (1982), however, seems promising in its accuracy, and since his children are still in the middle of the process, we may get the real longitudinal study badly needed, covering the whole period up to adulthood.

It has been one of the serious problems that many studies do not go on beyond the age of three, and thus leave unrecorded many interesting features of children's later linguistic development. Even though we are interested in details of the early phase of development, for practical reasons many parents would like to know more about long-term consequences. What happened when the child started school? Did the child succeed in maintaining (or developing) the same level of proficiency in both languages? What was the child's later attitude to her own bilingualism? What other long-term consequences (linguistic, psychological, social) did bilingualism have for the child? Questions like these remain unanswered – there are no case studies where the investigator has later gone back to the same child when she is a little older or grown-up and made a new detailed investigation – not even cross-section studies. Even though there are many very good descriptions of the bilingualism of young people and, in particular, of adults, with fairly detailed statements of linguistic preference and so on, the subjects examined are not those whose linguistic development was studied in childhood. And that is a pity.

The earlier studies, in which tape recording was not used, are also unsatisfactory in that we can never be sure of the reliability of the data they are based on. Especially when observing one's own child, but also in collecting other observational data, the risk of error is considerable. One may "hear" what was not in fact said, one may fill in and correct utterances without any conscious falsification. What one sees (or does not see or hear) depends to a large extent on what one is interested in or listening for at the moment, and one's own hypotheses have a considerable effect on the selection of data. The parent especially will be adept at interpreting her or his own child, so that the parent will believe that something the child has in fact communicated by non-linguistic means was actually communicated verbally. The parent is of course better at interpreting what the child tries to say than an outsider who knows the child much less well. But in an eagerness to be critical (since we know, of course, how easily observational data can be distorted) the parent may also be over-critical and hear "mistakes" where they do *not* occur. Similarly, an over-reliance on the technical aids at one's disposal may cause one to ignore or leave unreported details which are indispensable to a proper understanding: non-linguistic communication taking place, for example, or the external circumstances in which the verbal utterances occur. One may in this case find that even some of the verbal utterances recorded, no matter how good the reproduction is technically, become unintelligible.

7.2.2   Some case studies

The earliest detailed case study we have is the one of Louis Ronjat who had a French-speaking father and a German-speaking mother. His father (who was a linguist, and who reported on his son's bilingual development, Ronjat 1913) and his mother were both of them very careful to speak only their own mother tongue to their son. They often also spoke their respective mother tongues to each other, but also often German. Louis started talking fairly early and he did not mix up his two languages. At the beginning when he learnt a new word, he "tested" it by saying it both with a German and a French pronunciation, in order to get feedback as to which language it belonged to. This testing procedure lasted for a week at the most for each word, and the boy began with this procedure at a very early age, before he was two years old. After the word had been tested it seemed then to be placed securely, so that it did not occur in the wrong linguistic environment in his speech. Nor was there much interference in his pronunciation, although he was a little slow in his development here – it was not until the age of 3 years and 5 months (3:5) that he was able to produce all the phonemes in both languages. There was occasionally some syntactic interference in his speech, but in general his two languages were clearly separated.

In the development of vocabulary, German, his mother's language, was at first the stronger. But even at an early stage, Louis began consciously to balance his vocabulary in the two languages, so that as soon as he had learnt a word in one of them, he would ask what it was in the other. There was no evidence that his vocabulary was smaller than that of the equivalent monolingual child in either language, once he had overcome his initial difficulties with French. Louis was quite capable of switching languages without apparent effort. He soon categorized all the adults in his immediate environment as either French or German speakers, and did not make the mistake of talking to them in the "wrong" language. Vildomec reports in his book on multilingualism (1963) that at the age of 15 Louis Ronjat was pretty completely bilingual and spoke both his languages entirely fluently. He preferred, however, to use French for technological subjects and German for literature. Ronjat emphasized in his study the importance of the one-person-one-language principle and he thought the careful observing of this principle was the reason why his son hardly ever mixed up his two languages. He believed, too, that the observing of this principle made the learning process easier, so that his son did not seem to have any difficulty in learning the two languages. He cited the contrasting example of another child who had had a great deal of difficulty in becoming bilingual and gave as one of the important reasons for the difficulty the fact that the child's parents were not consistent in speaking their respective mother tongues.

A very interesting recent case study is that by George Saunders (1982), an English-speaking Australian who studied German both at school and at university, as well as staying in Germany doing field work in connection with his PhD. His wife is also a native English speaker. The two sons, Thomas and Frank, now 9 and 7, were brought up bilingually, with the father speaking German to them and the mother speaking English. Saunders' book, which is also meant for parents, gives a fascinating and varied account of the bilingual development from a sociolinguistic and psycholinguistic point of view, supported with a lot of transcripts from recordings and with test results. In the conclusions Saunders characterizes the results as very satisfactory. "Both children, it is true, are more fluent and accurate in English, but have approximately equal vocabularies in German and English. In the home they function equally well in English and German. Outside, they can be indistinguishable from monolingual English-speaking peers, and can also communicate effectively with German-speakers. Moreover, their German has been acquired at no expense to their English, the official language of their country. Knowing German has not impeded the children's speech development in English, nor has being able to speak, read and write German had any deleterious effect on their educational progress in an English-speaking school" (p. 244). Saunders emphasizes that he has spent "as much time as possible talking to and playing with them" to ensure that they are exposed to as much German as possible, and that "some effort and perseverance had been required to establish and maintain German in the home in a predominantly English-speaking environment" (p. 244), at the same time as he concludes that the effort "is more than compensated for by the rewards" (p. 244). The unusual factor in this case study (except that it makes for really fascinating reading for laypeople, too, though it is an accurate scientific account) is that German was not the native language of either of the parents, even if the father's command of it seems to be excellent (he is taken for a native speaker by many Germans, p. 24), and he seems to have a very positive integrative attitude towards German. Even though Saunders himself recommends the same method to other parents (but without a discussion of the principle of speaking an L2 to one's children, and specifically mentioning parents who speak languages other than the dominant language of their community and want to pass on their languages), it would seem that this is still a case of élite bilingualism, if applied to parents neither of whom is a native speaker of the language they want to pass on. But for families with two native languages the book contains invaluable information.

In a different kind of case study, adult bilinguals describe their childhood, and much of the sociological material in reports of this kind may be reliable even if linguistic details are lacking. Ilonka Schmidt-Mackey gives us a good example of this with an account of her own multilingual childhood in an article on linguistic strategies in bilingual families: she always spoke German to her grandfather (who was multilingual, with German as his main language), and felt at ease doing so. Her father, who was bilingual in German and Hungarian, always spoke Hungarian to her mother but German to Ilonka. Her mother, too, spoke German to her up to the age of nine, when Ilonka moved to a different school where the language of instruction was Serbian. After that she spoke Serbian to her mother when they discussed school, German when they discussed other things. After high school she spoke almost only Serbian to her mother, who replied in Serbian or German.

Ilonka tells us that she understood Hungarian right from the beginning, even though her parents did not discover this until she was about four. She always liked Hungarian best, but accepted the fact that Hungarian was her parents' language and that they expected her to speak German to them. She says she felt like an outsider and that she was sometimes jealous of her mother, who seemed to enjoy a greater share of her father's love than she did. Without resort to any interpretations based on the Oedipus complex she blames the language for it. When she went up to university she started speaking Hungarian to her father. This brought father and daughter closer together, and gave her a feeling of warmth and tenderness that had always been lacking in her German relationship with her father. After that her father spoke German to her only when reproaching her or when they discussed academic topics (Schmidt-Mackey, 1977: 134–35). Even if as outsiders we may suggest explanations other than linguistic ones, it remains that the daughter's explanation fixes upon language – a nice example of what one may miss by not speaking to one's child in one's mother tongue. It is clear in this case that there was no question of Ilonka not knowing German very well or of her being unable to develop a good and loving relationship with a German speaker (her grandfather, after all, was a German speaker), but the point was that Hungarian was her father's mother tongue (even though German, which he had a perfect command of, might by the criterion of competence, have been regarded so, too).

In several other case studies the principle that one person should always speak the same language to the child has been strongly emphasized. This is so in Pavlovitch's account (1920) of his Serbian- and French-speaking son, who kept his languages well separated; and in Hoyer & Hoyer's description (1924) of a Russian- and German-speaking child who heard only Russian from the mother and German from the father, and began to speak intelligible words at the age of eleven months. The principle is also emphasized, by a description of the consequences of ignoring it, in Smith's report (1935) on eight children of an American missionary family where the parents spoke English and Chinese interchangeably to the children and the children mixed up the two languages. Similar unfortunate consequences, of a high level of interference, and sometimes, too, of fairly late linguistic development in one or both languages, in situations where the two languages have not been consistently kept apart or not kept apart at all, are also reported by Burling (1959) writing about Garo and English, by Tabouret-Keller (1962) on French and German, and by Murrell (1966) on Swedish and English. Good comprehensive accounts and tables of studies of the bilingual development of children, both in bilingual families and in situations with one language at home and another outside, can be found, for example, in McLaughlin (1978), in the introduction to Hatch (1978), and in Saunders (1982), to name only a few of the best and most easily accessible.

7.2.3 Similarities and dissimilarities in the case studies – which principles do children follow?

In his excellent survey of different studies, McLaughlin (1978: 86–98) discusses the sequence of development in children's acquisition of the two languages. He tries to establish the points at which most of the children show a similar pattern of development in both their languages and in comparison with monolingual children, and where there are differences between the languages as well as between the bilingual and the monolingual child. My discussion in what follows is partly based on McLaughlin's survey.

As regards *phonology*, the bilingual child usually has to learn more sounds than the monolingual.[1] Moreover, the bilingual child has to learn to which language each of the phonemes belongs. The process of phonemic acquisition is apparently approximately the same as with a monolingual child, though the bilingual child may experience many kinds of difficulty both in learning the large number of phonemes and especially in assigning them to the appropriate language. Many investigators report that there is an initial period of mixing or confusion (for example, Leopold, 1947; Rūķe-Draviņa, 1967). This seems to happen especially when both the languages have several difficult phonemes. If we compare pairs of "corresponding" phonemes in the two languages, it seems that the child first learns the easier of the pair, and uses that sound for a time in the other language also (for example, Murrell, 1966; Rūķe-Draviņa, 1965). Stankovski found the corresponding phenomenon in cases where a language was being forgotten: Serbo-Croat-speaking children in Sweden first lose the "difficult" phonemes of Serbo-Croat, which have no exact counterpart in Swedish, and substitute for them the most nearly corresponding Swedish phoneme (personal communication).

The balance between the two languages also seems to affect the acquisition of phonemes. If a child has a nearly equal command of both languages, the period of mixing may be relatively short, and often not occur at all (for example, Engel, 1965). If one of the two languages is very dominant, then its sounds may be substituted for the sounds of the non-dominant language in the process of phonemic acquisition. I have seen similar phenomena in the written language: one can see in the compositions of many Finnish children in Sweden who have learnt to write Swedish but have had little or no practice in writing Finnish (which however they apparently speak fluently) the substitution of the Swedish grapheme å for the Finnish o, so that they write *kåti* for *koti* (home). Many children seem to be conscious of their shortcomings at an early stage. Celcé-Murcia (1975) reports that children may systematically avoid words which are difficult to pronounce in one of the languages. We may compare this with children who, for instance, have a lisp or difficulty pronouncing /r/ and who learn fairly systematically to avoid words where their difficulties show.

In their *syntactic* development, too, bilinguals seem to exhibit the same sequence of development as monolinguals. Since there are apparently certain universal features characteristic of syntactic development in any language (albeit it is difficult categorically to specify what these are), there will be a considerable degree of similarity with regard to some fundamental syntactic distinctions between what the bilingual child learns in each of the two languages. The child often learns features common to both languages first. Where the two languages express things differently, the child will usually learn first whichever of the two forms of expression is easier. Syntactic constructions which differ in the two languages are often learnt later by the bilingual child than by the monolingual in her one language. Much the same is true of morphology.

As regards *semantic* development, things are more complicated for bilingual children. They must simply learn more words than monolingual children if they are to be as competent. The ideal of equivalent competence, step by step with the monolingual child, is not always reached either, but it is perfectly possible for a child, even if it requires more deliberate planning of the child's experiences and contacts with different kinds of social institution than would be necessary for a monolingual child. The child, too, must make a greater effort. The kind of "difficulties" bilingual children may have can, for example, involve using a word over too large a semantic range (too large an extension) for a longer period than or in a way other than the equivalent monolingual child, especially in cases where words have different extensions, ranges of application, within the two languages. An example cited by Leopold is the English word *brush,* which can be used of a clothes brush, shoe brush and paint brush, whereas the German word *Bürste* cannot be used of a paint brush, but must in this case be replaced by the word *Pinsel*. Again, the German *Tuch* (cloth) can be used both for a handkerchief, towel and napkin, where English has three different words. In such cases it will be difficult for a bilingual child to sort out the different segmentation or portioning out of reality used by the two languages. The influence of the other language will make it easy at first to use the extension of the more widely applicable word with a word in the other language, which corresponds to *one* of the meanings: thus to use the English *towel* to mean also *napkin* and *handkerchief.*

The *awareness of using two different languages* seems to develop at somewhat different stages with different children. The difference here seems to depend upon how consistent the speakers in the child's immediate environment have been. In his 1960 study, Imedadze judges that the child is aware of using two different languages as soon as she begins to use them separately to communicate with different individuals. It is, according to Imedadze, precisely the constant effort to find approximate translation equivalents that makes the child aware she is using two different languages. The use of synonymous word pairs, according to Imedadze and many others, need not mean that the child is yet aware that the two languages are different: at the beginning the child will often use a word from either of her languages, whichever is easiest to remember, irrespective of which language it happens to belong to.

Volterra & Taeschner (1975) reckon there are three stages in the development of this awareness (this applies to children who mix their languages right from the beginning). During the first stage the child develops a single vocabulary in which a specific meaning is expressed by means of either one or the other of the two languages but not by both. At the second stage (with the child in their study) the child has developed different vocabularies in the two languages but continues to use a common syntactic system – this was at about the age of two. The third stage was reached by about the age of two and a half: here both vocabulary and syntax are differentiated and the child uses different languages when speaking to different people.

The extremes suggested by various researchers for the emergence of this awareness of two distinct languages vary between about eighteen months (Ronjat, 1913) and three to four years.[2] The difference is to some extent due to the fact that slightly different criteria for awareness are being used. After the age of three or four, however, most children can keep their two languages apart when necessary, that is to say when they are speaking to monolinguals and not other bilinguals. When speaking to other bilinguals they may still mix the languages since they know they will be understood.

The conclusion must be that different children develop along fundamentally similar lines, even if different circumstances affect the speed and the final results.

7.2.4   Practical hints

If parents wish to help a child growing up in a bilingual family, there are a number of practical things that can be done:

■ Talk to the child as much as possible and as early as possible. Even babies a month or two old may like to listen to poetry, just as they like hearing someone singing. Even though they understand nothing of what the words mean, other things are being communicated to them, by rhythm, by closeness, by contact, and by observing the interplay between linguistic and non-linguistic expression.

■ Try to organize for the child as many varied linguistic situations as possible in both languages, including literature and songs. Make sure that the child has contact both with adults and children in both languages. Try to help the child to learn (and experience) in one language whatever she knows also in the other.

■ Play linguistic games with the child. Help the child discover that language is exciting and that it's fun to learn to pick out linguistic and cultural differences and similarities.

■ Try to arrange for the child to get mother tongue instruction in *both* languages, not only instruction in one as a mother tongue and in the other as a foreign language, which is often what one can get in the best case, the situation frequently being that there is no instruction whatsoever in one or the other of the languages.

■ Try to show the child in practical situations, not only by discussions, how splendid it is, how useful and rewarding, to be able to participate as a native in two different cultures. Try to give the child a chance to be proud of her bilingualism and her cultural competence.

But what if the parents have already started speaking only one language to the child? If one of the parents has abandoned her or his language and started speaking the other's? This is often the situation in families where one of the parents speaks the majority language and the other another language. There is then great pressure from the environment upon the parent who speaks the minority language to switch languages, especially if the majority speaking parent cannot manage the minority language. Or what if the parents have adopted one single language simply out of ignorance? Have they harmed their children? Is it possible for the parent who has changed to revert to her or his mother tongue even when the child is no longer very young? These are questions often asked.

Many of us have made precisely the "mistake" of switching to the majority language – I am one of them. Had I known 20 years ago when I was expecting my first child what I now know about bilingualism – or even what I knew 10 years ago – I would have spoken Swedish, one of my mother tongues, consistently to my children, since they would in any case have learnt Finnish, their father's language, which happens to be my other mother tongue, both from him and from the surrounding community in Finland. I did not do this, and now it is too late (even though both of them anyway are quite fluent in Swedish – but not native).

There is no point in bewailing what one has not done and what cannot now be done; better to try to find out what can be done now.

Here is a typical pattern of development that I have heard described by many parents who have abandoned their own language:

At the beginning everything goes well. You love your wife or husband and want to speak her or his language to your child. You discover new words (and experience constantly new things about your child) together with your partner. In any case it does not feel quite natural to speak your own language to your child when your partner is present because she does not understand it, and you do not want to exclude the one you love.

You feel you can manage fairly well in the other language; you can say most of the things you want to say when your child is still young, at any rate almost up to school age. Perhaps it feels a little strange when you are reading stories to your child in the evening or talking to the child about serious things, because you are perhaps not quite able to express yourself with sufficient subtlety and precision in your adopted language, but by and large you feel able to communicate what you want to say.

Sometimes there may be the vague feeling that you would be able to cope with a disciplinary problem with more humour if you were able to interject some quick comment to show your child that while you were quite serious about demanding something, you knew too that the child knew you were both playing a game at the same time, you in the role of parent and she or he in the role of child. You would be able to convey then that while your role as parent obliged you to make some unwelcome demand of the other person playing the role of the child, there were still real human people behind these roles who were buddies. All this it would perhaps be beyond you to convey in your adopted language. Then it might well start to happen, too, that your child begins to correct your speech, both pronunciation and other things. It is usually possible to see the funny side of this, but not perhaps when you are tired or when your wife/husband joins in and corrects you too – you may suddenly get unreasonably rather cross.

It is later, when the child is eleven or twelve years old, that you begin to notice a lot of negative things. Your child will in a number of areas have a larger vocabulary than you have – and even if the same thing is happening to your partner, that she or he is finding some of the words the child brings home strange, you are left with the feeling that you would be able to make something of some of these new words if this were your own language and you could draw on the slang of your youth. Your child also begins to correct you much more than before and sometimes you may see or hear a directly scornful reaction to your inadequacies in the language. You may feel rather hurt, and a bit helpless. Some parents find that their children can on occasion be ashamed of them and not want to talk to their friends and so on. And when with puberty all the difficult matters emerge, you may find it really very difficult to talk to your child, and this is just when talk is all the more important since bodily contact is often much diminished. You do not know how much is the effect of puberty and how much of language, but you may feel rather bitterly that you have lost your child. And when the child is grown up or nearly grown up, and you would like to show her something of what has been important to you, the child has no chance of understanding or sharing, because of language.

Adults I have spoken to have told me that as children they looked down on their mother or father, thought that she or he was stupid, did not want to bring friends home or felt they had to make jokes about their mother or father speaking with an accent, felt disloyal, but had to do it anyway, thought their mother or father was being sentimental in going on about "my culture, my own country" – and then they had to pretend to be very self confident and *de haut en bas* when they visited *that* parent's home country, all the while really feeling stupid themselves for not understanding what people said there. But at the same time they saw their own mother or father become a different person in this other country, cheerful, humorous, joking, altogether more fluent – someone they did not really recognize and who seemed altogether more competent than the parent they had known. And that made them think and sometimes even ask accusingly, "Why didn't you teach me your language?"

Most of the parents I have talked to who abandoned their own language have said that now they would do things differently. It was just that it all seemed to go so well in the beginning. If there had been difficulties then, they might have been able to change back to their own language, but by the time they realized what the difficulties were going to be, it was already too late. Many parents have told me, too, about half-hearted attempts to change the situation, or that they only abandoned their language when their children refused to speak it; but the end result was the same: they had the feeling their children knew only a small part of them, and that they themselves had partly lost their own children.

What, in practical terms, can be done if one *has* abandoned one's own language but wishes to reverse the process and start speaking it again? How does one start again? Are there guidelines to be followed?

If one does not wish to follow the one-person-one-language principle, there are other principles that can be tried instead. The important thing is that the child's sense of security is not disturbed. The child should always know quite clearly what is going to happen, what is expected of her and what she in turn can expect. One can devise a principle for oneself, preferably together with the child if she is old enough. This may be based on distinction of time, place, subject or a number of other things (see section 5.2.3.3). For example: "We'll always speak Swedish in the kitchen and bathroom, and Greek in the other rooms." "We'll speak English every evening between 6 o'clock and 8 o'clock, and Swedish for the rest of the time." "When we're cooking and playing we'll speak Urdu, and Norwegian the rest of the time."

"On Sundays we'll speak Arabic, the other days Swedish." "When there's someone here who speaks Turkish, you and I will speak Turkish too, otherwise we'll speak Danish." "When Mummy's at home we'll all speak Danish, but when you and I are alone at home together we'll speak Kurdish." "During the summer and in the other school holidays we'll speak Finnish, and Swedish for the rest of the time."

One should make a cautious and natural start with the new arrangements. If the child is old enough, one can prepare the ground in advance by discussing what a good thing it would be if she could speak Mummy's or Daddy's language, and how pleased Mummy or Daddy would be to be able to speak their own language for part of the time. One can tell the child about all the nice things she could do once she knows the minority language. In order to motivate the child one can try to organize situations where she particularly enjoys herself and where the minority language is spoken. A start could be made, for example, when the family has been on holiday in the country where the minority language is spoken and where the child has heard everybody (or at least a lot of people) speaking it, including Mummy or Daddy; or alternatively in connection with a long visit, a visit which the child is expecting and looking forward to, from someone who does not know the majority language ("now that Grandma's coming – you know she can't speak any Norwegian – you'll want to be able to say something to her, won't you? What do you think would happen if Grandma came along and asked you something you didn't understand, like 'haluaisitkos sinä lähteä minun kanssani ulos ostamaan suklaata?' " [*would you like to come out with me and we'll buy some chocolate?*]).

It is important to make language learning fun, something exciting and that comes naturally, and to make sure the child's security is not disturbed, as well as giving the child a natural pride in her knowledge of another language ("We've got to speak Swedish now when X comes, because he only knows Swedish, poor man. The two of us who know both Swedish and Greek should be kind to him. The poor man can only speak *one* language, so we should show generosity and speak the language he understands").

When the child has learnt enough of the minority language, one can begin cautiously to enlarge the occasions for its use, and gradually make them as varied as possible in order to avoid functional differentiation.

If none of the adults in the family speaks the majority language but they speak *different* minority languages (the mother, for example, Finnish, the father Arabic (and French), and the family lives in Sweden), then the situation becomes more complex and demanding. In such a case the parents should try to think hard about their future plans (if planning seems possible):

■ Do they think they are going to stay in Sweden, or will they move to one or other of the parents' home countries?
■ Is it possible to arrange for either or both of the parents' mother tongues to

be the language of instruction and/or a subject at nursery school and at school?

■ Can the child get further support (in addition to the parents' support) for her development in the parents' two mother tongues (literature, records, associations, visits to the home country, extended visits and possible schooling in the home country at some stage, radio, television, etc.)?

■ Does the child have the opportunity to play with other children and meet adults who speak either of the two languages?

■ What is the status of the languages in Sweden?

■ Which of the two languages will the child perhaps be able to learn actively later if she remains passive while she is young or is not allowed to develop at that stage?

■ How important is bilingualism or trilingualism going to be for the child's social relationships?

■ How well do the parents command each other's languages (and are they willing to learn them?), and how well do they know the majority language?

It is difficult to give general advice, but the principle holds good here, too, that the languages that get less support in the larger community need all the support they can get from parents and the various institutions like day nursery and school, if they are to develop to a high level of competence. It is perfectly possible for an ordinary child to become trilingual or more, but this requires more patience, consistency and long term planning from the parents than would be needed from parents of a monolingual child. The rewards too are much greater, however, even if the child does not have a native command of *all* the languages (provided that at least *one* of the languages is allowed to develop fully).

7.3   Children from linguistic majorities

7.3.1   Limitations

As has already been mentioned several times, I am excluding two groups almost entirely from my discussion: élite bilinguals and children who only have lessons in a foreign language at school where the aim is in no way that they should become bilingual, but rather that they should acquire some command of a foreign language. This also means that a number of élite schools are being excluded from the discussion, such as the Kennedy School in West Berlin, as well as French, German and Russian schools in Scandinavia, and the like.

So far as schools are concerned whose aim is to make "ordinary" majority children bilingual, I shall consider only the sort of research that sheds light on the Scandinavian situation, especially from the minority point of view.

According to Richard Tucker (1974: 102–3), educational programmes that try to give majority children a grasp of a foreign language can be divided into four groups: (1) traditional foreign language lessons at school, (2) a system in which the traditional foreign language teaching is supplemented by the teaching of one subject through the medium of the language in question (English-speaking children, for example, might be taught geography in French in the sixth grade), (3) early immersion, and (4) late immersion. Later in the same article, Tucker mentions a fifth possibility, that is the placing of single individuals in schools whose language of instruction differs from their own, in classes where the rest of the pupils speak the language of instruction as their mother tongue. I shall concentrate on early and late immersion, alternatives 3 and 4.

Since it is important for us to acquire some overall picture of the experiments with majority children, I shall not present specific experiments but will content myself with a brief summary of the organization and results. The immersion programmes, especially the Canadian ones, are among the very best researched and controlled language teaching experiments in the world, and there is a great deal written about them.[3]

7.3.2 Early immersion

An immersion programme involves children from the linguistic majority of a country (with a high status mother tongue) choosing to be taught through the medium of a foreign language. The first immersion programme of this kind was started in September 1965 at the St. Lambert School, with two pre-school classes of English-speaking children who were taught in French by bilingual French-speaking teachers. These programmes have multiplied in the more than 15 years since then, so that Quebec and Ontario in particular have a large number of them (for example, both in Montreal and Ottawa even in 1976 more than 20% of all English-speaking children started their schooling in early immersion programmes – Barik & Swain, 1976a) but they are often to be found in the other provinces as well. The number of children enrolled in early immersion programmes in 1981–82 across Canada was 88,000 (Swain & Lapkin, 1982: 4). One must add to this total those children who are now above elementary grades and those who have already left school after an immersion programme. The programmes are slowly spreading to other countries (mainly the U.S.A.) and languages other than French (Spanish, German, Hebrew, Ukrainian – see Lambert & Taylor, 1982 and Lambert, 1983).

All *teaching* in these programmes was from the beginning conducted in French only, and all the children spoke English as their mother tongue. Since in each case the teacher understood the children's mother tongue (even though she never used it when speaking to them), the children were not obliged to use the foreign language, before they felt secure enough to do so, in order to make known their basic needs. Instead they were able to continue speaking their own language. At this stage, according to Lambert (1974), the teachers concentrated on developing the children's listening comprehension and vocabulary in French, as well as running all the usual pre-school activities. At the end of the first year, the researchers and the teachers tried by observation to establish how much French the children knew, but it was not until the first grade that formal tests were used. By the end of the first year most of the children had a fairly extensive passive vocabulary in French, and they were themselves trying out some French words and even sentences. In first grade the children learnt to *read and write French* and their parents were specifically asked *not* to teach them to read and write English at home. However at this stage, before English was introduced into the school curriculum, many of the children had in fact learnt to read and write in their mother tongue too. The teaching of the mother tongue, normally in two 25 minute periods a day, was introduced in second grade – it was thought that to introduce English any earlier might disturb the children's learning to read and write in French. This system did not seem to affect the children's knowledge of their mother tongue, even if other studies have revealed shortcomings in children's grasp of their own language, usually in cross section studies with no opportunity to check again a few years later to see whether the damage was permanent (for example, Ruoppila, 1973; Engle, 1975). In some of the immersion programmes devised later a practical subject such as music or physical education was taught through the medium of English right from the first grade, but most of the programmes omitted English altogether until the mother tongue teaching started. *The English language element* was gradually *increased* so that some subjects began to be taught in English. In those programmes where the transition was quickest, sometimes half the subjects were taught in French and half in English by the fifth year, but more usually French was dominant until a little later. It was common, for instance for geography or history to begin to be taught in English in grade 4 or 5, while the rest remained in French. In some of the programmes, the subject studied in English varied from year to year. In most programmes, however, only half the subjects were being taught in French by grade 7 or 8, with the rest in English. Some of the children then continued their education in French-speaking schools, but very many also in English-speaking schools.

Many of the programmes were extremely *thoroughly evaluated.* Each spring the children were tested, both individually and in groups, using not only the standard school tests common throughout Canada but also specially devised ones. The St. Lambert programme, for instance, used a number of language tests both in English and French, listening comprehension tests, speech production tests of all kinds, tests to measure different aspects of morphology, syntax and semantics, to evaluate pronunciation, and to measure the children's ability to discriminate between different sounds in other foreign languages, besides all the usual tests in English and French, mathematics (done both in English and French), and the other school subjects, and tests for flexibility and creativity, for verbal and non-verbal intelligence, and to evaluate the children's attitudes towards their own group and other groups. Both French- and English-speaking control groups were often used, very carefully selected and matched for age, sex, social group, verbal and often also non-verbal intelligence. The organizers also often tried to find control groups of children who were taking part in other educational experiments (for example in mathematics), in order to eliminate the Hawthorne effect, i.e. not knowing whether what is done in the experiments or the fact itself of taking part in an experiment is responsible for the results. And finally, in some of the programmes, children were included in the control groups who had wanted to take part in the immersion programme, but who had been excluded because of lack of places (this in order to check the effect of motivation, to check for the possibility that the parents and children in the test group might have been more enthusiastic about the children learning French than those belonging to the control groups).

In general the children in the early immersion programmes, with certain exceptions in the lower grades, did as well in their mother tongue *English* as the control group children, or better (and in the standardized tests often slightly better than the Canadian average). The immersion experience thus not only allowed the children's mother tongue to develop "normally", but also seemed to have a considerable transfer effect on the mother tongue. There is of course also the "risk" that the parents, knowing their children had very little English at school, talked to them more than they would otherwise have done at home; but this could hardly explain the good results in the more formal aspects of linguistic command. The small number of children who showed some uncertainty for instance about punctuation and other such things normally reached the monolingual level in grade 3 at the latest. Results showing an improvement over the monolingual attainment in English began to appear usually in grades 4 and 5. We may compare these results with those for children in maintenance programmes, for example in the Rock Point experiment, who also began to show transfer effects in grades 4 and 5, even overtaking monolingual children in the language *not* used for instruction (which in maintenance programmes would, of course, be the majority language which is not the children's mother tongue).

The results in *French* have varied to some extent, depending on the different experiments. In a few programmes the children did even better than monolingual French children in certain subjects, particularly after grade 3. But mostly the children have done equally well or less well, compared to French-speakers, and in some such tests even considerably worse. However, in all the programmes the command of French shown by even the "weakest" children was much better than that of children who were learning French as a foreign language at school. The tests in which the children performed worse than monolingual French children measured more difficult aspects of French morphology (gender, concord, tense), or aspects of language only acquired properly as a result of prolonged and varied contact with native speakers (for example, certain features of intonation or speech production in carefully preprogrammed contexts where the children themselves could not influence the choice of words or subject matter).

In all the different *school achievement tests* too, the children performed well in both languages, as well as or better than monolingual children. The results of *attitude measurement tests* varied considerably, depending on the particular programme and also the stage at which the tests were given. It was possible to see, especially in the attitudes of the older children, some reflection of the general political climate of relationship between French and English speakers in Canada. Overall the children had a positive attitude both to their own linguistic group (they did not feel any less English Canadian for taking part in the programmes) and towards French Canadians (and the European French), as also mostly towards other nationalities. But the *great* enthusiasm for things French which perhaps at first was expected did not materialize, the children's attitude tending to be fairly realistic. Lambert says that these children have, as it were, been given a second overcoat which they can comfortably put on and take off at will. When children in the various programmes were asked, for instance, whether, given the choice again, they would take part in such programmes, or whether they would prefer monolingual English education, and whether they would recommend immersion for other children, their younger sisters and brothers perhaps, their answers were overwhelmingly in favour of the immersion programmes. Initially the children taking part in immersion programmes in Canada were exclusively middle-class. But after a very short while, programmes were organized in which working-class children and children with special linguistic and/or psychological difficulties took part. According to the researchers, the results from these programmes were as good as those for middle-class children.[4]

It is thus clear that it is possible to teach majority children through the medium of a foreign language so that they become fairly proficient bilinguals. Their grasp of their mother tongue does not suffer, on the contrary it tends to benefit. Their knowledge of the second language will not reach the standard expected of monolingual speakers of that language, with the help of teaching at school only, but this could be easily improved if they spent some of their free time with children and adults from that foreign language group. Their ordinary school subjects do not suffer by being taught through the medium of a foreign language, and their attitude to their own and to other linguistic communities is positive. Both in their general cognitive development and in certain specific aspects of it they achieve results as good as or better than corresponding monolingual children, which is what the threshold hypothesis would predict. I think we in Scandinavia should seriously consider following the Canadian example in organizing immersion programmes for majority children. There are no risks involved, and there is a great deal to be gained (see Skutnabb-Kangas, 1983a). Immersion programmes have spread from Canada to other countries, above all to the U.S.A., but they have not always been as "pure" in conception and planning as the Canadian ones, and the results have tended to be more varied. The social group factor has not always been so carefully controlled, and support from parents and the local community has not always been as unproblematical. Children speaking the language of instruction as their mother tongue have also been introduced into the classes, often at a fairly early stage. Consequently, many of the American programmes are more like partial than total immersion programmes – and the results from partial immersion programmes are not as good, as will be clear in section 7.3.4.

7.3.3   Late immersion

Experiments with late immersion have been conducted in Canada for children whose parents were worried that their children's English and general school achievement would suffer in early immersion programmes, but who still wanted their children to acquire a better knowledge of French than they would with conventional foreign language teaching. Late immersion programmes have involved teaching children in grade 7 or 8 everything (or at least most of the subject matter, except, of course, English) through the medium of French for one or two years.

The late immersion programmes have varied a great deal with respect to the children's knowledge of French at the start of the experiment. In some programmes the children have already had traditional foreign language teaching from a fairly early stage at school, often from grade 3, but there have also been programmes involving children who had started French only in the previous year, having 20 minutes of French a day during most of that year, and in the last few months of the year before the transition to the immersion programme having an hour (or, in some programmes, 40 minutes) of French a day.

Some of the children have gone back to their ordinary English-medium programme after the immersion, while others have continued to do one or two subjects in French.

The results have varied considerably. In a few programmes they appear not to have been much better than those in ordinary foreign language teaching. However, in most of the programmes the children's French has improved considerably, and because the children have been older, they have made slightly more progress in French than children in early immersion during the *same period of time* (older children are better at most aspects of language learning than younger children). But because children in early immersion were taught through the medium of French over a much longer period, it is hardly surprising that the overall results obtained from early immersion are considerably better. This is particularly true in that area of language learning that young children are anyway better at, the development of surface fluency and good pronunciation; but it is also true for most other aspects of language command. Late immersion has been found to have no adverse effect on the children's English, but hardly any beneficial effect either – again, precisely what the threshold hypothesis would predict. Children in late immersion programmes do not even approach a native speaker's competence in their second language, French. But even in late immersion children do acquire a better grasp of French than children taught in traditional foreign language classes, without any negative influence on their mother tongue or on school achievement.

7.3.4   Partial immersion

The "worst" results seem to have been achieved with partial immersion programmes. These schemes are the result of anxiety on the part of parents, children or school that the children's knowledge of their mother tongue and/or their school achievement would suffer from complete change of the language of instruction. Therefore, the change has been partial, with for instance half the instruction given in the foreign language, or some other combination with both the mother tongue and the foreign language as the medium of instruction. Here, too, there has been considerable variation, as to the starting point of the experiment, how long it has lasted, what proportion of the instruction has been in each language, how the teaching has been organized (whether the same material was repeated in both languages, whether different subjects were taught in different languages or whether the language was changed in the middle of the day, every other day, every other week, and so on – see Mackey's typology). What has not varied so much has been the results: the children's command of their mother tongue has been no better than that of comparable monolingual speakers, and sometimes worse than that of the control groups. Their knowledge of the foreign language has often not developed as rapidly as was expected. A comparison with results from early or late immersion where such comparisons have been possible, suggests, too, that children in partial immersion programmes do not make the progress these other programmes would suggest was likely as the result of the period of time they have been taught in the foreign language. It has often been shown also that the children's school performance, especially in subjects taught through the medium of the foreign language, has suffered by comparison with that of monolingual children and children in other kinds of immersion programme.

Results for partial immersion programmes have been more variable in countries other than Canada; and in some third world countries where children from the linguistic majority have been taught by partial immersion a foreign language that was the former colonial language, or one of the so-called world languages, the results have sometimes been slightly better.

This is presumably because both the teaching materials in one of these "great" languages and the teacher training in how to teach in and through the medium of these languages has been better developed than in the children's mother tongue.

Some of the general factors responsible for the poor results with these partial immersion programmes are those which perhaps also might be taken to apply to minority children in the situation most like that found in partial immersion: that is, compound classes in which minority children are being taught in their own language for some of the time and in the majority language together with majority children for the rest of the time. If a constant change of language at school, which allows neither language the opportunity for a quiet and settled pattern of development, can be bad even for majority children, we may fear that it is even worse for such minority children (and this can be seen in the few evaluations that exist).

7.3.5 An attempt to compare the effect of some important factors on achievement in language learning

In what follows I shall try to assess the relative importance of some of the factors that affect the learning of a second or foreign language. The number of factors we know influence the learning process is considerable, so I shall again be highly selective. By calculating the correlation between different factors it is possible to establish their relative importance in explaining the results of learning. Since my aim here is pedagogical, I am most interested in those factors which can be influenced by the way the learning is organized. It is interesting for me, of course, to know that such things as the child's age (i.e. absolute age, not the age at which the instruction starts), sex, length of stay in the new country, nationality, the social group of the parents, all affect the child's performance in learning the second language (see Ekstrand, 1978c: 5). But if I want to know what to do in school, it is not particularly helpful for me to know that the results would be better if the child were an older girl with middle-class parents than a younger boy with working-class parents. These are factors the school can do nothing about. I am therefore mostly interested in things that something can be done about.

The factors I shall try to weigh against one another are these:

- Is the language *medium* or *object* in the learning process?
- Is the learning context *functional* or *abstract*?
- Does the learning of the second/foreign language start when the child is *younger* or *older*?
- Is the *intensity* of the teaching high or low?
- Is the *duration* of the teaching long or short?

7.3.5.1 Medium or object?

The most fundamental difference between traditional foreign language learning and immersion from a methodological point of view is that in the traditional programmes the language itself is the object of study: you study the language in order to study the language! By contrast, in immersion programmes the language becomes an instrument, a means by which knowledge (hopefully interesting) and skill are acquired and contact is made. We know that this difference is important. If the aim is a really good grasp of the language, it is not enough that that language be the object of study; it must also be used as a tool for *real* communication and for acquiring knowledge in *real* situations. This is to some extent attempted in the best of the traditional foreign language classes, but in spite of the teacher's best efforts, the allegedly real situations in which the language is used are generally very artificially constructed, foreign to reality. It is, of course, also important that language should be the object of conscious attention, but if it is no more than that, then bilingualism will not be achieved, only at best a good knowledge of a foreign language. We learn languages by living in them and if the school cannot offer real, non-simulated opportunities for using a language so that the activity comes to be more important than the fact that it is conducted through the medium of a foreign language, then the result at best will be a kind of school bilingualism, and not natural bilingualism. I am assuming for the moment, of course, that the learning process takes place only at school (and this is not the case with second language learning by immigrant children).

7.3.5.2 Functional action context or abstract context?

Especially in the early stages, languages are learnt better in some real life context demanding action than in the abstract. This is one of the few insights that remain unchallenged after the bitter controversies of the last few decades about the best methods of teaching foreign languages. The context of action, however, must here, too, be real and not simulated. That adults who move to a foreign country seem at first much slower to learn the new language than their children is probably largely to be explained by this very fact: they are able to develop strategies for avoiding the use of the new language even in real contexts (see Ehlich, 1980), whereas their children learn the new language in the process of actively functioning in this new environment to which they have often been brutally exposed, without a chance of evading its demands upon them.

The language use of adults is often to a higher degree in situations where meaning is conveyed by linguistic means alone; verbal expression is used not only (or not at all) to accompany physical action but rather with an independent function of its own. The words often transmit the message by themselves. When an adult moves to Finland from some southern country and learns the Finnish word for snow, "lumi", she may be looking at snow through the window or seeing a picture of a snow-covered landscape and being told about the characteristics of snow, while her child touches the snow, makes snowballs and throws them, wades through the stuff, gets wet, makes a snow woman and a snow castle, tastes the snow – and learns the word at the same time. If as many contexts involving action could be organized for the adult as children have, the foreign language learning for adults could probably be made much faster. On the other hand, much of what an adult has to learn in a foreign language is so abstract that it is difficult or impossible to set in any context of action. And often the only action for which certain expressions can be used is itself abstract and verbal.

And again, the context of activity may also actually *hinder* the learning process if the teacher is not very observant. Karin Aronsson has shown (1977, 1978a) that an intelligent immigrant child can behave in a meaningful way in a Swedish class, as if she understood the *linguistic* part of what happens, with just a minimal grasp of Swedish or with the help of a few phrases. This is just because of the action-oriented context. The teacher simply does not need to notice how little Swedish the child actually knows. The child is greatly helped by recurrent routines, non-verbal activities of various sorts, by the use of paralinguistic features, by accurate and careful observing of the teacher and of other pupils and the skilful use of contextual clues and of elimination strategies.

A good pre-school and elementary school pedagogy in Scandinavia builds very much on the child's experiences. Experience, i.e. the child's knowledge of the world, helps the child to understand discussions about that world even without understanding the language that those discussions are in. Language is in the elementary classroom often something that accompanies action, and the concept validation may often be empirical only or both empirical and verbal (whereas it becomes verbal only in the higher grades – and many minority children start failing at that stage). An example which I often use here and which many teachers and children will recognize is the following:

The teacher says something and the child does not understand or understands only a few words. On the basis of her knowledge of what usually happens in the classroom or what is likely or possibly may happen, the child starts making assumptions about what it could have been that the teacher said. Most children are realistic, and learn very quickly the rules and restrictions pertinent to a classroom setting. The child knows, for instance, that it is not likely that the teacher has said: "There is a red elephant flying in the clouds and it is going to come in through the window and swallow you, so you must climb up to the lights in order to be saved." The child then starts to evaluate her hypotheses on the basis of what the teacher and the other children do, what the situation is and how others react to what the teacher has said and what the child herself does. Some hypotheses are then ruled out and rejected, some remain, and the child tries an intelligent guess among the remaining ones, and watches the feedback. It can, for instance, be like this: Since it is not Monday, the teacher cannot have said x. Since we just had a break, it cannot have been y. Since nobody stands up, it cannot be z, nobody takes a book, it cannot be a. Since the window is open, it cannot be b, nobody knocks on the door and nobody looks in that direction so it cannot be c. Since we have boots on and it rains, it cannot be d. And so on, until a few hypotheses remain. The child starts slowly doing something to try it out and watches closely the reactions. If there is any negative or surprised looking feedback, for instance a raised eyebrow, or "What are you doing?" or the like, the child concludes that it was the wrong hypothesis, and tries the next one, which then happens to be right. And so the child mostly does the right thing, without having understood anything or only very little of the *verbal* parts of the message, and the teacher says: "but Fatima understands perfectly well everything I say, she always does everything right". Even Fatima herself may sometimes think that she understood the verbal part, instead of being able consciously to analyze the way in which she used contextual cues and her knowledge of the world (i.e. of what usually happens in the classroom) for inferring the message. Fatima may herself say "yes" when asked if she understands what the teacher says (from Skutnabb-Kangas, 1982c).

Organizing a context of actions is not sufficient, then, for foreign language learning. The activity must also be put into words, verbalized – and this is one of the things that immersion programmes have striven to do.

7.3.5.3 Optimal age

The discussion, at different times and in different countries, about the best age for foreign language learning used to centre on the learning of a language as a school subject. The tendency has usually been to lower the age at which children are introduced to a foreign language, hence the emergence of something like the FLES movement (Foreign Languages in Elementary School) in the U.S.A. To begin with, people were very enthusiastic about teaching foreign languages to young children and thought children's understanding of other values and openness towards them would also be greatly improved by the early introduction of a new language. This was a period of optimism and of increasing contact across national boundaries – but FLES proved a disappointment (as is clear from the title of Theodore Andersson's book *Foreign Languages in the Elementary School: A Struggle against Mediocrity,* 1969).

Even though in Scandinavia all children begin to learn their first foreign language much earlier than in the majority of other countries (in Finland and Sweden in grade 3, in Norway grade 4 and in Denmark grade 5). An even earlier start has also been advocated. Tentative experiments have been carried out (the EPÅL project – EPÅL standing for English in the primary school – in Uppsala has been the most ambitious of these, with English being introduced in grade 1 – see Holmstrand 1975, 1978a, 1978b, 1979a, 1979b, 1980).

The early introduction stems from a belief that in many ways younger children are better at learning foreign languages, and that it is a pity not to make use of their greater capacity. To begin with, this belief was simply based on observation: young children seemed to learn very easily to speak a foreign language, fluently and with a genuine accent. Adults on the other hand took a long time to learn a new language, it needed great effort, and the results were far from fully satisfactory. Later, another kind of evidence seemed to support the same belief. Neurophysiologists put forward different theories about the structure and development of the human brain, its plasticity, the process of lateralization, and so on. Most of these theories pointed to a fairly early optimal age for language learning. It was thought that lateralization was completed fairly early, and that the plasticity of the brain then began to diminish, so that the ability to cope with certain aspects of foreign language learning was weakened. It was above all Penfield & Roberts (1959) and Lenneberg (1967) who put forward the biological theories which influenced linguists; but behaviourist orientated psychological theories about the learning process itself (for example, Ervin & Osgood, Skinner) were also used to support the belief in an early optimal age. Practical pedagogical experience, too, whether the evidence here was presented systematically or not, contributed an element to the discussion. Young children are better able to imitate than older children or adults, and less afraid of making mistakes. They are also more willing to copy example, and less critical of the long-term usefulness of what they are learning. They are more enthusiastic and more easily motivated, at least in the short term. It was typical of the early debate about language learning that linguistic ability was thought of as some kind of single indivisible entity: either there was an optimal age for language learning (though with some room for variation), or there was not. One writer who tried to introduce some distinctions was David Stern (in an article entitled "Optimal age. Myth or Reality?" – 1976). He concluded that there are perhaps different optimal ages for different aspects of language learning. Stern's view more or less resembles the most recent conclusions, according to which the ability to learn foreign languages improves with age, like other abilities.

The conclusions of a large number of more recent studies (see the references in Ekstrand 1979b) are that older learners are better, quicker and more efficient at most aspects of foreign language learning. Only in a few areas can it be shown that young children have an advantage over older children and adults. But most of the advantages enjoyed by younger children can be compensated for in older children and adults by different kinds of pedagogic arrangement in the teaching situation. Studies which deal with immigrant children (and most do not, but rather are concerned with foreign language learning at school) produce the same results; in particular, after Jim Cummins' re-analysis of Ramsey & Wright's data (1980). Ramsey & Wright's study (1974) was one of the few comprehensive enquiries to show that immigrant children who were younger when entering learnt the new language better than children who arrived in the host country shortly before, during or after puberty. However, Cummins' re-analysis of the same data with length of residence (LOR) kept constant shows that this was not so: where LOR was the same, the older children had learnt relatively more English than the younger.

It seems, too, that the whole question of an optimal age cannot be discussed in isolation, without regard to other factors. What comes to be important for minority children is also the question of what is gained or lost by an earlier or later introduction of *formal* instruction in the second language. If a later introduction has distinct advantages, then perhaps the second language should be introduced later, no matter what the optimal age discussion says. And later introduction of the second language does indeed seem to have great advantages for many minority children, and little in the way of disadvantages.

It is the question of what happens with the child's mother tongue because of the intrusion by L2 that is chiefly to be considered when weighing the advantages and disadvantages of early instruction through the medium of a new language. If introducing L2 threatens the opportunities for development of the mother tongue, then it should not be done early. If, on the other hand, it seems that mother tongue development is likely to continue reasonably, then early introduction of L2 may be desirable. In the case of majority children, it is likely that the mother tongue will develop anyway, even if they are taught in a foreign language right from the pre-school stage, as the results of immersion programmes show. However, in the case of minority children this does not seem to be the case, and *this* is what may make it wise to delay teaching *through the medium* of an L2, and indeed to some extent also formal teaching *of* L2.

"If formal teaching of L2 to immigrant children is delayed, this facilitates the continued development of L1, without having any bad effect on their proficiency in L2. This is because the greater learning capacity of older children when they begin with L2 compensates for the shorter time they have to learn it" (Cummins, 1980a: 13–14). The same conclusion emerges also from a recent long overview by Cummins (1983). Older pupils are better at learning foreign languages because their overall cognitive capacity is greater. The programme of education that "most effectively facilitates the children's general cognitive development will also be the most efficient in developing their ability to learn L2", as Cummins says (1980a: 13). If the language the child knows best is her mother tongue, as is the case with most immigrant children when they have their first contacts outside the home (day nursery, kindergarten, school), then it is in that language that she can also best interact with her environment in a way which develops her cognitive/academic language proficiency most (see section 5.2.2.5). And since "the most important factor affecting the formal development of L2 in school situations is the individual's level of conceptual development" (Cummins, 1980a: 13), then the kind of educational programme which fails to encourage the optimal verbal level of conceptual development, i.e.

teaching immigrant children through the medium of L2, will be seen to directly *counteract* its own aim, the learning of L2.

The optimal age question is, in fact, a double one: it has to do both with the learning of the foreign language *and* of the mother tongue. From the point of view of mother tongue learning, then, what is the optimal age for the introduction of L2? We have seen that an early introduction of L2 is quite all right, provided that this does not threaten the development of the mother tongue. But let us suppose that the child's mother tongue *is* under threat: what, then, is the optimal age? Can we speak of critical periods of development or can we say at any one stage or another that here the child's hold on her own first language is "secure" or so "fully developed" that L2 will pose no threat to it?

A language develops satisfactorily and is not forgotten if it is used enough – so much should be clear. But what is enough? We may begin with the extreme cases. There was the instance of a woman at the Finno-Ugrist congress in Tallinn about ten years ago. She spoke a language which, so far as was known, was spoken by only two people in the world at that time: she herself and a linguist who had learnt the language from her while he was recording it in writing. She came from a linguistic group consisting of only a few hundred speakers. At the age of twelve, because of the Russian revolution, she had been separated from her group, most and possibly all of whom had been killed. In any case, for the rest of her life she had had no contact with any of them. This meant that from the age of twelve onwards she had had no living soul to speak her own language to, until, at the age of nearly seventy, she taught the linguist her language. According to him, her language was rich and varied, with a large vocabulary. Her recipe for how to manage to retain it for over fifty years with no one else to speak it to had been to speak it to her God every day. ... At the other extreme (as I would describe it) are those immigrants who have left their own country as well-educated adults, who have every opportunity (as Finns, for example, have in Sweden) of maintaining their language, of hearing and reading it every day, but who after a few years speak their own language so that some of the phonemes have been replaced by Swedish phonemes with many very common words not only replaced by Swedish words but actually "forgotten", making grammatical mistakes, and finding even informal everyday conversation difficult. Neither of these extremes is representative, but they serve to show the relativity of how much or how little support the mother tongue needs to flourish or to die. Extreme cases are interesting as objects of research, but their experiences cannot be generalized to be valid for the majority.

When discussing the stabilization of the mother tongue we must make a distinction between different aspects of language. By the age of three or four the child has usually "mastered" the syntax of the languages she speaks (see, for example, Brown, 1973; McLaughlin, 1977). She can express the most central syntactic relationships, can use subject, predicate, object, predicative, and so on, and the child's language is beginning to resemble adult language not only by containing the semantically important words but also by making use of a large proportion of those rather "empty" elements which express formal properties and relations between sentence elements.

Morphology and syntax usually develop along parallel lines. Even if children are familiar with most of the simple morphological patterns in their L1 by the age of three or four, they tend to achieve full mastery of them only when they reach school age (see, for example, 1977 Ruoppila and its bibliography). The mastery of grammatical patterns (for Finnish) also correlates with the degree of linguistic stimulus the child is exposed to (how much she hears adults and friends talk, how much and in what way she is talked and read to, etc.). We know that children from higher social groups, only children, and the older children in families with several children perform better than children from lower social groups, children from families with more than one child, and younger children with older siblings. This is true even for grammatical patterns, but above all for vocabulary. Vocabulary differences may be very evident even at the pre-school stage, but the important thing to note is that *all* children have mastered the vital vocabulary they need to express most of their needs adequately before they reach school age (surface fluency, BICS).

The child can usually also cope with most of the sounds in her mother tongue as early as the age of three or four, and in most cases at the latest before starting school (i.e. in Scandinavia at 7).

Most of the functions of language that Halliday lists as fundamental are probably mastered by children very early (Halliday, 1973):

■ *the instrumental function* ("I want", using language to get things done);
■ *the regulatory function* ("do as I tell you", using language to regulate the behaviour of others);
■ *the interactional function* ("me and you", language in social interaction between the self and others);
■ *the personal function* ("here I come", using language to present one's own identity) – these functions develop probably very early, and in the elementary form in which they occur in children the differences between social groups are perhaps not very evident before school age. Clearer differences, however, may emerge with:
■ *the heuristic function* ("tell me why", using language to learn about things, to investigate reality, to ask questions);
■ *the imaginative function* ("let's pretend", using language to create one's own environment); and
■ *the referential (or representational) function* (informing about "facts").

However, the fact that a child knows a great deal of her mother tongue before reaching school age does not mean that the language is as fully stabilized as that of an adult. Many aspects go on developing throughout one's lifetime. Vocabulary is the best example of this, but it is also true that a speaker may become more skilful at managing many of the functions

Halliday distinguishes, even in middle age. We must not conclude from this, though, that it is impossible to say anything about the stabilization of the mother tongue. There seem to be certain stages which are particularly related to the various stages of children's cognitive development. We can here distinguish between at least two aspects.

The more complex syntactic structures of written and more formal language, features which require a more extensive grasp of speech planning and analysis, are obviously only mastered by children after the age of 10–12, at the stage when, according to Piaget, the transition occurs from the stage of concrete operations to abstract, formal operations, in cognitive development. Grammatical phenomena like passive and agent, complicated nominalizations or prepositional phrases, and generally constructions involving many transformations and embeddings seem to cause children difficulty as late as the age of 10–12, and often later too, even into adult life. In a similar way, very many words which stand for abstract concepts, forming part of a complex hierarchical structure will be learnt by the child only at the same point of transition to the final stage in intellectual development. The late appearance of ability of this kind is in no way unique to linguistic development: for example, the ability to take in a general view of a traffic situation which is necessary for cycling in heavy urban traffic (the ability to calculate the consequences of different alternatives, to change a decision after a quick reassessment of the situation, and so forth) appears at about the same age, and children should not be sent out alone in traffic before this.

There is no escaping the fact that linguistic development does *not* proceed at a steady and even pace. But this does not justify our suggesting it is immaterial at what age intensive foreign language medium teaching is introduced, in conditions where the mother tongue has only severely limited chances of developing outside school. It is rather the case that we must allow for a jerky pattern of development. It is only *after* the child is beginning to approach the final stage of cognitive development that we may speak of an evenly progressing movement. From this point onwards, the gathering of new experience and the exposure to new situations for the rest of any individual's life will bring about quantitative change in linguistic command, but no longer qualitative change of the fundamental kind that some of the early experiences represented.

Let me refer here to the discussion about surface fluency and the acquiring of cognitive tools in section 5.2.2.5. Command of the fundamental aspects of language, of the phonemes of one's own language, the central syntactic constructions, and the central vocabulary, would be roughly equivalent to fully developed surface fluency, and signify that the individual had reached the first plateau. Since individual differences in achieving this fundamental ability are not great, we may assume that most children reach this phase before school age. Most of the aspects of linguistic command which develop later (expansion of vocabulary, the more complex syntactic categories, the ability to use language decontextualized, without a concrete context in cognitively demanding situations) are strongly influenced by the environment, and particularly by those factors that affect children's general cognitive capacity. It is here, as a consequence, that considerable individual variation becomes apparent in the developmental process.

As I have mentioned before, this later development of language as a vehicle for thought shows significant correlation with the child's school achievement. If the child is deprived of many of the institutional opportunities (school, for example) for developing this capacity linguistically (if the child is put into a situation where the interchange between her and her environment is not optimal) then there is the risk that this linguistic/cognitive capacity will not get the opportunity to develop in an optimal way in any language.

To define in quantitative terms the point at which the mother tongue is "secure", in terms of the amount of use the child must have made of it, is of course impossible. But the question can be posed in qualitative terms: at which point has the child come to a stage where it is possible to develop a language which is comprehensive enough to resemble adult language?

But even if the child *has* the possibility of developing to this point it is not to say that all children *do* so.

Let me summarize my discussion like this: If the immigrant child is taught mainly in her own language (with possibly some foreign language teaching) up to the age of 10–12 years, then her mother tongue will be given the chance of a good start. If teaching *through the medium of* the majority language, and in some cases perhaps even formal teaching *of* the majority language, is postponed to this point, the child will still enjoy most of the advantages in learning a new language that young children have by comparison with older children and adults. Thus she will still be able to learn to speak the new language without any foreign accent, even if she has not heard it spoken in her environment before. Even more will this be the case where, as is common in Scandinavia, the child has been exposed to the foreign language every time she has gone out of the front door. This inevitable exposure to the majority language will ensure that the immigrant child achieves surface fluency in it, whether formal teaching of it is delayed or not. And if the child acquires L2 before puberty, she has every chance of speaking it without any accent. The other advantages which may be enjoyed by very young children in learning a new language can be "compensated" for by the way the teaching is organized; provided that the older children feel secure and accepted in a monolingual mother tongue class, and provided that as a consequence they have a series of experiences of success in their school work and feel self-confident, then they are happy to risk imitating, to make mistakes, and so on. Long-term motivation may also improve where children are allowed to progress in L2 at their own pace without being forced, but where at the same time they have ample opportunities for using L2 when they want to. The difference between the younger and the older child will then be a difference between external motivation (young children *are obliged* to speak L2 because no one at the day nursery understands their language) and internal motivation (which may yield better results in the converting of input to intake). A child's motivation may be much improved if she can choose the situations in which she will use L2, rather than being forced into situations where, for instance, problem solving at school has to be done in the foreign language – see further in 10.2.3.

A child's motivation may also be improved if the second language is set in the context of activity of some kind. Again, it will help greatly if the new language can be used as an instrument with which the child manipulates and interacts with her environment. Also, if the introduction of L2 is delayed until a bit later, then there is an excellent chance for the best possible interaction between the child's cognitive and linguistic development. And this again makes it possible to analyze the material presented and used in L2, in an efficient way – something where older children and adults have the clearest advantage over young children. It can thus be said that children of about 10 to 12 years old have begun to enjoy most of the advantages adults have in learning a new language, without having lost many of those advantages which are peculiarly the property of young children. And what has begun to be lost can be compensated for by organizational means in a monolingual class in the children's mother tongue.

7.3.5.4 Summary: the weighting of various factors

The age of the child when L2 is introduced, and the intensity and duration of the teaching seem to operate together. Each of these factors has to be attended to, but what seems to be more important is the way in which they are combined.

It appears that late introduction of L2 improves the results, provided that the other factors remain constant. If teaching starts at the age of 10–12, the results seems to be particularly good in relation to the time spent in teaching. But the assumption here is that it will then really be possible, for a few years, to give as much time to L2-learning as would have been spent on it had the whole process of learning been begun at an earlier age.

The more intensive the teaching is, the better the results seem to be if measured against results achieved with the same number of teaching hours spread over a longer period. Again, if all other factors remain constant, the results seem to be better, the longer the teaching continues, as one might expect. The varying relations between these three factors seem to be decisively important in foreign/second language learning, but these relations have seldom been isolated for scrutiny in research studies.

If we look again at the teaching of majority children with the importance of the relation between these three factors in mind, the results we considered earlier will be clearer. The best results have been achieved in early immersion programmes, where age of introduction is low, intensity the highest possible, and duration long. The next best results have been achieved with late immersion, where age of introduction is high, the intensity also very high but the duration short. Less good results have been achieved with partial immersion where the age of introduction has varied, but is often low, where the intensity is often fairly low, and the duration often but not always long. Fairly good results have been achieved with programmes in which one or more subjects are taught in the foreign language: low starting age, fairly low intensity, and long duration, but with the difference that the language is used as a medium of instruction and not just as the object of study, as would be the case in traditional foreign language teaching.

As has already been shown, the distinction between foreign languages and second languages, as well as between high status mother tongues and low status mother tongues, is also important. A second language, which the child hears spoken all around her anyway, may well be formally introduced later, especially if this gives a low status mother tongue the chance to develop. By contrast, if we are dealing with a foreign language that the child hears (almost) exclusively at school, and if the child speaks a high status mother tongue which has a good chance of developing normally in any case and which thus needs no more than the formal kinds of grammatical support from the school, then the age of introduction can be made even very low, since this lengthens the duration and perhaps also the intensity.

7.4   Children from linguistic minorities

7.4.1   Background

When looking at how to evaluate programmes for minority students in different countries, the differences often seem to me to be so great that it simply is impossible to speak the same language. In the U.S. Baker & de Kanter in discussing the criteria for good studies, have as their starting point that their decision "recognize the need to prepare language-minority children to function successfully in an English-speaking nation" (p. 5), leading to a conclusion where "a programme that produces mediocre English performance while maintaining the home language skills will be judged a worse programme than one that produces better second language performance while ignoring home language skills". Their "over-riding concern in evaluating instruction for bilingual students is how well they learn English" (p. 5). Their students "*communicate to the test* what they already know" (p. 7) (my emphasis) and they "limit the conclusions reached . . . to those that do not require assuming some underlying explanations for the results" (p. 14).

When there are more than 20 million non-English or limited English speakers, a nation cannot without qualification be called English-speaking, especially if one thinks of *speaking*. A more important goal could be to prepare language-majority students to function successfully in a multilingual nation. The whole ideology behind the statements is assimilationist, stating clearly that minority mother tongues have no value and stressing the importance of English. There is plenty of evidence that children do not communicate to tests but with people. And knowing that "policymakers had one set of goals and assumptions (orientated to transitional bilingual education) and Chicano community groups had another set of goals and assumptions (orientated to mother tongue maintenance and cultural self-determination)" (Matute-Bianci, 1982: 18), it does not seem reliable to discuss and try to evaluate transitional bilingual programmes without even mentioning this discrepancy and without trying to assess what role it could play in explaining contradictory results for transitional programmes.

In contrast with this American way of evaluating we could take a European conference with representatives from different European community countries, discussing the evaluation of programmes set up for migrant minority children after the EEC-directive in West Germany, Belgium, France, Britain and The Netherlands (Nieke, 1981). A self-evident starting point in the discussions is, for instance, that a value free or neutral science and research does not and cannot exist (p. 108) and that the value judgements of the researcher, even if she tries to hide or overcome them, influence the results. The methodological discussion about evaluation tries to set out the principles which govern the ways in which the insight and motives, the "erkenntnisleitende Interesse" (Habermas, 1968) of the researcher can be best presented, discussed and its consequences controlled. It is according to this type of ethics of evaluation obligatory to present in every evaluation the interests and motives of both the evaluator, the people being evaluated and the body paying for the evaluation, for the evaluation even to approach any kind of reliability. This methodological conflict, between the type of evaluation of minority education represented by, for instance, Baker & de Kanter and many Europeans, makes a content discussion of different evaluations almost futile as long as the principles behind evaluation methodology are not clarified. These questions are further discussed in Skutnabb-Kangas, 1982a and Cummins & Skutnabb-Kangas (eds) (in preparation).

In the Swedish version of the book I discussed different possibilities of presenting some of the evaluations of studies about the education of minority children, and rejected the way many researchers have used, namely giving tables or lists with plus and minus studies, an approach which has been used in other areas of study (there are examples of this type of good tables for instance about child language research in Hatch and McLaughlin or about the influence of the teacher in Bratt Paulston – see the bibliography). But in the case of the experience of minority children at school, I feel such a list would be more misleading than helpful. There is a risk that one might begin to classify studies fairly mechanically as either for or against a certain position, knowing little about their transfer value. If, as Lars Henric Ekstrand did at a public debate in Stockholm held on 1.12.1980, somebody presents a number of studies which show that bilingualism has beneficial cognitive consequences, without making it clear that most of these studies are of children from bilingual families, majority children in immersion programmes, or majority children learning a foreign language at school and then goes on to use these results as an argument for teaching immigrant children in Sweden through the medium of Swedish from as early an age as possible, so that these beneficial consequences should follow, the argument can only be thoroughly misleading. Those actually present at the Stockholm debate who did not know that the studies mentioned were not in fact of immigrant children had no chance of knowing what it was they were actually evaluating.

In the Swedish version I therefore chose to present a few studies (Modiano, 1966; Hebert et al., 1976; Vorih & Rosier, 1978) more thoroughly and to discuss some of the principles behind them, and then to give some references for further reading. But since both those studies and many others are easily available in English (while they are not in Scandinavian languages) and especially since there are many good reviews, I want here only to refer the reader to some of those reviews, and then proceed to present some of the Scandinavian studies. The principles behind some of the good studies have been discussed in so many ways in this book already that a repetition here seems unnecessary. I shall only touch upon some of the points which are not mentioned elsewhere in the book.

One of the interesting findings in Modiano's study is concerned with the teacher variable. It is not possible, though, to say categorically, that it is *always* better to have a teacher from the children's own group (even if that is what Modiano's study shows). It seems to depend to a large extent on whether the teacher has the same class background as the children taught, and whether she shows solidarity with them and their parents. An assimilated middle class teacher from the same ethnic and linguistic group, teaching lower class children who are opposed to assimilation, can produce bad results (see, for example, Paulston, 1977: 107–11 and Oxman, 1971, quoted in Paulston). By contrast, a teacher from the majority group who respects the children's ethnic and cultural background, who has the same kind of ideological background or standing as the parents, and who tries to learn the children's language, may quite possibly achieve excellent results even though she is not a member of the minority group.

The results from the study of Francophones in Manitoba (Hebert et al., 1976) are going to be of great interest when different countries come far enough so that the fight is not any more about the right to mother tongue medium teaching but rather about the amount spent on teaching through the medium of either language. Especially in countries where a transitional model is applied (like the U.S.A.) or where experiments are starting about the best way/time/division of time if the children are to be transferred at a fairly late stage, i.e. after the first 6 grades (as in Sweden, see the recommendations in SÖ September 1982), the percentages of time spent through each language deserve careful consideration. I quote Hebert's summary:

"The results of the research show clearly that those programmes which operate with a high proportion of French (more than 71%) have the best chance of guaranteeing a high level of bilingualism among French-speaking pupils in Manitoba. ... If we want to define that school situation which offers the best chance of success in both languages, our research indicates that it will be the situation in which French is used as the language of instruction for all subjects except English. 'Mixed' programmes, where both languages are used in the teaching, usually produce less satisfactory results in French; moreover, they seem to lead to linguistic confusion among a large number of the pupils. Linguistic confusion hinders these pupils not only in the two languages themselves, but also in the other school subjects. It appears therefore that in Manitoba, a community which is overwhelmingly English-speaking and where French is a language difficult to maintain, educational programmes which have a large proportion of the teaching in French offer the best chance of ensuring that the pupils become efficiently bilingual, as well as performing satisfactorily in other subjects" (Hebert et al., 1976: 21–22).

The Rock Point Navajo study should be seen in the light of the fact that many American and Canadian Indians fear that their mother tongues will die out in the process of assimilation. This can be seen in the following resolution from National Indian Brotherhood (1972) – it is a counterpart to many similar resolutions written, for instance, by Inuits and Same, and the same sentiments have also been expressed by World Council for Indigenous People at its meetings:

"Language is the outward expression of an accumulation of learning and experience shared by a group of people over centuries of development. It is not simply a vocal symbol, it is a dynamic force which shapes the way a man looks at the world, his thinking about the world and his philosophy of life. Knowing his maternal language helps a man to know himself; being proud of his language helps a man to be proud of himself. The Indian people are expressing concern that the native languages are being lost, that the younger generations can no longer speak or understand their mother tongue. If the Indian identity is to be preserved, steps must be taken to reverse this trend."

One of the interesting things in the Rock Point study (which showed that Navajo children initially instructed through the medium of Navajo did considerably better than the English-medium instructed controls even in English in grades 4, 5 and 6) is the comparison between teaching in the majority language with good, ready-made materials and teachers well trained, and teaching in the minority language with hardly any teaching material available and teachers trained inadequately or not at all. The fact that better results were still obtained from teaching in the minority language should embolden us to start experiments even where what is necessary in the way of teachers and materials does not yet exist. In such cases there must be a great deal of reliance during the first few years of the experiment on the suggestion that bad materials and insufficient teacher training can be compensated for by the involvement of teachers, parents and children, if the advantages to be gained are important enough. And the simple fact of teaching through the medium of a language not before accepted at the school will in itself usually be a great step forward, a sufficiently valuable gain. This would apply in the case of a number of indigenous and especially immigrant minorities in Scandinavia: different Same groups, Romanies, Kurds, and so on. But it is also important to emphasize that in order to ensure good results even after the first enthusiasm has subsided, it is vital that from the very beginning there should be a serious attempt to remedy deficiencies in the teaching materials and in teacher training.

There is a wealth of material for further reading in this area. Good older surveys are Paulston (1975a and b, 1977, 1978), Cohen (1975), Engle (1975), Cohen, Fathman & Merino (1976). For references and state of the art descriptions the five volumes in *Bilingual Education, Current Perspectives* (1977) provide a useful synthesis, as do the bibliographies by the National Clearinghouse for Bilingual Education, and by M. Jungo (1978). More recent reviews are Troike (1979), Rist (1979), Dutcher (1982), Hedman (1978), Yletyinen (1982) and Cummins (1983), just to mention a few. Many countries have excellent surveys with bibliographies about the situation in their own countries – for instance in Germany the Deutsche Jugendinstitut Dokumentation-series (see for instance Weidacher 1981) and publications by the research group ALFA, or for Britain in Klein 1982, *Race and Education in Britain 1960–1977*, Mullard 1981, Bourne & Sivanandan 1980, Sivanandan 1982. When looking for bibliographies one can go to the Commission for Racial Equality, the Institute of Race Relations, the Centre for Multicultural Education at the University of London Institute of Education, the Runnymede Trust, the Centre for Urban Educational Studies, the Centre for Information on Language Teaching and Research, all in London. There are also good descriptions and comparisons of either different European countries or world-wide. For instance Niete, Budde & Henscheid (1982) is written about Germany, with counterparts about Britain and France. SOPEMI reports tell about changes year by year, and reports like Hammar (ed., forthcoming) and Churchill (written for OECD, forthcoming) compare countries in a detailed way. It is surprising that so little in the way of practical reforms has come out of all the rich documentation. Cummins & Skutnabb-Kangas (eds) presents some of the more innovative recent empirical studies (vol. 1) and discusses problems and differences in evaluations (vol. 2).

Scandinavian studies
    When comparing studies in Scandinavia with the criteria set out by

Baker & de Kanter (1982) for "acceptable studies" of the outcome in minority education, we can easily see that there is not a single study in Scandinavia fulfilling their criteria! According to their criteria the acceptable studies should be "true experiments" (i.e. what Göte Hanson calls "rat research"), there should be a random assignment to experimental and control groups (if children *want* to participate they cannot be studied), all the appropriate statistical tests should have been used (i.e. only quantitative data are data), norm-referenced tests should not be allowed, nor grade-equivalent scores. There are two main reasons we have no Scandinavian studies of this kind. One is that there are simply not enough children at one place of the same national and linguistic group to permit a longitudinal study with random assignment. The other, more important one, is that there are few researchers in Scandinavia who would agree to undertake such studies, because of ethical and ideological and paradigmatic reasons. Especially in questions where there are very definite opinions about the desirability of certain types of model of schooling (as there is in minority education), it would be extremely difficult to conduct a positivistic type of "true experiment", and the ethics of many follow-up studies even without any intervention have also been fiercely debated in Scandinavia. In what follows I will briefly present a few studies and tell the reader where additional information is available.

The only long-term Scandinavian project involving mother tongue classes is the Södertälje project, under the direction of Göte Hanson from the Department of Psychology at Stockholm University. This project, has been in progress since 1972, like the Lund project. The final report is not yet available, but a number of articles and minor studies have appeared, most of them in Swedish. In this project, three experimental classes have been followed from the first grade. The children had no pre-school education and it seems reasonable to suppose that the results for the children would have been even better if they had attended a Finnish pre-school class. The local authority's view that mother tongue classes provide a good and reliable solution is evidenced by the fact that such classes have increased in number during recent years. In 1980 there were 31 Finnish mother tongue classes in various schools (Hanson, 1980a) and additional classes in Serbo-Croat and Spanish.

Teaching in the Finnish classes took place entirely in Finnish during the first two years, with the exception of music where both Finnish and Swedish were used. Swedish as the second language was not introduced until grade 3 when it was allotted five hours a week in the timetable; woodwork was taught in Swedish from grade 3. From grade 3 onwards, mathematics, gymnastics and, from the spring term onwards, social studies were taught in both languages, with the Swedish teacher present. English was postponed until grade 4 when it was given two hours a week to begin with, this increasing to five hours a week in grades 5 and 6. Social studies were still taught in both languages in grade 4, whereas all other subjects (except, of course, Finnish) were taught in Swedish from grade 4 onwards. However, there were six hours a week of Finnish in grades 4 and 5, and four hours in grade 6. In grade 7 the children were taught in exactly the same way as the Swedish children, and the language of instruction was Swedish. They also still had mother tongue teaching in Finnish. With different pioneer classes different models were tried out in grades 7–9, partly depending on organizational matters. Pioneer 1 were taught together with Finnish children who had been taught through the medium of Swedish from the beginning. Pioneer 2 were taught together with Swedish children, and also compared with a completely Swedish parallel class. Pioneer 3 were kept together, with no other children added, but taught entirely through the medium of Swedish – Hanson compares them with the Finnish children who were also the comparison group for Pioneer 1. The information I have given here is derived from the teaching programme for "Finnish classes" in the Södertälje municipal district (1980).

Göte Hanson says in a number of his articles (1980a, 1980b, 1980c) that the children have attained "a native command of the two languages after five years in a mother tongue class" (1980b: 17); or in another place, that after six years they speak, read and write Finnish and Swedish nearly as well as children in Helsinki from comparable backgrounds (1980a, b). The children are linguistically active, and they switch languages without difficulty when necessary (I can myself confirm that this is true as a result of talking with some of them). Some of the children choose the more advanced English course in year seven, even though they have had less English than the corresponding Swedish children. They have "a good bilingual balance".

The following tables show the comparisons now available for the three pioneer classes when they were in grade 9, i.e. the last year of the Swedish comprehensive school. The grade points obtained at the end of grade 9 are the ones which the youngsters use when competing for further education. The scale is 1–5. In English and mathematics there has been a choice between a general course (GC) and an advanced course (AC) and the number of pupils who have chosen each is given in the table. The advanced course is required for some of the longer theoretical studies, in upper secondary education. Social studies include civics, religion, history and geography, natural studies include biology, chemistry and physics. Hanson suggests that pioneer 3 be compared with comparison 1, Finnish children in a Swedish class.

Both the children themselves and their parents are satisfied with the level of achievement. It is important to the parents that their children, having learnt Swedish, also speak Finnish, so that they can talk to them and discuss problems with them in their own language. The children are happy at school and are pleased to be able to speak both languages, both of which they identify with. Bullying by Swedish pupils is rare, and where it has occurred, the children have been able to cope with it because of the strong support they have had from their mother tongue class. Göte Hanson takes as his starting point the psychological need the children have to feel secure, to

TABLE 5

	Pioneer 1	Com-parison 1	Pioneer 2	Com-parison 2	Com-parison 3	Pioneer 3
Finnish	2.80	2.10	3.85	—	—	3.65
Swedish	2.33	1.50	3.00	2.94	3.00	2.53
Maths GC	2.71 (7)	1.43 (7)	3.43 (6)	3.00 (9)	3.07 (15)	2.64 (14)
Maths AC	2.38 (8)	3.33 (3)	3.17 (6)	2.88 (8)	3.30 (10)	3.33 (3)
English GC	3.00 (2)	1.86 (8)	3.33 (2)	2.00 (7)	3.00 (10)	2.40 (10)
English AC	2.69 (13)	3.33 (2)	3.50 (10)	3.50 (10)	3.27 (15)	3.29 (7)
Social st.	2.83	1.90	3.31	2.83	3.12	2.85
Natural st.	2.56	1.87	3.36	2.82	2.98	2.70
N	15	10	12	17	24	17

Comparison 1 – Finnish children, grades 1–6 in Sw. class, 7–9 in the same class with pioneer 1.
Comparison 2 – Swedish children, grades 1–6 in Sw. class, 7–9 in the same class with pioneer 2.
Comparison 3 – Swedish parallel class, grades 1–9 in Sw. class.

(Compiled from tables 1, 2 and 3 in Hanson 1982b, on the basis of information given in Hanson 1982a.)

belong to a group and to be appreciated. The result of the project is that "the majority of the pupils are completely bilingual for their age, are at the same standard in other subjects as their Swedish counterparts in the parallel classes, have a personality where the main characteristics are that they feel self-assured and secure", (1980d: 4). The explanation of this is "that in mother tongue classes the pupils understand what their teacher and their classmates are saying. As a result they can keep up with the school work and be active. They are spared the humiliation of failing to cope with the work: a common experience in a class where they do not understand what is being said. The children thus have the chance day by day of experiencing success in their school work rather than failure and defeat" (1980d: 4). "The children themselves attribute their success to the fact that they have felt secure in their class, because they have understood everything that was being said and done, and because their teachers and their parents have demanded of them that they work hard at school, which was tough going but good" (1980e: 2). And "when you make demands of the pupils, you show that you believe they can achieve something worthwhile. Not to make demands of them can be to give the opposite impression. This is testified by pupils who have 'failed'. The pupils' self-confidence has a chance to grow as they are able to meet the demands made of them at school" (1980d: 4). Göte Hanson also discusses the question of segregation and integration in connection with mother tongue classes, a matter which has attracted much attention. Hanson makes a distinction between what I call physical and psychological integration, and he reserves the term integration for the second, psychological integration, and calls physical integration "school placement". In his view we should try to place a child so as to enable the child to do the integrating herself – no one else can do the integrating *for* anybody (which shows that the basis for a real integration is not a forced but a voluntary motivation to integrate). Hanson describes the children in his project as being *functionally* integrated; they use the same resources at school as the Swedish children, and are surrounded by Swedish pupils. They are *socially* integrated: they participate in certain activities with the Swedish children and "belong to" the school; they have the same social framework of reference. And they have started their *societal* integration: as adults they will have the same opportunities as the Swedish children. According to Hanson, the children are ready to integrate themselves by themselves (1980a). A more thorough presentation of the project, with comparisons also from Finnish-medium classes in two other towns, will be available in Cummins & Skutnabb-Kangas (in preparation).

The project *Models for the Bilingual Education of Immigrant Children* (Lund University, Department of Education) (1972 to 1980) studied Finnish children in a monolingual Finnish kindergarten (with some teaching of Swedish), and in mixed classes (in Sweden called compound classes) in the lower forms of school proper. Although "models" in the plural was used in the title of the project, in fact only one model was investigated, although it is true that in the very first year of the investigation, before the project was properly under way, the pre-school children were placed in three Swedish schools and also taught by itinerant Finnish teachers. This particular model was soon abandoned as unsatisfactory in many respects. Even so, in general it is still the most common pattern of teaching for pre-school immigrant children. . . .

This first, "integrated" group of children had one year only of pre-school education, and since their experience of the pre-school stage was quite different from that of the other, later groups, the results from this group should consistently have been reported separately; but this was not done in the final report on the project (Löfgren & Ouvinen-Birgerstam, 1980). The other three groups all went to a Finnish medium kindergarten for three hours each day, and during the second of these three hours there was a "Swedish instructor" at the school who took one or more children at a time into an adjacent room where they were "initiated into Swedish children's culture by listening to fairy tales and records, by singing Swedish songs, dancing Swedish dances, and acting out and retelling the typical fairy tales. The Swedish instructor also conveyed to the children the kinds of distinctively Swedish concept she thought of as central for starting school".[5]

In grades 1–3 the Finnish children were integrated into two parallel Swedish classes. About half the children in these classes were Swedish, the rest Finnish immigrants *as well as* immigrant children of other nationalities.

The team of teachers for the two parallel classes for any one term consisted of two Swedish class teachers for all the ordinary subjects, one Swedish teacher who taught all the immigrant children Swedish, and a Finnish teacher: that is, three Swedish and one Finnish teacher in all. The Finnish children were first taught to read and write in Finnish, the other children in Swedish. All the mathematics teaching was in Swedish, though in the first year the Finnish teacher was present at these lessons for two hours each week. There were only two hours weekly of teaching in Finnish in social studies during the first two years (of a total of five or six hours a week of social studies teaching) in addition to the regular teaching of Finnish. The teaching of Finnish in grade 1 and the autumn term of grade 2 amounted to eight hours a week, with seven hours a week in the spring term of grade 2, and two hours a week (plus two hours of auxiliary tuition in Finnish) in grade 3.

The aim of the teaching was to make the children functionally bilingual. Functional bilingualism was defined as follows: Functional bilingualism means that children whose mother tongue is something other than Swedish are able to function in different Swedish language situations as well as children with otherwise equal prerequisites but whose mother tongue is Swedish. At the same time the children are expected to be so proficient in their mother tongue that they can function naturally in environments where their mother tongue is used, as well as having the cultural and linguistic groundwork for a possible return to the country of origin" (Löfgren & Ouvinen-Birgerstam, 1980: 2). Another definition used was this: "an ability to understand and speak two languages, and participate in two cultures, which gives an opportunity to live and function in two countries" (Löfgren & Ouvinen-Birgerstam, 1980: 13). How was success in achieving the objectives measured? What is known about the children's ability to function well in different Swedish language situations? What is known about how they function in situations where their mother tongue is used? What of their prospects in case of return? What of their participation in the two cultural worlds and two countries?

The material collected by the project consists of test results in Swedish, Finnish and mathematics, an IQ-test, school reports, observations by teachers, and one interview with each of the children's parents conducted in 1974–75. This means that the only situations known are test situations. But what proportion of ordinary children's linguistic situations are test situations? No attempt was made at any kind of measurement of anything else that the project said it aimed at. This in itself means that there is no secure basis for comment about the degree of functional bilingualism among the children. The groups, too, were very small. Again, for it to be possible to say anything significant about how well the mixed classes worked, something would have to be known about the children's performance at the junior and secondary school stage, after the special programme for them had been discontinued. From grade 5, there is a little evidence (standard test results, school reports, one Finnish test result) for the ten children who attended the Swedish pre-school class (Group 1), and who thus, of course, cannot be compared with the other children who took part in the project. The only evidence from grade 5 (apart from the non-representative group 1) are the test results for *four* children who took the ITPA test (Illinois Test of Psycholinguistic Abilities, which has been translated into Finnish). From grade 4, with the exception of some evidence for Group 1, there are only the results of two Finnish tests for the same four children and seven others. There are no results for Swedish, no school reports, nothing else. From grade 3, if Group 1 is discounted (it is put together with the other groups with which it is not comparable, in the report) there are school achievement tests in Swedish and mathematics, school reports and three sets of results from Finnish tests for 11 children, but still no results from special language tests in Swedish. A few Swedish language test results are recorded from grades 1 and 2.

On the basis of this evidence, far-reaching conclusions are drawn in the summary about the children's knowledge of their mother tongue and of Swedish, about the relationship between these two and about the effect of the teaching model on their bilingualism. The report says, for example, that "the bilingual teaching model developed in the project has improved the Finnish pupils' chances of becoming functionally bilingual" (summary). The authors have recently repeated their conclusions in English (1983), and therefore it is important to look more closely at the evidence for these conclusions.

In a number of cases no test results are available, even though they should be. The explanation given is that "for various reasons a whole group was not tested, or the testing failed". I know from discussions with the teachers that the standard tests for the particular year of schooling were sometimes too difficult for the children, so that the teachers did not want to conduct them. Sometimes the time limits prescribed in the tests were not observed (so that the children were given more time to complete, which of course improved their results). If the children had been regularly tested, and if the time limits had been strictly obeyed, then the results would probably have been much worse. Now we have no idea which of the gaps in the record of results are contrived and which are "real".

We do not know either whether the children always sat the tests prescribed for their age level, and this is nowhere stated. However, as a result of the information I compiled in the spring of 1977 about all the Finnish tests carried out in the project, one can see that for instance in the spring of 1977 tests were used for grade 4 which had been designed for grades 2 and 3 (these were Finnish vocabulary test reading tests, and tests of mechanical arithmetic ability), and for grades 1 and 2 (Finnish dictation and mathematical problem solving). Naturally, the results obtained are better when tests are used which were intended for younger children, and when the results are assessed on the basis of what younger children should be capable of. The report does not even mention that this practice of using simpler tests was ever resorted to, let alone how common it was.

The results obtained were compared with the results obtained by Finnish classes in Kari Lasonen's studies (1978b), and it was concluded that the children in mixed classes in the project did just about as well in Finnish as did the children in entirely Finnish classes in Sweden. The comparison is in fact quite misleading because the children involved in the project went to a Finnish medium kindergarten (which might be expected to have improved their grasp of Finnish); but we simply do not know what kind of educational experience the children described in Lasonen's report had before they started in the Finnish classes at school. Many of them may well have attended Swedish medium kindergartens, which were not likely to have helped their Finnish. One cannot fairly compare groups of children with different prerequisites.

Let me, to end, quote a few examples of the many conclusions in the final report on this project which are simply untenable, or unsupported by the evidence:

It is concluded that the language spoken at home had no decisive effect upon the development of the children's Swedish (Löfgren & Ouvinen-Birgerstam, 1980: 81). However, it was also said that all the parents spoke to each other exclusively in Finnish, and to the children predominantly in Finnish. How, then, was it possible to learn anything about the effect of the home language on Swedish if most of the children in the project had virtually the same linguistic home background?

It is concluded that "the children's development of a proficiency in Swedish was not a direct result of their level of proficiency in their mother tongue", and that "the children's proficiency in Swedish in the first year was a good guide to their degree of proficiency in Finnish" (p. 84), and that "the children's early command of their mother tongue . . . was not related to their achievement in Swedish in grade 3". Moreover, it is stated that "the children's intellectual ability was more important than any purely linguistic factors in accounting for their performance at school". All this is said in spite of the fact that *the results of the intelligence tests show a very weak correlation with* the results of the standard tests in grade 3 in Swedish and mathematics and with the school reports in Swedish, mathematics, social studies and Finnish, whereas *the results in Finnish tests* show strong correlations with all those results (between 0.50 and 0.70). It is also mentioned in passing that "in grade 3 there was a fairly strong positive correlation (0.63) between Finnish comprehension and the results of the standard test in Swedish" (p. 86). In spite of the fact that the results reported show clearly a positive correlation between mother tongue development and both the command of Swedish and school achievement in general, such a link is denied in the conclusions, and the impression is given that other factors were the decisive ones and that mother tongue development was of no importance.

The investigators are obliged to admit that the children fell "slightly below the average of the Swedish group" in mathematics, Swedish and Finnish (p. 68) and that "the average in the linguistic tests is one standard deviation lower than the average of the norm groups, i.e. monolingual Finnish children in Finland and monolingual Swedish children in Sweden" (p. 68). Nevertheless it is maintained that "the majority of the children can be judged to be functionally bilingual according to the definition of bilingualism adopted in the project" (p. 102), and that "the bilingual teaching model developed in the project has improved the Finnish pupils' chance of becoming functionally bilingual".

If the aim of the project was to ensure that the children did worse in Finnish, Swedish and mathematics than monolingual children from either country, then it was indeed successful.

We know from educational and other research that if children become the objects of intensive scrutiny (with researchers present, extra teachers, smaller classes, extra careful planning of the teaching, not to mention the kind of money – 2 million Swedish crowns – spent on this project), then they tend to produce better results.

If then, in spite of all the extra effort for the period of eight years during which the project was running, the results have been below normal, we may draw two possible conclusions:
▪ that Finnish working-class children in Sweden (or other immigrant working-class children) are so very much more stupid than the average monolingual child that they cannot reach the same educational level, no matter what effort is put into teaching them, or
▪ that there is something wrong with the way they have been taught.

This last conclusion, which questions the efficacy of mixed classes, is in my view the only possible interpretation. But since the project was intended to provide support for the National Board of Education's advocacy of mixed classes at a time when the immigrant organizations had begun more and more emphatically to press for mother tongue classes, the project organizers could not afford to admit that their experiment had not turned out to be successful, this in spite of the fact that the National Board's view has now changed, to the extent that mother tongue classes are now found wholly acceptable (see further my articles, 1981a & b, and about the National Board's latest views where in fact mother tongue medium classes are recommended as the norm for the first 6 grades, SÖ 1982). See Skutnabb-Kangas 1982b for a discussion of the impact research has had on decisions about the education of minority children in the Swedish setting.

The only other long-term project reported is the Västerås project, evaluated by Sirpa Arwidsson (1977), comparing Finnish children in Finnish medium and Swedish medium classes in the same municipal district. The preliminary and partial reports suggest that the children in the Finnish classes, who were worse at Swedish and better at Finnish than the Finnish children in the Swedish classes (as might have been expected – compare the Rock Point investigations), have made better progress in both languages than the Finnish children in the Swedish classes. This is suggested by beginning and end of term tests.[6] At the beginning of the project the Finnish children were much weaker in Finnish than the Finnish control group in Lahti, Finland. This is hardly surprising, since the children had not been to Finnish pre-school classes. On the contrary, most of them had been to Swedish pre-schools, and very few of them had had Finnish childminders. In most of the tests they were still not performing comparably with the control group in Finland by the spring of grade 2 (and this agrees well with the results Kari Lasonen has obtained from single tests of pupils in various Finnish classes – Lasonen, 1978a, b). But the children in the Swedish classes lagged much further behind in most of the Finnish tests than the children in the Finnish classes. On the other hand, these children in the Swedish classes were well ahead on the Swedish language tests and reached average norms in some of them. They performed fairly well in comparison with their Swedish classmates in certain tests where comparisons were made. *If* a final report on this project appears (and the project has had no official financial support of any kind), it should be of interest to the reader of this book.

It is to be expected that the results show a cumulative effect even after the Finnish-medium teaching has been discontinued, just as in the study of Turkish and Moroccan children in Holland (see Altena & Appel, 1983), where the experimental group continued to show gains compared with the control group after the mother tongue medium instruction (which only lasted a year, in grade 1) was finished, and where the experimental groups outperformed the Dutch-medium instructed controls in Dutch at the end of grade 3.

The relative failure of the earliest language shelter programmes in Sweden to achieve *all* that is possible in the way of positive results (see for example Lasonen & Toukomaa, 1978; Toukomaa & Lasonen, 1979; Toukomaa, 1980) is largely explained by strictly extrinsic factors: the children started on the programmes too late and continued with them for too short a time. And the evaluations also stopped too early, just as in the Västerås project. The programmes have now started to show more and more positive results – see the article by Tingbjörn in Cummins & Skutnabb-Kangas (eds), vol. 2.

There are very few long term projects to do with day nurseries and pre-schools. Summaries of what has been done can be found in various publications by Britt-Ingrid Stockfelt-Hoatson and in a recent large report from the Ministry of Health and Social Affairs (1982).

There are a number of cross-sectional studies, some good, some less good. Some of the better ones are by Pertti Toukomaa, Kari Lasonen, Timo Särkelä and Jorma Kuusela (see bibliography). Pertti Toukomaa's early studies especially (see bibliography) were extremely influential, partly in pointing out how poorly Finnish immigrant children in Swedish classes performed, both in language tests in both languages and in general school achievement, but especially in developing the interdependence hypothesis and discussing the importance of mother tongue development for learning an L2. Only some of these studies are reported in English (which has led to a peculiar reaction in Baker & de Kanter where they talk about "a high attrition rate in the authors' sample" and say that "missing data pose a particularly severe problem" (1982: 16). Even if it seems incredible, it is not unusual to find oneself in a situation where somebody points out that what is not reported in English does not exist (even if it is reported in other languages, for example Finnish and Swedish, as in Toukomaa's case – see bibliography). Some of Toukomaa's most influential studies are partly reported in English and I refer the reader to them. – There is a plethora of minor studies in Scandinavia, and I refer the reader to the bibliographies for different Scandinavian countries for them.[7] The tendency seems to be partly towards mere descriptions, with mostly but not always very little theoretical foundation, even if some of these descriptions may be extremely thorough. Partly there are also new studies, ongoing or already reported, which have a more "understanding", ethnographical approach but which seem to be difficult to generalize from. Few of them have had educational questions as their main focus of interest.

Most evaluatory studies have unfortunately not dealt with the relationship between teaching in the mother tongue and in the second language as an independent variable. A number of the official evaluations have also suffered from other shortcomings – of a kind that make it evident that the issue of bilingual education touches upon important economic and political considerations. This is true for instance of the extensive AIR report (which maintained that bilingual education had no measurable effect whatever, criticized, for example, in Cárdenas, 1977 and Leyba et al., 1978). It is also documented that the decision as to who should carry out this particular evaluation was dependent on the willingness or otherwise of supporting the president's election fund (Cervantes, 1979). The recent Baker & de Kanter evaluation, also much criticized (see a summary of the criticism in Cummins' article in Cummins & Skutnabb-Kangas (eds) vol. 1), also shows some of these deficits, as does, surprisingly, Christina Bratt Paulston's recent (October, 1982) report for the Swedish National Board of Education.

Just as many of the American evaluations suffer from different types of bias so do many other studies which have pointed to the negative effects of teaching in the mother tongue. Some of the most important errors in this regard have been of the same kind as those already discussed in sections 7.1.1–3. Some additional ones that could be mentioned are the following:
■ The distinction between majority and minority has not been made properly or not at all. Thus the extensive investigation carried out in Rizal in the Philippines treats the children's mother tongue Tagalog as a minority language and English as the majority language, even though Tagalog is an official language in the Philippines which receives massive support from the

community at large and is in no danger of extinction or of losing ground to English. Although English as a "world language" and a language of international trade enjoys high status as a consequence of the economic strength behind it, both children's and parents' lives are for the most part lived through the medium of Tagalog, even outside home. The children's situation is thus better regarded as being like that of majority children learning a minority language, a second language. It is true that the children have opportunities both of learning and using English outside the home, but nevertheless the situation much more closely resembles that of majority children learning a foreign language at school than of minority children learning the majority language.

■ In many of the experiments the results are measured after too short a time has elapsed. The most striking example of this I know was a study in which the investigators tried to measure the results after *five weeks'* teaching, and were very surprised to find that the group receiving bilingual teaching did not score much better results than the control group taught in the majority language (this was a Spanish/English experiment conducted somewhere in the United States; the precise reference escapes me). As Christina Bratt Paulston has strongly emphasized in several of her publications, it would be unreasonable to expect results until the experimental teaching has been going on for four to five years. Many of the studies producing negative conclusions have measured their results after one to three years' teaching.

■ In many of the experiments only the data that are easily operationalizable and easy to measure are counted as results. As a consequence, some of the probably most important advantages for minority children of being taught in their mother tongue have not been evaluated at all in the negative investigations, simply on the grounds that they are difficult to measure. Criticism directed against that school of thought which takes the view that "if a concept cannot be measured, it does not exist" (Paulston, 1981: 29) has intensified during the present decade, and the view of different paradigms (represented also by differences in the demands made on evaluations) has become steadily more and more subtle.

A number both of major and minor studies show that when minority children are mainly taught in their own language, when, that is, they take part in *maintenance programmes,* they perform better at school and in general, both in their two languages, and also more generally in the other subjects. They are also happier, more content, more open, and more self-assured. Co-operation with their parents is better, as is the relationship in general between the minority group and the school, and possibly between the minority group and the rest of society. Many of these studies are not in fact well controlled (nor for that matter are many of the studies giving the opposite result: that minority children do *not* perform better if part of the teaching is in their mother tongue); but, together with better planned investigations, they nevertheless in my view establish a trend of evidence clear enough not to be mistaken.

I do not know of a single well-controlled and sufficiently long-term study, in which the methods of evaluation have included both quantitative and qualitative elements, and in which the elementary and necessary distinctions discussed early in this chapter have been made, which shows that minority children with a low-status mother tongue have performed less well when taught through the medium of their mother tongue than when taught through the medium of the foreign or second language.

In recent large-scale evaluations of minority education in 32 municipalities (covering more than a third of all minority students in the country) made for the Swedish National Board of Education (see reports by Tingbjörn, Enström, Källström, Ekström, Edberg and Holmegaard (and different combinations of these writers) in the bibliography, and SÖ September 1982 for the Board's summary, conclusions and recommenda- tions) the conclusion is that "positive experiences (of mother tongue medium classes) preponderate on the whole" (Enström, Källström & Tingbjörn, 1982). None of the respondents in the municipalities (school authorities, teachers etc.) reports exclusively negative experiences, many of the negative ones are qualified with things like "possibly" and "in special circumstances" and all replies report positive experiences. "The great majority of positive viewpoints are concerned with social/psychological advantages, while organizational and linguistic-developmental advantages come next" (p. 16). "The school management in districts with home language classes (i.e. mother tongue medium classes, my remark) appear to be in favour of this type of class" (p. 20). "Problems connected with the pupils' social development in their interaction with Swedish pupils (the risk of isolation, in other words) and staffing problems of various kinds are considered to be the greatest disadvantages." The National Board of Education is careful to point out, though, in their summary (SÖ, 1982) that the reported disadvantages are *fears* of problems, not actually experienced problems, and that the risk of isolation is discussed just as much in connection with students in compound classes, with Swedish students in the same class. "Another concrete and serious problem concerns the transition from a home language class at intermediate level to a senior level class in which most instruction is in Swedish" (p. 20). According to the summary of teacher answers, "the majority regard the home language class (i.e. language shelter, my remark) as the best way of encouraging bilingualism" (p. 26). Many of the factors I have summarized in a table earlier (for instance in Toukomaa & Skutnabb-Kangas, 1977: 37) seem to be repeated often in teacher answers. It is clear that many of the conditions necessary for successful teaching in L2 are not present for minority children in submersion programmes, while they are there in both immersion and language shelter programmes. [8]

TABLE 6

Immersion	Submersion	Maintenance
Additive bilingualism	Subtractive bilingualism	Functional bilingualism
Teaching through the medium of L2	Teaching through the medium of L2	Teaching through the medium of L1
Linguistic majority	Linguistic minority	Linguistic minority
High status mother tongue	Low status mother tongue	Teaching through the medium of L1 gives it status
Often middle-class parents	Working-class parents	Working-class parents
Voluntary programmes, strong motivation	No alternatives, weak motivation	Voluntary programmes, strong motivation
L2 not a threat to children's L1	L2 a threat to children's L1	L2 not a threat to children's L1
Bilingual teachers who speak L2 only in class but who understand L1	Monolingual teachers (L2) who do not understand the children's L1	Bilingual teachers who speak only L1 in class but who understand L2
Children monolingual in L1 at the beginning	Both L1 and L2 children mixed	Children monolingual (or dominant) in L1 at the beginning
Progress in L2 compared only with progress of other L1 speakers	Progress in L2 compared with progress of native L2 speakers in the same class	Progress in L2 compared only with progress of other L1 speakers
No auxiliary teaching in L2	Compensatory auxiliary teaching of L2	No auxiliary teaching of L2, but ordinary second language teaching of L2 for the whole class
No one stigmatized for inadequate knowledge of L2	L1 children are separated and stigmatized for inadequate knowledge of L2	No one stigmatized for inadequate knowledge of L2
Parents active, often initiators of the programme	Parents are made passive, language difficulties, often opposed to the programme	Parents active, often initiators of the programme
Children need not feel ashamed of L1	Children often ashamed of L1, do not want to learn it	Children are not ashamed of their L1, they want to learn it
High teacher expectations	Low teacher expectations	High teacher expectations
Healthy self-confidence, sense of security, self-assertion, positive self-image	Low self-confidence, sense of insecurity, lack of self-assertion, negative self-image	Healthy self-confidence, sense of security, self-assertion, positive self-image
Positive bilingual, bicultural identity	Conflicts of identity, rootlessness, marginality, alienation	Positive bilingual, bicultural identity

Notes to Chapter Seven

1. It would, of course, be possible hypothetically to propose a comparison between a bilingual child learning two languages with some of the smallest phonemic inventories in the world and a monolingual child learning a language with one of the largest phonemic inventories: in this case the monolingual child would actually have to learn more phonemes than the bilingual.

2. For example, Leopold, Elwert, 1960; Geissler, 1938; Imedadze, 1960; Rūķe-Draviņa, 1967.

3. The reader interested in further detail may go further and choose (and the titles will often indicate the kind of investigation involved): Lambert & Tucker, 1972; Swain, 1974, 1976a, 1976b; Swain & Bruck, 1976; Swain & Burnaby, 1976; Swain, Lapkin & Barik, 1976; Sweet, 1974; Stanley, 1974; Wilton, 1974; Hildebrand, 1974; Genesee, 1976; Edwards & Smyth, 1976; Spilka, 1976; Cohen, 1975, 1976; Maurice & Roy, 1976; Tucker, 1976; Tucker, Hamayan & Genesee, 1976; Tucker, Lambert & d'Anglejan, 1973; Gulutsan, 1976; Harley, 1976; Edwards, 1976; McInnis, 1976; Halpern, 1976; Trites & Price, 1976; Stern, 1976; Paulston, 1975b, 1976, 1977b.

4. See Tucker, Lambert & d'Anglejan, 1973; Bruck, Tucker & Jakimik, 1977; Cziko, 1975; Genesee, 1976; Bruck, Rabinovich & Oates, 1973; Trites & Price, 1976.

5. There is an interesting piece of information here: the kindergarten continued even after the children involved in the project had left it (in 1976), but without any of the Swedish instruction. ... Löfgren & Ouvinen-Birgerstam, 1980: 35.

6. Examples: DPI listening comprehension in *Swedish,* where the raw scores for children in Finnish classes was 40.2 and 43.4, thus an increase of 3.2 scores in one term; and for children in Swedish classes 46.3 and 47.4, an increase of 1.1 score. Tasola's word/picture association test in *Finnish*: 29.7 and 33.0, with an increase of 3.3 for the children in the Finnish classes; and 27.7 and 29.9, with an increase of 2.2 for children in the Swedish classes (Arwidsson, 1977: 75–77).

7. We can start with the two bibliographies edited by David Schwarz: Invandrar- och minoritetsforskning. En bibliografi 1973 and Invandrar- och minoritetsfrågor. Nordisk bibliografi, 1976. Then there are the various publications issued by Immigrantinstitutet: Elisabeth Engström & Ann-Margreth Millesten, Tvåspråkighet och invandrarbarn i för- och grundskola. En kommenterad urvalsbibliografi, 1977; Lena Böök-Cederström, Kristina Eriksson & Kerstin Fredriksson, Invandrare i Sverige, 1965–74. En bibliografi, 1977. For Finland, see Olavi Koivukangas & Simo Toivonen, Suomen siirtolaisuuden ja maas-samuuton bibliografia. A Bibliography on Finnish Emigration and Internal Migration, 1978; and Krister Björklund, Förteckning över litteratur rörande finlandssvenska samhällsfrågor, 1966–79.

EIFO has also published a bibliography edited by Tomas Hammar and Kerstin Lindby: Swedish Immigration Research. Introductory Survey and Annotated Bibliography, 1979. Now and then small bibliographies are published in Norway, most recently Oversikt over migrasjonsforskning i Norge. Nylig avluttede, igangvaerende og planlagte prosjekter, a bibliography circulated at the 5th Nordic Conference on Migration Research in Oslo (see Ringen, 1980) and Migration Research in Norway (see Backer *et al.*, 1981). For Denmark, more general bibliographies should be consulted: Danmarks Paedagogiske Bibliotek: Fremmesprogspaedagogik, Katalog over bibliotekets litteratur 1980, or the unofficial list of literature about immigrants to Denmark, available in a duplicated typescript, or the new bibliography from Mellemfolkeligt Samvirkes Dokumentation om indvandrere, by Helle Leth-Møller and Lone Pontoppidan.

8. While this book was in press, several new descriptions of children in bilingual families came out:

KIELHÖFER, BERND & JONEKEIT, SYLVIE, 1983, Zweisprachige Kindererziehung, Stauffenberg Verlag, Tübingen.

TAESCHNER, TRAUTE, 1983, The Sun is Feminine.
A study on language acquisition in Bilingual children. *Springer series in Language and Communication* 13, Springer-Verlag, Berlin.

PORSCHÉ, DONALD C., 1983, Die Zweisprachigkeit während des primären Spracherwärbs mit einer Zusammenfassung in englischer Sprache, Gunter Narr Verlag, Tübingen.

8 How is bilingualism measured?

8.1 Why should it be necessary to measure bilingualism?

Even though it will already have emerged several times that I consider attempts to describe bilingualism and bilingual individuals to be more useful than attempts at measuring, and even though I believe that we are not yet able to describe bilingualism in individuals securely enough to be able to base any principle of measurement on sound foundations, I propose nevertheless to describe in this chapter the kinds of measurement that have been attempted. Let me emphasize very strongly, however, that simple measurement in isolation may do more harm than good, and that measurement will always do some violence to the subtle texture of reality.

Just like definitions of bilingualism, measurement can assess features and abilities in individuals or communities. In the case of communities, a measurement can be to count how many individuals are bilingual and to what extent (and in estimating that, individual measurement will be necessary), or to what extent communities function in several languages. Many demographers and political scientists have published detailed discussions relating to the description and measurement of bilingual communities (see e.g. McRae – references in the bibliography). I shall not concern myself here with the measurement of community bilingualism but only of individual bilingualism.

There are many reasons other than research reasons for measuring the bilingualism of individuals. It is important, for instance, to know who is *sufficiently monolingual, that is, little enough bilingual, to need or to be entitled to some degree of language service.* This applies to the placing of minority children in schools, the right to the services of an interpreter, the right to language teaching, the right to demand service in one's mother tongue, and so on. It is also important to know who is *sufficiently bilingual to qualify* for positions where bilingualism is expected (or a good knowledge of a language other than the mother tongue). This may apply to a number of occupational demands: to be able to function as a teacher, interpreter, translator, diplomat, holder of scholarships abroad, student, immigrant adviser, civil servant in a bilingual country (or in a monolingual country that uses a language other than the applicant's mother tongue) or region or office.

When the degree of bilingualism is measured for such purposes as these (to determine, that is, whether or not a person is sufficiently bilingual or monolingual for something), all that is usually produced is a single measurement. But we need also to be able to measure the degree of bilingualism repeatedly over a period of time if the aim of the measurement is to *determine what changes occur as the result of deliberate attempts to influence the situation.* The most common situation will, of course, be the attempt to make an individual bilingual or more bilingual by a process of education and teaching. In such a case, the individual's *degree of bilingualism* (in most cases only the knowledge of the more foreign of the languages) *before, during and after* the process of instruction is measured. And measurement of this kind happens in foreign language teaching in schools or language courses.

8.2 Different ways of classifying the measurements

Linguistic behaviour is to a high degree unconscious, beyond conscious control of detail. No comparison has been made between the degree of conscious control exercised by monolinguals switching between different social or regional variants, and bilinguals switching between two different languages. But just as switching between two languages is easier to observe than switching between varieties of one language, so it seems natural to assume that bilinguals themselves are perhaps more conscious of their linguistic behaviour than monolinguals. The reports by monolingual individuals as to the linguistic norms they observe and their language use show a very weak correlation with the ways in which they actually in practice use their language (see, for example, Blom & Gumperz, 1972; Labov, 1966, 1972). Individuals tend to think they are reporting their linguistic usage when they are in fact reporting the linguistic norms they think they *ought* to observe in speech (Labov, 1972a; Thelander, 1974: 44, 68; Widmark, 1973: 20), without *consciously* distorting the evidence. Something like this can also be observed in diglossic communities, but on the whole we can assume that linguistic behaviour among bilinguals is more conscious than among monolinguals, *provided* there is no external pressure. The evidence available as to the greater metalinguistic awareness of some bilinguals (see references in the section on bilingualism and intelligence, 9.4.3) points in the same direction. This is why it is assumed that reports by bilinguals about their own linguistic behaviour can be used, with certain reservations, as a measure of their bilingualism.

In what follows I have chosen to separate the different sorts of measurement of bilingualism into *reported* and *observed* linguistic behaviour. I classify as reported behaviour all information provided by a bilingual speaker herself, either in questionnaire or interview form, as to linguistic use and knowledge: this will consist of various kinds of *background data*, of *self-assessment*, and of *the results of measurements of attitudes*. Among the background data, of course, is the relevant demographic information, which the researcher need not obtain directly from the informant, but which at one time or another the informant has supplied to the authorities or to other researchers. I classify as observed behaviour information gathered from observation of the informant and her linguistic performance. The period of observation may be a short one, as for example during an interview (when it is possible to make some assessment of the linguistic performance of the individual being interviewed), or it may be a long one, for example participant observation where the researcher seeks confirmation of reported linguistic behaviour. The most important form of observed linguistic behaviour consists of different kinds of language test.

The tests used in the measurement of bilingual linguistic proficiency are of two kinds: 1. tests which are also used for measuring the *linguistic proficiency of monolinguals*, and which use the monolingual as a norm. Such tests measure the bilingual individual's proficiency in her two languages separately; and 2. tests which are used only to measure *a bilingual proficiency*. Such tests measure the bilingual's two languages in relation to each other.

8.3   Reported linguistic behaviour

8.3.1   Background data

Information about when, where and to whom the bilingual speaks each of two languages is usually collected by means of interviews or questionnaires about background data.

The first carefully constructed questionnaire focusing on the linguistic background of bilinguals, the Hoffman Bilingual Schedule, was published as early as 1934. For decades it was the model for similar questionnaires aimed at collecting background data, and it is still used (for example by Zirkel, 1972: 70). Hoffman's well-tested questionnaire contained questions about the spoken language, about reading and writing, about the informant's own active language use ("which language do you speak to your mother?"), about the language of the rest of the family ("which language does your father speak to your mother?"), and about activities outside the home ("how often do you listen to talks given in L1?"). Hoffman weighted all these questions equally, and his measure of bilingualism (bilingual score) is the average of the points scored. More recent research has been critical of this kind of questionnaire in some respects. Einar Haugen believes that a more *detailed* differentiation would provide a more reliable picture of the background variables. Haugen would prefer to construct a bilingual profile, or use more precisely limited and defined measurements, each of which would describe *one* aspect of the complex of background factors (1964: 15). Macnamara divides the background questions into five categories, relating to the language use of the different speakers (informant herself, father, mother, siblings and the environment). According to Macnamara, nothing of the reliability is lost if all five categories are combined into a single evaluation of the background factors (Macnamara, 1969: 85–86). A serious criticism levelled against this sort of questionnaire is that it combines such different kinds of information without any proper weighing of the relative importance, attributing equal importance to data which, in my view, are non-comparable. Factors which have been given equal weight (where I think they should not) are for example length of residence, whether or not the mother works outside home, whether or not the child speaks L2 with friends, whether or not the child listens to talks in L2. Very important factors affecting the parents' knowledge of L2, like sex, education and age at the time of migration are not discussed at all, for instance, in Hoffman's scale (see Municio & Meisaari-Polsa, 1980, describing how these factors differentially affect the knowledge of Swedish among Finns, Poles, Turks and Yugoslavs in Sweden).

We can also criticize the failure to make any adequate distinction between *knowledge* of L2 (or L1) and the actual *use* of it, to distinguish between competence and performance. Such a distinction is not brought out sufficiently clearly if we only ask which language the informant speaks to the father without asking an additional question about how well the father speaks this language. Parents may for reasons of prestige and for other reasons choose to speak to their children in a language they do not speak particularly well, in order to help their children to learn it (Jaakkola, 1973a). In Sweden it still happens that teachers tell immigrant parents to speak Swedish to their children, even if their Swedish should be very poor and thus provide a very poor model for their children (Häkkinen, 1974; Jauho & Loikkanen, 1974: 63). And even academic researchers have been known to give such advice! Macnamara gives an example of social pressure to exaggerate the use of L1: the Irish government used to pay £10 per year per child to the parents of children who spoke Irish at home. The temptation in this case to say one did when one did not speak Irish at home must have been great (Macnamara, 1969: 86). The opposite case is also found, for instance in the Finnish-speaking districts of the Torneå Valley in Sweden:[1] speakers report that they speak L1 less and L2 more at home than is really the case, or they may entirely suppress the fact that they use L1, or feel offended at the suggestion that they speak the majority language of the district (Hansegård, 1972; Loman, 1974a). The status of a language, the attitudes to its speakers, the official attitude, and so on, all greatly affect the reliability of background data. However, in many investigations the background data do show a fairly strong correlation with other measurements of bilingualism (see, for example, Arsenian, 1937: Pintner & Arsenian, 1937; Kolasa, 1954; James, 1947; Sahlman-Karlsson, 1974). If the above caveats are borne in mind as to the possible sources of error, background data can be used as one kind of measurement of bilingualism. The collection of background data is the easiest way of acquiring information about the *use* of languages. A more reliable way would be a lengthy period of participant observation but few linguists will have the opportunity for this unless the informant is a member of their own (extended) family.

Other common kinds of measurement of bilingualism, by self-assessment or linguistic tests, do not usually measure language use but linguistic proficiency, competence.

8.3.2   Self-assessment

In self-assessment an informant is asked to assess her own knowledge (or use) of L2 or of both languages. One may ask for a fairly *well-differentiated assessment* (see the examples below) or be content with an *overall judgement*. One may distinguish between *primary* and *secondary skills*, or between *receptive* and *productive skills*. *Each* language may be treated *separately* or questions may relate only to the more foreign of the two. The *languages* can be investigated *in relation to each other*, i.e. questions can be asked about the degree of bilingualism. Here particular scales may be used which start from the notion of a *balance effect* (they may be scales based on the assumption that a speaker knows one of two languages better and therefore the other one less well, or scales which accept the answer "both equally well" as unproblematical, that is, as evidence of the fact that knowing both languages *equally well* means knowing both of them well). Or scales may be used which make no *assumptions about the balance between the languages* in advance, so that all possible combinations are taken into account, even the possibility that the speaker may know both badly.

Self-assessment seems to be a fairly reliable way of measuring bilingualism.[2] In the investigation carried out by Invandrarutredningen (the Swedish Immigrant Survey), in which self-assessment was compared with observed behaviour (the judgement made by the interviewer), the two kinds of measurement were found to differ only in minor ways. "Only in the case of the extreme values on the scale was there a certain discrepancy: interviewers used extreme values more often than interviewees, who tended to prefer the intermediate values" – thus the result is summarized by Municio & Meisaari-Polsa (1980: 18–19).

We should, however, be aware of certain reservations about the reliability of self-assessment, as about the reliability of background data. If one of the languages enjoys much higher prestige, informants tend to exaggerate their knowledge of it, and to minimize or completely suppress their knowledge of the less prestigious language (for examples of this, see Hansegård, 1972: 111; Jaakkola, 1973a, and section 8.3.1). Self-assessment tends to be more realistic if both languages enjoy more or less equal status, if a proficiency in one or the other of the two languages does not lead to positive or negative sanctions, i.e. if the sociolinguistic climate is relaxed. The amount of contact with L2 also influences the assessment so that a speaker who is frequently in a position to hear and speak L2 will have a more realistic notion of her ability than another speaker who more rarely uses L2. It is easier for a Finland Swede to over-estimate her knowledge of Finnish if she lives in Pargas/Parainen (where about two-thirds of the population report themselves as Swedish-speaking) and only rarely comes into contact with Finnish speakers, than if she lives in Kokkola/Gamlakarleby (where less than one-fifth of the population is Swedish-speaking) and uses Finnish daily at work (Sandlund, 1970, 1972). Swedish speakers' assessment of their knowledge of Finnish is more reliable in Finland than Finnish speakers' assessment of their knowledge of Swedish (Lindman & Alho, 1971), because the Swedish speakers probably more often come into contact with their L2, Finnish, than do the Finnish speakers with *their* L2, Swedish. In the case of children of school age, it has proved that their grade at school in the language in question affects their self-assessment (Macnamara, 1969: 86), and this has to be taken into account when the results are interpreted.

The expectation an individual herself or others have of her knowledge of L2 may also vary. There may be lower expectations as to someone's knowledge of a language if the individual lives in a country or a locality where there are fewer opportunities of using the language in question. A speaker may also come to expect more of herself without being aware of it if she is faced with a subtler and more varied range of the language than before. A speaker may thus think less of her grasp of a language at a later date than she did earlier, even though, objectively speaking, she has learnt more of it in the intervening period, because during that time she may have faced novel situations which revealed that her linguistic grasp was inadequate in some areas.

Friendly native speakers, who with a beginner in their language may be very understanding and loud in their praise, expect more as the stranger comes to be more integrated, and they may occasionally be irritated when even after a couple of years the foreign speaker still does not understand everything or finds it difficult to express herself in writing. Language difficulties may also at the beginning be used as an excuse, but after a while it becomes less easy for native speakers to identify as language difficulties what they take to be simple stupidity, ignorance, defective logic, or an inability to think out properly formulated sentences. And this will, of course, also affect the bilingual speaker's own estimate of her linguistic ability. The discrepancy in children between pronunciation (which may be absolutely accurate) and the rest of their proficiency in the language can be just as confusing (see sections 5.2.2.5 and 7.3.5.2). Surface fluency affects children's self-assessment to a very high degree, even leading them to insist that they do not need help with L2 at school. However, it is more usually the case that immigrant children, or at any rate slightly older immigrant youngsters assess their knowledge of L2 as being rather worse than their teachers do: the pupils say that they have language problems whereas the teachers will say that they speak Swedish as well as the average Swedish child would. Even adults who speak with a good accent can in the same way lead native speakers to think that they know the language well, despite the fact that they may themselves say that they have difficulties. The discrepancy prevails above all between speaking and writing. If the speaker's self-assessment is based on both primary and secondary proficiency in L2 (where the former is good and the latter poor) and the observer bases the assessment on primary proficiency only, the correlation between the two is of course poor. This is more often true of speakers from oppressed minorities than from stationary indigenous minorities educated in their own language. An overall judgement should therefore not be used when assessing them, but primary and secondary proficiencies should be kept separate. The expectations that native speakers have of how well foreigners should command their language, also affect the non-native speaker's self-assessment and wish to try to speak the language. People who have been able to force other people to learn their language often have high expectations of foreigners (who often do not dare to try to speak the foreign language, because of negative experiences of the tolerance of the L2-speakers), while people whose languages are seldom learnt by foreigners often show foreigners good-will which is out of proportion to the foreigner's actual knowledge of the language – and this encourages them to learn more. All this also affects the self-assessment.

Many sociologists take the view that the conceptions informants themselves have of their knowledge of a language are more important as objects of study in sociological investigations than the actual state of their knowledge, since their assessment (both of their own linguistic knowledge and of their interlocutors') is decisive for their choice of language and their linguistic behaviour in general (Pipping, 1969: 217; Sandlund, 1970: 10; Broo, 1974: 6).

8.3.3   Measurement or description?

Where background data and self-assessment are used in *descriptions* and not in *measurements* of bilingualism, different kinds of information are often collected which throw light on the choice and use of language by informants in various situations. Good surveys of the variables that might form part of such a description have been made by William F. Mackey (1970) and Joan Rubin (1970: 525–27). In Rubin's questionnaire the components are organized hierarchically so that later alternatives are determined by earlier choices. In many models the factors affecting language choice are separated into cognitive, affective and action components. When background data and self-assessment are used for the *measurement* of bilingualism rather than for its description or for producing a bilingual profile (Haugen, 1964: 95; Mackey, 1970), the variables have to be very much restricted in number, so that one single measurement can be produced. Just as with the construction of a social index, so with an *index of bilingualism*, it is the most decisive variables which must be focused upon so that they can then be combined into one index. And in both cases the choice of variables is crucial, and will at the same time also be a measurement of the researcher's ideological and political priorities.

Some researchers collect information about only one of the languages in measuring bilingualism, others about both. If we assume that an informant always has at least *one* complete language, L1, then whether or not we believe that complete bilingualism exists, we can be contented to collect information about L2 only. If, on the other hand, we suspect that *both* languages may be more or less incomplete, then we should preferably have information (and especially test results) relating to both languages. An index of bilingualism based on one language can only be used if there are other types of evidence that the informant has a "complete" command of the other language (the language not measured in the index), or at least of those aspects of it which the index measures.

8.3.4   Attitudes

8.3.4.1 Limitations

In studying attitudes towards different languages, we can focus upon monolingual speakers' attitudes to foreign languages as well as upon bilingual speakers' attitudes to their two languages. *Attitudes towards languages* are very often, if not always, impossible to separate completely from *attitudes towards speakers of those languages*. To try to do it is in part artificially to wrench language away from its use. But again, studying attitudes towards language *users* is the topic of other books, books about prejudice, discrimination and racism at the individual level, leading to studies about power relationships and racism at structural and institutional levels which are important prerequisites for understanding language questions. But here I have to limit myself to attitudes of individuals not groups, towards languages not language users.

Many studies have been made of the attitudes of monolingual speakers (i.e. majority speakers – minority speakers are mostly bilingual) towards foreign *languages* in the attempt to discover what kinds of attitude lead to the best results in foreign language learning.

Most of the investigations which concern themselves with the attitudes of monolingual speakers towards *users of various languages* elucidate these attitudes by asking questions simply about attitudes towards *various languages*. Such studies try to map out the contours of prejudice, racism, ethnocentrism, and so on. Studies of this kind are still relatively rare in Scandinavia.[3]

8.3.4.2 Instrumental and integrative attitudes

The Canadian psychologist Wallace E. Lambert, studying the role of attitude and motivation in L2 learning, especially (but not only) in bilingual environments where the groups come in contact with each other, has distinguished between what he calls instrumental and integrative motivations. An *instrumental* orientation emphasizes the utilitarian aspects, an *integrative* the desire to learn (and capability of learning) to know the other linguistic group and perhaps to a certain extent to identify with it, become a member of it (Lambert, Gardner, Olton & Tunstall, 1970: 473–74). The inegrative motivation seems to be more durable in the long drawn out labour of L2 learning, when intelligence and language aptitude are kept constant (Gardner & Lambert, 1972: 193–94).

In what follows we will discuss some of the attitudinal factors which create good relationships between minority and majority students. The first question is whether or not contact with the speakers of L2 and knowledge of L2 create a more favourable attitude towards it and its speakers. Results are here divided. Gardner & Lambert show that students doing well had parents with positive *attitudes* towards other language groups, but their attitudes did not correlate with their *knowledge* of other languages or their *contacts* across the linguistic border. Arne Trankell (1974: 158–62) indicates the exact opposite, showing a connection between contacts with foreigners and positive attitudes (more generous, less fearful and less discriminatory) towards immigrants. Mirko Takač (1978) again points to very negative attitudes among Swedish-speakers towards immigrants (but less *vice-versa*) in school districts with a great deal of contact. Lambert also discusses the direction of the correlation and assumes that the positive attitude in students which gives rise to an integrative motivation is primary and results in a good command of L2, but he cannot exclude the opposite possibility: that an individual who knows an L2 well will also develop a positive attitude towards its speakers.

It seems that part of the answer lies in the *type of contacts* one has – the amount does not seem to be decisive. In a Canadian experiment English speakers who had learnt French at school were asked to communicate with what they thought were invisible French and English speakers (in reality tape recordings made beforehand) who both launched into informal discussion and also invited a more formal style of response much like the one the informants had learnt at school during French lessons. The informants were asked to judge both the French and English speaker with regard to various characteristics in both the formal and the informal situation, and to say what kind of impression they thought they themselves had made on the partner. They felt more ill at ease themselves, thought that they had seemed more unfriendly, less intelligent and less self-confident, and gave the partner more unfavourable traits of character in the *informal* discussion in French, while they thought positively of both themselves and the partner in the informal discussion in English (Segalowitz, 1976; reported in Segalowitz & Gatbonton, 1977). If the learner of L2 with an integrative attitude tries to come into contact (or is forced into contact, like many minority children, regardless of their attitude) with speakers of L2 before she has a *good* command of the style of informal speech, she may find the experience off-putting and may be discouraged from further attempt at contact. If a minority child in Scandinavia who has just begun to learn the most basic school vocabulary in L2 is placed in a situation where she is forced to communicate informally with Swedish/Norwegian/Danish children, all the negative and defensive psychological mechanisms may swing into operation. The child will feel stupid and helpless, will attribute to the native speaker a lot of negative characteristics, and will experience such a sensation of unease as is likely to influence her response for long afterwards, no matter how encouraging teachers, peers and other partners are. It would often seem better, then, to delay informal contacts until the child has reached the stage of being able to cope with them linguistically as well without any damage to the self-confidence – this is a further argument for not being in too much of a hurry to integrate immigrant children with children who are majority speakers.

Two pedagogical implications seem to follow from a number of studies. It should be clear that negative attitudes and racism cannot be informed away – they spring from economic and political causes, and these basic causes are reflected for instance in majority speakers' negative attitudes towards minority languages and speakers. If one wants, nevertheless, to try to do something at the individual level, contacts between majority and minority speakers should be organized so that both (but especially the one who has to function in an L2) can feel secure and self-confident in a natural way, i.e. be in a position where it is possible to do justice to the knowledge and skills that each brings with her. Again, forcing minority children into situations where they are made to feel incompetent, both linguistically, socially and in terms of content, in majority medium classes, does not seem to be conducive to fostering positive integrative attitudes in minority *or* majority children. With the differences between prerequisites and results among different children trying to become bilingual in mind (discussed in section 4.2) we could also predict that majority students learning a minority language as their L2 (for instance English children or adults in Britain learning Gujerati) should be able to tolerate more situations where they feel incompetent in Gujerati, than minority students learning a majority language as their L2 (Gujerati children in Britain learning English), because the whole endeavour is a game for the former and bitter reality for the latter.

When studying a bilingual's attitude towards her two languages it is important to distinguish between a majority group bilingual with a clearly dominant mother tongue and a much less good command of L2 (who can be studied much in the same way as a monolingual learning an L2), and either one with approximately equal command of both, or a minority bilingual. The decisive factor seems to be whether or not we can assume that the speaker has a positive or "neutral" attitude towards L2 (whether it is an enrichment, much like a game, where it is not connected with a central value in the speaker's life). If L1 is a minority language with low status, then a negative attitude towards L2 may be felt by the speaker as defending and preserving her language and identity.

The distinction between instrumental and integrative motivation is particularly useful in situations where a distinctly non-integrative attitude to L2 is judged to make for this preservation of the identity or even the existence of a minority group. Here one might nevertheless expect a strong, instrumentally orientated motivation to learn L2 since the minority speaker needs the majority language as an instrument.

The difference between minority and majority group informants (whether monolingual or bilingual) has not always been sufficiently taken into consideration when results have been interpreted. In Gatbonton (1975; as reported in Segalowitz & Gatbonton, 1977) Francophones hearing French Canadian voices reading English, ascribed pro-Anglophone attitudes to the speakers on the basis of a native or near-native English accent, while voices with a more marked Francophone accent were ascribed pro-Francophone attitudes (which did not show any correlation with the real attitudes of the voices). The more "nationalistically" minded informants chose the most fluent sounding speakers only for positions with connections with Anglophones (i.e. purely instrumentally) while the least "nationalistic" subjects tended to choose the voices with the most native-sounding English accents for all leadership roles, regardless of the amount of contact the roles implied with Anglophones. The existence of a certain sociolinguistic pressure is revealed in the study: a minority speaker whose accent in the majority language is "too" genuine might be chosen for roles where the command of L2 is instrumental, but her loyalty to her own group may also be questioned by the group because of the accent. Another study with the same type of experimental design (but with both Francophone and Anglophone voices, with different degrees of accent in their L2) by Genesee & Holobow (1978) had both bilingual (immersion) and monolingual Anglophone children as informants. There are many interesting details in this well-controlled study, but the interesting thing from the point of view of the discussion here is that Genesee & Holobow, who in many respects record results that contradict those of Gatbonton & Segalowitz, do *not* interpret them as a difference between minority and majority group informants, which to me is the natural interpretation. The majority group, whether bilingual or monolingual, has no reason for feeling linguistically threatened by the minority. It needs to have recourse to no boundary-preserving mechanisms, and an integrative attitude, a desire to identify with the minority group, is not for it in opposition to a desire to identify at the same time with its own majority group. There would be very little risk that positive attitudes towards Francophones and the desire to mix with them socially would lead an Anglophone to abandon her English for French. Nor is there any risk in Canada that the Anglophone population *as a group* might be absorbed into the Francophone group, and cease to exist as an independent entity. Thus for the majority group there is no risk entailed in combining positive attitudes towards *both* linguistic groups. For a minority, on the other hand, such attitudes may objectively bring with them the risk of the dissolution of the minority group because of the relative strength of the majority group.

We also need to discuss to what extent it is *language* and to what extent other factors that influence attitudes. Language functions as a symbol of group membership. Usually a number of other features are associated with that linguistic symbol, even where, to judge from outward appearances, the language difference seems to be the only one separating two groups (as with Finland Swedes and Finnish-speaking Finns). Other associated features are, of course, particularly in evidence where the linguistic border coincides with other borders (ethnic, racial, economic, political, etc.). That language need not be the most important symbol informing attitudes towards other groups is clear from Allardt, Miemois & Starck's thorough study (1979) of the Finland Swedes (912 subjects from Metropolitan Helsinki). When asked which groups they most and least identified with, only 7% of them gave Swedes from Sweden (speaking the same language) as the group most identified with, whereas Finnish-speaking Finns from Helsinki were by far the group most often identified with (28%) – and 34% gave Swedes from Sweden as the group they had the weakest feeling of affinity with (whereas Swedish-speaking Finns from other regions in Finland and Finnish-speaking Finns from the area around Helsinki occupied intermediate positions on the scale). Eric Allardt's interpretation of the answers stresses the *existence of multiple identities,* that an individual feels she belongs to several different groups (without feeling that there need be any kind of conflict between them). He stresses similarly the great *importance of local and regional ties*: an individual feels greater affinity with others *from the same country who speak a different language* than with individuals *from a different country who speak the same language,* to give the two extreme examples.

The same tendency for language as a factor to lose its importance in circumstances where the language question is not felt to be very problematical (as it *could* be if the official status of the two languages were highly unequal) is also clear from other investigations. One of them

(Sandlund, 1971), carried out by Ulf Berg, investigated which conflicts 454 Finland Swedes regarded as the most serious in Finland (conflicts between language groups, urban and rural dwellers, social classes, employers and employees, the last two classified together in the analysis as class conflicts). They were also asked whether they thought that the language conflict was going to grow or diminish in the future. The results indicated that those in more homogeneous Swedish-speaking areas, with a less secure grasp of Finnish, and from the lower social classes tended to emphasize the language conflict and be pessimistic (quite understandably because it is more difficult for them to get work in Finnish-speaking areas because of language if they become unemployed, one reason for Finland Swedes being over-represented among immigrants from Finland to Sweden), while those from bilingual areas or closer to the capital tended to emphasize the class conflict and think that conflict between the language groups was bound to diminish. Bilingualism may thus lead to a lessening of the importance of the language factor itself, provided that the standing of the two languages is similar (as it is in Finland), and one can afford to emphasize other solidarities and conflicts. This represents a more instrumental and relaxed attitude to the languages in question and can be found in situations where the need for boundary-preserving mechanisms is no longer so great and where there is a possibility of attaining some type of instrumental integration (or structural incorporation) into the majority. It need *not* imply any less of an ethnic awareness, as Allardt points out – it merely lessens the risk of serious conflict (Allardt, Miemois & Starck, 1979: 22). A good way to avoid conflict and assist integration in multilingual schools would thus also be to make the status of the minority languages as high as possible, so as to equalize them with the majority language – that is bound to give a basis for positive attitudes in *both* minority and majority students.

8.4   Observed linguistic behaviour

8.4.1   Limitations

Much of the information that can be obtained by collecting background data, reported by a bilingual informant, can also be obtained or confirmed by observation, systematic or unsystematic. The most important way of getting a measurement of bilingualism by "objective" observation, however, consists in the measurements of proficiency by means of *tests*.

The usefulness of language tests depends completely upon what one tries to measure with them, and the purpose for which the results are required. Many linguists still doubt that we know enough about language, language learning, and linguistic proficiency to be able to construct adequate, varied, objective linguistic tests (see, for example, Gumperz,

1972: 204). The value of measurement as such is questioned by some researchers, especially if measurement, the collection of "hard evidence", is not combined with other, more descriptive kinds of observation: "soft evidence". In spite of all my reservations about the use of tests in an area about which we know too little to allow any great confidence on our part that they can be made reliable, they merit some discussion here. For more comprehensive kinds of discussion see, for instance, Oller, 1979.

I have already above classified tests used to measure the linguistic proficiency of bilinguals into those which are (or can be) also used for monolinguals and which take monolingual proficiency as the norm, and those which are designed solely for the purpose of measuring bilingual proficiency. Certain tests which fall into the first category may, as an unintended side-effect, also bring forth features which are particularly characteristic of the bilingual, for instance, interference. If, however, the purpose for which the test was designed is to measure something else, for instance certain syntactic constructions, and the measurement of interference was not part of the intention (test material could for instance be designed with the help of contrastive analysis so as to be likely to produce interference), then the test clearly falls into the first category. It is the purpose for which the test was designed (and the linguistic norm envisaged), not the results, which decide the category to which it belongs. It should be said that by the use of monolinguals as a norm, two quite different things may be meant (the two may sometimes be combined in the same test, but sometimes only one kind of use is involved):

■ In the first case, the linguistic proficiency aimed at, and which the subjects' knowledge of a language should approach and be comparable with, is the kind of proficiency that a native speaker of the target language possesses. The *native speaker of the target language* is assumed to be *monolingual*, and it is she who sets the norm for the person whose proficiency in the target language is being tested.

■ In the second case, the individual from whose language teaching and learning situation one starts is the monolingual speaker: she is in process of learning the target language as a school subject or in some other pedagogic situation, and is thus being subjected to a conscious process of instruction; she is not learning the language in "natural" circumstances. There is no attempt made to focus upon the kind of circumstances in which a "natural" bilingual would have acquired L2, and to test a language most probably to be acquired in those circumstances. Rather what is being tested is the pedagogically presented *knowledge* about the language that teachers have *tried to impart* quite consciously, by ordinary instruction. Here the *subject being tested* is *monolingual*; and the norm for proficiency in the target language is the kind of command a monolingual speaker might expect to have of a foreign language.

When tests of the first kind are used, one wants to compare the bilingual's linguistic proficiency with that of a monolingual. The implicit assumption is thus, that a bilingual can achieve an equal command of one or both languages to that of a monolingual. One is interested in measuring everything the bilingual has *in common* with the monolingual. With tests of the latter kind one is more interested in measuring the *differences* between the monolingual and the bilingual. One is looking for those specific features which are *characteristic of a bilingual* (as opposed to monolingual) *language proficiency,* and that is our main interest here.

8.4.2   Tests which use the monolingual as the norm

Tests of this kind have mainly evolved in three different sorts of context:

1. There are *pedagogically* orientated tests, which measure the prerequisites for participation in a language teaching programme (initial behaviour), or the results of the teaching of a foreign language or the mother tongue (terminal behaviour at the completion of the programme); often these tests start language teaching. In a number of countries tests have been developed for placing purposes. They determine, that is, whether a student is monolingual or bilingual enough to benefit from a certain kind of teaching (see, for example, the discussion and the references in Cummins, 1980b and in Dulay & Burt, 1980). The L1 of the learner is in most cases left out of account completely.

2. There are *linguistically* orientated tests, which earlier often measured simply grammatical competence, as defined by intra-lingual structural criteria.

3. There are *psychologically* orientated tests, which are based on investigations of the verbal factors of intelligence, and which are constructed with the cognitive and sometimes affective processes in mind that are manifested in linguistic behaviour.

Since my intention here is not to discuss the ordinary test *construction* at all, I shall confine myself to a consideration of such aspects of tests as tell us something about them as instruments for the measurement of bilingualism.

Many of the pedagogically orientated tests have been criticized for not being bas d on any linguistic theory, which could predict or explain the relation between the variables in the test. The variables to be measured have often been intuitively chosen, without reference to any theoretical model of linguistic proficiency (Wrede, 1971: 3); or they have been adopted because the grammar books use the corresponding categories, without any discussion as to whether these categories have any psycholinguistic relevance (Teleman, 1974). Linguists, too, are often guilty of this sort of procedure. Many tests constructed by linguists and psychologists are also used for pedagogical purposes.

The rapid progress in the last few years in both foreign language pedagogy and contrastive analysis, error analysis and especially interlanguage studies has led increasingly to a tendency to make use of the learner's own production as an own "norm", attempting to establish through which phases the learning develops. In interlanguage studies errors are not seen as negative but rather as necessary positive stages in the process in which the learner constructs her own grammar as it gradually approaches the monolingual norm. Deviations from the monolingual norm are interpreted as indicative of the learner's trying out different rules and strategies in making the best possible use of a limited competence and repertoire (see Færch, Haastrup & Phillipson, 1983; Færch & Kasper, 1982, 1983; Haastrup & Phillipson, 1983). So far it has been mainly the *attitude* (and not the actual test construction) that has changed (and more in the formative than the summative phase – see Bloom, Hastings & Madaus (eds) 1971, especially Cazden), but interlanguage studies have contributed towards improving the theoretical foundation on which pedagogically orientated tests could be based, and some easing of the norms which have been unfair to bilingual speakers. Partly this is because it is linguists, people who know something about *language* and *language* learning (and not educationalists, who know about language *learning* and (language) *teaching*) who have worked with interlanguage. Even *linguistically* orientated tests have hitherto often been constructed by educationalists, psychologists or teachers. Many linguists have had decidedly little interest in testing (partly because they do not as a rule learn anything about it in their studies).[4]

The criticism that is now beginning to be directed, particularly by sociolinguists, at linguistically orientated tests is that they do not take into account how language is used in natural situations, and that tests provide an unnatural social situation, and thus produce distorted results. This should not, of course, be taken to mean that tests involving language used in so-called natural situations are always to be preferred for all purposes to tests in which more formal aspects of linguistic and cognitive competence are measured (see Cummins, 1980b). Quite the opposite – often more formal, CALP-type tests may be more informative when minority children's L2-proficiency is assessed for placement purposes.

Psychologically orientated tests have above all tended to consist of verbal parts of intelligence tests and further developments of these. Here, too, attention has begun to be focused upon making the test situations more meaningful by presenting the subjects with real tasks and with people they really have to communicate with.[5]

Many of the new developments are at a description stage only, and there are very few attempts to quantify. A combination of developmental (cognitive, linguistic) and situational (psychological, social, pedagogical) aspects, with both qualitative, in-depth data based on a longitudinal approach, and more quantifiable cross-section data, seems to be the ideal, but we are still far from it, and many of the attempts made at, especially, quantifying have attracted severe criticism.[6] Forthcoming reports from the 5-year project on describing communicative competence at OISE (the

Ontario Institute for Studies in Education) Modern Language Center (Merrill Swain, Jim Cummins) will be of interest for the testing of bilinguals.

8.4.3   Tests which are used to measure bilingual linguistic proficiency

8.4.3.1 What types of test have been used?
The use of methods of measurement which test each of the bilingual's two languages separately, with monolingual proficiency as the norm, implies the two-code theory (5.2.1), as should be clear. The two-code theory is also clearly behind some of the methods of measurement used to try to isolate the characteristic features of bilingual competence. This reflects the negative attitudes: bilingualism thought of as something undesirable, as a transitional phase to be worked through as quickly as possible, almost as some kind of pathological linguistic condition. Attitudes like this were responsible for the description and enumeration of the characteristics of bilinguals as though they were the symptoms of a disease, a deviation from the healthy norm represented by monolingualism, deviations from two different norm systems. It has been said that the term "interference", for instance, carries with it this impression of bilingualism as something abnormal and unpleasing (Fishman, 1968: 29–30; Haugen, 1970: 1–12). As more and more sociolinguistic investigations made it plain that bilingualism is a permanent feature of many societies (Gumperz, 1964, 1967, 1969, 1971; Fishman, 1966, 1968, 1972c), theories about one single bilingual repertoire/one code developed. The adoption of such theories necessarily entails the development of special methods to measure the *bilingual code,* different from methods used to measure a monolingual code. Many different kinds of test have been used, and different researchers classify them in different ways (for a more detailed survey, see Skutnabb-Kangas 1975a). Linguists have often been particularly interested in measuring interference. Psychologists have developed different kinds of speed test and tests to measure automatic functions: how fluently a speaker speaks, how quickly she switches languages, how flexible she is, and to what extent one of the two languages dominates. Sociologists have examined to what degree and in what situations a bilingual speaker uses both languages. And educationalists have often been interested to measure the size of the repertoire in both languages. Some are trying to measure bilingual proficiency directly, some more indirectly.

        If we survey the development in the last few years of tests to measure bilingual proficiency, we find that in fact, for all this research interest, disappointingly little has happened. A number of attempts have been made to construct methods of measurement specifically for bilinguals (for example, Burt *et al.*, 1975), but these seem to represent little improvement on the older tests, and to reflect little in the way of any new theoretical thinking. Many of the new ideas are coming from interlanguage studies and from studies of testing in immersion programmes. In what follows I propose to discuss briefly some of the central notions that lie behind many of the tests and to draw attention to some difficulties in relation to them.

8.4.3.2 Dominance versus balance

The balance between the two languages has been used as a measurement of bilingualism, the assumption being that the more equal the balance between the languages the more bilingual the speaker is. We may doubt this for two reasons at least. Fishman has sharply criticized the use of balance between languages as a measure of bilingualism on the grounds that this defines balanced bilingualism as the ideal (Fishman, 1968: 25–26). In his view, bilingualism as a stabilized phenomenon can only exist where there is functional differentiation between the languages, diglossia. No society, he affirms, needs two languages for the same range of functions. He believes that a bilingual society produces exactly those kinds of bilingual whose one language is dominant in one area and whose other language is dominant in another. Such a society will *not* produce bilinguals whose languages are in balance. So a method of measurement with balance as the ideal is unrealistic. Moreover, balance as a measurement of bilingualism entails the assumption that a speaker whose languages are in balance commands both well. The possibility is ignored that a bilingual might have a poor command of both languages, speaking both equally badly rather than both equally well (see also sections 10.4–5 for a discussion of the quantitive aspects of double semi-lingualism).

The method used to measure dominance has also been criticized. In principle this involves subtracting the score for the language the informant knows less well from the score for the one she knows better. There may also be additional operations. In this way the attempt is made to eliminate that area of linguistic command which is common to both languages, the cognitive operations which function in the same way in the two languages. The validity of the hypothesis upon which this attempt is based may be questioned. The way the mediating operations function (see Osgood's model in section 5.2.2) is far from clear, even for monolinguals and even less so for bilinguals. We do not know whether it is the influence of the g-factor (g = general) or only the verbal factor that the dominance measurement tries to keep constant through the subtraction operation. It is very difficult as a consequence to say how relevant dominance or balance between the languages is as *measurement of bilingualism*. Finally we may also criticize the measurement of dominance on the grounds that the dominance in any case is largely determined by the *selection of content* used for the test, at any rate for natural bilinguals who will always show a degree of functional differentiation determined either by external circumstances (the opportunities for using the two languages) or by themselves (certain preferences more or less chosen by themselves). Before the dominance measurement can be used as a measurement of bilingualism, the bilingual's linguistic ability should be tested in a number of different domains to guarantee that the content of the test material is representative at least to a certain extent. As long as the dominance measurement uses material that takes no account of the domains in which a bilingual might be dominant in which language (and variations between speakers are likely to be so great that individual adjustment will have to be made for each speaker), the measurement of dominance that results will be largely a matter of chance.

8.4.3.3 Speed

The use of speed as a measurement of bilingualism (sometimes measuring the verbal speed of reaction in one of the languages only; sometimes as a measure of dominance, the difference in reaction speed between the two languages) has also been criticized. Speed has been chiefly used by psychologists (for example, Ervin-Tripp, Lambert), and criticized by sociologists (for example, Fishman). The tests used in the measurement of speed can be divided, for instance, into those that measure language comprehension and those that measure production. In order to know how quickly comprehension has occurred, the informant has to be asked to react in some way, so that it becomes clear that she has understood. Comprehension tests, and in particular production tests, have at times compared bilinguals' results with those of monolinguals, but it has often been a matter of determining the relative degree of bilingualism, i.e. of comparing the performance in each language (rather than using any external criterion), and thus obtaining a measurement of dominance. In fact, speed seems to be quite reliable as a measurement of dominance.[7] However, the general objection still applies, that dominance is an uncertain measure of the degree of bilingualism, especially if performance in the two languages is much the same. With production tests, we may also say that relative speed tests measure more the degree of functional differentiation than the degree of bilingualism – the results depend to a large extent on the area from which the test material is drawn.

Besides, there may be changes when children grow older: there may be a generalized speed factor in younger children, which becomes more specified in older children, so that different group factors may account for, for instance, speed in physical and motor tasks as opposed to speed in verbal tasks (see Wissler, 1901; Burt, 1973a). Eysenck also shows that speed manifests itself importantly in information processing, and not in simple experiments with speed of reaction (1973: 247–51).

Fishman regards speed as a very ethnocentric kind of measurement: if the culture in which the bilinguals live does not value speed highly, it is pointless to use speed as a measurement (Fishman, 1968: 24–25; Liungman, 1970: 159). In many cultures slow, thoughtful speech is valued highly, and the kind of verbal speed normally measured in these tests will relate hardly at all to language command. Many of the measurements seem to measure a quite primitive, often almost automatic speed of reaction. Other tests have measured, for example, how quickly informants are able to obey instructions in both languages, how many words they can remember correctly after seeing (or hearing) them for a limited period of time (or how long it takes them to learn the words by heart in the two languages), how many words they produce within a certain period of time in response to certain stimuli, and so on. Tests like this are often combined with dominance tests. The assumption has been that the more rapidly an individual can function in a language the better command she has of it, and that the language in which she reacts the more swiftly (or in which her production per unit of time is the greater) is the dominant language; a fairly primitive model. It is common for the reaction time of bilinguals to be slightly longer either in both or at least in one of their languages than that for the equivalent monolingual, and this is easy to understand, since the bilingual has more to choose between. This difference seems to apply above all to tests where the stimulus is ambiguous, in that it could belong to either language, or to tests in which the subject does not know in advance in which language the stimulus is going to be. The difference is less noticeable where the subject knows in advance which language is going to be involved. But, as Edith Mägiste says: "this delay is hardly a handicap if it is set in relation to the great gains a command of a new language confers. ... Tenths of seconds, which may be of decisive importance on the athletics field, are of no practical importance in most linguistic contexts" (Mägiste, 1979: 99).

8.4.3.4 Code switching, translation and interference as measures
Many researchers have used as one of the criteria for bilingualism the bilingual's ability to switch quickly or automatically between the two languages (see the definitions of bilingualism in section 4.3). This requirement may apply only to the primary proficiencies, so that one is able easily to *understand* discussions which alternate between two languages and is able oneself freely to switch from *speaking* the one to speaking the other when needed; the requirement may also be extended to the secondary proficiencies of reading and writing. The degree of interference ("instances of deviation from the norms of either language which occur in the speech of bilinguals as a result of their familiarity with more than one language, i.e. as a result of language contact" (Weinreich, 1967: 1) has also been used as a measurement of the degree of bilingualism, especially by linguists. The more interference, the less bilingual, in this view – absence of interference has even been required in definitions of bilingualism. I disagree profoundly with this view, which seems to be based on the rigid use of monolingualism as the norm, making bilingualism and bilinguals negatively deviant.

We can discuss code switching and translation as instruments for the measurement of bilingualism starting from the assumption that these skills are usually learnt and practised by bilinguals. If we accept this assumption, then code switching and the ability to translate are good measurements of the degree of bilingualism. We may also start from the assumption that these are special skills which are acquired by special training; if this is the case, then they might correlate only weakly with other measures of bilingualism, and the ability to switch codes and to translate would not be a reliable measurement of degree of bilingualism. Interference can be discussed likewise: is it bad command of L1 or L2 (or general sloppiness) that causes it (good measure) or is it used by most bilinguals in certain situations (then it would be a bad measure)?

It should be pointed out here that I will discuss code switching, translation and interference only from the point of view of how accurately they measure the degree of bilingualism. There is a huge general theoretical and empirical literature about them for the interested reader, both more purely linguistic and sociolinguistic (see for instance Clyne, Dittmar, Haugen, Hasselmo, Oksaar, Poplack, Sankoff, Vildomec, Weinreich in the bibliography, just to mention a few). Many of the case studies of bilingual children describe interference and code switching in detail, too. I will not discuss where the borderline is between interference and switching, neither structurally/situationally nor historically, nor the fact that the norms of bilingual speech communities are (and should be accepted as) different from the norms about interference (and what constitutes interference in *langue* and *parole*) in monolingual communities (although I have a section on that in the Swedish version of the book).

One of the main functional differences between interference and code switching on one hand, and translation or interpretation on the other hand is that the "same" content is reproduced in the latter but usually not in the former. Bilinguals who commonly use both their languages in speech must have considerable opportunities to practise code switching, except in those rare cases where the bilingual commutes between two wholly or nearly monolingual communities at fairly long intervals. If the community is bilingual, with or without diglossia or monolingual in one of the bilingual's languages and at the same time diglossic so that the bilingual's other language is used only in unofficial contexts (at home, with friends, etc.), then the bilingual must switch codes. How skilful at code switching a speaker becomes seems to a large extent to depend upon how widely separate from each other the situations are where the different languages are used, and upon how many bilingual situations and speakers the individual comes into contact with. Probably the most demanding situation is the one involving many bilingual and multilingual speakers as well as monolinguals, representing a variety of languages, and where a speaker must switch rapidly from one language to another as different individuals are spoken to, and where there are no clear rules as to which language is expected of one in conversation with other bilingual speakers. The situation is one where languages are switched rapidly, and where it is difficult to predict which language one will hear and which one will have to answer in. A test situation which uses code switch as a criterion for the degree of bilingualism is an artificially accelerated version of a very demanding situation of this kind.

For this reason, code switching, especially when linked to demands made on speed, probably is more a measure of the number of times a speaker has had to cope with situations where rapid code switching was required, than being a measure of the degree of bilingualism itself. Code switching tests can also be said to measure learning contexts. If we call to mind for a moment the distinction between compound and co-ordinate bilingualism, then it will be clear that an individual who has learnt the two languages in wholly separate contexts will probably find it more difficult to switch rapidly than someone who has learnt both languages in the same environment, and possibly from the same speakers.

In the same fashion it has been discussed whether translation as a skill should be wholly distinguished from bilingual ability (Halliday, McIntosh & Strevens, 1970: 142), or whether the ability to translate well (simultaneously and successively) is simply evidence of such complete bilingualism that only a few speakers ever achieve it. Many experienced teachers testify to the superiority of translation as a method of measurement. But on the other hand there are many bilinguals who complain that they find translation very difficult. This might be true in particular for co-ordinate bilinguals. There is, of course, a need for translation even in diglossic communities. Only in communities where everyone is bilingual does the need not exist, and according to Fishman, communities of this sort will tend to become monolingual. But even the contact between two monolingual communities necessitates translation. Therefore it seems reasonable to suppose that most naturally bilingual situations should produce bilinguals who are capable of translating, at least to some extent, or at any rate of interpreting between the two languages, with no exact details required. On the other hand, it is also clear that translation and interpretation at a high level are abilities that require special training. Simultaneous and successive interpretation even requires regular practice, since the act of translation is here performed at very high speed, as is not necessarily the case with written translation or less formal interpretation. Here, too, the environment is influential. A young child can be fairly skilful at translation if it has grown up in a bilingual family and gone through the phase of running back and forth between the parents and translating. The teaching at school is also important. If one of the bilingual's languages is taught as a second or foreign language while the other is the language of instruction, the child will probably get a good deal of practice at translation.

If exact and subtle equivalence is not part of the requirement, and if great speed is not expected, then translation may perhaps be used as a measure of bilingualism. But on the one hand, a very skilled bilingual speaker need not be a good translator, especially if speed is required; and on the other hand, an individual with a fairly limited knowledge of an L2 may nevertheless produce an acceptable translation, with the use of dictionaries, and given enough time.

I have described how, in bilingual families, many children both mix languages and have all sorts of interference in the beginning. Most of them can keep their languages apart before school age, and mix them thereafter mostly only when speaking to other bilingual speakers. It is important to investigate those situations in which bilinguals think that it is necessary to mix languages to some extent. According to many researchers a speaker may in certain informal situations make a rather unfavourable impression, be thought of as self-important and remote, or signalling detachment, domination or formality if her speech is "too pure". Many discussions among Swedish-speaking mother tongue teachers of the minority of Finland Swedes suggest that their pupils are interested in observing in which situations a mixture of languages is required and approved of, and in which situations it can create negative feelings in the listener and counteract the speaker's purpose by irritating the listener unnecessarily, for instance in an official situation where the pupil is in a weaker position than an adult partner.

There are contradictory reports about the awareness of bilinguals themselves of using interference, where third or fourth generation immigrants who are clearly dominant in the language of the new country seem to be unable to tell "correctly" to which language certain items belong "originally" (see Hasselmo, 1974). With more recent immigrants, stable indigenous minorities and individuals who have grown up in bilingual families the awareness seems to be greater, and many of them use code switching and interference consciously and elegantly for different stylistic, situational, etc. purposes. When interference signals a weaker command of one of the languages it often seems to be a situation which the individual knows of and may try to remedy (for instance asking about a word she doesn't know – see examples in Saunders 1982, especially the chapter "Departing from normal language choice in the family").

With a bilingual norm it becomes pointless to try to measure the degree of interference (in the monolingual understanding of the term), and to use this as a measure of the degree of bilingualism. If we are to use the monolingual's norm in deciding what is interference (every deviation from the L1 or L2 norm which is due to the speaker's familiarity with another language), then sociolinguistically sensitive bilingual speakers will be classified as less bilingual if they speak naturally, especially if the tester is bilingual, and thus leads the sensitive bilingual being tested to function according to the bilingual norm.[8] If we use a bilingual norm in deciding what constitutes interference (failure to adhere to the bilingual community's own norms in the choice of language varieties: L1, L2, or L1 + L2), then what we are measuring is not the degree of bilingualism, but sensitivity to the bilingual norm and willingness to adhere to it.

If this argument is accepted, then the only way to use interference as a measure of degree of bilingualism is to explain in the test instruction that the test situation requires the bilingual speaker to speak L1 or L2 in as "pure" a form as she can, because the communication partner is absolutely monolingual. But there are difficulties about this too. Who will decide, for example, what kinds of interference actually impede intelligibility, and what kinds perhaps have the effect of making the language more varied, enjoyable and creative?[9]

To summarize, in my view use of the amount of interference as a measurement of the degree of bilingualism rests on a negative view both of bilingualism and interference, a one-dimensional and puristic attitude which can only be harmful. To my mind this kind of measurement is at worst actually objectionable and at best problematic in that it tends to penalize linguistic creativity and social sensitivity and to define this as "less bilingual". Measurement of this sort should be used with very great care, if at all.

What I have said holds equally for interference (or transfer, as it is called in language learning studies) as it occurs in learner language, whether it is children or adults who are learning a second language, i.e. in the process of becoming bilingual. There are many different opinions as to how much the learner's deviation from the target language is the result of influence from L1. Burt & Dulay's calculations suggest a figure for syntax as low as 5%, for example, though most other researchers put the figure higher. In spite of the diversity of view here, interlanguage studies have helped to establish a more positive view of interference. The learner's use of the resources of L1 in situations where the norms of the target language are still unclear is seen as one positive communication strategy rather than as an illicit intrusion into the territory of the target language, even if it does not always help (see Haastrup & Phillipson, 1983).

8.5 To test or not to test – that is the question

As I have said before, different attitudes are possible to the business of testing bilinguals.

▪ First we may say: tests are unreliable, they give a distorted picture of reality, they reduce the individual, they can never measure or capture what one is capable of doing with language in real situations, and tests can never catch all the important features anyway. The devising or use of tests is something one ought not to get involved with.

Let me give you an extreme example my friends were discussing once when I was in Berlin (West). The experts on immigrant language in Germany had been brought together to decide how immigrant guest workers in West Germany should be tested in German when they applied for German nationality. In the first place, all my friends were absolutely opposed to the idea that a good knowledge of German was necessary for the obtaining of German nationality – they felt that this condition was unjust so long as ordinary guest workers in the country had so little opportunity of learning the language. Secondly, they thought it impossible to construct and administer a test that was multi-faceted enough to reveal in real terms how the subjects, for example, would manage in German in their place of work. Thirdly, they thought it grossly unfair to put workers through a test in standard German who had learnt their (non-standard) German at work – but of course it would have been impossible to devise tests for all the variety of dialects and sociolects. On the other hand, if they were to refuse to devise a test, then the command of German would be tested by police officers with no linguistic training whatever, and simply in the course of a conversation, or the police might devise a test. It is often a matter of choosing the least bad alternative rather than agreeing only to co-operate if something really satisfactory could be done or refusing to co-operate. If we don't do the testing, someone else might, who might know even less than we do about bilingualism. P.S. My friends chose to devise a test. . . .

■ Second we may say: since there are no really good tests anyway, I will make use of this kind of enquiry, which is not a test, but which will still provide me with some information, with the practical data I want. This is not a test, it is no more than . . . whatever you like to call it. And so we use something we have put together ourselves (without enough scrutiny of it) or have taken over from a colleague, something that fails to meet even the most elementary of the requirements for a satisfactory test or questionnaire. Something that could have been improved had we had any acquaintance at all with research on testing procedures. There are frightening examples of "tests" and "questionnaires" of this kind used in official enquiries. The information they provide is often likely to be more misleading and mischievous than no information at all, since those who are given the results (and unfortunately sometimes even the very people who have conducted the enquiry) believe they derive from the use of solidly respectable tests and testing procedures and provide, at any rate, reliable basic information. Testing in these cases has undoubtedly been a choosing of the greater evil in a situation where there is no really good alternative available.

■ Or we may as a third alternative concentrate so much on refining the instruments to be used for measurement that this task comes to occupy more of our attention than the real problem that measurement was supposed to elucidate. This kind of attitude is well illustrated, to my mind, by the rather alarming way in which the discussion (one might almost say the agitation) about Pertti Toukomaa's remarkable investigations of immigrant schoolchildren has proceeded. The attacks made upon him have been full of errors and untruths (see further my critique of Ekstrand's methods in Skutnabb-Kangas, 1979c and 1980a). "These attacks have in general avoided discussing directly the problem he focuses upon, its social origins and consequences, and have instead concentrated on discussing matters of technical pernicketiness. For example, psychological tests used for sociolinguistic and educational purposes have been discussed as though their purpose had been the technical, linguistic one of revealing exactly where and how immigrant children's linguistic ability is deficient. The problem that should be discussed is *why* immigrant children do so badly, worse than majority children, in different kinds of measurement of linguistic ability and school achievement, and what the long-term consequences of this may be, for them and for our society. By comparison with this, the question of how the different tests are constructed seems quite immaterial: immaterial too because these are tests that are also used (and standardized) for monolingual children. For immigrant children to be able to cope well in schools where abilities of the kind that these tests measure are required, they *must* acquire them, *whatever they are*. By concentrating on a secondary question, by reducing the question about immigrant children's poor school achievement and its causes to a question about testing technique, the real issue is avoided. It may indeed be interesting to discuss technical matters for their own sake too, and we do need discussion about the validity of various methods of data collection, but if these technical discussions are used (by the researchers themselves or by others) to deflect attention from the real problems and to discredit critical research which on the basis of theories about minority education tries to view the problem in its whole social context, highlighting the reasons for and the consequences of the present state of affairs, then we are guilty of just such mistakes ... as characterize the analytical positivistic philosophy of science attitude at its worst" (Skutnabb-Kangas, 1979b: 172–73).

The reader interested in questions of pedago-political consequences of minority education research and its different philosophy of science paradigms, ideologies and methods can find a detailed account in a book comparing North American and Scandinavian debates (Cummins & Skutnabb-Kangas, in preparation).

The three different attitudes I have described may be seen to run parallel with the three different stages in the development of language testing described by Bernard Spolsky (1976): the pre-scientific; the psychometric – structuralist; and the psycholinguistic-sociolinguistic. The pre-scientific attitude would be the one characterized by an uncritical reliance upon an intuitive view of what are the important variables to be measured, with no attempt made to systematize them or give them a basis in theory about language as a system, language use, or bilingualism. The psychometric-structuralist stage brought technical precision and dexterity, and statistically reliable methods, but with little attention paid to the material in the tests, or the purposes for which the tests were being used. This tendency in its extreme form led to the quite barren discussions in Scandinavia about the concept of semilingualism. At the more psycholinguistically-sociolinguistically orientated stage we begin to see both how difficult testing is (and sometimes to refuse to test for this reason), and also to try to develop ways of describing language usage which might provide a basis for more realistic methods of measurement. We begin, too, to take into account for which purposes and in whose interest tests are used.

There is a further danger worth pointing out here, that in our eagerness now to test what people actually *do* with their languages (instead of or in addition to testing what they *could* do), we only test what people do in concrete everyday communication situations. We construct tests which imitate certain types of ordinary communicative situations: for example, explaining something to another person in a "real" situation (where the other person is dependent on the explanation given – typical examples are tests where two subjects are separated by a screen with the same kind of landscape before them, and one of them is asked to give the other directions as to how to reach a certain goal). Or we test children to see whether they understand the basic vocabulary and syntax used in school textbooks. All this is in reaction against the "unreal" tests which required conscious manipulation of language in a way that is not demanded by everyday face-to-face communication. The danger with this more sociolinguistically orientated kind of testing is that we forget that language is also used for purposes other than everyday communication, and that a child who can manage only this ordinary sort of communication (giving someone directions, for instance) might not in fact have a good enough command of the language to be able to use it for academic work at school. Jim Cummins has warned us particularly of this where language tests are being used for school placement purposes (see section 5.2.2.5 and Cummins 1980b) where often only the child's surface fluency has been tested and not the ability to use the language as a cognitive tool.

Notes to Chapter Eight

1. Here is an example from my own experience. I met a teacher, a Finnish-speaker, from the Torneå Valley, Sweden, at a course for teachers, who at the beginning of the course denied in rather hurt tones that she knew any Finnish. The course was on bilingualism: among the things dealt with were attitudes, the consequences of long-term linguistic oppression, a colonized consciousness and the shame individuals feel at belonging to a linguistically oppressed group. After a few days at the course, she began to speak lively but slightly halting Finnish, and of her own accord took up with me the question of why she had denied she had any Finnish at the beginning.

2. See, for example, Koiranen, 1966; Macnamara, 1969: 86; Jaakkola, 1969: 80–86; Lindman & Alho, 1971: 34; Sandlund, 1972: 13–14; Sahlman-Karlsson, 1974: 140.

3. An example is provided by the investigations conducted by Arne Trankell and the IMFO group of the prejudice Swedes feel towards immigrants (see, for example, Landén, 1971; Montelius, 1971; Trankell, 1971, 1973, 1974). Another example, where children's attitudes have been studied, is the research carried out by Mirko Takač and his group in Gothenburg (see Carlsson & Valík, 1979; Takač,

1978). There are very many elaborate and less elaborate descriptive reports on attitudes to immigrants in Scandinavia, for the most part concentrating on Sweden. The reports from the Commission on Discrimination (Sweden) summarize a number of them. I refer the reader to them.

4. Though they have been quick enough to criticize, often knowing very little about test construction – see, for example, Bengt Loman's critique of tests used by Pertti Toukomaa in Loman, 1978a: 39–40, where it emerges that Loman does not know that the test manuals normally set out the criteria for scoring, i.e. give criteria for and examples of acceptable and unacceptable answers.

5. See, for example, the tests to measure communication in schizophrenic families developed by Rolv Mikkel Blakar and his group in Mossige, Pettersen & Blakar, 1979, these have also been used for measurement of sexual differences (Blakar & Pedersen, 1980a, b).

6. See, for example, the discussion that followed Norbert Dittmar's lecture introducing implicational scales, that is, scales in which the attempt is made on the basis of frequency of occurrence to arrange different rules about verb phrases in order of learning, so that the knowledge of a "later" rule implies an "earlier" rule already (partly) learnt (Dittmar, 1978).

7. For example, Lambert, 1955; Lambert, Havelka & Gardner, 1959; Preston & Lambert, 1969; Rao, 1964; Mägiste, 1979.

8. I often find it difficult to trust results about the language use and linguistic competence of bilinguals if the test has been conducted by someone who does not speak both languages – and this is to direct fairly fundamental criticism at most Swedish projects on bilingualism, which have been conducted often by Swedish researchers with no knowledge of the immigrant language they were investigating. Here, too, Hansegård is an exception, with his excellent command of Same and Finnish.

9. I believe, for example, that some of the Danicisms that I have started using in my Swedish make it richer – they are immediately intelligible to all Swedes, even though it is quite clear that my use of them depends actually on my familiarity with Danish.

9 Bilingualism, cognitive development and school achievement

9.1 The threshold hypothesis

In a number of studies in which bilingual children's cognitive ability has been measured, both by various kinds of intelligence test and other tests, contradictory results have been obtained. According to the earlier investigations bilingual children perform much less well than monolingual children. According to a number of more recent studies they perform as well or better. Various circumstances which bear upon this inconsistency and on the school achievement of minority children will be discussed in this chapter, some have already been dealt with in the discussions of immersion, submersion and language maintenance. First I want to concentrate on only *one* aspect of these contradictory results, and that is the influence upon children's cognitive development of bilingualism. One attempt to explain the divergent results has led to the development of the threshold hypothesis (Cummins, 1976a, 1976b; Toukomaa & Skutnabb-Kangas, 1977).

In his first version of the threshold hypothesis, Cummins suggests that the level of competence attained by a bilingual child in L1 and L2 may function as an intervening variable mediating the effects of the child's bilingual experience on cognitive growth (1976a: 23). He sees both bilingualism and monolingualism as instruments, tools, which a child uses to operate upon the environment, i.e. she investigates and organizes the environment in the Piagetian sense. The bilingual instrument is more complex and so more difficult to master, but once mastered, it may also have greater potential than the unilingual instrument for promoting cognitive growth. But if for a long period a child is forced to operate with the help of the less well mastered language, it is likely that her interaction with the environment, both input, processing and output, may be less conducive to cognitive growth (see 10.2.3). The child may fail, then, to comprehend much of the content transmitted in class, and may also find difficulty in expressing her developing intelligence and operating upon the environment verbally through L2. A possible consequence of this is a decrease in intellectual curiosity (Cummins, 1976a).

Cummins then goes on to suggest that there may be a certain level of L2 competence (and mother tongue competence which is assumed here to be high) which must be attained to allow the potentially beneficial aspects of becoming bilingual to influence cognitive development. He calls this level the threshold level. In his first article on the threshold level, Cummins also suggested that there might be two thresholds, and that the attainment of the lower "would be sufficient to avoid cognitive retardation, but the attainment of a second, higher level of bilingual competence might be necessary to lead to accelerated cognitive growth" (Cummins, 1976a: 24).

The hypothesis has been further developed and compared with results of a number of studies in the attempt to explain them. The starting point for these attempts has been the following diagrammatic representation of the hypothesis:

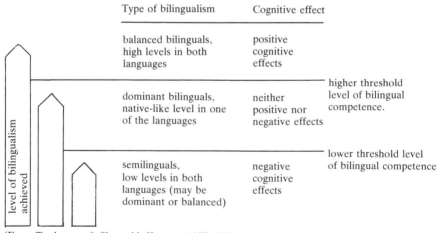

(From Toukomaa & Skutnabb-Kangas, 1977: 29)

We suggest that children who have attained a very high level in both their languages (native or near-native) belong to the group that shows positive effects when various aspects of cognitive development are measured. Those children, on the other hand, who have reached native competence in one language only, normally their mother tongue, but with a much less good command of the other language, will show neither positive nor negative effects, i.e. their achievement will not differ from that of monolingual children. Those children, finally, who achieve a native level in neither of their languages and who are forced during a prolonged period to function in a less well mastered language in those situations which have been designed to further cognitive development (at school, for instance), would according to the threshold hypothesis show negative effects, i.e. do less well than corresponding monolinguals. In what follows, I shall survey a number of studies suggesting variously that bilingualism has positive or negative cognitive effects, to see whether they can be interpreted with the help of the threshold hypothesis.

9.2   Bilingualism and negative cognitive development

9.2.1   Early studies of bilingualism and negative cognitive development

The early studies of bilingualism and cognitive development (intelligence) were often attempts to investigate why bilingual children did badly at school. And since it was thought that intelligence was the decisive factor in school achievement (there was general enthusiasm for the relatively simple explanations of intelligence that seemed to have emerged over the broad front of enquiry and confident reliance on the developing procedures for intelligence testing), a number of studies were carried out in which the performance of monolinguals and bilinguals in various types of intelligence test was compared. Such investigations were being made on a large scale as early as the 1920s and they still form part of many psychologically orientated bilingual research projects, albeit in a rather more sophisticated form. At the same time, however, the widespread critical scrutiny to which in some countries (including Scandinavia) the undifferentiated use of psychometric data in general and intelligence tests specifically is being subjected has begun to influence the study of bilingualism so that "softer", more observation-based methods are now beginning to be preferred (as was made clear in the chapter on the measurement of bilingualism), or at least some combination of both types (see Cummins, 1980c). Many of the kinds of mistake that were made in the 1920s are still being made today in investigations of bilingualism. Therefore I will very briefly discuss some of the earlier research first. The investigations involving intelligence testing may be summarized under three headings:

1. Investigations using *verbal tests in the bilingual children's L2*, where the IQ of bilingual children was compared with that of monolingual children, with no attention paid to the type of test used, and no account taken of the language in which the test was *not* conducted, the children's mother tongue. Since the tests were verbal, they implied understanding and use of the test language, which in most cases was the children's school language but not their mother tongue.

2. Investigations using both verbal and non-verbal tests, in the children's L2 where their IQ was compared with the IQ of monolingual children in both kinds of test.

3. Investigations using either *verbal or non-verbal tests, or both, in both languages*, where the results were compared as between the two languages; and for each of the two languages individually with the results gained by monolingual children.

A few words about the design, results and mistakes in each type. When bilingual children were tested with verbal tests in their L2 (type 1), their IQ-scores were much lower than monolingual means (in Hirsch, 1926, 85.8 and 98.5, in Mead, 1927, a difference of more than 27 points and only 6% of the bilingual children reaching the monolingual average, etc). In many of these studies the children's level of bilingualism was inadequately or not at all controlled. The child could be counted as bilingual if she had immigrant parents (Hirsch, 1926) or a "foreign" surname (used as criterion also in Zirkel, 1972) or if a foreign language was spoken in her home, regardless of who spoke it (Mead, 1927; Rigg, 1928; Saer, 1922, 1923). The children's sex, age and SES was seldom properly controlled.

The second test type, both verbal and non-verbal tests in L2 were usually better controlled in relation to factors discussed above. The results showed usually that monolinguals scored approximately the same in both test types, while bilinguals did less well at verbal tests (their average IQ could be up to 20 points lower on verbal than non-verbal, for example in Jamieson & Sandiford, 1928) and as well as monolinguals at non-verbal tests (or sometimes even better).[1] Some researchers maintained that children who had been taught through the medium of the test language at school, did not suffer any linguistic handicap in verbal tests even if they were tested in their L2 (for instance, Arthur, 1937), but most researchers agreed that verbal tests in L2 were unfair to bilingual children and should not be used (Sanchez, 1932 – who went to great trouble trying to prove this with word list comparisons from basic vocabulary lists, from Stanford-Binet's intelligence test and testing bilingual Spanish speakers – Arsenian, 1937; Seidl, 1937; etc). Arsenian's conclusion after his thorough investigation echoed the views of many researchers that bilingualism and IQ had not been found to correlate in any way.

The third type of test, in the children's two languages, showed that they registered higher IQ-scores when tested in their L1 than when tested in L2 (Brown, 1922; Yoshioka, 1929; Mitchell, 1937; etc). But there were a number of difficulties in using verbal tests in both languages, such as making them equivalent and standardizing them. Conclusions which could have been drawn already from research material dating from before the Second World War were: Bilingual children score better in nonverbal performance tests than in verbal tests, and better in their mother tongue, L1, than in language learnt later, L2. Bilinguals often do as well as monolinguals in performance tests, but usually worse than monolinguals in verbal tests, often in both languages. Verbal intelligence tests do not give a fair picture of the intelligence of bilingual children, whichever language they are tested in, and should never be used alone anyway.

9.2.2   The consequences of neglecting what should have been learnt from the early studies

Even though many researchers into bilingualism have long accepted and now take practical account of these conclusions, they do not seem to be clear to all psychologists engaged in the measurement of IQ and in other psychometric studies who have no special interest in bilingualism. One finds, even in the most recent literature, an amazing ignorance about the nature of linguistic problems, especially in the USA but also to an increasing extent in other countries with both new and old minorities. There is an attitude towards other languages than one's own which seems to me to be a quite incomprehensible inability to see the value of other languages. This cultural imperialist attitude which one sometimes encounters especially with speakers of so-called great world languages (but not only among them) is the more deplorable as it is reflected both in research and in the recommendations researchers make, with often disastrous consequences for linguistic minorities. That the following self-evident fact should need to be *pointed out* in a serious scientific publication (Seng, 1970: 113) is evidence of the gravity of the problem: "If a child is not proficient in Standard American English but his cognitive structure is complex in terms of concept formation and integration, that child *is* intelligent." Because of an increased interest in schoolchildren socially and linguistically "handicapped" lively discussion has again recently arisen both in Scandinavia and internationally as to the *general* justice and validity of measurement of intelligence, and school achievement, and the demands made at school. This large topic is now debated on all sides and that may be why perhaps sometimes the overall view and the historical perspective seem lacking. In certain cases, there has been a clear regression in opinion, a neglecting of the knowledge already available to us and that we should have. Psychologists have again begun to suggest that verbal tests should be used in testing bilingual children. In Sweden, too, immigrant children are in many cases tested in Swedish: performance tests are used (with Swedish instructions if testers in the children's L1 are not available) but sometimes also verbal tests, even if in many cases performance tests are available in the children's mother tongue. Pertti Toukomaa has shown, though, that Finnish immigrant children in Olofström are several years behind their monolingual peers in verbal tests both in Swedish and in their mother tongue, while their intelligence as measured by non-verbal tests (with Finnish instructions) is quite normal (Toukomaa, 1972b, 1973a, 1975c). It looks as though every country is going to insist on its separate right to make the same old mistakes many others have made in this area as in other matters to do with the position of minority children. Rather little is known about what has been done in other countries earlier, and even where something is known, that foreign experience is thought irrelevant to us in "our country". So it is that in Denmark, too, tests in Danish are used in evaluating the placement, abilities and needs for auxiliary measures of immigrant children, even though some psychologists and some immigrant organizations have begun to protest. These attitudes also influence, among other things, the placing of immigrant children in special remedial classes in the schools, even though the central authorities, in Sweden, for example, try to impose guidelines on how children should be tested before they are put into remedial classes. One investigation in Botkyrka municipal district showed that Finnish children were over-represented in such classes at every level (Kuusela, 1973). In the USA, too, minority children are over-represented in such classes (Civil Rights Commission, Linguistic Reporter 1974: 1, references in the last years of Forum). The same tendency can be seen in England (see, for instance, the Rampton Report, 1981) and in West Germany (see references in Yletyinen, 1982). It is increasingly clear, too, that researchers are aware that this does not reflect differences in intelligence, but unfair methods of assessment (Liungman, 1970) – the title of the by now classic book by Coard (1971) is symptomatic of this: *How the West Indian Child is Made ESN in the British School System* (ESN = educationally subnormal). (On some of the more informed discussions about the causes see Mullard 1982a, b; Sivanandan, 1982; Green, 1982; and Katz, 1982, just to mention a few, with somewhat different views.)

9.3 Bilingualism and positive cognitive development

There are also a number of studies that show bilingual children performing *better* than monolingual in tests that measure different aspects of cognitive and linguistic development as well as various kinds of non-verbal aspects of communication. This better performance has been particularly evident in the areas of (1) general intellectual development, (2) divergent thinking, (3) a tendency to observe and analyse various aspects of language, a type of metalinguistic awareness and (4) sensitivity to feed-back cues and to non-verbal communication (Cummins, 1976a).

9.3.1 General intellectual development

Peal & Lambert's classic study (1962) was one of the first well-controlled studies in which bilinguals scored better than monolinguals. It thus broke away from the otherwise uniformly negative pattern of results for bilinguals. It showed a positive connection between bilingualism and general intelligence. Moreover, the intelligence profile, according to different subtests, was more differentiated for bilinguals than for monolinguals. The study involved 10-year-old French-Canadian middle-class children. Lambert's colleague, Anisfeld, tried reanalysing Peal & Lamberts' data (1964) to discover which aspects of intelligence were most positively affected by bilingualism, and she eliminated some of the test subjects until she could match the rest into bilingual/monolingual pairs according to IQ. The bilinguals still did better than the monolinguals in a number of such tests, even if the differences were now somewhat less pronounced. Anisfeld also reported new results where the bilinguals were in particular better at tests requiring symbolic manipulation and mental agility.

Several other studies have later come to similar conclusions, showing that bilingualism promotes general intellectual development.[2] Even though all these studies have controlled factors like age, sex and SES, the bilingual and monolingual subjects have not always been matched with respect to other important background variables, as they were in Peal & Lambert's study. On the other hand it is difficult to say which IQ measurement is likely to be the most neutral independent variable in investigations which after all are measuring *general* intellectual development, and where the dependent variables are also cognitive measurements of various kinds. But on the other hand, it is perhaps more interesting to investigate precisely those aspects of the general cognitive development that bilingualism may positively affect, rather than to study intellectual development as a whole. Bain & Yu (1978a), for instance, set out to investigate the point of contention between Piaget's conception of the relationship between language and thought, where language is assigned a secondary role, and Vygotsky's view, which allots language a decisive role. They matched monolingual and bilingual children from Canada, France and Germany, according to IQ, SES, school reports, age and sex, and investigated what they called contemplative performance by tests where the subjects were to discover the rules of the game on the first test occasion and to apply them on the second occasion in the solution of similar problems. Their investigation (which also involved sensitivity to non-verbal signals, Bain's portrait sensitivity test – see 9.4.4) involved children both in the pre-operational stage (where the bilinguals discovered the rule much more quickly than the monolinguals) and in the concrete operational stage (where the trend was also in favour of the bilinguals). The transfer time (the time it took to begin to apply the rule) was the same with bilinguals and monolinguals, once they had discovered the rule.

9.3.2   Divergent thinking

Divergent thinking, one of the intellectual operations Guilford (1959, 1973) has discussed in his non-hierarchical model of intellectual structure, is one type of linguistic creativity, an ability to reorganize: a very fruitful concept which is however difficult to isolate by testing (Liungman, 1970: 202–3). A number of studies have produced results showing that bilinguals score better in tests for divergent thinking than monolinguals. Let me give some examples.

In Landry's study (1974), "bilingual" children in grade 6 (they had foreign language teaching for between 25 and 45 minutes each day) obtained significantly higher numerical results than monolinguals in the Torrance Test of Creative Thinking, in both verbal and numerical subtests. It should be mentioned, though, that Torrance himself obtained different results in Singapore (Torrance, Gowan, Wu & Aliotti, 1970), where the bilinguals performed less well than the monolinguals in the subtests for fluency and flexibility, but better in tests for originality and elaboration. In the matter of fluency, the results agree well with the theory that those aspects of language that have to do with accent and fluency show weak correlations with language used as a cognitive instrument (see the section on surface fluency and language as an instrument of thought: 5.2.2.5). As regards other aspects of Torrance's results, the reader is referred to section 8.4.3.2 on dominance. Anisfeld's study (1964) reports no differences for divergent thinking between monolinguals and bilinguals, either.

In an analysis of data from St. Lambert immersion children Scott (1973) found that the bilingual children's command of French in grade 6 showed high correlations with tests for divergent thinking in grade 3. The results in the divergent thinking were better predictors of their later knowledge of French than the results in non-verbal intelligence tests. Scott's analysis also lends support to the possibility that divergent thinking may have been positively affected by immersion programmes. It is, in fact, impossible to judge whether high scores in divergent thinking tests are a *result* of functional bilingualism or *one of the reasons* for high levels of functional bilingualism.

Cummins & Gulutsan (1974), investigating monolingual and bilingual grade 6 children, reported significantly better results for the bilinguals in tests for linguistic originality, but no difference in four other tests of divergent thinking. In a further analysis of the same data, Cummins (1976a) found that it was the balanced bilinguals with a high degree of proficiency in L2 who did well, exactly as the threshold hypothesis would predict, whereas the children who were very dominant in their mother tongue did less well.

Carringer, in a study of 24 Spanish/English balanced bilinguals matched with 24 Spanish monolinguals (1974), showed that the bilinguals were significantly better in the divergent thinking tests. Cummins, however, (1976a) criticized Carringer's study on the grounds that neither IQ nor SES were sufficiently well controlled.

9.3.3 Linguistic analysis and metalinguistic awareness

A number of studies have investigated different aspects of the way monolinguals and bilinguals analyze language, and particularly their awareness of the specific nature of language as a system. I shall briefly describe a few of these.

Werner Leopold, who has written the most comprehensive study so far of a bilingual child's linguistic development (Leopold, 1939–50: 1–4), observed a number of years ago that his daughters (especially the elder, Hildegard) were able to separate sound and meaning, name and object, earlier than monolingual children. He assumed that habitually hearing an object given two different names, one for each language, forced them to attach more importance to meaning than to the word used to express the meaning (149, 199). Imedadze (1960, 1967) and Vygotsky (1935 translated 1975, 1962) express similar opinions. Anita Ianco-Worrall (1972) studied 30 children bilingual in Afrikaans and English between the ages of 4 and 9, from bilingual homes where the parents were strict about the one-person one-language principle. Each child was matched with two monolingual children, one Afrikaans and one English, with respect to age, sex, SES and intelligence. The bilingual children did much better than the monolingual in tests for sensitivity to the semantic properties of words (by contrast, for instance, to interpreting similarities between words in terms of their acoustic properties: choosing, let us say, which of the two words "can" or "hat" most resembles the word "cap"). The bilinguals were also more aware of the arbitrary nature of words, when they were asked to decide whether something could be called by another name (for instance whether the names for "cow" and "dog" could be exchanged). First they were asked without comment, and later in the form: "If you had to find names for things, could you call a cow a dog, and a dog a cow?"

Jim Cummins wanted to check whether this type of answer where the children perceived the relationship between word and referent as arbitrary was because the bilingual children really were more aware of the arbitrariness of the link than monolinguals, or whether it was because they were more sensitive to the tester's attempt to get them to think further by asking additional questions (so that the children, for example, said that the names could be changed in other circumstances because the bilingual children perhaps had grasped that this was the answer expected of them). He did a similar experiment with Irish children in grade 3 and 6, matched with monolingual children by age, sex, SES and IQ. In his study the children were asked to give reasons for their answers. The children also had to make up their minds about various contradictory and tautological statements. The bilingual children did better with all the statements except the tautological ones (where there was no difference, all the children found them difficult). Cummins' conclusion was that bilingual children have a better developed awareness of some of the properties of language and are capable of more rigorous analysis of certain kinds of linguistic statement (Cummins, 1976a, b, 1977c).

Sandra Ben-Zeev (1972, 1975, 1977a) assumes that this greater awareness and a more intensive analytical ability towards language develops as a consequence of bilingual children's attempts to keep their two languages apart, to avoid interference. She studied 98 Hebrew/English middle-class children and 188 Spanish/English low SES children, again with age, sex, SES and IQ controlled. The bilinguals did better than monolinguals at different kinds of language game involving substituting words for other words and answering questions but preserving the meaning of the old word:

"This is named plane, right? (Experimenter holds up toy aeroplane) In this game, its name is turtle.
Can the turtle fly? (correct answer: yes).
How does the turtle fly? (correct answer: with its wings)".

In more difficult exchanges, the subjects also had to violate different kinds of grammatical rule, for example, rules of concord or sub-categorization:

"For this game the way we say *in* or *into* is to say the word *clean. . . . See this doll? See this house? Tell me where the doll is going* (experimenter pushes doll inside of house).
(Correct answer: *The doll is going clean the house.*)
Does the dollhouse get cleaner, dirtier, or does it stay the same when the doll does that?
(Correct answer: *It stays the same.*)
(Ben-Zeev, 1977a: 34).

In tests of this kind, which according to Ben-Zeev require an ability to treat sentence structure analytically and to be linguistically flexible, the bilingual children performed better than the monolingual. By contrast, they were not better than the monolinguals at using the rules of ordinary grammar, for example in Berko's morphology test (Berko, 1958). Berko's test involves applying morphological rules to nonsense words: for example: This is a lod. Here is another lod, what are these? (Experimenter points to two of them) (correct answer: lod*s*). The Spanish/English bilinguals also did less well than the monolinguals in vocabulary tests.

As I have said, explanations of bilingual children's greater analytical ability suppose that bilingual children, in their observation of two languages (a form of contrastive analysis) and in their endeavour to keep them apart, come to pay more attention to language itself, its structures and the central properties defining it, than do monolingual children. There are suggestions, too, which have been tested to some degree (for example by Ben-Zeev, 1975), that this greater analytical ability may transfer to areas outside language.

9.3.4   Sensitivity to feed-back cues and non-linguistic communication

Various types of feed-back cues related to linguistic performance or performance expressed via language may come from within the language itself and its structure (a child says "I runned" and the adult in the next sentence says "perhaps you ran too fast and you fell down, did you?"); or they may come from different non-verbal details in the situation (the child does not get what she has asked for, somebody does not understand what the child is trying to say, somebody expresses disapproval or amazement, etc). To be sensitive to feed-back cues involves alertness, speed in interpreting them, rapid awareness of possible errors and alternative ways of re-organizing. Sensitivity to non-verbal communication is really a subdivision of this overall sensitivity and involves an ability to interpret facial expressions, gestures, intonation, situations. Various tests have shown here, too, that bilinguals do better than monolinguals. In her Spanish/English study (1975), Ben-Zeev had several different tests to measure this sensitivity and the bilinguals consistently did better than the monolinguals. For example, the children were given tasks like these:

■ They had to classify objects according to different principles, such as shape, and so on. When they were asked to reclassify the objects according to another principle, the experimenter gave various cues suggesting reclassification or as to which principle should be used. The bilinguals responded to these cues more quickly than the monolinguals.
■ They were asked to spot defects in a number of details in pictures in the Wechsler Intelligence Scale for Children Picture Completion Test. Again the bilinguals did better.
■ They heard the same nonsense word again and again and were asked to say whether it was the same word or whether it had changed a little. The bilingual children identified changes in the same way as adults, i.e. reacted in a more "mature" adult fashion than the monolinguals.

In a study by Genesee, Tucker & Lambert (1976), monolingual and bilingual children were asked to explain how a game was played to two partners, one blindfolded and the other not. The bilinguals proved to be able to take better account of whether the partner was blindfolded or not. Both Bruce Bain (1975a) and Jim Cummins (1975) report significant differences between monolinguals and bilinguals in a test developed by Bain in which children were asked to interpret the feelings being experienced by individuals in 24 portraits by classical painters. This same kind of sensitivity to feelings conveyed by facial expression has been found to be greater in women and girls than in men and boys (see the references in Thorne & Henley, 1975). It emerged from Torrance *et al.* study (1970) that bilinguals often noted details that were important for the transfer from one picture to the next when they were asked to describe a sequence of events they saw in a series of pictures. The explanations for this greater sensitivity are rather like those suggested for cognitive flexibility and divergent thinking. Most explanations are based on the need bilinguals have to learn to switch codes and to know when to do so. The bilingual speaker needs to notice and take account of very small often not verbalized cues and to modify her behaviour accordingly. Sometimes it will only be she who draws the appropriate conclusions from these cues; the speaker sending the cues may be quite unconscious of doing so. Various very small changes in a social situation may be observed more closely if their effect is to require a code switch; and so the bilingual gets more practise than the monolingual at paying attention to the fine detail of a social situation and at reacting in various ways.

9.3.5   Summary

In summary, then, we can say that bilingualism may have positive or negative consequences for cognitive development, or none at all. What the consequences are, depends upon the circumstances in which children become bilingual. Even in the present condition of society it is possible to increase the number of bilinguals experiencing positive consequences:

■ We could make sure that people are better informed about how children become high-level bilinguals in various circumstances.

■ We could ensure that minority children were given proper opportunities, before starting school, and during and after their schooling to learn their two languages well. It requires much greater emphasis on their mother tongue, as a medium and also as a subject.

■ We could give majority children more opportunity to participate in immersion programmes.

■ We could in general always set high standards for *both* languages, rather than aiming at dominance in one of the languages.

All these recommendations seem to follow from what we can conclude from the positive studies. In most of them children have had high levels of proficiency in both or at least one of the languages, while we either know or can suspect that this has not been the case in the negative studies – and this agrees well with the threshold hypothesis.

9.4   Class as a mediator in school achievement

Most of the investigations throughout the world which have been concerned with bilingual children (or children that were thought to be or were to become bilingual) show that it is common for them to do badly at school. The evidence is convincing and depressing as one can see in most books on bilingualism. Only recently has this pattern started to change, and in the same way as in the earlier chapters we have to make the distinction again: the children who seem to break the pattern are élite bilinguals, children from immersion programmes and most recently also children from language shelter programmes.

Even though the reasons for this poor school achievement have been studied since the beginning of the century, it still does not seem to be quite clear to everybody why bilingualism and poor school achievement correlate so strongly. Many researchers and education officials still behave as if the correlational link were a causal one, i.e. as if bilingualism were the cause of poor school achievement. One can still read that bilingualism may "have a negative influence on children's intellectual development", "hamper intellectual activity, not only in the languages themselves, but in all other subjects as well", "prevent children from thinking clearly" and so on – the quotations are from a report from a Council of Europe symposium, see Oestreicher, 1974: 9. I shall here try to discuss further this kind of opinion and how its emergence might be explained, and explore further reasons for the fact that many bilingual children do indeed perform badly at school. Since immigrant and guest worker children form the largest group of bilingual children performing poorly at school in Europe, I shall again concentrate on them. In order to put flesh on the bones of the discussion of poor achievement at school I shall also look at actual examples from some countries in chapter 11, presenting a typical guest worker country, West Germany, and a typical immigrant country, Sweden, in order to see how school achievement is directly affected by these different policies. In this chapter I shall discuss first some of the more general social factors affecting school achievement from the minority children's point of view, and then the role of different kinds of bilingualism in school achievement.

As with IQ tests, so with school achievement, it has been convincingly demonstrated that children from lower social groups as a group generally perform less well. Their marks are worse, more of them are in remedial classes, they choose shorter and less prestigious sets of programmes with fewer theoretical subjects, and they more often drop out. The situation seems to be the same all over the world (see for instance Matute-Bianci 1982 for Spanish speakers in the U.S.A.).

Economic factors affect or are the direct cause of all other factors mediating good achievement both in IQ tests and at school. It is well known, too, that all the elements used to make up the SES rating show strong correlation both with IQ and school achievement: the occupation, education and income of the parents, the physical (and thus also often psychological) conditions of the home (number of rooms, modern conveniences, cultural stimuli, etc.), and the general housing environment. The economic reasons for poor school achievement can be discussed at a variety of different levels, but to do this would be outside the primary interest of this book. There is a great deal of literature on the subject (see for example Apple, Bernstein, Bowles & Gintis, Bourdieu, Jencks et al.). All I want to do here is to establish that one of the main tasks of the school system is to reproduce in the younger generation the present power structure, to sort out some children. The class character of the educational system affects those groups worst to which most bilinguals belong – and it is among them we find the ones who are on the way to becoming the European *lumpenproletariat*. Some of the psychological and educational mediators of intellectual underdevelopment and poor school achievement (see Pettigrew, 1964: 111; Watson, 1973b: 366–67) will be briefly discussed here and some specific ones in chapter 12. These mediators affect the results of intelligence tests and affect school achievement, so that the children's performance does not do justice to their potential.

Stress and anxiety have a negative effect on test results and school achievement.[3] To live in a world dominated by the majority and to belong oneself to a minority, which is the experience of most bilinguals in the world, can easily produce a chronic state of stress, which makes performance worse. Stress in test situations tends relatively to improve the capacity for associative learning, but to impair the capacity for abstract reasoning (Watson, 1973b: 374; Jensen, 1973: 241). This alone would explain the differences that are, according to Jensen, found between different SES classes in the distribution of level 1 and level 2 thinking processes. Stress theory further claims that individuals who react to stress by becoming introvert and passive (which is what low SES children often do) show a more serious disturbance of their intellectual functions in test situations than those who react by becoming extrovert and aggressive, as high SES children tend to do (Watson, 1973b: 375). Some aspects of stress have been discussed in section 5.2.4. The subjects' opinion of their own chances also affects test results. Minority and low SES children tend to have a more modest idea of their abilities than majority and high SES children. This depresses their performance, and the performance in its turn further undermines their self-confidence, and lengthens the odds against them (even if many minority children despite this may have a perfectly sound self-confidence – one way of resistance, see Stone, 1981). Lack of self-confidence also leads to poor motivation. Teachers' expectations, which have been shown to have a dramatic effect on children's performance (see Rosenthal & Jacobson, 1968a, b), also tend to be lower with minority and low SES children. Teachers are often prejudiced against low SES children and assess their personalities, achievements and prospects less encouragingly than with high SES children (Lawton, 1970; Osterrieth, 1974; Rogers, 1967; De Coster, 1974). And in the case of minority children, the racism of both teachers and majority peers, and especially the racism of the whole school system (organization, curriculum, materials, ideology) is often claimed to be the most important factor explaining poor school achievement (see e.g. Mullard, 1982a, b; Sivanandan, 1982). The most important thing in creating an atmosphere which is motivating and encourages children to learn, is to feel that they are accepted by their teacher. Parents of low SES children often have lower expectations and aspirations *vis-à-vis* the children's school, sometimes also less interest, which reflects the fact that the school is not organized so as to suit *their* children – and the parents know it. But even so many low-SES-parents *do* encourage their children, and schools often legitimize their own lack of will or inability to do anything by blaming the parents. The children will come to make their own the low expectations teachers (and parents) have of them, and failure becomes a self-fulfilling prophecy, with the children able to do little themselves to affect the situation.[4]

The age, sex, race and ethnic group of the teacher or the examiner, as well as her SES in relation to the children's, also seem to have an effect upon them. Minority and low SES children often have less in common with teacher or tester, and this will frequently (but not always) affect their performance adversely.[5] A conscious teacher who accepts the children on their own terms, does not have to be like them in order to achieve good results (see Saville–Troike, 1973; Paulston, 1976).

The forms of praise and control used in school may also be more foreign to low SES than high SES children. What may act as a strong inducement to high SES children, for instance verbal praise, or reference to future reward (a good report, the opportunity of further education, a better job) may be meaningless for low SES children, who may more often be used to the idea that work is its own reward. Perseverance may suffer because relevant feed-back is lacking.

The artificial system in most schools where things and principles are discussed instead of getting out and doing the things in real life, and trying out the principles to see whether they hold good, favours middle-class children who are probably more used to the fact that concept validation does not necessarily need to be empirical. Much of what happens at school may for low SES children seem irrelevant and unreal operations, may fail to engage their attention and involve them, so that they derive no incentive from it to change their behaviour and perform. And why should they – even if they do, they do not get the same rewards, as for instance Jencks *et al.* have convincingly shown, or Willis (1977) in the book about why working-class children get working-class jobs.

9.5   Bilingualism as a mediator in school achievement

9.5.1   From independent to mediating variable

The assumption has often been that bilingualism itself is for bilingual children simply the cause of their poor performance at school. Earlier literature about the whole subject is full of judgements to this effect. Other theories have then been evolved to explain the relationship between bilingualism and poor school achievement. Perhaps my own developing thinking about the matter will illustrate the various stages in the evolving discussion: When I first began to be interested in the study of bilingualism in the early 1960s, I only felt it was strange that there were writers on the subject who thought it had negative consequences. I experienced my own bilingualism as something tremendously positive, something that gave me a perspective and a sense of relativity which I did not always encounter among monolinguals. It was a source of enrichment to me, too, meaning that I was able to feel at home both with Finnish-speaking and Swedish-speaking friends and with the two different cultures. I was puzzled that all this could be thought to put me at a disadvantage, so I began to read what was written. By the beginning of the 1970s I had come to the conclusion that it was not bilingualism *in itself* that was responsible for bilingual children's poor performance, but the fact that they happened to live in social and economic circumstances that would have affected their performance badly even had they been monolingual (Skutnabb-Kangas, 1972a: 94). But then I started to think: bilingualism *in itself* – what on earth was *that*? Bilingualism, after all, is *always* part of a set of socio-economic circumstances of *some* kind. It cannot strictly exist by itself any more than can any social phenomena. At this stage a number of explanatory macrosocial models began to appear. We who were working on bilingualism among immigrants began to speak more about the larger societal reasons for trying to enable or prevent people becoming bilingual (see, for example, Paulston, 1977a; Skutnabb-Kangas, 1977b; Toukomaa & Skutnabb-Kangas, 1977) and to treat bilingualism as a mediating variable. And then syntheses began to appear, attempts to take into account the objectives of the school system, the social and linguistic context in which education took place, and the curriculum as a process – a more differentiated model (Cummins, 1977a).

In sum, then, if we begin by saying that bilingualism – or some variety of it – is the *cause* of poor results in tests and at school, we are in fact beginning in the middle of a causal chain, as Christina Bratt Paulston has many times pointed out (1976, 1977, etc). Then we are treating bilingualism as an independent variable. But it cannot be treated as a dependent variable either, so we only state what kind of education best leads to bilingualism for different groups. Bilingualism – or monolingualism for that matter – is never a goal in itself. I see bilingualism as an instrument (to be) used in achieving more general societal goals. It has been, among other goals, used to prepacify or attempt to pacify sections of the population which would otherwise be difficult to control, or to forestall trouble in these areas. Bilingualism can be used to prevent equality (if it is of a kind which has negative consequences, for instance, for school achievement) or to help to create equality. I have already discussed bilingualism in these terms in my typology of bilingual education (section 6.5), and shall look further here at the notion of bilingualism as a mediating variable.

9.5.2   The reproducing circle in bilingualism

Since we know that the school system is one of the means used by the ruling groups to attain certain societal-political goals (for example, to select individuals for the needs of the (capitalist) labour market) we must ask the question: what are the goals of different societies as they try with the help of the school to make various groups bilingual or to prevent them from becoming bilingual? I classify here in four categories the goals a society may

TABLE 7

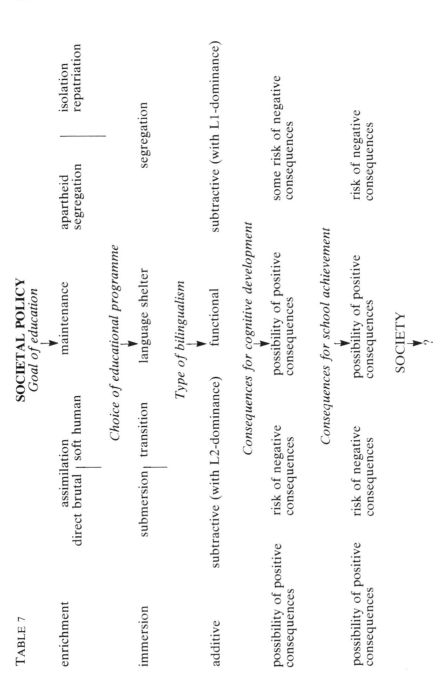

SOCIETAL POLICY
Goal of education

enrichment	assimilation direct brutal | soft human	maintenance	apartheid segregation	isolation repatriation

Choice of educational programme

immersion	submersion | transition	language shelter	segregation

Type of bilingualism

additive (with L2-dominance)	subtractive	functional	subtractive (with L1-dominance)

Consequences for cognitive development

possibility of positive consequences	risk of negative consequences	possibility of positive consequences	some risk of negative consequences

Consequences for school achievement

possibility of positive consequences	risk of negative consequences	possibility of positive consequences	risk of negative consequences

SOCIETY → ?

have for an education which claims that it intends to produce bilinguals – see Table 7.

The more macrosocial-political goals have already been discussed in my typology in 6.5. Education directed at children from linguistic majorities has as its objective the *enrichment* of the children's linguistic repertoire. Ordinary foreign language teaching at school is in fact also a very modest form of linguistic enrichment, an expansion of children's linguistic potential. Education directed at children from a linguistic minority may have several different goals. *Assimilation* may be direct assimilation, as with the Romanies in Finland, whose children are placed in Finnish schools without any special consideration for the Romany language or culture, with no teaching in L2 (Finnish), no mother tongue teaching or any attempt to present the history and culture of the Romanies to the children, let alone to Finnish-speaking Finnish children (Weckman, 1980). Most immigrant children also experience this direct brutal assimilation. Or there may be transitional assimilation, more indirect, a little more humane and less painful, where the L1 of the children is used as a subject or even a medium for a few years, to be phased out when the transition to L2 is completed. *Segregation* can also be of different kinds, one more brutally physical, as in apartheid systems, one a combination of physical and psychological, as in guest worker ghettos. But from another angle one can also look at repatriation as an aspect of apartheid – Kreutzberg then might be considered West Germany's Soweto, and Turkey West Germany's largest Bantustan, producing future workers who are allowed to stay in the power centre only as workers and have to go back to the periphery which cannot feed them when there is no work. . . . *Maintenance* of the minority as a minority may also be the goal: to support and develop the minority culture and language and allow it to flourish on its own terms, in co-operation with the majority and to the benefit of both. In this case the majority language and culture are not learnt at the expense of the minority's own distinctive character and language, but in addition to them.

If the educational aim is enrichment of majority children, an *immersion programme* is chosen and the children are taught through the medium of L2.

If the aim is assimilation a *submersion programme* is chosen: the minority children are placed in what are called "ordinary" majority language classes (with or without some initial teaching of the language) where all the instruction is by means of the majority language – that such classes are called "ordinary" reveals the ethnocentric perspective very clearly: everything that happens in other than Danish or Norwegian, or German (where the classes are "Regelklassen"), or Swedish is beyond the ordinary. It is still often the case that an "ordinary" class is defined as one without immigrant children in it, though in many places such classes are themselves becoming the exception.

If the aim is segregation or/and repatriation, a *segregational programme* is chosen: the child is taught through the medium of L1, in a segregated school or environment, with bad teaching or no teaching of L2 and few if any possibilities of (meaningful and equal) contact with L2-children.

If the aim is the maintenance and further development of minority children's language and culture in interaction with the majority culture, a *language-shelter programme* is chosen. The Finland Swedish school system is a good example: A Finland Swedish child can often attend a Swedish day nursery, go to a Swedish school, and even have her further education (occupational training school, college of one kind or another, university) in her own language, Swedish, while at the same times she studies Finnish as a second language at school and often speaks it daily to her friends if she lives in a Finnish or bilingual district (see Gunnel Knubb-Manninen's recent study of the linguistic characteristics of pupils in Swedish-medium schools in Finland, 1982).

Which kind of educational programme a child has experienced will have consequences for the result. Immersion programmes usually result in an *additive* type of bilingualism: the child's mother tongue is intact, or develops even better than in majority medium programmes, even though the child has not been taught it as much as monolingual majority speakers. This shows that there is probably a possibility of a transfer effect between languages if the individual reaches a high level in both (if, in terms of the threshold hypothesis, she reaches the higher threshold level of bilingual proficiency). It also shows that a language spoken by a large proportion of speakers in the child's immediate environment, a language she hears every day in varied situations and which enjoys a high status, probably develops to a great extent outside the school and without its help. To this well developed majority language mother tongue, the immersion programme adds another language which in no way threatens the first. Many of the positive results recorded in studies of bilingualism and its effect on cognitive development and school achievement derive from just these sorts of additive situation, as can be seen in earlier sections.

In submersion programmes, the situation is *subtractive* (Lambert, 1975): language learning takes place so that the child's linguistic proficiency constantly reflects a process where a second language gradually undermines L1, is substituted for it. And the learning of the second is a slower process than the forgetting of the first (see, for example, Toukomaa, 1977a). Or a child, born in the country of production – Swetland, 1979; Catani, 1982 – never learns L1 to the level of proficiency of monolinguals. The development in both languages is fragmentary and incomplete. Subtractive bilingualism is what has often been called double semilingualism in Scandinavia (Hansegård, 1972), or it may also be called "disruptive bilingualism" (Bain & Yu, 1978b), on the grounds that the development of the mother tongue has been disrupted by L2.

All the negative results for bilinguals in different kinds of investigation into IQ, in language tests and in measurements of school achievement seem to occur in connection with subtractive bilingualism in submersion situations. Often it may be exactly the situation suggested by the threshold hypothesis where the child has not reached the monolingual level in any language. The child is especially at risk when she is forced to function for a long time at school in her weaker language, while the mother tongue is given no institutional or societal support (see 5.2.4).

Language shelter programmes seem to produce a positive kind of bilingualism which I call functional: the child can manage in both languages in accordance with the society's demands and her own wishes. One of the differences in relation to additive language learning situations has to do with the fact that the criteria decisive for what is learnt in which language may differ. At any rate in the beginning, the extent of an immersion child's use of L2, the language of instruction, for natural communication, can be relatively restricted and more dependent on the child's own active efforts (and choices). Children in language shelter programmes, by contrast, usually live in the midst of an environment dominated by the majority language, so that demands from the outside rather than their own preference decide what of L2 they learn most quickly. They also encounter situations at an earlier stage where they are obliged to function in L2 and this determines to a large extent the kind of repertoire they find it most useful to learn. The input they get in L2 is thus largely determined by the society outside the school. Immersion children, on the other hand, will sometimes have no contact at all with L2 outside school hours, at any rate during the first few years, and they are therefore very dependent on which parts of the L2-reality the school chooses for them to learn. In contrast again, children in segregational programmes may live surrounded by L2-speakers (guest workers) or may not (children in Bantustans), but racism and segregation prevent them from either participating in L2-activities or at least choosing how much and in what type of activities they want to participate. Functional bilingualism, like the additive variety, brings with it a good chance of positive cognitive development and success at school, while there is a distinct risk of negative consequences in submersion and segregational programmes. For details see section 7.4.

9.6   Circumstances conducive to second language learning – a comparison between different programmes

In 5.2.3, 7.3.5 and earlier in this chapter we have already discussed many of the important factors influencing second language learning and tried to summarize them in various ways. Here we will try to give another type of summary and then see how the different programmes just discussed compare in organizing circumstances conducive to the best possible L2-learning for the child. The starting point in the discussion is that the most important process in both learning and acquiring L2 is to convert input (what the learner receives when she is being exposed to L2) to intake (i.e. to something that is processed and retained).

There is no guarantee whatsoever that all input will become intake. In fact, there are many situations where the amount of input may be large but the intake extremely small. This is the case with those adult migrants who have lived in the country of production for years, sometimes a decade or more, without learning much of the majority language (see e.g. Kotsinas, 1981), even though they have been surrounded by it at their place of work, in shops, in the streets, on television, etc. Likewise there is evidence that there is no guaranteed intake even in the case of children, regardless of the amount of input (e.g. Aronsson, 1978a). Dorothy Legarreta-Marcaida's observation (1981: 88) from a kindergarten with 14 Spanish-speaking children taught through the medium of English is typical: "The school program was eradicating Spanish and teaching very little English – though children were 'exposed' to it all day long."

If we try to assess what type of conditions or prerequisites are conducive to converting input to intake, the following points can be suggested:
- The input must be *comprehensible* to the child, at least to a large extent. Factors influencing the comprehensibility have to do with the child's *level of cognitive functioning, linguistic proficiency* in the language concerned, *knowledge of the world*, and with the *chance to infer from contextual cues*. The relevance of the first two is almost self-evident. Knowledge of the world has already been discussed to a certain extent. The less the child understands verbally of the input, the more she must know and/or be able to infer from the context. A decontextualized situation, like the one already described in the higher grades, provides fewer cues for making the input comprehensible, and therefore the child's knowledge of the world (here among other things, and most importantly, her knowledge of the subject matter) becomes more crucial. Specialized knowledge of the particular topic (and setting, situation) where the input is being given in an L2, helps to make the input more comprehensible.

An example given by Stephen Krashen in a lecture introducing Krashen 1981 (San Francisco, 15.1.1982) illustrates the role of knowledge. Krashen was temporarily attached to a French-language university in Canada, and his French was low intermediate school French. He also attended faculty meetings. He claims that he could understand more, i.e. he received more comprehensible input, than a French-speaking man-in-the-street (or woman-in-the-street, my remark) would have received in the same situation. Such a man (or rather woman) would probably not know anything about faculty meetings, their usual content, style of discourse, etc. while Krashen, who is an old hand in university contexts, could make out a lot even with his incomplete knowledge of French. Knowledge of the world can, at least to a certain extent, make up for lack of linguistic competence in a foreign language, and thus make the input the person receives more comprehensible.

And if the input is more comprehensible, it is more likely to become intake, i.e. to lead to learning or acquisition.
- The *affective filter must be low*. In Krashen's terms this means that the *anxiety level* must be low, *motivation* and *self-confidence* must be high.
- The child – and especially the adult – must have an *instrument for analyzing the input*.

It is also important to look at the role of input in foreign and second language lessons. In most Western European countries with migrants, the majority language is still taught to migrant children, when special classes in it exist, using the same methods as those used in foreign language teaching, because many of the languages concerned have never been taught as second languages, only either as mother tongues or as foreign languages. In foreign language instruction the classroom is often the main source of input, because the learners by definition do not live in an environment where the foreign languages are spoken by large numbers of native speakers. The task of the classroom teaching is here to provide both the input itself, and the means of making input intake. If the language lessons are abolished (or postponed to a later stage in the child's school career), the input and, accordingly, the intake, disappear, and the child does not have any chance of learning the language.

The situation is altogether different in a second language class, except at the very beginning when the learner does not understand *any* of the input outside the classroom. Even if there are adults with limited and perhaps topically restricted input outside the classroom, and children who are so much socially segregated from the majority children that their out-of-school input is small, a second language learning situation mostly means that the learner gets (or can get, if she does not consciously try to avoid it because of earlier negative experiences) a huge amount of input outside the classroom. It is an utter waste of time, then, for the teacher to spend time providing input. The task of classroom teaching in a second language instruction would be twofold:
- to make at least some of the incomprehensible input that the learner gets outside school more comprehensible (for instance by providing key vocabulary, with translations, etc.), and
- to give the learner the instruments needed to make input (which the learner is supposed to get outside classroom situations, to a great extent) intake (for instance by giving the learner as much knowledge as possible about those worlds that the learner comes into contact with outside the lessons – and this is naturally most efficient if it is done through the mother tongue).

If instruction through the medium of the second language is reduced, completely abandoned or postponed, the learner still gets massive amounts of input. The second language learning results then depend on whether or not the learner had adequate instruments to make that input intake. If the time saved from cutting the instruction through the medium of the second language (which may have given the learner a lot of incomprehensible input) can be used more efficiently, for instance, to give the learner the instruments needed, through the medium of the learner's mother tongue, then cutting the instruction through the medium of the second language and teaching the child through the medium of her mother tongue may result in more intake, i.e. more learning and acquisition of the second language.

It is useful to remember, when looking at the child's situation in a submersion class, that "a small amount of comprehensible input, even one hour per day, will do more for second language acquisition than massive amounts of incomprehensible input", and "understanding is a prerequisite to acquisition. Thus, the more context or background [knowledge] we can provide, the more acquisition will take place" (Krashen, 1981: 66–68).

We could try to summarize some of the conditions for optimal L2-learning as follows, and then try to compare the programmes we have discussed – and I would like here to remind the reader also of the discussions in 5.2.4 about the input, processing and output through the medium of a channel not yet fully mastered in decontextualized cognitively demanding situations.

1. *requirements for making the affective filter low* (affective factors)
a low levels of anxiety, springing from a feeling that the child is being given credit for her real performance and judged in a fair way, where her imperfect command of L2 is not interpreted as a deficiency but where interlanguage is seen as natural for a learner;
b high internal motivation, reflecting an acceptance of the child, her language and culture. A possibility of reacting and being understood both non-verbally and through the medium of L1, and getting help from bilingual teachers when the child's attempts to produce or understand something in L2 fail (compare e.g. Lozanov, 1978);
c high levels of self-confidence, based on acceptance, a feeling of having a fair chance to succeed, together with experience of success.

2. *requirements for getting comprehensible input in L2* (cognitive-linguistic-social L2-related factors)
a input in school which is adapted to the linguistic level of a learner of L2 (together with other learners, not native speakers of L2), especially in the beginning of L2-studies when the child does not get much out of outside-school-input;
b input outside school from understanding peers, with a possibility of gaining high status and being accepted on an equal footing.

3. *requirements for developing instruments to analyze the input and make it intake* (cognitive-linguistic–social-L1-related factors)
a adequate cognitive development in the mother tongue, in order to give the child good possibilities of inferring, of using contextual cues, of analyzing, etc. and in order to help the development of the common underlying basis for all language development, L1 and L2; means of analyzing the input;

b adequate linguistic development in the mother tongue, in order to be thoroughly familiar with ways of realizing cognitive categories linguistically at least in one language (including familiarity with more complex standard language, and good reading and writing skills);

c enough background knowledge, knowledge of the world, given through the medium of the child's L1, so that the child is familiar with the topics discussed in L2 in order to understand more and get more comprehensible input;

d help from a bilingual teacher, who can explain, give examples, compare and give rules when the child asks for it, after first having defined something as a problem.

TABLE 8

Requirement	Programme			
	immersion	*submersion*	*segregation*	*maintenance*
1a low levels of anxiety	yes	no	no	yes
1b high internal motivation	yes	no	no	yes
1c high levels of self-confidence	yes	no	no	yes
2a input adapted to student's level	yes	no	yes?	yes
2b input from equal peers outside school	no	no	no	yes?
3a adequate cognitive development in L1	yes	no	yes?	yes
3b adequate linguistic development in L1	yes	no	can be	yes
3c enough knowledge of the world given	yes	no	can be	yes
3d help from a bilingual teacher	yes	no	can be	yes

As we can see, the situation of a minority child in a submersion programme is the worst possible one from the point of view of L2-learning. Even if the child here is exposed to L2 more than in any of the other programmes, the exposure is not of the kind conducive to L2-learning. In fact we may speculate how much of the L2-learning of those who have managed anyway is despite the school (for instance in peer contacts outside the school) and not because of it. And if the child does not master the most important instrument of learning in those cases where it is L2, the possibilities this gives for school achievement are poor. This takes us back to looking at our circle again.

9.7   Synthesis

With the passage of time, we come full circle: society gets back the negative consequences of what it set going itself by organizing the education of minority children so badly. The children who achieve little at school and have little or no further education grow up to be adults who have difficulties on the labour market, difficulties in understanding why their situation is disadvantaged, and difficulties in doing anything about it. Now society should bear the responsibility for them, because it influenced their chances in a negative direction. Instead, society makes the minority members pay, in quite concrete ways, both economically and psychologically (and often repatriates those who are unproductive over longer periods of time – see Chapter 11). And in any case, the minority members (instead of society) are blamed, and made to believe that the bad results are their fault. Of if they refuse to believe it, they are at least prevented from protesting in any effective way (Chapter 12). But even if those parts of society which are responsible for the failures refuse to accept the responsibility, they are affected too. The failure of many minority members ultimately affect the whole society, possibly in rather disruptive ways if the poor system of education continues. Some of these more societal perspectives are discussed in Chapters 11 and 12.

It is quite clear that our ideas about the ways in which bilingualism, especially early foreign or second language learning, affects children's development, have become much more subtle and refined in the last few years. It should be clear that it is impossible to speak about the benefit or the harm done by early bilingualism *in general*. What is decisive is the conditions under which and the reasons why L2 is being learnt, i.e. bilingualism must be seen as being caused by something and aiming at something.

But if we try to see bilingualism as something constantly changing and developing (as I also tried to do in the definitions of both L1 and bilingualism) we also need to be able to explain how a child's proficiency in the two languages leads to different results *during* the schooling process (and section 5.2.4 tries for instance to start a description of one of the details). To this end we must dissect the degree and the level of bilingualism and treat them in different ways in the different phases of the process. A general, synthesizing model for the evaluation of the results of education programmes aiming at bilingualism has been proposed by Cummins 1977a. He suggests that L1 and L2 abilities should be treated *firstly* as an independent variable, in relation to choice of programme. The social and linguistic conditions of the child before starting school (minority/majority, low/high status mother tongue, etc.) will determine the child's linguistic level in each language when she starts school. These abilities should be treated as a causal variable in the choice of a suitable educational programme. L1 and L2 abilities should *secondly* be treated as process variables because they mediate the child's experiences at school and determine the academic outcome. At the end of the school year L1 and L2 abilities should *thirdly* be treated as a dependent variable, i.e. the child's abilities in the two languages are seen as one of the outcomes of the education she has received, along with cognitive and academic outcomes. Cummins provides the following diagrammatic illustration of his model (1977a: 84):

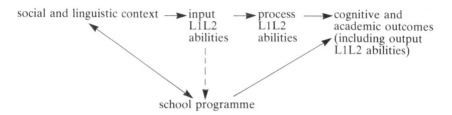

The concrete experiences of different school situations in Chapter 11 should be fairly easy to place within this kind of framework, so that a better understanding of the relationship between bilingualism and school achievement is arrived at.

Notes to Chapter Nine

1. Darsie, 1926; Graham, 1925; Jamieson & Sandiford, 1928; Pintner, 1923; Pintner & Keller, 1922; Lester, 1929; Barke, 1933; Havinghurst & Hilkevitch, 1944; Shotwell, 1945; Darcy, 1946; Jones, 1952; Anastasi & Cordova, 1953; Fitch, 1966.
2. Bain, 1975a; Balkan, 1970; Cummins & Gulutsan, 1974; Liedke & Nelson, 1968.
3. Watson, 1973b: 367, 373; Katz, 1973a: 382–83; 1973b: 257–61; Labov 1972a: 191.
4. Tyler, 1965: 100, 118–19; Goldman, 1973: 353; Watson, 1973b: 367–68; 1973c: 281–82; Katz, 1973a: 378–81; 1973b: 263–64; Pettigrew, 1964: 128; Osterrieth, 1974: 39–40.
5. Katz, 1973b: 256–65; 1973a: 385–86; Watson, 1973b; 368–69; Labov, 1972a: 205–6; Kangas, 1972b: 140–41.

10 Double semilingualism – does it exist?

10.1 Double semilingualism and other deficiency theories

Double semilingualism has become a dirty word in the Scandinavian debate. Parents and teachers use the term: parents usually to express their worry about their children, and teachers sometimes in a negatively labelling way (about their pupils) but more often in speaking of their worry about a kind of diagnosis which is very imprecise and not promising. Teachers, in using the term, also express a helplessness in a situation where they simply do not know what kind of assistance to give the children. If occasionally some people use the term of themselves, it can be in very different situations. Occasionally it may be used in the spirit of bitterness and defeat by someone who feels linguistically and otherwise helpless, powerless, and deprived of opportunity – someone about to give up. More often it is said as a joke by someone who is in fact highly bilingual (with a certain often freely chosen functional differentiation) – such a speaker can afford to joke about her linguistic abilities. At the precise moment she cannot remember a word in the other language. Again, the term may be used in a half-ironic or half-bitter way by someone who is clearly repeating someone else's judgement of her, not her own identification. However, as used by researchers semilingualism is certainly a dirty word, something we are not supposed to say. One may encounter an almost moral indignation in other researchers if one uses the term.

I ought to make it clear that I think it has been a good slogan word and that it has done its duty, which was to stimulate a practical discussion as to what should be done. In the scientific debate the word has outlived its usefulness and should go. But *only* if we really do begin to investigate what the phenomenon actually is that it tried to describe. In my view there is something real behind it, but a phenomenon that is very difficult to pin down using the crude mesh of research concepts and methods that we have at our disposal – at the moment it indeed seems impossible.

248

Many of those who have never met children who possibly might be referred to as semilingual suspect that the whole concept is a fiction, more depending on the prejudice of observers than the child observed. It is easy, especially for researchers of a progressive cast of mind, to brush aside the whole concept and to declare that it must be the same kind of middle-class construction as was once the description, for instance, of black children's English as a deficient and inferior variety of white middle-class English, which of course it is not. This is usual practice with the middle-class bias which enables those in power to define the speech of the working class, of black people or of other powerless groups as deviant and consequently deficient, simply because it does not happen to resemble the variety they speak. We can see this with researchers who have worked to dispel prejudice, for instance, about Black English (Brent-Palmer, 1979; Burling, 1981), but who are not very familiar with the Scandinavian situation (in addition Burling seems to think that semilingualism describes interference, language mixing, which is of course completely incorrect). Again, they may say, this is another deficit theory using monolingual white middle-class norms in a markedly ethnocentric fashion to force those norms on bilingual immigrant working-class children, and then to label them as inferior, deficient, or at least different.

This is a very tempting intellectual position, and I wish with all my heart that semilingualism could thus be explained away. It would then only be necessary to change those observing and not the observed (who has been labelled as semilingual). But I can be as careful as I can to guard myself against distorting prejudice of any kind; and the phenomenon can still not be explained away. What it seems to me to be important to stress is that semilingualism cannot be regarded as a deficiency inherent in the *individual* but should rather be treated as one result of the (linguistically and otherwise) powerless circumstances, the (linguistic) oppression in which she has lived. Even if we might be able to speak of it in terms which say something about language (and I am not even sure this is possible, at any rate yet), and particularly in terms which say something about the individual's opportunities for using language for all those purposes language should be able to serve for people, I do not consider semilingualism to be a linguistic or scientific concept at all. In my view it is a political concept, so far at a pre-scientific stage of development. It properly forms part of an argument about power and oppression. But it should be the duty of researchers towards those who suffer its consequences to subject the whole notion to careful scientific study. And until the conditions that produce semilingualism disappear, we should continue to point to the phenomenon they produce (see Wande, 1977; Skutnabb-Kangas & Toukomaa, 1977).

Double semilingualism is one of the ways in which the shortcomings of the school system are projected on to the individual child, to be experienced as the child's shortcomings both by herself (see Chapter 12 on patterns of violence) and by others. It is the child who comes to be the scapegoat instead of school and society. As soon as the minority itself gets control over the way the school system is organized, semilingualism can be eradicated. But if we are to understand anything very much about the whole phenomenon and the debate about it in Scandinavia, we must begin by looking back for a moment at the origins of the concept. This also seems to me to be a useful exercise because there are so many misunderstandings about the concept in other countries – it is treated as if it had a scientifically proven status (and well supported by empirical studies) and then questioned; rather we should all be trying to discover what the phenomenon actually might be.

10.2   The origins of the concept

The term double semilingualism first appeared in the Scandinavian debate about bilingualism at the beginning of 1962, when a radio talk by Nils Erik Hansegård was announced in *Röster i Radio/TV* entitled "Tvåspråkig eller halvspråkig" ("Bilingual or semilingual"). The term was taken up by Håkan Ringbom (who had taken part in the work of Nordiska sommaruniversitetet – the Nordic university summer school – in 1962 when Hansegård lectured on semilingualism) in *Finsk Tidskrift* (1962) in a review of different theories about language shift. He wrote: ". . . when an individual abandons her mother tongue completely in favour of another language, there will always be a period of 'double semilingualism', when the two languages get in each other's way" (Ringbom, 1962: 267). There is no evidence that the concept or the term has any connections with the early Finnish nationalist movement in the mid-nineteenth century which advocated that Finnish should become a national language in Finland, even though some writers, ignorant of Finnish history, have suggested it.

Quite what the term might mean was little discussed until the appearance of Nils Erik Hansegård's book, *Tvåspråkighet eller halvspråkighet*, in 1968. In this book Hansegård drew attention to the linguistic situation of the Torneå Valley Finns and the Same, and accused the Swedish school system of being an instrument for language shift for those whose mother tongue was not Swedish.

When Christina Bratt Paulston, in November 1974, introduced the notion of "semilingualism" in America, she made the point that the phenomenon had been noted by Bloomfield as early as 1927, even though he did not use the term "semilingualism" to describe it (Bratt Paulston, 1974: 28). Bloomfield described the speech of an Indian called White-Thunder in these terms:

"White-Thunder, a man around forty, speaks less English than Menomini, and that is a strong indictment, for his Menomini is atrocious. His vocabulary is small; his inflections are often barbarous; he constructs sentences of a few threadbare models. He may be said to speak no language tolerably. His case is not uncommon among younger men, even when they speak but little English. Perhaps it is due, in some indirect way, to the impact of the conquering language."

Dell Hymes in 1974 also made a similar observation about the Quechua Indians who "so to speak gave up their Quechua before they had learnt Spanish" (Hymes, 1974: 72). Terms like subtractive bilingualism (Lambert) non-lingual (Pfeiffer) 1975 – see the description of Kee in 12.2 – or disruptive bilingualism (Bain & Yu) also refer to the same type of phenomenon. The phenomenon, then, is not particularly new to researchers, nor particularly Scandinavian.

10.3   Different definitions

Most writers who have used the term semilingualism (except Hansegård) have made little attempt to define it properly, and many would be reluctant to admit that what they have said about it amounts in practice to a definition. This is a further indication, in my view, of how emotional and pre-scientific the discussion has been. Nils Erik Hansegård is still the writer who has made the most thorough attempt to define what he means by semilingualism. The attempts at definition can, even if they are helpless, at any rate be arranged as definitions by competence and by function. Most definitions of semilingualism are by competence: "The imperfect command of a linguistic system" (Loman, 1974a: 9). "Linguistic proficiency is defective both in Finnish and Swedish" (Pinomaa, 1974a: 122). "Partial command of Swedish and partial command of the mother tongue" (Hansegård, 1972: 128). "These children know neither Finnish nor Swedish properly, they have become semilingual" (Heyman, 1973: 107). "Immigrant pupils ... have acquired only the superficial everyday language. They do not understand the deeper meanings of words. Finnish immigrant pupils are ... usually very backward in linguistic comprehension and vocabulary both in Swedish and Finnish ... their linguistic development has come to a halt, they have become semilingual" (Toukomaa, 1972b; cf. Cummins, 1980b – here, too, Toukomaa was ahead of his time ...). "The child never learns to express himself fully in either language but becomes semilingual" (Resolution ... 1973). "Knows neither the mother tongue nor Swedish well" (Schwarz, 1973: 4).

Other definitions concentrate on the function of language, and consider how well (or rather in this case how badly) the individual succeeds in communicating by means of the two languages. Most definitions by function are set against a background of a functional differentiation between languages, diglossia, which has been transferred from the community at large to the individual, so that she has a command only of those aspects of either language that she actually needs in the diglossic community. Neither Torneå Valley Finns nor immigrant children at Swedish schools are able to

use both their languages in all the situations in which language is called upon,
at all levels, in all spheres of activity, in all functions. This is the kind of fact
reflected in the definitions by function:
  "Apparently, the teaching in Sweden leads, at best, only to
  'semilingualism' . . . they learn to talk about subjects connected with
  school in Swedish, subjects to do with home they talk about in Finnish.
  After a time neither language will be usable in all contexts" (von
  Sydow, 1970: 1799).
  "What is specific to diglossia is that each of the languages has *mutually
  complementary* functions, just as different styles fulfil different
  functions in a monolingual community. . . . They are in other words in
  some way two linguistic halves. Instead of bilingualism we should rather
  speak about *semilingualism* or partlingualism in diglossia. This
  semilingualism entails a limitation of an individual's communicative
  ability outside the community: in a monolingual community in which
  one of the diglossic languages is spoken the bilingual's repertoire may
  prove to be too limited in a certain area, either the official or the
  unofficial" (Jaakkola, 1973a: 21).

10.4   Hansegård and semilingualism: both quantifiable and qualitative aspects

I think it is important to try to see what Hansegård meant and what type
of description he has given about semilingualism, in order to understand the
very emotional debate. One of the important differences I see in the
semilingualism debate compared to many other deficiency concept debates
is that it has usually been a monolingual middle-class standard speaker who
has defined and used the concept, not one of those "labelled". Most deficit
concepts has been used in a way which has been negative to the minority in
question, in order to legitimize the fact that no measures or too few measures
have been taken, by explaining that the "condition" is incurable and the
people's own fault. In the case of semilingualism we can see the opposite.
Hansegård, even if he comes from the Swedish-speaking majority, is a near
native speaker of both Finnish and Same, the language groups he has
described (he held a chair in Same at the University of Umeå) and lived for
decades with the people he describes. Even though he is a philologist and
linguist by training, he has used mainly anthropology-related methods and
written mainly in an anthropological and historical tradition (in addition to
detailed linguistic accounts, for instance, about the Same language). Also it
seems to me that those minority members who have used the semilingualism
concept in discussions, have had (and expressed) the same feeling described
by, for instance, Dale Spender about something everybody knows (in her
case something every woman knows – another minority) and that now

becomes easier to talk about because it has got a name. Even if there might have been some negative labelling also, the concept has certainly drawn attention to the educational concerns of minorities in Scandinavia, especially Sweden, and may also have contributed to the fact that Swedish immigrant education is one of the best in the industrialized world.

What has Hansegård said, then, about semilingualism? Nils Erik Hansegård summarized the views elaborated in his book, *Tvåspråkighet eller halvspråkighet?* (1968) in an article with the same title (1975). Here he divides linguistic command into six aspects and says that what he means by semilingualism is "a defective command by bilinguals in these six areas" (Hansegård, 1975: 8). The first three aspects he isolates are more quantitative and have more to do with the "langue" side of linguistic command; the last three are more qualitative and have more to do with the "langage" side. "Langue" and "langage" are Saussurean concepts (de Saussure, 1959): the first refers to individual languages, concrete linguistic systems like Finnish and Swedish; the second refers to the general human ability (which distinguishes woman from the animals) to use language as a means of communication. Hansegård suggests that it is the first three of his six aspects which have been the focus of attention in discussions of semilingualism; he himself, by contrast, is more interested in focusing on the last three, on the "langage" element (Hansegård, 1975: 8). These are Hansegård's six aspects:

1. *Size* of the repertoire of words, phrases, etc. understood or actively available in speech.
2. *Linguistic correctness*, i.e. the ability to understand correctly and to realize in a speech act such elements of a language as phonemes, intonation, stress, suffixes, etc.
3. The *degree of automatism,* i.e. the extent to which understanding and active use of a language take place without conscious deliberation, without blockages or other impediments.
4. *Ability to create or neologize.*
5. Mastery of the *cognitive, emotive and volitional function* of language.
6. Richness or poorness in *individual meanings*, i.e. whether reading or listening to a particular linguistic system evokes lively and reverberating semantic images or not (Hansegård, 1975: 8).

Hansegård continues:

"We may, if we consider the matter from the 'langue' side, describe a bilingual individual as semilingual, if he/she shows quantitative deficiencies (smaller vocabulary, etc.) compared with those who speak the languages as their only language, and who have the same individual prerequisites (social group, school education, etc.), and if the bilingual in addition to this deviates more from the normal for the two languages and has a lower degree of automatism than monolinguals (see aspects 1–3 above). This is probably what many people have understood

semilingualism to be . . ."   (Hansegård, 1975: 8)
Hansegård describes semilingualism in terms of the three aspects more
central to him like this:
"We have a case of semilingualism (aspect 5) if an individual cannot
give full linguistic expression to her feelings, or is not fully affected
emotionally by a language. I have for long periods been in contact with
Torneå Valley Finns (and with Same) with a kind of inner silence and a
defective emotional contact. An individual may well speak Swedish
correctly and fluently but the emotional experience behind the flow of
words seems meagre. The explanation of this lack, and others relating
to aspects 4 and 5, can lie in a poverty of individual semantic
experiences (aspect 6)."

(Hansegård, 1975: 8)

10.5   What has been investigated?

10.5.1   The quantifiable aspects

We might ask first exactly *what it is* that has been investigated to
produce results which begin to say something about the phenomenon. Most
studies deal with Hansegård's first three aspects, the ones he did not
consider so important. Let me discuss a few of them.

A collection of nine articles by Magdalena Jaakkola, Irina Koskinen,
Mogens Baumann Larsen, Bengt Loman, Kerstin Nordin, Mirja Pinomaa
and Gunnel Wrede was edited by Bengt Loman under the title *Språk och
samhälle 2, Språket i Tornedalen* (Language and Society 2, The Language in
the Torneå Valley) in 1974. The contributions presented one part of the
results of an interdisciplinary project designed to give as fully detailed a
picture as possible of the Torneå Valley both on the Finnish and Swedish
side of the border that runs through it, and to study the effect the border has.
The articles in Loman's volume focused upon both the intralingual (regional
and social) and interlingual (Finnish-Swedish) variation in the Torneå
Valley as well as upon the inhabitants' linguistic attitudes. The question that
became the most important one to answer was whether the inhabitants of the
Torneå Valley were really doubly semilingual when their Finnish was
compared with that of native speakers in Finland, and their Swedish with
that of native speakers elsewhere in Sweden and among the Finland Swedes.
The linguistic material consists of transcribed interviews in both Finnish and
Swedish. The informants were first interviewed in Swedish about their
children's schooling and a year later in Finnish on the same subject. A
macrosyntactic analysis of the material was carried out using a method
developed by Loman and others for an earlier project on the syntax of
spoken Swedish, *Talsyntax* (Loman & Jörgensen, 1971). The complexity of
the material (sentence length, number of subordinate clauses), its

correctness (number of correctly and incorrectly constructed sentences, incomplete sentences, or errors in sentence construction), and its completeness (number of complete sentences as compared with the number of fragmentary sentences and interjectional macrosyntagms) were all analyzed.

The comparison showed that the adult informants' Swedish was as correct and complete and almost as complex as the Swedish of informants from the corresponding social group elsewhere in Sweden and in Finland, measured in the terms described. The results showed too that in its macrosyntactic characteristics the informants' Finnish was much like their Swedish (there were no results describing the macrosyntactic structure of Finnish-speaking Finns). The interference in both their languages is described and it may be noted that they have the same kind of interference in their Swedish as the Finland Swedes have.

A comparison between the performances of different groups of eighth grade children (bilinguals from the Torneå Valley, Finns who had learnt Swedish as a school subject only, and Finland Swedes) in different Swedish language tests showed that the Torneå Valley children were not in any way handicapped, and did better than the Finnish-speaking group in most subtests.

Nothing has appeared in this investigation that can be said to lend support to the semilingualism hypothesis. Bengt Loman concluded his thorough case study of a single individual's linguistic ability with these words: "if her linguistic ability is representative – then the whole notion of semilingualism is based on a fiction" (Loman, 1974c: 78). Bengt Loman himself tries to find why the "myth" should have arisen. He points out that "people from outside the Torneå Valley tend to classify its inhabitants socially on the basis of the degree of Finnish substratum in their pronunciation [of Swedish]." In the social assessment

"there are likely also to be latent evaluations of an individual's education, perhaps also of his general competence. Corresponding tests have also shown that assessment made of an individual on the basis of an anonymous voice and speech sample tends to be influenced by superficial features especially – how self-assured the speaker sounds or how fluently he speaks – rather than by the more substantial aspects of speech, namely grammatical form and content. There is a possible vicious circle here. People from the Torneå Valley often say they are made fun of because of their pronunciation; this creates insecurity, and these factors are perhaps enough to maintain, both among the people in the Torneå Valley themselves and among outsiders, the myth of their linguistic inferiority" (Loman, 1974a: 14).

Loman also points to the possibility that the people in this region may misjudge their own linguistic ability, and that they may have exaggerated notions of the verbal proficiency of monolingual outsiders. He discusses their sense of inadequacy, especially in more formal public speech. He also discusses the possibility that the conclusions may be based on random or inadequately collected materials, on influence on the informants' linguistic behaviour of a great distance (linguistic or other) between interviewer and informant (Loman, 1974c: 78–79).

All the kinds of factor Loman mentions may well play a part in perpetuating the notion of semilingualism. But most of the investigations that seem *not* to support the hypothesis that such a phenomenon exists concern themselves entirely with *syntax*. And even if a speaker's syntax is complete and undistorted by comparison with that of monolinguals other aspects may still tend to suggest the possibility of semilingualism.

As against Loman's results we can cite the results of vocabulary tests in the same book. Magdalena Jaakkola used synonym tests in Finnish and Swedish (Jaakkola, 1973: 86, 1974) and found that the bilinguals showed the poorest performance in both. In Pertti Toukomaa's studies of Finnish immigrant children (Toukomaa, 1972b, 1973a, 1975c; Skutnabb-Kangas & Toukomaa, 1976), the children's performance both in the Finnish tests (vocabulary, synonyms, word groups) and in the Swedish tests (DPI tests, listening comprehension, reading comprehension, dictation) was at the level of the lowest 10% of the monolingual children (Skutnabb-Kangas & Toukomaa, 1976: 51–77). In most of the studies of immigrant children and of speakers from the Torneå Valley, there has been either a test of some kind or an assessment of language proficiency, sometimes only in Swedish but often in both languages, as part of the information gathered about school achievement. In the majority of these studies the children's language proficiency, either in Swedish or mostly in both their languages, has been below the monolingual norm.[1] Even though Wrede's investigation did not reveal any differences (see Wrede, 1974, or for more detailed data, Wrede, 1971), the rest of the empirical evidence is so substantial that it must be taken to be a proven fact that bilingual speakers can fall below the monolingual norm in vocabulary. (A detailed discussion of various possible sources of error in Wrede's investigation and in other similar studies may be found in Wrede, 1974.) We can state then, that immigrant children at least, and to some extent also Torneå Valley speakers, perform less well than monolingual speakers in item one of Hansegård's list. In the matter of items two and three, quantitative investigation has so far shown up no differences of consequence, but observation testifies to the fact that immigrant children seem to speak less correctly (aspect 2) and seem to react with a less easy automatic response (aspect 3) than monolinguals (what is observed is linguistic uncertainty, silence, reluctance to speak, a tendency to speak only in whispers, a more than "ordinary" need to hunt for words, etc.). Moreover, if we recall what was said in section 5.2.2.5 about surface fluency and the use of a language as an instrument of thought, one could also imagine that some of the features Hansegård discusses under 2 and 3 would *not* need to show any deficiencies.

This applies in particular to pronunciation, that aspect of correctness that has to do with "sounds, intonation, stress" (Hansegård, 1975: 8) – by contrast with aspects of correctness involving larger linguistic units like suffixes and syntactic and semantic correctness – and features relating to automatism and fluency in ordinary everyday oral situations in face-to-face contact. Hansegård should perhaps have specified a little more the various features under his second and third aspects, because especially for speakers who have heard both their languages from childhood, surface fluency is seldom a difficulty. This often contributes to teachers' misjudgements of children's command of the language more foreign to the children, and leads the teachers to believe that the children's proficiency is better than it is in reality.

10.5.2 The qualitative aspects

The last three of Hansegård's six aspects of linguistic command, the aspects referring to the "langage" side of language, have been much too little investigated, though Hansegård himself thinks that they are the more important ones. The reason they have been investigated so little is plain: we do not yet know very well how to do it. The whole area is in the borderland between linguistics and psychology, even psychiatry, and so far only some tentative forays into it have been suggested (by means of association tests, and Osgood's semantic differential . . . Loman 1975, Hansegård 1975, Skutnabb-Kangas 1976e), but almost nothing done. There have been a lot of discussions but very few empirical studies. A few of the discussions will be mentioned.

Hansegård's aspect 4, creative and neologizing ability, can be looked at from many angles. One possible approach remarked upon in a debate (see transcript in Skutnabb-Kangas, 1977c) could be through linguistic creativity as it finds expression in literary activity. The dearth of Finnish writers on the Swedish side of the border in the Torneå Valley was remarked upon in the debate. This lack is the more striking when one looks at the Finnish side of the border where a fair number of notable writers have grown up and lived, writing a good deal about life in that part of the country (for example, Timo Mukka, in his book *Maa on syntinen laulu (Earth is a Sinful Song)*). We might also think about creativity and neologizing from the point of view of rigidity of norms. Children are usually allowed to create words, to make up new words and new compounds and to expand the use of existing words – in many cases these new creations pass into internal family use because they seem so "attractive". This is particularly so with names used for people (what the child calls herself, her grandparents, her godparents, and so on – the new coinage is often the fossilized shape of the child's first attempts to get the proper word out) or with objects the child comes into contact with day by day, with names for parts of the body, words which in certain milieu may have a taboo character (for the sexual, digestive or excretory functions, for instance). But many foreigners must have experienced the feeling that *they* are not allowed to be creative in the foreign language – their creations are not socially accepted. And if one tries a linguistic joke in a foreign language, as often as not one is corrected "you can't actually say that", or "one doesn't say that in X". The same way may well be true for a bilingual who is trying to be creative in the language she speaks less well. And after enough in the way of negative feed-back one simply gives up trying. Just how rigid norms many people have and just how unaware the monolingually naive are of the fact that language is an agreement which can be changed, and that new words and expressions, new linguistic conventions can be introduced, if one wishes to do so, simply by starting to use them and by promoting and spreading their use, has become *abundantly* clear in the course of work in women's movements to change the patriarchal language (see, for example, Blauberg, 1978; Rekdal & Skutnabb-Kangas, 1979). It is probably impossible for us at the present moment to say how much the lack of creativity and neologizing in the language of speakers whose conditions of life may be suspected of not giving the development of their bilingualism the best possible chance is due to a lesser degree of actual ability, and how much due to monolingual intolerance of the coinages of non-native (or bilingual) speakers.

In regard to Hansegård's *fifth* aspect, discussion has largely centred on the cognitive and emotive rather than the volitional functions of language. In the consideration of the cognitive function, the threshold hypothesis is of interest (see section 9.1). The hypothesis suggests that those bilinguals who do not reach the lower threshold of bilingual competence which is needed to avoid cognitive deficiency, belong to just that group which according to Hansegård's description of semilingual speakers could show deviation in cognitive aspects of language, compared with monolinguals.

The problem of the possible effect of semilingualism on children's cognitive development is difficult to approach, but an awareness of it should be central in any discussion of different models for bilingual education, particularly in relation to what consequences may ensue if children are forced to function for long periods in the less well mastered language in educational situations whose function is among others to encourage the development of language as a cognitive instrument.

Reaction to the question of a possibility of negative cognitive consequences has sometimes been simplistic and emotional, but moral indignation at the possibility of cognitive consequences helps no one. What is needed is basic research. It is especially in this area that the popular debate about semilingualism has often produced foolish statements and indefensible generalizations displaying conceptual confusion and imprecision.

As regards the emotive function of language, the debate in Scandinavia has centred on the question whether L2 can take on as much of an emotive function as L1, whether the second language can be emotionally charged for the speaker as her own mother tongue is (see Stolt, 1975a, b; Hansegård,

1975). Hansegård maintains that "it can hardly be doubted that the language first acquired is in a special position" (1975: 11), and that: "the mother tongue has an immediacy and spontaneity that can hardly be fully attained in another language. When it is a matter of expressing one's feelings, one's mother tongue functions with an immediacy that can be almost reflex-like" (Hansegård, 1975: 11). However, he does also admit that "the superiority of the mother tongue – in emotive functions and in other respects – is not a hard and fast rule without exceptions" (Hansegård, 1975: 11). Birgit Stolt believes that:

"it could be unfortunate if the emphasis on the emotional value of the home language gave rise to the idea that Swedish must of necessity come to be a solely intellectual, cold and abstract medium. On the contrary, we must try by all the means at our disposal to give Swedish a positive emotive function – that must be fundamental to any learning process that is to have good results" (Stolt, 1975b: 25).

Stolt maintains further that emotional contact does not only take place through language (and few would feel inclined to dissent), that L2 may well come to be charged emotionally by new experiences particularly linked with that new language. Stolt would like to see situations created to produce just such an emotional charge, for instance by teaching mothers and children Swedish together – a procedure which Hansegård, for his part, takes to be an even more refined version of that process of total linguistic assimilation, taking away a speaker's mother tongue, than the prohibitions and punishments which were used when the Finnish speakers in the Torneå Valley were made Swedish, undergoing "a cultural genocide" (Hansegård, 1975: 127).

It is probably the case that most immigrants who arrive as adults have their most highly charged emotional experiences in the medium of their mother tongue and are best able to convey their private and cultural heritage to their children by using that language. There may be exceptions among those who live together with people from the new country and who daily experience and verbalize new emotions in the new language, etc. or among refugees, etc. who want to have nothing more to do with their old language and country. In the first case, the children can acquire two mother tongues, each emotionally charged and it would be a pity to deprive them, by a decision that even the immigrant parent should use only the majority language, of the enrichment and intellectual stimulation of two mother tongues and two native cultures. In the latter case, as Birgit Stolt says, a great attempt must be made to give the majority language a positive emotional function, even though this generally does not seem to be very easy.

We must remember that a large part of children's socialization before school age will be in terms of their mother tongue. It is in their mother tongue that their deepest emotional security is anchored, and this sense of security is vitally what makes it possible for them to respond positively to new experiences. The new positive connotations that the children of course should get in learning denotative meanings in the new language, should preferably be connected with situations where the use of the new language is a natural and functional thing, that is, together with native speakers of it. If the parents also switch to the new language in order to create positive connotations in it, and in order, as they think, to help their children learn it better, then they risk moving to a "subtractive" language learning situation (Lambert, 1975), with L2 gradually taking the place of L1, rather than "additive" with L2 being added to L1 and with both languages being maintained. Bilingualism will in this case become a negative transitional phase rather than a source of permanent enrichment. Most of the unfortunate consequences of bilingualism spring from the subtractive kind.

A child is then certainly able to experience both languages as charged with positive emotion: the one language need not exclude the other. But just as the new language cannot properly be built on a vacuum (see the metaphor of the water lilies) so "emotional functions" cannot be built up without the corresponding natural, functional, positive experience in the new language. The true basis for new positive experience is the child's sense of security deriving from the acceptance of her social and personal identity by the group she is part of, and intimately connected to and conditioned by the socialization in the mother tongue (Skutnabb-Kangas & Toukomaa, 1976, 1977; Toukomaa & Skutnabb-Kangas, 1977).

Hansegård's final aspects had to do with richness or poverty in individual meanings, i.e. whether reading or listening to a particular linguistic system evokes lively and reverberating semantic images or not (1975: 8). Many of the examples I have given above and in my discussion of the mother tongue earlier in the volume illumine just this aspect and the feeling of something cold and impoverished in the second language even if the speaker has in other respects a good command of it. Antti Jalava, a Finnish writer living in Sweden, who came to Sweden as a 9 year old, then in adolescence almost completely forgot his Finnish, describes this very well in his articles, stories and books – see the passage from his "Nobody could see that I was a Finn" in Section 12. But how do we investigate these feelings? I for one do not know.

As we think over Hansegård's six aspects again, the conclusion is that there is evidence that his description of semilingualism describes something that may exist but something that we know close to nothing about. The further question to be asked then is what we as researchers accept as evidence, and that is what the debate has latterly centred on. There has been a fairly vigorous discussion of the methods used to elucidate the phenomenon of semilingualism.

10.6   The debate about methods

Those who have come most under attack have been Nils Erik
Hansegård and Pertti Toukomaa. The attacks have come from two
directions, both of which may be described as positivist, but since latterly the
argument has been more concerned with the organization of education for
immigrant children and not so much with semilingualism, I shall restrict
myself here to the accusations levelled at Hansegård.

Loman accuses Hansegård of a "tendency, in a discussion about the
linguistic situation of the people of the Torneå Valley, to allow generalizing
statements to replace attempts to elucidate empirically or to document
scientifically formulated hypotheses", and he goes on to say:
"There may of course be deficiencies of one kind or another in
individuals – but I react against Hansegård's tendency to ascribe all
these defects to the people of the Torneå Valley in general. . . . The
assertion is all the more serious as it is presented without any attempt at
scientific documentation. Hansegård invokes his contact over 20 years
with the people of the Torneå Valley in all kinds of situation – but he has
not given a single concrete example of how this defective linguistic
ability is manifested. Still less has he tried to conduct a systematic
investigation of their linguistic competence. And obviously he has least
of all realized the importance of comparing data from the bilingual
population of the Torneå Valley with data from some monolingual
control group, for example in Central Sweden (with consideration also
of social variables). Instead he is content to repeat crude generalizations
based on subjective assessments (Loman, 1975: 27).
In his English summary of his response to Hansegård, Loman
characterizes Hansegård's work as speculation with no empirical evidence
and supported by no data (Loman, 1975: 28). Hansegård himself writes as
follows:
"The statements about the semilingualism of the people of the Torneå
Valley made in it (Hansegård's book, my comment) are mainly based
on observations made over a period of more than 20 years and on a
study of the history and living conditions of the people. The method I
have used is thus largely the same as is used by social anthropologists
and ethnographers, namely participant observation. This method must
surely have the same value as when used in the disciplines of social
anthropology and ethnography. . . . It is a prejudice to suppose that the
humanistic sciences must use the methods of the natural sciences to be
more true and valid, for instance, by approaching their laboratory
techniques" (Hansegård, 1975: 10).
Hansegård further points out that he has studied the "phenomenon of
language mixture in Same over a period of 7 years on the basis of over 6,000
authentic recorded utterances of Same in all kinds of situation" (Hansegård,

1967), and has "corrected and graded nearly 10,000 compositions in Swedish written by Swedish and Finnish (and a smaller number of Same) pupils at the secondary school in Kiruna". He also says that he has not conducted any tests or made any measurements of linguistic ability while at the same time admitting the value of checking subjective observations by more objective methods (Hansegård, 1975: 10).

As I see it we have here a very nicely illustrated case of two philosophy of science and methodological traditions in conflict. I see a connection between the ideology of the researcher (both political and philosophical), the paradigm of science she uses and the methods. It is clear that most of us do not do "pure" "uncontaminated" research with no influence from other paradigms – a lot of research and researchers represent rather eclectic approaches. But I think that the following diagram (which I have used in connection with other debates between different paradigms in minority education) is illustrative of these debates as well:

socialist political ideology	liberal/conservative political ideology
is often	combined with
materialist/phenomenological-existentialistic philosophical ideology	idealistic/logical-analytical philosophical ideology
which is often	connected with
critical/hermeneutic paradigm of science	positivistic paradigm of science
which often	leads to use of
theoretical-scientific thinking, based on developing scientific concepts, which describe the essence of phenomena and try to explain, understand and criticize (and possibly change)	empirical thinking, based on developing empirical, everyday concepts, which describe/register the appearance of phenomena and try to explain apparent, superficial correlations only, not to understand or criticize (or change)

(from Skutnabb-Kangas, 1982a)

Christina Bratt Paulston's and Rolland Paulston's (1976) discussions about the different paradigms are a case in point here. Bratt Paulston instances a number of situations where the researcher relying wholly on quantitative data will fail to understand, or misunderstands, or will ask the wrong questions. In the final analysis it is not a question of data but of opinions and world view, she says (1981). She also advocates the use of a combination of qualitative and quantitative data (and gives a good example of such an attempt, using a table of attributes of the qualitative and quantitative paradigm, p. 32), stating that "quantitative studies gain from 'rich descriptions' and qualitative studies can benefit from quantitative concerns for reliability and validity" (p. 34). But what has been destructive and dishonest in the Scandinavian debate about methods has been that strong proponents of the quantitative approach have treated qualitative research like Hansegård's as though it were no more than bad quantitative research, and have labelled it unscientific, rather than judging it on its own terms. The proponents of a qualitative approach have so far tried to defend themselves in a constructive way by demonstrating patiently that it is a question of different paradigms and methods, and that each must be judged on its own criteria, not the other's. Now that patience seems to be about to be exhausted (see Hanson, 1980a). The energy expended in the debate about semilingualism could have been put to a better use in attempts at combining different methods than in futile arguments where one party does not even acknowledge what the debate is all about. The debate between Göte Hanson and Lars Henric Ekstrand is a close parallel to the earlier one with Hansegård and Loman, but even more devastating – and there are very close parallels in the U.S.A. also. Some of the issues in these controversies will be dealt with in Cummins & Skutnabb-Kangas (eds) (forthcoming) and I refer readers to them.

All the important empirical work clarifying the issue about semilingualism is still ahead. While we are waiting for it we can look at what functions it has come to serve that many minority children do not do as well as monolingual children, either in language tests or at school.

Note to Chapter Ten

1. See for example the discussion in Wrede, 1974: 170–73; Henrysson & Björkquist, 1963; Henrysson & Ljung, 1967; Johansson & Wikström, 1974; Lasonen, 1978a, b.

11 The function of immigration – a comparison between different countries

11.1 Background

In this chapter we shall discuss various frameworks for immigrant education at a societal-political level and from one particular angle: we shall ask what economic and political interests the children's poor performance at school has come to serve. One of the main tasks of the school system in any society is to participate in reproducing the power structure – the school, of necessity, works to preserve the institutional structure of society as it is.

It is important, I feel, to try in some way to make a connection between our analysis of what happens with the individual and with society as a whole. Otherwise we shall be drowned in details and see every child *only* as an individual. Even if, for instance, we might think that the problems experienced by indigenous working-class children are very like those experienced by immigrant children, there are special circumstances involved in immigration, which make the immigrant child doubly oppressed in the school system by comparison with the indigenous working-class child. We should not, then, treat the problems (and joys) of the immigrant child simply on the individual level; neither should we treat them simply as a class issue. The class aspect should be weighed together with the fact that immigrants and guest workers form a special underclass within the working class in most European countries, a kind of *lumpenproletariat*.

11.2 Why immigration?

At the end of the 1960s, and even as late as the early 1970s, many observers still believed that the guest worker and immigrant system was a good thing for the countries from which the immigrants and guest workers came, and to some extent for the countries to which they came. The guest worker system was seen as a form of development aid given by the rich industrialized countries to "less developed" countries. The following main advantages were seen to accrue to the countries of origin:

1. The unemployed, who could not make a living in their own country and who were a burden on its economy, were given work and were thus able to support themselves and their families, relieving the pressure on their own country's economy and social welfare system.

2. Those who came to the industrialized countries would get an industrial training, which they would be able to apply on their return, in order to build up industry in their own country. The developing countries would acquire industrial skills so that they would be much less reliant on the "experts" from the industrialized countries.

3. The remittances (money sent back to their own countries by the guest workers and immigrants) would on the one hand improve the poorer countries balance of payments and on the other be used for investment which would ensure that work was waiting for the returning immigrants when they went back after a few years.

Certainly it was admitted that the whole system was a convenient way for the industrialized countries to find temporary labour during a period of industrial expansion, but the system was chiefly seen as an act of benevolence, developmental aid. It was calculated that the guest workers and immigrants and not the host countries were the real beneficiaries. This whole view is plainly evident in documents relating to immigration from the Council of Europe, the OECD, and so on (see, for example, the early reports of the proceedings of the Nordic seminars on migration research, and the literature referred to there).

The more qualified view that is now beginning to predominate has considered whether the advantages claimed for the countries of origin have in fact materialized, and what negative consequences emigration has had for them. The countries of immigration have come under scrutiny as well: what advantages have they derived, in particular economically, and perhaps also politically from the system, and what is the mainly social price that has been paid, and is increasingly being paid (and should be paid, if the immigrants are ever to be on remotely the same footing as the indigenous population)? There has been some discussion of what the countries of production have gained or could gain culturally but few countries have made use of the possibilities offered here. There has also been some discussion about the possibility of compensation to the sending countries for the reception of some of their best labour – Sweden has had such discussions mainly with Finland and Yugoslavia. Another topic as yet little more than mentioned, but which will no doubt be much more vigorously debated in the next decade, at least in Sweden, is about what can be done to remedy all the bad consequences of the guest worker and immigrant policy of the kind conducted by all Western European immigration countries, which have produced what has been called a lost generation, a generation of young people entirely disabled for life in these countries.

Even if it must be admitted that the emigration countries have benefited to some degree (and many of the *individuals* who emigrated *did* benefit economically), the benefit derived has been counterbalanced by the negative consequences of emigration (Hamberg, 1981). Emigration even of unskilled labour involves the loss of workers in their best working years. This alters the age distribution in the emigration countries, and affects the economic foundations of society at the local level. When that section of the population with the most purchasing power disappears, the economic basis for various kinds of service disappears also. We can see this happening, for instance, in many small villages in Finland where the shops, the post office, the chemist, the local branch library have been closed down, and where the doctor has left, to be replaced by a travelling nurse, where there are fewer buses but higher local income tax since people began to leave. Whole villages have almost emptied, boarded up houses wait for the summer when they come to life again for a month or so during the industrial holiday period, the shutters opening when the factory gates open.

In the matter of education and training for the immigrant workers, we may say that most of the hopes have been shattered. The guest workers and immigrants have generally had jobs requiring no training whatsoever. If we compare the education and training many immigrants had before they came with the jobs they have found, we may fear that the reverse has happened: those with occupational training already have found no use for it, and those with no training have not received any in the new country. The only change that may be presumed to have occurred is that people from the countryside have been urbanized, becoming accustomed to industrial work (but without getting a training which would have qualified them for more skilled work).

Neither has the money sent home been used in a way which would have created new jobs, and on the whole it has not improved the balance of payments (Hamberg, 1981). Rather than being used for productive investment, much of it has gone to the purchase of property that has not provided the owners with work, or of desirable consumer goods, this contributing in its turn to an increased flow of imports which has counteracted any positive effect on the balance of payments that might have been expected. Money sent home has also sometimes been used to keep uneconomical farms going, so preventing a structural rationalization which might have made the economy more like the Western, with the positive and especially negative consequences that might have from an ecological and human ecological point of view.

Emigration has certainly contributed to the ever-widening gap between the Third World and the industrialized countries in the 1970s. Even though immigration has led to increased social expenditure in the countries of production (and this is likely to increase in the 1980s), the balance of advantage derived from the whole system nevertheless remains with them. Let me try to give a summary of what the function of the guest workers and immigrants has been, as well as noting changes in that function (among the literature I have found particularly illuminating here, I should mention as introductions for amateur economists like myself, Castles & Kosack, 1973; Castles, 1980; Horst, 1980; Nikolinakos, 1973 and Sivanandan, 1982). Some of the economic arguments were discussed in 7.4.

According to Stephen Castles (Castles & Kosack, 1973; Castles, 1980), immigration after the Second World War fulfilled two main functions for capitalism. On the one hand, during a phase of rapid industrial expansion and capital accumulation, it made available a cheap labour force which was mobile, untrained, unorganized and unable to demand its rights. On the other hand, the presence of immigrants helped to promote social, economic and political division within the working class itself: the indigenous working class became more bourgeois as a section of it moved up one rung into lower middle-class jobs, to blue collar jobs and away from the heaviest industrial work and the dirtiest service jobs. Because of this movement and because of language difficulties the indigenous working class could not even start to develop any solidarity with immigrants and guest workers. And this along with the fact that immigrants were deprived of most political rights, weakened the working class.

Let me give just one example of who stood to gain. Jan Ekberg, who in an earlier report investigated how immigrants and Swedes made use of, and financed through their taxes, local services in Växjö (Ekberg, 1979), in a more recent investigation summarises the results of calculations he has tried to make for the whole of Sweden:

"Over the years considerable sums have been transferred, via the public sector, *from* immigrants *to* the Swedish population. This can also be expressed by saying that the available income of the Swedish population is greater or that it has access to public services at a lower price (paying lower taxes) because of the immigrants" (Ekberg, 1980: 1).[1]

During the 1970s, however, the function of immigrants changed. The labour intensive expansion which, in part through the exploitation of the labour of immigrants, had made possible the accumulation of capital, could no longer continue at the same rate in the industrialized countries. The most advanced sectors began to find it more profitable to export capital to the underdeveloped countries, with low wage levels, than to continue to import labour. The textile industry is a good example. When the Swedish and imported immigrant women were too few or would no longer tolerate the poor working conditions, firms moved some of their production to countries where the wage level was lower, to Finland, mostly to Ostrobothnia, where the local authorities were generous, giving land and help with the building of factory accommodation (see Sandlund & Sundén, 1975 on the workers at Algots in Närpes). The firms inherited the old machines (which were no longer good enough for Sweden) and the old advertising slogans "It's enough just to say Algots".

A survey of the factory accommodation built by the local authorities in Kainuu, Lapland and Ostrobothnia from 1963 to 1975 revealed that these regions in Finland attracted 312 different industrial companies during those years, a large proportion of them Swedish. The companies, most of them in textiles and ready-made clothes, moved into new factories built and owned by the local authorities. The survey counted only firms that had moved into the rural districts, not those in towns.

"In Sweden the NJA-group (a progressive song and theatre group) composed a song for the enterprise-minded:
Have you heard of the lovely country
which is flowing with labour;
They give you your factory and everything free,
the best you've ever had.

The businessmen coming ashore in Finland were not in fact given their factory buildings quite free, but there were many advantages in that lovely country. The local authorities put a lot of money into building factory accommodation, they put up security for loans, they helped to arrange training courses, and they built houses for the employees" (Sahlström, 1977: 20).

There are not many textile factories left in Ostrobothnia now. When the women began to demand better working conditions and when it became advantageous for the firms to move production even further away (all or part of it) to countries where the wage levels were even lower and where the women were not organized, the move was made to Portugal, Hong Kong, South Korea, India, Latin America. Let me borrow some extracts here from a poem written by Anja Leppinen from Finland, a worker in one of these factories who has more recently had great difficulty in finding a job because she was actively involved in the struggle for better working conditions. She writes the poem about three women, Berit from Sweden, Alice from Portugal, and herself. They all worked for Algots, each in her own country:

The pattern
We met each other in Portugal
three women from different countries
Berit from Sweden
Alice from Portugal
Anja from Finland
It was just before spring 1978.

We worked for the same employer
the capitalist Johansson af Sweden
whom the Swedish state had fed with money, kept going.

Were new machines bought for the money?
Were the jobs guaranteed?

On the contrary.

One day the news of the bankruptcy reached us in Finland.
A few lines on a tiny piece of paper one early spring day in 1977
– A multitude of thoughts fled through the brain:
Uncertainty – unemployment
– And then a feeling of relief crept over one
– There was no feeling of regret
– No more harassment
no more inhumanity,
harshness,
sneering devilishness
from the management
from their lackeys
with their scorn and satanic intrigues.

In the shock announcement it said
that there was money left for one week's wages only,
but the recommendation was: Keep on sewing!

We were allowed to stay on in the Finnish factory, Algots,
the Swedish state took over.
There was fresh hope of better conditions.
The hope was extinguished after negotiations
and remarks about problems which can be solved
if the will exists.

It didn't exist.

Profitability,
high production:
that was the main thing
even if the methods are old-fashioned
the Swedish employer thought.

This was Finland.
How about Portugal?

Closing down at the end of 1977.
The people who had worked and toiled
kicked out
unpaid wages
there they stood without unemployment benefits
these didn't exist.

Other jobs, then, things people did before Algots?
No, to be sure, what existed before Algots
did not exist after it.
Girls who had worked for farmers

wouldn't do any more.
They had the mark of "Algots" upon them.
Branded as trade union activists
Subversives
because they had not accepted the way Algots treated them.

Unity, solidarity
this the Portuguese workers had learned.
They had gone on strike to get rid of the worst bosses.
Together they had been standing waiting outside the gates
until the comrade was let in
whom the company had kicked out.

Our meeting in Portugal
arranged by Swedish Educational Radio
in February 1978
was for the Portuguese workers.
The fight for survival

Berit from Sweden, then,
the country with the high standard of living?
Norrland – an underdeveloped area
where few industries
had established themselves.
Reasons of convenience?
Better to be where everything in society
is concentrated.
Cutbacks of the Algots units
the factories up north.
Closing down.
How do the women feel,
when they have first got out
become gainfully employed
become wheels in the machinery
had a feeling of participating in the society –
and then be kicked out?

They had even, after all, liked their jobs.
From the very beginning they were united
they demanded human treatment.
Those methods which are still applied in the Finnish factory
didn't do any more in Sweden.
Unanimously they had decided on a strike
in solidarity with the Portuguese workers
when the struggle was about
getting rid of the factory boss Donna Mariana

Sometimes Berit and I cried
for Alice and her comrades in Portugal.
There is though enough to cry about in our Nordic countries.
Tears do not help
but sometimes the feelings become so strong
that they demand release.

They asked me,
my Portuguese and Swedish comrades
in the same company:
Do the workers in the Finnish factory support you unanimously
when you fight for their rights in the union?
An honest answer must be no.

Then I felt ashamed of my home town conception
of conditions of employment
the lack of awareness
the indifference
The word solidarity is still an unknown concept.

Now I am unemployed – after Algots
in Finland of the eighties
I am branded by Algots
just like the Portuguese workers.

We met each other – three women
from different countries
with the same employer.
Geographical distances
separated us and the factories.
The pattern was the same.
(Anja Leppinen, *Folktidningen Ny Tid*, 16.10.1980,
translation: Robert Phillipson and Tove Skutnabb-Kangas)

According to Castles (1980: 37) the export of capital has led to "a
decline in industrial employment in Western Europe which was intensified
in the mid-1970s by the decline in growth, starting with the so called 'oil
crisis', and, in the late 1970s, by the rapid introduction of microprocessors".
Despite loud public calls, particularly from (extreme) right wing parties for
all immigrants/guest workers to be sent home as unemployment rates
continued to rise among the people of the host country, this has not
happened to any appreciable extent. This attitude can be seen in all Western
countries. Some examples;

"Foreign drug pushers and pimps are destroying Swedish youth and
exploiting Swedish girls. . . . Foreign drug pushers, murderers, pimps,
gambling bosses, rapists and other criminal elements should be expelled
from our country for ever. Privileges enjoyed by immigrants, like
preferential treatment on the housing list, free accommodation in

hotels, subsidies for furnishing flats, paid for by social welfare, generous 'cultural subsidies' for expensive newspapers in foreign languages (all this paid for with your money), should be stopped. A Swede should not be discriminated against in his own country, and in any case, Sweden can't afford to pour vast sums of money down the drain. What we need is a determined effort at organized repatriation of non-European immigrants who are making no real contribution in Sweden. This should be done humanely but resolutely" (from a leaflet entitled "Bryr du dig om ditt land?" [Do you care about your country?] published by the organization Bevara Sverige svenskt [Keep Sweden Swedish]. For information about more or less racist, fascist and neo-nazi organizations in Sweden, see Nagy, 1979).

"How comes it that the German Federal Republic is obliged to maintain this scum, and even pay it, at the expense of the German taxpayer? . . . guest workers, political refugees, gypsies. We should do as they do in other countries – hysterectomy for the women, or castration for the men – stop them breeding like the flies and vermin they are."

"You should open the floodgates as soon as you can and pump in millions more of these refugee down and outs, so that every last German will know it isn't worth working your guts out here just so these savages can live it up day after day at our expense" (extracts from letters sent to the Ministers for Domestic Affairs, Baum and Gries, published in *Der Spiegel*: 15.9.80).

There has in fact been no large-scale repatriation of immigrants or guest workers, even though attempts have been made in various countries to get it started. Different countries, rather, use different methods. The industrial countries of Europe all have some kind of immigration quota and increasingly various kinds of additional restriction, all more or less along racial lines. This is clear, for instance, in Great Britain, which since the 1962 Commonwealth Immigrants Act has introduced various restrictions on the rights of members of the British Commonwealth to come to the United Kingdom. The control was tightened up within the existing legislation in 1965; East Africans, especially Ugandan Asians, were prevented from entering i.. 1968 (by a new act hurried through Parliament in three days); and in 1971, more particularly, the Immigration Act excluded from the country citizens of the New Commonwealth i.e. non-whites (for further detail, see Sivanandan 1982 and Smith 1977 or for individual case studies, see various minority journals published in Britain, and for the women's point of view, *Women's Voice*).

Similar methods have been adopted in Norway, with so-called "subsidiary markets" within the general labour market which are partly exempt from immigration quotas and where various unofficial criteria may apply, as Aud Korbøl explains in an article aptly entitled "Norsk race relations industry" (1979). Other methods range from the holding of a referendum in Switzerland, and money payment to foreigners leaving the country in France, to the questioning of foreigners' right to unemployment benefit in Denmark. In this latter case, it was maintained that unemployment pay should be withheld, even though the contributions had been paid, on the grounds that foreign workers who knew little Danish were not really available for employment; and workers thus forced to live on social security could after a year at the most, and sometimes immediately, have their residence permit reconsidered, with on occasion a one-way ticket home as the result. The law in Denmark stipulates that a foreigner who comes into a situation where she might need social security payments over a long period must be "offered help to return home" (for the Danish situation, see Klebak & Horst 1978, and an interview with these two writers in *Information*: 3.4.79; also statements from Forbundet af arbejdere fra Tyrkiet [the Association of workers from Turkey] on the subject of Turkish women in Denmark, whose situation was the immediate cause of the debate about availability for employment; see also Rahbek Pedersen, 1980b).

According to Castles, the reason immigrants and guest workers have not in fact been repatriated to any appreciable extent, in spite of loud demands for it and attempts to engineer it, is that the immigrant population has acquired a new function in addition to its older function. It is used as a buffer, shock absorber at the lowest layer of society, absorbing the worst of the consequences (the worst of the unemployment, for instance) caused by the restructuring of the capitalist world economy, and thereby protecting the higher layers from as direct and brutal an exposure to these consequences as they would have without immigrants. And whatever general truth there may be in the comparative misery theory, it may be taken that this is *one* way of helping to prevent the indigenous working class becoming revolutionary.

If the immigrant and guest worker population is to fulfil its two roles: as supplier of cheap, mobile and under-organized labour which helps to create a dividing gulf within the working class and weakens it, and as a buffer absorbing the worst shocks, then the children and grandchildren of immigrant workers must also be kept down in the same weak position which their elders had educationally, socially, economically and above all politically. And this is where the school system comes in.

The international experience about minority education is often referred to in the Scandinavian debate. One can often discern a tendency not to acknowledge how important political circumstances are for the way schooling is organized. For this reason I shall turn to describe two sharply distinct situations, where different recommendations as to the best ways to organize minority education are needed. Regardless of what the political situation is, certain basic facts are true. But I want to show that measures taken in different countries in most cases are not based on these facts. A researcher recommending measures must be aware of this.

In what follows, I will try to show that the ways in which the education of immigrant and guest worker children is organized are logical consequences and reflections of the wish to enable capital to continue the exploitation of immigrants/guest workers, and that this aim is achieved, despite the different methods used. The methods seem to vary with the variation between different countries as to the point reached in the process of development which was outlined earlier. And that, too, is why the methods used to fight the oppression which immigrants and guest workers are subjected to must vary.

The recommendations researchers make for the education of minority children are absolutely opposite in Scandinavia and West Germany. I disregard the fact here that there is disagreement between researchers within these countries (see Haberland & Skutnabb-Kangas, 1979 and Skutnabb-Kangas, 1979b). In Scandinavia it is recommended that *immigrant children should be taught through the medium of their mother tongue*, with Swedish/Danish/Norwegian as a second language. The immigrant organizations are united with the researchers in demanding teaching through the medium of the mother tongue (see, for example, the resolution on migrants from the Alternative Women's Conference in Copenhagen in July 1980). They are above all against distributing immigrant children directly into Swedish/Danish/Norwegian classes. In West Germany most researchers recommend a fairly *rapid "integration" into German classes*, and are opposed to the kind of national, mother tongue classes now found, for instance, in Bavaria. The immigrant organizations are rather divided in their attitudes; for instance, Greeks demand (and do have many) mother tongue medium classes of the "Scandinavian" type (see Skutnabb-Kangas, 1982a and Tsiakalos, in preparation, for details). In both countries researchers believe they are recommending what is *best for the children in the present political circumstances*.

11.3   A comparison of some aspects of a guest worker policy and an immigrant policy

Before we turn to look at the way differently organized educational systems can lead to similar results, we must first examine some of the fundamental dissimilarities between a guest worker policy and an immigrant policy, since they affect both measures taken at schools and methods and recommendations one can (and must) follow if one wants to improve the bad results. I shall try to summarize some of the factors in West German guest worker policy and Scandinavian immigrant policy that make contradictory recommendations both realistic and necessary. I want to show, too, that the education the minority children receive, despite the very different circumstances, contributes to the reproduction of the powerless status of the parents at the same time as it helps to maximize profitability, minimize costs and retain control over the future destiny of the migrants.

Before I summarize the main differences in policies, I shall give a few details about the various countries so as to provide a context in which they can be considered. Estimates of migrants in Western Europe vary between 14 and 18 million, not counting naturalized immigrants. The latter figure also includes an estimated total for so-called illegal migrants – a recent Council of Europe meeting estimated their number to about 2 million. The EEC-commission also says that an additional 20% should be added to the official figures in the EEC-countries (SIV-Dokumentation, October 1980: 1). In *West Germany* there are approximately 4.63 million foreigners (Statistisches Jahrbuch, 1981) plus an additional number of "illegal" migrants. Foreigners make up 7.5% of the population but 10% of the labour force. More than 25% of them have lived over 10 years in the country, and approximately two-thirds of the rest more than 8 years. About 1 million of them are under 16 years of age. Turkish nationals are the largest group (in the middle of 1981 33.4%), and the six most heavily represented countries of origin (Turkey, Yugoslavia, Italy, Greece, Spain and Portugal) account for three-quarters of all foreigners (TIP 1/1982). The number of foreigners is increasing rapidly, regardless of the halt on migration and the process of repatriation, particularly because of the high birth rate and the fact that most migrants are young. Of all children born in 1978 13% had foreign parents (Schmitt, 1981: 17). In West Berlin the foreigners account for 10% of the population but 31% of all births (Spiess, 1979: 47). The number of foreign children in many schools varied between 50–70% (Bericht zur Lage der Ausländer in Berlin, 1978: 18) and many schools have close to 100% foreign pupils.

At the end of 1981 Sweden had 414,001 foreigners, 4.97% of the population. Roughly 114,000 of them were under the age of 15. 4.5% of Swedes but 6.9% of the foreigners are aged 0–3 years, and in some groups like Turks, Greeks, Chileans, the percentage of children is even higher. While 17.3% of the Swedes were over the age of 65, only 2.4% of the foreigners belonged to this older group (SIV-Dokumentation 29.3.1982). Granted that 400,738 foreigners have been naturalized between 1948–1981 (SIV-Dokumentation 23.3.1982) and that their birth rate has been higher than that of Swedes, the following often cited figures are probably reliable: there are 1.2 million people in Sweden with an immigrant background now, there will be one in four in the year 2000 (the total population of Sweden is 8,323,033) and every other child born in the year 2000 will have an immigrant background (whatever that may mean – there is a lot of criticism, rightly, about the use of the terms). Even in Sweden many school districts and schools show the same kind of variety as in Germany. There are schools where around 50 different mother tongues are represented (there are close to 150 of them in Sweden altogether), and for instance in Tensta-Rinkeby (a Stockholm suburb with the highest concentration of immigrants in Sweden) 80% of the children on the waiting list for day care now have foreign parents.

Norway and Denmark both have roughly 100,000 foreigners, 2% of the population. The largest groups of foreigners in Denmark come from Turkey

(60–70% of them are Kurds), Norway, West Germany, Britain, Sweden, Yugoslavia and Pakistan. In Norway the largest groups come from Denmark, U.S.A. Britain, Sweden and Pakistan.
The absolutely largest group in Sweden comes from Finland, 41.5% of all foreigners. The other countries of origin heavily represented are Yugoslavia, Denmark, Norway, Turkey, Greece, West Germany and Poland.

11.3.1 Permanency of stay

The crucial distinction, decisive for whether we should call a policy a guest worker or immigrant policy, is the question of permanency of stay. In a guest worker policy, *circulation* rotation is hoped for. Ideally it is hoped that young, healthy, able-bodied, single male workers will come to the country of production (Swetland, 1979), work hard there for a few years, with no thought of anything other than work (and preferably overtime work as well), live in barracks, make no demands on the social services, and return home after a few years, but in any case before they are worn out, old or ill, to be replaced by new healthy male workers exactly as the needs of the labour market determines. In an immigrant policy, on the contrary, the point of departure is that those who have been allowed to come, also have the *right to stay*, and that most of them will probably avail themselves of this right.

The way things have developed in Sweden is typical. At the beginning, Sweden too, had a guest worker policy, even though there was experience of other forms, too, for example in the final stages of the Second World War and just afterwards, when a large number of refugees were accepted. The guest worker policy did not last long in Sweden, however, by contrast with most other European industrialized countries. We can follow the development of official attitudes by examining the terminology used in Sweden in official reports on the new arrivals. At first they were called "imported (foreign) labour" – this during the time when Sweden was actively recruiting in other countries. What is imported can also be exported when no longer needed. The power of words over thought! We were lulled into illusions that it was a passing thing. Too many people even today think so. Gradually the expression "imported labour" was phased out, to be replaced by "foreign labour", and then by "foreigners", and finally by "immigrants". The term "immigrant" was introduced deliberately in the middle of the 1960s to indicate that those who had been allowed to enter were once and for all accepted if they so wished. In other words, the idea that the situation was a temporary one was set aside. The purpose has not always prevailed. . . . The term "minority" has by contrast not been easily accepted in ordinary use, even though the Swedish Parliament in 1975 laid down guidelines for a "policy towards immigrants and minorities" (Kjell Öberg, former director-general of Statens Invandrarverk [National Board of Immigration and Naturalization]).

11.3.2 Legal status

An insecure legal status is characteristic of a guest worker policy (from now on abbreviated GWP), compared with the much *more secure legal status* in an immigration policy (IP). This particularly applies in the following areas:

a) *Residence permit*: this, it is true, is difficult to obtain both in a GWP and an IP, but in an IP there are clear rules specifying entitlement, the permit is valid for a longer period (at least usually) and there are fewer restrictions attached to it. In an IP it is much more difficult to withdraw a residence permit once granted, and again there are rules specifying the circumstances under which this can be done. By contrast, in a GWP the threat of withdrawal of residence permits can be used by the authorities as a way of disciplining "awkward" guest workers.

b) *Work permit*: in a GWP this does not usually come automatically with a residence permit, but must be applied for separately (in West Germany, for instance, the children of foreigners with residence permits must themselves apply for work permits, which may not necessarily be granted them). In a GWP, the unemployed foreigner runs the risk of having the work permit, and with it the residence permit, withdrawn. In a GWP the work permit often has conditions attached to it. It may specify a particular place of work or employer. This makes it difficult for guest workers to take part actively in trade unions, to organize, etc. When foreign workers risk being repatriated if they change jobs, their condition is little better than that of serfs.

c) *Regulations covering unemployment*: in a GWP the guest worker (GW) risks repatriation if unemployed, either immediately or after a period of time, or withdrawal of the work permit or receiving no unemployment pay at all, or at least not under the same conditions as a citizen of the country (even though a GW is usually required to make the same social security contributions).

d) *Entitlement to social security benefits*: in a GWP the GW who receives such payments (or who is in a situation where a citizen of the country would receive such payments over a long period) may run the risk of repatriation, or face other difficulties (on application for naturalization, for instance). This often means that a GW does not dare to apply for the social security payments she is entitled to, even in very desperate situations, but will try to make do as best she can, by going into debt, depending on relatives, etc. The usual social security benefits for GWs, too, are less generous than for citizens.

e) *The authorities in administrative charge*: in a GWP these are usually the police and in an IP usually the civil authorities. In a GWP the distinction between the legislative and the executive authority is sometimes not clear.

f) *Rights of appeal*: a GW often has no right of appeal at all in a court of law against an expulsion order or other similar official act. The only possibility of appeal will often be to the same authorities who served the order, or to some closely related official body, rather than to an independent, more impartial body. A GW can often be deported before the appeal has been finally decided on, as has happened on more than one occasion in Denmark. In a GWP there is often a double punishment for any criminal offence: the GW serves the prison sentence and is then deported despite that. This last can also happen with an IP, but in many other respects immigrants will have the same rights as native citizens.

11.3.3 Naturalization

Naturalization, change of nationality (with possible retention at the same time of the original nationality) is difficult or impossible in a GWP (see, for example Franz, 1978, 1979). According to Franz, the annual total of naturalizations in West Germany is very small, and many of those naturalized are married to Germans or are very highly educated. There are hardly any GWs among them. In a GWP the rules governing naturalization are often arbitrary and they are not openly published. In an IP they are mostly both clearly defined and made public, so that it is possible to find out about them in advance, and they include a right of appeal.

During the years 1945 to 1981, about 400,000 foreigners obtained Swedish citizenship (SIV Dokumentation) and the annual figure is now about 24,000 (Statistik om invandring och invandrare, October 1980). Since in the last four years the natural population growth has shown a decrease among Swedish citizens but an increase among foreign nationals, and since there has been a net surplus of immigrants (more immigrants than emigrants), "foreign nationals are responsible for the total population increase in the country" (Statistik om invandring och invandrare, October 1980: 6–7) (even if that increase seems to have diminished so that the whole increase in 1982 was no more than 3,500 persons and the birth surplus was only 900, the lowest figure in 150 years (Nordisk Kontakt 1, 1983: 64).

11.3.4 Which country's legal and educational system is to prevail?

In a GWP, (aspects of) the sending country's legal and educational systems are extended often to the recipient country, while in an IP the recipient country's system applies. This may mean that in a GWP the sending country selects, trains and sends out teachers (often via its embassy), and has control of the curricula and teaching materials, sometimes only in the matter of mother tongue teaching, but sometimes over the whole school system. The sending country often has its own examinations which it sets for its nationals in the recipient country, it may be both for adults and children. Many sending countries also contribute to the cost. In an IP there may also be co-operation, for example, in the acquiring of teaching materials or even teachers, but the recipient country controls the curricula, which are often exactly the same as for its native citizens once the immigrant children have been incorporated into classes with the majority children. Those classes, too, which are taught through the medium of the immigrant children's mother tongue will in an IP have the same curricula as for majority children. The only exception is, of course, with the actual teaching of the mother tongue and possibly with religious instruction. But here, too, in an IP curricula will be worked out that suit the children's situation in the new country, rather than simply being taken over from the sending country. The recipient country bears the whole cost of the teaching and makes the attempt to train the teachers for the immigrants (often these are recruited from among immigrants already in the country, and who know it well), and to give further education to teachers trained in the sending country.

Sweden has faced some delicate situations over the extent of co-operation with the sending countries, since it is only reasonable that the same policy should be adopted towards all of them in the opportunity they are given to exert ideological influence upon the immigrant children by means of teachers and teaching materials. Some countries, such as Yugoslavia, have actively tried to extend their influence, whereas others have not shown the same interest. The bilateral education councils that Sweden has with various sending countries are only advisory bodies. Since it is cheaper for recipient countries to allow the sending countries for example to plan and carry out most of the mother tongue teaching, a degree of interference is allowed here in the internal affairs of the recipient countries that would not be tolerated in other spheres. The recipient countries can thus save money that would otherwise have to be spent on investment in new forms of teacher training, the development of new teaching materials and so on.

As regards the legal system, the fact that in a GWP the sending country extends its authority to the recipient country may involve a degree of "co-operation" between the legal and police systems of sending and recipient countries. We see the effect of this in West Germany, where the Turkish police, and various Turkish extremist organizations which in Turkey function under the protection of the police (the Grey Wolves, for instance) are allowed to operate.[2] Let me give another recent example of "co-operation" from Denmark, a country still undecided as between a GWP and an IP. We were given money by The Nordic Cultural Foundation to organize a course in Kurdish for Kurdish teachers from all over Scandinavia, a course which would teach them to write Kurdish. In Turkey (where these teachers came from) Kurdish is a forbidden language and all Kurdish teachers receive all their training, both at school and later, through the medium of Turkish, which for them is a wholly foreign language.[3] The only Kurds who can read and write Kurdish have learnt to do so in various schools run by the underground movement. The man who ran the course, Mehmet Emin Bozarslan, now living in Uppsala, had been imprisoned for four months in Turkey for writing a Kurdish ABC book, ALFABE (later

published in Sweden by Invandrarförlaget, Kvarngatan 16, 50244 Borås).
None of the Kurdish teachers in Denmark knew how to write Kurdish.
The Turkish Embassy in Copenhagen tried to prevent the course by
pointing out that the participants were still Turkish citizens and were thus
not entitled to break Turkish law, whatever country they were in, and in
Turkish law Kurdish is a forbidden language (a legislative proposal to
introduce a more stringent form of the prohibition which had been in force
since 1923 was made on 16.8.66, was dealt with by the Minister for
Domestic Affairs on 3.1.67, was approved by the Turkish government on
25.1.67 and published in the official newspaper, *T. C. Resmê Gazete*, on
14.2.67). When the press asked the embassy official, Uğurtan Akinci, who
tried to stop the course, whether he was actually making threats, he replied
that he was only trying to "give good advice". So the official Turkish view
was that Kurds were not allowed to learn how to read and write their own
language even in Scandinavia. We held the course, naturally, and have held a
follow-up course, too. After the first course, in August 1980, Claus Bergsøe,
the Danish lawyer acting for the course organizer (Association for Workers
from Turkey), wrote a letter to the Danish Ministry of Foreign Affairs,
asking the Ministry to take action so that the same type of incident where a
foreign embassy interferes with cultural activities which are perfectly legal in
Denmark would not re-occur. We still haven't even had a reply from the
Ministry (February 1983).

11.3.5 Reuniting the family

It is not part of a GWP to encourage the reuniting of the family. On the
contrary, the policy tries to prevent this in order to ensure a circulation of
labour and to avoid social expense. GWs are often given permits for certain
kinds of job (for instance, as domestic workers in Great Britain) only if they
are unmarried and without children. And in a number of cases, women
brought in by various agencies, who have advised them to sign declarations
that they were single and without children, have been expelled when they
have tried to bring their children into the country (for examples of this, see
Women's Voice). The regulations, similarly, can be very hard on people who
get divorced: often a person is expelled for getting divorced after too short a
time from the wife or husband (already living in the country or even a citizen
of the country) she or he came into the country to join. Women in particular
have often in this way been placed in intolerable positions (as was pointed
out in the resolution on migrants passed at the Alternative Women's
Conference in Copenhagen). Both in Denmark and Norway (even though
officially Norway has an IP not a GWP!) there have been examples, in cases
like this, of gross injustice.[4] A typical new example comes from West
Germany, where the Federal Government introduced further restrictions on
2.12.1981. Now children over the age of 15 are not allowed to reunite with

their families anymore, neither are children who have one parent only in Germany. And if a youngster from the second generation marries somebody from the country of origin, she or he is not allowed to come in unless the spouse has lived in West Germany at least 8 years without a break, and even then not until the marriage has lasted 1 year (in Bavaria and Baden-Württemberg 3 years) (TIP 1, 1982). And according to the government representative in charge of foreigners there are plans to lower the age limit for children allowed to join their parents from 15 to 6 years! (Liselotte Funcke in Frankfurter Rundschau 25.2.1982).

In an IP (at least on paper) reuniting the family is seen as natural, even if there are restrictions with regard to age and time limits and often a stipulation about "suitable" accommodation (which in some countries has to be available before a foreigner may bring in the family – although it is often impossible to get a larger apartment before the family is actually in the country). Usually the definition of what constitutes a family is a very narrow one, a western nuclear family is taken as the norm. Elderly parents usually have to be above a certain age to be allowed to join their children, but the age limit is based on the general life expectancy in industrialized countries, so that parents from countries where the life expectancy is lower often do not live long enough to qualify for entry.[5]

The Swedish attitude to reuniting the family has probably been much influenced by those groups who have entered Sweden, i.e. refugees where naturally the whole family was allowed in at the same time and Scandinavians who make up nearly 60% of all foreign nationals in the country. Since the agreement on a free Nordic labour market in 1954, Scandinavians are allowed to settle and work in any of the Nordic countries with or without their families.

11.3.6 Housing segregation

In a GWP, there is often fairly strict housing segregation. The GWs often live segregated in hostels or barracks, near their place of work.[6] Typically GWs also live in the most run-down parts of the inner city, just like the blacks in the U.S.A. The GWs often pay extortionate rents, and sometimes several GWs share a single bed (see, for example, Berger & Mohr, 1975). They have no entitlement to accommodation (municipal or other social housing) as citizens of the country do, and they are often severely discriminated against in the housing market, as experiments have shown where two people with exactly the same background but one English and the other a minority member, have been treated differently (see Smith, 1977 and *Racial Minorities and Public Housing,* 1975).

With an IP, the foreigners often live in expensive new suburban housing or in condemned houses in the inner city. In most countries they pay more for less, that is, they pay more for a lower standard than the indigenous population (see Pedersen, 1975 and Puntervold Bø, 1980). Voices are often raised among the indigenous population demanding that immigrants should be spread out to prevent the creation of ghettos. The ghetto, in this view, is seen as undesirable in every respect. Few attempts, as might be expected, have been made to suggest that there are *advantages* in such concentrations: these suggestions have often come from anthropologists (see, for example, Ehn, 1975; Engelbrektsson, 1978; Hannerz, 1981 and Kramer, 1979).

Both in the GWP and the IP, attempts have sometimes been made to impose upper limits (absolute or proportional) on the number of foreigners who may live in any one area or in flats belonging to any one landlord (see, for example, Trankell, 1973; Invandrerrapport II, 1978, and I-Azam, Khan, Rigas, Siddiqi, Skutnabb-Kangas & Özcan, 1980). The reverse has also been proposed, most recently for example by the director-general of The National Board of Immigration and Naturalization in Sweden, on the grounds that centralization would make it easier to provide language-connected services.

The placing of immigrants in IP countries is often governed by the stipulation that "suitable" housing has to be available before a family can reunite. Many immigrants are forced to move to new suburbs with large expensive flats in order to be allowed to bring in their families. But a development can be observed after a few years: families move back into the inner cities, where there is older housing at lower rents, or where they are closer to relatives or to their fellow country(wo)men. No regulation, it can be noted, specify for the indigenous population the kind of housing they must have before they are allowed to marry and have children.

A final point about physical or psychological segregation should be made – it has already been mentioned in an earlier chapter and will be further discussed in chapter 12. What in physical terms is a ghetto may or may not be so psychologically. Again, the only black family in a white suburb may or may not be psychologically segregated from the neighbours. And if a lot of minority members living together is a worrying ghetto, why are there no loud public demands to spread out *all* minorities who live so, for instance, white upper-class families? It should also be clear that *neither* a forced concentration (a ghetto) *nor* a forced spreading out (upper limits) helps integration.

11.3.7 Political rights

It is the main characteristic of a GWP, as distinct from an IP, that the GWs have very few political rights. Even their right to form associations, especially politically orientated associations, may be restricted, if not officially then at least often in practice. This becomes very clear in the new West German legislative suggestions. Nowhere in the world do GWs have the right to vote in the receiving country. Locally they may have bodies that represent them in an advisory capacity but they are nowhere able to participate in the decision making process.

Add to all this the attempts made by some sending countries to extend their own legal systems to embrace their nationals in the recipient countries (which often means that GWs' opportunities for political action are restricted from yet another quarter), and the situation looks very bad: GWs, by and large, have no democratic opportunity to influence their condition, none of the political means available to citizens of the country they live in is available to them. Catani (1982) thinks that their situation can be compared to that of the slaves in ancient Rome. It remains to be seen how the European future will be affected by the fact that there are even now millions of people in Europe who have been deprived of their right to engage in political activity, and by the fact that a generation is growing up who see in their parents an example of political passivity or resignation, or by the knowledge that if one wants to influence one's situation, then only non-democratic means are open.

In an IP, foreigners are accorded more and more formal political rights. At least two factors, however, are at work that may tend to erode these rights. All over the world we can see how the decision making processes are being transferred from the democratically elected bodies to others (big financial enterprises, multinational companies, etc). We ordinary people have little opportunity of influencing our future when the parliamentary processes are steadily being undermined and their importance diminished.[7] Many of the decisions which vitally affect our future are being taken by individuals who have not been democratically elected, and the elected bodies seem not to be able to influence the decisions, sometimes indeed not even to be aware of them. In these circumstances witholding democratic rights from oppressed groups no longer seems of such consequence, when many of the important decisions are taken elsewhere, anyway. We should beware, however, of thinking that the granting of democratic rights to immigrants is a merely cosmetic exercise since parliamentary democracy is being eroded in any case: the right to vote in local and national elections does give *some* ability to influence people's daily lives by democratic means.

A second factor tending to qualify the rights is immigrants' lack of opportunity to exercise them. First generation immigrants are often in a worse position than equivalently educated native citizens because they simply do not know the system as well as they knew the system in their home country, and because for many of them it is too difficult to try to keep up with affairs in both countries (though many try to do this). Again, many immigrants are prevented from exercising their rights by language difficulties. The present younger generation of immigrants, too, because of poor education or other factors to do with a marginal or conflict situation may be worse placed to exercise their rights than the indigenous younger generation. Some investigation has been done into the political resocialization of adult immigrants, but it remains to be seen how children born in the new country will be able to act.[8]

11.4   Educational policy

11.4.1   Criteria for the classification of educational models

As will have become clear in previous chapters, there are a number of ways in which we might classify the organization of education for minority children. Different criteria may be applied. In what follows I shall use only three criteria in summarizing how education is organized, first in a typical GWP country (West Germany) and then in a typical IP country (Sweden) – with a glance at the other Scandinavian countries. The criteria I have chosen are:

1. *The language of instruction*: the children's mother tongue (L1) the majority language (the official language of the recipient country – L2) or both.
2. *The degree of integration or segregation*: (a) extent of integration or segregation – in relation to the indigenous children and to children of other foreign nationalities in the school as a whole and in the classroom
   (b) content in different subjects (which country's curriculum is followed; is the curriculum identical for indigenous and foreign children or are there modifications?); and
   (c) the ideological background of the teaching, manifested in teaching materials, training of teachers, and pedagogical and ideological principles governing the teaching.
3. *The goal of the education*: assimilation, transition or the maintenance of the children's own language. The goal can be seen both in the official rhetoric about the goal in the classes (where, for instance, some will have as their official goal the preparing of the children for a transition to majority language classes), and from the practical arrangements and results. The question as to whether the education is intended to prepare the child for life in the sending or the recipient country involves, of course, judgements about the educational goal (criterion 3) and ideological background (criterion 2).

Because the organization of education varies greatly, it is difficult to give a fair picture of all existing arrangements and that necessarily makes my presentation general. Readers seeking further information and more detail are referred to more specific sources: official reports and recommendations from different countries, statements of principle and reports of practice at the local level. There is a great abundance of such matter.

11.4.2   A typical guest worker country – West Germany: the organization of education

The guest worker children in West Germany can get their education in six different types of class (Reich, 1979: 8):
1. German "ordinary classes" (*"Regelklassen"*), classes planned for

German children, with minimal or no consideration given to the fact that all the children are not German-speaking German children.

2. "Special classes" (*"besondere Klassen"*) with GW pupils only, but with German as the medium of instruction, with German teachers and curriculum. The results ought to be the same as ordinary German classes. This type is common in West Berlin.

3. International preparatory classes, with children from several different nationalities, with no consideration given to their different mother tongues. The official goal is transitional. The children are supposed to receive instruction (including intensive teaching of German as a second language) which prepares them for transfer to "ordinary" German classes. This type is found especially in Baden-Wüttemberg.

4. 1–2-year national preparatory classes with children from one nationality only, but not necessarily with the same mother tongue. No account is taken of the fact, for instance, that Kurdish children from Turkey do not speak Turkish as their mother tongue: they are all taught as if they did, just as they would be in Turkey, where Kurdish is a forbidden and oppressed language (see 11.3.4, 12). The children are often taught both by a German teacher and by a teacher of their own nationality. The official goal is to give them enough German and a sufficient grasp of other subjects after about two years to allow a transfer to German classes.

5. National classes for several years, particularly in Hamburg and North-Rhine-Westphalia. These classes are mostly taught by a teacher of the same nationality as the children, and German is supposed to be taught as a second language. Some of the classes lead to a *compulsory* transfer to German classes (for example, in North-Rhine-Westphalia after grade six), which often means that children simply drop out of school after grade 6, because neither their German nor their knowledge of other subjects is good enough to enable them to follow the teaching through the medium of German in an ordinary German class. Some of the classes have an *optional* transfer, which often means that the children are not transferred either. Frequently neither the teachers of their own nationality (who are controlled by the countries of origin) nor the German teachers want the children to be moved, albeit for different reasons. The teachers from the children's own country often do not want the move because they would risk losing their jobs if all the children were transferred to German classes. The German teachers, for their part, do not want foreign children in their classes because they usually have no training in how to teach them, and they feel they have frequently failed in this task. It is, too, in many ways easier, of course, to teach an all-German class, where all the children understand the language of instruction. There is, in addition, pressure from German parents to keep the classes their children are in all-German. Parents often fear that the standard of teaching will decline or that their children will have less attention from

the teachers if there are many immigrant children in the class (though questionnaires actually show that teachers, even though they have the feeling they ought to spend more time with the foreign children, do not do so in practice – see for example, Nielsen, 1978). Some of the arguments put forward by parents and teachers to oppose the idea of foreign children in German classes are also openly racist. Exactly the same kind of fears have been expressed by parents in Great Britain, too – and have been used politically for racist purposes.

6. Complete national classes with teaching materials and curricula from the countries of origin and teachers sent out by the embassies. These classes also in theory provide for the teaching of German as the second language, but in practice this is often a dead letter. This type is found particularly in Bavaria, and this is what in earlier chapters has been described as a segregational model.

The *language of instruction* in the first three types is German (a language most of the children do not know), in the last two types the language of instruction is to a large extent their mother tongue or the official language of their home country. In type four a combination of both is used, with German as the dominant language.

The first type of class, the *German "ordinary" class* is integrative – assimilationist[9] since the GW children are mixed both with German children and with GW children of other nationalities, and since the teaching follows entirely the German pattern (both physical and subject matter/ideological integration/assimilation).

The second type of class, the *special class*, is integrative with regard to the content of the teaching, the ideology, and also physically with regard to other groups of GW children, but not with regard to German children. Much the same could be said of the third type of class, the *international preparatory class*, but here the content is not altogether the same as in German classes albeit ideologically entirely German-orientated. The last three types are physically *segregative*, as the children are neither mixed together with German children nor with other GW children. As regards content, type six, the *complete national class*, is the most emphatically segregative compared with the content and the ideology in German classes, while the German-orientated content increases as we proceed to types four and five.

If we consider the whole system *not* using West Germany and everything German as a point of reference, but from the point of view of the children's chance of returning and re-integrating in school (and life) in the country of origin, then all the signs are reversed. The types of class that give the children the best chance of re-integrating into the school system of their home country, both as regards the physical organization of the class and the content and ideology of the syllabus, are the national classes (even if the chance they give the children is nevertheless hardly a good one), while the German classes segregate and alienate them most, by assimilating them into German values and ideology.

Officially types three, four and five have a pronounced *transitional* goal, that is, their main function is to prepare the children for a transfer to German classes. Type two is not so much formally defined as transitional as naturally taken to be so. Only type six has the *maintenance of the children's own language and culture* as its stated aim.

The official statements of goal, however, bear little resemblance to what actually goes on in the various classes. Wilfried Stölting (1978) argues that the teaching of German even in those classes which are supposed to prepare the children for transfer has in fact decreased, so that even they are in the process of becoming segregative national classes, too, while the so-called integrative classes, at any rate finally, have assimilation as their goal, and the children are not even encouraged to attend the voluntary mother tongue instruction that is provided.

The evidence presented in this book makes very clear the great divide between the official aim and the reality: in reality the results of *all* the class types are catastrophically bad.

The following table is an attempt to summarize the aspects discussed:

TABLE 9

Type of class	Language of instruction	Goal	Integration/Assimilation		Content (CO) Ideology (ID)
			Physical		
			German children	Other GW children	
1. German 'ordinary' classes	L2	Assimilation	+	+	CO++ ID++
2. Special classes	L2	Transition & assimilation	−	+	CO+ ID++
3. International preparatory classes	L2	Transition?	−	+	CO− ID+
4. 1–2 year national preparatory classes	L2 + L1	Transition?	−	−	CO− ID±
5. National preparatory classes, several years' duration	L1	Transition?	−	−	CO− ID−
6. Complete national classes	L1	Maintenance	−	−	CO−− ID−−

11.4.3 A typical immigrant country – Sweden: the organization of education

Education for foreign children in Sweden can be roughly divided into three groups, according to the language of instruction used:

1. Instruction mainly through the medium of Swedish, in Swedish classes, with Swedish teachers, teaching materials and curriculum. This stage may have been preceded by a longer or shorter period in a preparatory class, with intensive teaching of Swedish as a second language. It can be supported by auxiliary tuition, either in Swedish (=language instruction) or in other subjects, through the medium of either Swedish or the mother tongue or both. The auxiliary tuition is compulsory for the child, if the

school decides the child needs it. Teaching of the child's mother tongue can also accompany instruction in Swedish classes. This is voluntary for the child, in spite of repeated demands from the immigrant organizations that it should be made compulsory just as mother tongue teaching is compulsory for the indigenous Swedish children. Municipal authorities, however, are obliged to make provision for such teaching of the mother tongue if a sufficiently large number of pupils want it. In the autumn of 1981 there were about 4,000 children not given this kind of teaching even though they wanted it. At that time 54,400 children – about 62% of those entitled to it – attended mother tongue teaching in grades 1–9, while 17,400 were given auxiliary teaching through the medium of the mother tongue. 8.5% of the foreign children in grades 1–9 were judged to be "without any knowledge of Swedish at all", or were judged "to understand only very simple everyday language". 51% of all children went to the compulsory teaching of Swedish as a second language, 87% of those in need of it (as decided by the schools) (all the figures are from SCB U 1982: 17).

This is still the most common form of teaching for immigrant children in Sweden, even though the efforts of the various immigrant organizations to get mother tongue classes established (see category 3 below) have begun to bear fruit in the last few years.

2. Instruction in classes with two teachers, one Swedish and one from an immigrant group and both Swedish children and immigrant children of one nationality only. These are so called compound classes (or co-operation classes, as the Swedish authorities have also called them, in an attempt to make them seem more attractive to the immigrant organizations, who would actually prefer mother tongue classes wherever there are a sufficient number of immigrant children to make them feasible. "Intercultural" classes or "Begegnungsklassen", new concepts for the same old transitional assimilation, have not yet come to Sweden). In principle, the groups are taught separately, each by its own teacher, through the medium of the mother tongue, for some part of the time, and together in Swedish for the remainder of the time. In practice the teaching the immigrant children get through the medium of the mother tongue tends to be fairly little. All the kinds of auxiliary teaching mentioned above also apply to this type of class. The share of teaching done in Swedish grows rapidly and the intention usually is that by grade four at the latest, it should be possible to teach the immigrant children entirely in Swedish (apart from the auxiliary teaching using the mother tongue, and the voluntary teaching of the mother tongue). We have here, in fact, a typical transitional model. In August 1981 there were 284 classes of this type.

3. Instruction mainly through the medium of the mother tongue, with Swedish as the second language (often from grade two or three onwards). The classes consist entirely of immigrant children of the same nationality.

They last for at least the first 3 years, but preferably through the first six grades with the number of Swedish periods progressively increasing. From many quarters has come the demand for teaching through the medium of the mother tongue in the higher grades as well (grades 7–9), and some classes have been set up. There have also been some demands that immigrants should be taught through the medium of their mother tongue right through their school career. This mother tongue medium model is the one the immigrant organizations prefer because it seems to produce the best results, with regard to the level of bilingualism and school achievement, as well as the children's general well-being at school. In August 1981 there were 600 classes of this type with 9,218 pupils, 10.6% of all immigrant pupils, and the number is rapidly increasing, in spite of resistance from some assimilation orientated researchers and from some of the authorities. Even if a large proportion of these classes are Finnish, there are many classes in other languages as well (Turkish, Arabic, Spanish, Greek, Serbo-Croat, English, Assyrian, Chinese, Polish, German).

The first type is clearly *assimilationist*, the second *transitional*, the third has as its goal the *maintenance* (and further development) of the children's own language and culture, while trying to bring them to the same level of general knowledge, proficiency in Swedish and grasp of Swedish culture that Swedish children have. The last model is thus mainly geared towards a bilingual, bicultural life lived in Sweden, because Swedish curricula are followed and teachers are preferred who have had their training, or at least their further training, in Sweden. The first two types are integrative both as regards ideology and the content of what is taught and also in physical terms (the first one in relation to both Swedish children and other immigrant children, the second, the compound classes, only in relation to Swedish children). The third type segregates the children physically to begin with, but *not* as regards ideology and the content of what is taught.

The following table summarizes the Swedish models:

TABLE 10

| | | | Integration/Assimilation | | |
| | | | Physical | | Content (CO) |
Type of class	Language of instruction	Goal	Swedish children	Other immigrant children	Ideology (ID)
1. Swedish classes	L2	Assimilation	+	+	CO++ ID++
2. Compound classes	L2 + L1	Transition	+	–	CO+ ID++
3. Mother tongue classes	L1	Maintenance + bilingualism	–	–	CO+ ID+

11.4.4 Denmark and Norway

The organization of instruction is largely similar in Denmark and

Norway. These countries have the same type of models which Sweden had in the late sixties and in minor municipalities also in the seventies. In Denmark only 29 municipalities out of 275 had more than 50 immigrant children in the school system in the autumn of 1979 – see Skutnabb-Kangas & Rahbek, 1981. The bigger municipalities with more immigrant children have reception classes, with intensive instruction in Danish/Norwegian as a second language, approximately 15–20 hours a week. Sometimes this also includes some subject-matter instruction, mainly mathematics. This, too, is given through the medium of Danish/Norwegian, which the children at this point master very poorly. There is, moreover, a possibility of having voluntary mother tongue lessons up to 4–5 hours a week, but this instruction takes place outside regular school hours. After a period of from 6 months to 2 years the children are transferred to Danish/Norwegian classes. For a very short period after the transfer they can get extra help, given mostly by a Danish- or Norwegian-speaking teacher, but in certain cases also by a bilingual teacher. Norway uses more bilingual teachers inside the regular school than Denmark. In smaller districts with fewer immigrants, the children are put directly or almost directly into Danish/Norwegian classes. They may sometimes be getting auxiliary teaching for a few periods a week in Danish/Norwegian, either in class or by being taken out of the ordinary class teaching, alone or together with other immigrant children, and usually with no account taken of their age, nationality or mother tongue.

There have been some attempts in Norway to introduce instruction through the medium of the children's mother tongue, and the first Danish experiments are also going on. The Danish and Norwegian models are *integrative*, both physically and in content and ideology. They are likewise without exception *assimilationist*.

11.4.5 Finland

There is almost no immigration of labour into Finland, and there is therefore no system or pattern for the teaching of immigrant children. The few foreigners (about 13,000) resident in Finland fall by and large into the following categories: (1) foreigners married to Finnish nationals; (2) foreign language teachers; (3) foreign students and academics often staying only a short time; (4) technical and other experts, working, for example, on the nuclear power stations; and (5) artists of various kinds on very short visits. There are also a very few refugees. However, it is possible to make a comparison between the teaching of immigrant children in the other Scandinavian countries and the education of the indigenous minorities in Finland, and of Finnish children who return from Sweden, often with an inadequate command of Finnish. The largest indigenous minority group, the Finland Swedes (about 300,000) is not a minority in the legal sense, but the other part of the founding population of the country, with the same constitutional rights as the Finnish-speaking part. The Swedish language is therefore not a minority language but one of the two national languages. The Swedish-medium educational system in Finland is structured on exactly the same lines as the Finnish, the only difference being that the language of instruction is Swedish. There is thus a complete network of Swedish schools, and in a number of fields students can continue to study in Swedish after their matriculation, at universities, colleges, and other educational establishments (see, for example, Hoffman, 1975; Törnudd, 1978, and the report of the Language Preservation Committee (Språkskyddskommittén 1971)). The other indigenous minority languages in Finland, Same and Romanes, enjoy very few rights. There is almost no mother tongue teaching available in Romanes, and there are only so far experiments with elementary teaching through the medium of Same even if the demands are growing. For children returning to Finland from Sweden there is the possibility in many of the coastal areas of parental choice to send them either to Finnish- or Swedish-speaking schools. There are in addition many kinds of auxiliary teaching available in both languages, and the teachers are always to some extent bilingual, never complete monolinguals.

In Sweden, Norway, Denmark and Finland, moreover, there are some schools teaching through the medium of a language other than the majority language: Sweden has the smallest number of them (in Estonian, German and French), Denmark the largest (for example, Bjørns internationale skole: see *Skolen hvor det er normalt at være anderledes* 1980). Since these schools, however, are exceptional and since they cater, moreover, for a very small and non-representative section of the immigrant child population (or the guest worker child population: for instance, the Kennedy school in Berlin), I shall not deal with them in this book.

11.4.6 Some results

In West Germany it is officially estimated (by the former prime minister of North-Rhine-Westphalia, Heinz Kühn, in a thorough report, 1979) that around 25% of the GW children of obligatory school age, living legally in the country, do not go to school. The Federal Government admits that the figure can be around 20% (*Weiterentwicklung . . .* 1980: 78). Probably very few of the children whose parents are in West Germany illegally go to school. Jonas Widgren's estimate, made for Unesco in 1975, of the number of school-aged migrant children not attending school in the industrialized countries in western Europe was 300,000 to 500,000. Estimates by different researchers and migrant organizations now talk about figures of around 800,000.

In Scandinavia there are no official figures for I children not going to school. There are certainly not as many children in Scandinavia, proportionally, not going to school, as in West Germany, France or Switzerland, but it is reasonable to assume that there are more I children than native children also in Scandinavia not attending school. We found out, for instance, when comparing the school statistics with the census that less than a third of young Turks in the last years of compulsory schooling, residing in Denmark, actually attended school (Skutnabb-Kangas & Rahbek Pedersen, 1981: 312–13).

Heinz Kühn estimates in his report that more than 50% of all GW children leave school without a leaving certificate – and here he is of course only talking about those children who *do* go to school. The government report says that around 50% of the GW children do not attend any vocational school, more than 50% do not get any kind of leaving certificate from any kind of school, and more than two-thirds of the roughly 45,000 foreigners who leave school every year receive no form of vocational training (*Weiterentwicklung . . .* 1980: 78). The official figure for GW children finishing compulsory schooling without a certificate in North-Rhine-Westphalia was 65% in 1977, compared to 20% of German children, mostly working-class children (according to FIDEF, 1978). In 1976 90% of all foreign pupils in Hauptschule in West Berlin left without a certificate (Bericht . . . 1978: 25) (Hauptschule is the 3-year school for 12–15 year olds where those children go after the 6-year comprehensive school who have not succeeded in getting into Gymnasium or Realschule). Of all German children, around 30% continued to study either in Gymnasium or in Realschule, according to FIDEF (1978), but only 4% of the Turkish children did so (or, if one takes only Gymnasium and the latest figures: 23% of German but only 3% of GW children – *Statistisches Bundesamt*, 1981 and Schmitt, 1981).

Even if the Scandinavian figures are not as alarming as the West German ones, the results for immigrant children do not seem to be as good as those for the majority children. According to immigrant school psychologist Sunil Loona only 1% of the immigrant children in Norway finish an education after comprehensive school (in an interview, Viten, 1982: 6). In Sweden 69% of pupils with mother tongues other than Swedish, compared to 80% of those with Swedish, went straight on to upper secondary school from grade 9 of comprehensive school, according to a study of all compulsory school leavers in 1979. The immigrant pupils are admitted to a lesser extent than the Swedish pupils to the 3- and 4-year theoretical courses and more to the vocationally oriented 2-year courses and shorter courses (SO, 1981-01-07). It is also well known that drop-out rates for immigrant pupils in upper secondary schools are higher than for Swedish pupils. The Danish situation seems to be no better than the Norwegian. Of all immigrant children from the two largest groups (Turkey and Pakistan) who left the obligatory school between 1975–78 only 1.8% had finished a further education by 1.10.1978, while 11% underwent some kind of further education, and 87% got no further education whatsoever. Not a single child from Turkey or Pakistan finished Gymnasium during that time in Denmark. Many children dropped out before the 8th grade or did not come to school at all, and should therefore be added to the figure of 87% not receiving any further education (Rahbek Pedersen & Skutnabb-Kangas, 1980).

There is also sometimes a tendency in all Scandinavian countries on the part of the authorities (especially in Denmark) and even a few researchers (mainly in Sweden) to deny the bad results. The Danish Minister of Education, Dorte Bennedsen, tells us that "the present measures seem to function perfectly well" (1980: 341, my translation).

There exists abundant evidence for the bad results in schools, of over-representation of phenomena which reflect psychological, social and academic difficulties among migrant children and young people both in schools and outside. According to Kühn even those GW youngsters who *do* have a leaving certificate from Hauptschule (less than half of those who attend) are without any chance of getting qualified jobs with possibilities of advancement. His opinion is that almost all foreign children and youngsters in West Germany are in a situation where they are about to assume the role of complete outcasts, pariahs in society, if very drastic measures are not taken (Kühn, 1979: 88–91). And it seems that the latest measures in West Germany rather increase than decrease these negative possibilities. In all Western European countries we are forcing part of the migrant youth to become a new type of bitter, physically violent *lumpenproletariat.*

Again, even in Scandinavia where the results in schools, especially in Sweden, are better than in West Germany, the same type of figures showing over-representation in unemployment statistics, etc. exist. SIV-Dokumentation 23.4.1982 from the National Board of Immigration and Naturalization in Sweden says that the unemployment rate for foreigners is twice as high as for Swedes (unemployment statistics, nr. 22/82). Unemployment has risen for both groups, but the relationship remains the same. And the situation is much worse in Denmark and Norway.

This becomes more understandable when we look at different rates of development in different countries. Minority children simply fail earlier (and more brutally) in typical GW countries, while immigrant countries may give the children an (illusory?) better start, a better chance in the beginning. In GW countries the school already tells the foreign children what their future place is. In immigrant countries other societal forces, like discrimination on the labour market, guarantee that they don't get good jobs anyway to the same extent as native youngsters, even if they succeed in getting the same training. In an American book, "Who gets ahead" (1979), Jencks and others, according to Apple, "document the fact that not only are economic returns from schooling twice as great for individuals who are economically advantaged to begin with, but for, say, black students, even finishing high school will probably not bring any significant benefits. Thus, even if we could alter the school to equalize achievement (and that is one of the goals in mother tongue classes, my remark) the evidence suggests that it might not make a significant difference in the larger framework in which schools exist." So, even if minority children did get as much as majority children out of the school (and they don't) that might not help them in getting a good job. And this is clearly shown in the Scandinavian unemployment statistics, while in West Germany the failure comes earlier. Next we are going to discuss what function the failure has for the different types of policy. Here we can see a GW policy mainly as an answer to the earlier policy phase (= exploit cheap flexible labour), while an immigrant policy can be seen as an additional answer to the new development (= develop and retain a new native underclass to function as a buffer in the restructuring process of the capitalist world economy).

Since, according to Castles, the old function of guest workers presupposes that they are mobile, even the children must be educated to be mobile, ready to be sent back whenever their parents' (or their own) labour is not needed any more. They should be prevented from being educated to stay and to be integrated. Considered, however, as a social buffer group, the children of immigrants on the other hand must be *made* to stay and must be prevented from going back. Even if both are educated to be used as cheap labour (because as non-educated or badly educated they cannot choose their jobs), this conflict in function explains why the goal is monolingualism in different languages for the two groups: *monolingualism in the minority language in segregation programmes* makes the children linguistically "equal" (in the same weak position, unable to demand any rights, or better jobs, or more education) to their minority-language-monolingual mobile parents, and easy to send back. *Monolingualism in the majority language in submersion programmes* prevents the immigrant children from going back and *forces* them to stay, at the same time as by assimilating them to the values of (parts of) the majority society it prevents the development of solidarity with others with the same low status.

The GW children are kept unintegrated by preventing both organizationally and linguistically any real integration in the German classes and in German society. This is aided by the use of syllabuses, teachers (sent and controlled by the embassies) and teaching materials from the country of origin. The immigrant children are prevented both from wanting to return (because they are not taught enough of their culture, language etc. to know anything about the country of origin and because they are made to feel ashamed of their origins and to regard everything in the new society as better) and from being able to return (mostly because they don't know the language well enough). These aspects are further discussed in 11.4.7.

Because of the different functions GWs and immigrants fulfil, different countries also use different methods to make children fulfil these functions. Therefore researchers in West Germany and Scandinavia must also make different recommendations, if they want their recommendations to be scientifically sound. In West Germany enemy number one of the GW in the educational field is *forced segregation*. In that situation THE ONLY WAY TO ENSURE NON-SEGREGATION IS TO PUT THE CHILDREN INTO GERMAN CLASSES, i.e. into submersion programmes (which we know do not work), and eventually to force the German classes to change, so that the needs of GW children are met better. That should, in time, lead to a new "segregation" of the children (as has already happened with many Greeks in West Germany – (see Tsiakalos)), but then with a completely different goal.[10] But for the time being putting the children into German classes is the only way to ensure, especially for Turkish children, that they (a) learn at least some German, (b) receive instruction which at least is not directly undemocratic and strongly authoritarian, (c) receive instruction which can give them the same qualifying content which German children get, (d) can become familiar with both other GW children and German children and *vice versa*, and (e) get access to the same economic resources which German children get. In Scandinavia, especially Sweden, the worst enemy is not segregation, but *forced assimilation*. There is minimal risk that those recommendations which suggest a physical segregation of limited duration could be misused to promote a negative segregation of a Gastarbeiter-type.

German researchers have to balance between different demands. By using what from my point of view is a defensive strategy, namely recommending "integration" of GW-children into German classes (something they know is not the best possible alternative from the individual child's point of view) they try to prevent even worse things from happening, from the whole GW-group's point of view. They also have to make their recommendations so that on the one hand, they don't argue against what they know is good for the child, namely mother tongue classes, when trying to push for "integration" (a mistake I think, for instance, Boos-Nünning makes), but on the other hand don't offer the authorities a chance of using research results and recommendations which might be useful in an assimilationist immigrant policy, to legitimize and even strengthen a segregatory GW policy. Some of the Scandinavian research is, for instance, sometimes presented by German authorities as support for the segregatory Bavarian model, which it does *not* support, regardless of the superficial similarity of using L1 as the medium of instruction in both Bavarian Turkish classes and, say, Finnish mother tongue classes in Sweden.

Even if the climate for analyzing this type of problem has become harder even in Scandinavia during the last couple of years (especially in Sweden) and the level of the debate is extremely low (especially in Denmark), it still seems to me that many of us Scandinavian researchers use a more offensive strategy in tackling the questions of minority education. Having more clear-cut lines in one aspect should give us a better chance than we have had until now to deepen the analysis in other respects – and differentiation is badly needed. It would be naive of researchers or school authorities or immigrant organizations to believe in one global model, generalizable to minority education in all countries, for all minority groups and during all the different phases of economic and political development. Nice global theories are not worth much. But it is even more dangerous to say: let's be liberal and offer a lot of models. Random choice and repeating the same old mistakes which many other countries have made is something other than differentiated choice preceded by a thorough analysis.

11.4.7. Educational policy as a reflector and reproducer of societal policy

We can discuss the earlier exploitation of guest workers and immigrants in terms of three maxims, each describing how the societal policy tried to continue the exploitation of GWs and immigrants:
1. Maximize profitability.
2. Minimize the (social) costs.
3. Retain control.
In the following I will discuss educational policy, especially the organization of the classes, from two aspects:
- In what ways does the educational policy try to fulfil the aims that the maxims are an expression of?
- In what ways does the educational policy reflect the changes in the function of migration? A typical GWP can as just stated here be seen as an answer to the earlier stage (exploit cheap mobile labour!) and a typical immigrant policy as an answer to the present stage (develop and maintain a new indigenous underclass, which functions as a buffer, a shock absorber, in the restructuring of the capitalist world economy!).

Some of the important aspects which the industrialized countries must try to retain control over are:
1. sending back/going back (repatriation/return);
2. possibilities of protesting, and;
3. possibilities of developing solidarity between different immigrant/guest worker groups and between them and the native working class.

I will try to see how school helps to retain control over these aspects. In relation to *sending guest workers back home* it is imperative in a guest worker policy to keep the children unintegrated, prepared to be sent home (even by force) whenever their parents' labour is not needed any more. This is done by preventing a real integration in German classes and in German society. It is also done by making as much use as possible of syllabuses and teaching materials from the country of origin (and the latter reduces costs, too, because it is cheaper than producing new materials which would apply under guest worker conditions). The same applies to the use of teachers from the sending countries and to letting the embassies send and control them. All these measures could under different conditions, with a different motivation (and with different results) be good for the children. That would be the case if it was a positive instead of a negative segregation, and if the children and parents were given a genuine choice. Now all these measures function in a negative fashion only.

In relation to *giving immigrant children a possibility of returning* it is in the interest of the immigration country in an immigration policy (where the immigrants and their children are needed as a buffer) to prevent the children from having any real possibility of returning. This is done by not giving the children any real possibility of learning their mother tongue (which in the Scandinavian immigration policy is a voluntary subject for the children). It is also done by preventing the children from developing a cultural and national identification with their own group and its culture, and from feeling proud of the group, and by making the children feel ashamed of their origins. All this is partly a result of the organization of the school, where the focus is on everything Swedish/Norwegian/Danish. All status-giving activities are connected with the language and culture of the majority.

In relation to the *possibilities of protest* the pattern is the same in an immigration policy and a guest worker policy (except that the latter is more direct and more brutal). One doesn't protest if one has a bad education and hence difficulty in getting information about the world, about one's own place in it, and about the reasons for one's misery. One doesn't protest if one, because of lack of economic and political opportunity on the labour market and in society in general has no access to channelling a protest in a constructive way (constructive for whom? a good question . . .) so that it is heard. One doesn't protest if protesting implies a risk of consequences for one's residence permit or for relatives in the home country (and in many cases even being organized can have negative consequences – there are many examples of that even in Denmark). In an immigration policy the will to protest can also be undermined by giving the immigrant children the impression that their failure is their own fault (see next chapter). It is also done by seeing to it that the values of the majority society are so much underlined by the status given to them by the school, that those immigrant children who succeed in the majority school have internalized the majority norms (and do not, consequently, have any need to protest).

With adult immigrants, official unanimity about objectives (which may sometimes be found in a country which denies the existence of conflict between classes) may also function as an obstacle to protest. We can observe a trend towards this in Sweden. Officially, the Swedish Government, Parliament, and the immigrant organizations are unanimous about the aims of the school system: it is to make the immigrant children actively bilingual, to give them the same educational opportunities as Swedish children have, and to help them to maintain and develop their own culture. The offical aims are so formulated that the immigrants, too, can support them. When these fine aims are not realized, either the immigrants have only themselves to blame (since they have been party to the decisions and are thus partly responsible for carrying them out); or they must blame the government, their partners in the whole enterprise, for not putting fine ideas properly into practice or for working against them in some direct or indirect way (and, of course, the immigrant organizations are unwilling to believe ill of the government, or to criticize, since they and the government are *at one* in supporting the objectives). If the immigrants do in fact accuse their government partners of making less than honest efforts at the objectives, then they are often silenced with remarks about impatience, troublemaking, disruption of the generally harmonious atmosphere, and they are accused of imperilling the basis for fruitful co-operation. There is a good recent example of this where Christina Bratt Paulston, writing an official report for the National Board of Education in Sweden (1982) calls the Finnish immigrant organizations militant because they persist in their demands for mother tongue medium classes. . . .

A harmony model (as opposed to conflict model) of society where one no longer knows (or has to pretend that one doesn't know) where the enemy is, thus prevents protest at least as effectively as more direct measures. Differences between groups as to their culturally determined norms about the way conflicts are solved and co-operation established can make protests even more difficult. Rita Liljeström's description of the kind of relationship there may be between Swedish teachers and immigrant children (1979: 49, reviewing Shibutani & Kwan, 1965) may also cast light on the relationship between Swedish decision-makers and representatives of immigrant organizations. The distance between the groups (for instance with regard to power relationships) is maintained "by maintaining a social distance, even in frequent and repeated contacts. This happens if:
- At meetings only the matters under consideration are discussed.
- Rules and formalities are strictly observed.
- Contacts are kept at the conventional level.
- A friendly and liberal exterior is presented: a distancing friendliness hides both sympathies and antipathies.
- Standardized feelings are expressed and standard jokes are made.
- Culturally determined roles are played (for instance, the role of the teacher [or of the official – my remark].
- The role-taking is non-reciprocal.

Contacts are kept at the level of a purely superficial awareness. By contrast, informal and relaxed forms of social contact where people are spontaneous and personal, and reveal their real selves to each other, are very dangerous. They lead to a sympathetic sharing in other people's experiences. You come close to the point where you feel a real emotional involvement. It begins to become a concern of yours. It influences and affects you."

Rita Liljeström says that she does not want to caricature the Swedish school system, she wants only to "question the instrumentalism characteristic of a great deal of Western education". No more do I wish to caricature the Swedish authorities. But I recognize her description, in a concrete and subjective way, from a number of occasions on which immigrant parents and organizations have tried to make the authorities understand. I think of the Swedish authorities rather than of other groups of human beings I have come into contact with, when I read Rita Liljeström's

account of Ottomeyer's description (1978) (or Ottomeyer himself) of human relationships under the capitalist system:
"There is co-operation under the pressure of competition and insecurity about the future. Partners with different interests both trying to outwit each other. The game assumes that mutual indifference towards the other's personality is concealed behind a mask of amiability" (Ottomeyer, 1978: 48).

If one of the parties in a situation of conflict has the power to draw up the rules for the game (like official authorities in relation to immigrants), then those forms of protest to which one is accustomed may be defined as inadmissable by the rules of the game and those who perhaps do not master (or accept) the new rules, are thus prevented from protesting.

As regards *solidarity* among the GWs/immigrants themselves, and between them and the indigenous working class, the aim of dividing them is also achieved using different methods. In a GWP, integration of adults is being prevented, for instance, with the help of the housing policy and by the poor provision for the learning of German. With the children it is the same, because they are kept *negatively* segregated in their classes (without any of the benefits that a *positive* physical segregation could give) and away from contact with the German classes. The children are prevented from having social contact with German children or with immigrant children of other nationalities (in both cases their only means of communication would be German), because of poor or non-existent German teaching in the schools and because training programmes for teachers of German as a foreign language are only just beginning in West Germany (for information about teacher training, see Reich, 1979). And German children, for their part, are prevented from having any social contact with foreign children on equal terms because on the one hand they never get to know them very well ("Keep German classes German"), and because on the other hand the foreign children's achievement at school is so poor that German children find it difficult to respect and appreciate them.

With an IP, solidarity is prevented by assimilation. Rather than being presented, as would be the ideal way, as equal but a little different, immigrant children are made into inferior kinds of Swede, with low status. Swedish/Danish/Norwegian children are told very little about their foreign schoolmates' background and culture, and there often seems to be an underlying fear of any open discussion of conflicts: problems of this kind are rather referred to school counsellors and psychologists. Nor are the immigrant children told enough about their own language background and culture and the reasons for their poor performance at school, to be able to develop within their own group a feeling of solidarity and pride in themselves, which is necessary for solidarity with other oppressed groups. What is common both to a GWP and to an IP is that the *children* are made the scapegoats, they are made to believe that their failure is their own fault.

Thus they internalize the negative image that the majority society has of them.

In the case of the other two *maxims, maximize the profitability and minimize the (social) costs* we can see both similarities and differences between a GWP and an IP. The similarities concern general policy; and the common factor here is the exploitation of cheap labour, even if that labour is more mobile with a GWP (and can thus better be adapted to the needs of the labour market) than with an IP. The topic of the general economic exploitation of guest workers and immigrants falls outside the primary scope of this book (see Sivanandan, 1982 for references), and the question is therefore only going to be discussed briefly and as it affects the school system.

With a GWP it is simple to see how savings are made. They are made, for instance, by accepting the fact that many of the foreign children do not go to school at all. There have been no properly co-ordinated measures in West Germany, for instance, to get the children of illegal immigrants and others who do not attend school into the schools. The new policy recently adopted in the government plan of 19.3.80 does make some proposals, and the planned reorganization at ministry level seems to indicate a new awareness of the extent of the problem. But at the same time it seems now (March 1983) that only a few young people are going to profit from the new measures which seem to me to have twofold aims: to prevent as many as possible from coming and to throw out especially those who seem to become too expensive on the one hand, and to try even harder to assimilate the others, the possibly more profitable ones, on the other hand. If we only consider what proportion of the guest workers' taxes is saved by not having to employ teachers or make buildings and teaching materials available for those children who at the moment do not go to school at all, we shall see that the saving must be considerable. According to a calculation made by FIDEF (1978), North-Rhine-Westphalia saved about DM 100 million during the academic year 1977/78 in teachers' salaries alone, because it was accepted that about 50,000 guest workers' children of school age did not go to school in that particular Land (according to official statistics).

The authorities have also accepted a very high drop-out rate because it has been assumed that the social expense that will be incurred in making provision for guest workers' children without any kind of occupational training, for those who will be knocked out of the race in the preliminary heats, will be largely borne by the sending countries. This has been the assumption because it was thought that circulation of labour, with the consequent return of the problem children with their parents to their home country, was both desirable and achievable. If the children did not in fact go home, it would always be possible to withdraw their residence permits or refuse to issue them with work permits, which would come to the same thing; the unemployed, and otherwise undesirable young foreigners could simply be sent "home" if they became a burden on the state, and that is what is happening just now.

Savings are often also made in West Germany in two other even more directly discriminatory ways: the foreign children's classes and schools are often in poorer buildings than the German (and the foreigners in any case, of course, tend to live in the poorer urban areas, away from the well provided for owner-occupier suburbs); and the teachers of foreign children are often much less well paid than ordinary teachers. This last is partly (but not wholly) owing to the fact that some of the mother tongue teachers are paid on the salary scales in force in their own home countries. Savings are also made by resorting to short-term temporary solutions to problems, which do not require expensive teacher training, further training, or the development of teaching materials; and by making inadequate provision for the supportive and corrective measures needed to keep the system running.

Many countries with an IP practise some of the same kinds of cost cutting. But with a typical IP it is accepted from the beginning that families must be kept together (the reasons this is accepted may be various, they may be demographic, or humanitarian, or other – in Sweden, to give one example, it was actually impossible to stop Finnish families from entering because of the terms of the Scandinavian agreement about the free movement of labour (1954), that whole families would be allowed to move and settle in other Scandinavian countries). It was clear from the start in countries with an IP that the cost of supporting those who dropped out of the system could not be transferred to the sending countries. This made for a greater preparedness to spend money on social provision right from the beginning. The sums involved, in any case, are more than covered by the profit to the national economy deriving from the presence of immigrant workers (see Ekberg, 1983).

More recently, it should be noted, in the more "developed" stage of capitalism in the Western world, "costs" have begun to be defined differently. It is more and more accepted that the capitalist system will produce a large number of individuals who have been cast aside. It is beginning to be accepted that some individuals are from the very beginning destined to be "educated" for unemployment and failure. But in the place of any attempt to change a system that "requires" such failure, there is a tendency to try (by means of taxation) to transfer the costs incurred by this failure to groups other than those who make the big profits, as well as to demand, more and more cynically, cuts in the provision of social welfare services for those who have "failed". Few writers have defined the function social policy is formulated to discharge as honestly as Ritt Bjerregaard, a former Danish Minister for Social Services (in a speech at a conference arranged by the OECD in Paris, reported in Information: 13.11.80):

"This function: to alleviate the effects of capitalism and to disguise the causes of societal conflict, is constantly the task of social policy. . . . The reason why we in the capitalist countries have social policy and welfare systems is that without them we would not be able to secure law and order. Social policy is probably the most effective, that is, the cheapest and in human terms the best method of ensuring the continued peaceful functioning of a highly developed and complex society."

The minister sees social policy as an alternative to (though fulfilling the same functions as) the more violent apparatus for suppressing discontent: the police and the army. If social policy does not fulfil its task, its primarily political function, as she defines it, then in her view it is useless: and then other institutions of society must take over: "more policemen, more prisons, more law and order". As long as the social policy works, things remain satisfactory – it is precisely part of the function of social policy to prevent protest.

If protest is to be effectually prevented, then it becomes important not to allow the social services to become too professional: if too many individuals who *have* (some kind of) chance to protest come to know exactly how it is the system works, for instance in relation to immigrants, they become dangerous. In this context it can be seen that the movement away from state welfare provision towards more private forms of care and support (look after your drop-outs yourselves!) is also an attempt to prevent protest (although at the same time such a movement has many things to be said in its favour).

To summarize: immigration and guest worker countries have more or less consciously created a generation where many cannot support themselves by any legal means. But this generation is not going to be satisfied. Until now the dissatisfied in our capitalist societies have been controlled by two different types of means: social political measures, and bad conscience, shame and guilt (and these last will be the topic of chapter 12). Social political measures (social benefits) have prevented people from starving to death and from seeing how rotten the system is. The task of social political measures in a capitalist society is to take care of those non-succeeders, outcasts, that the system produces. Social political measures thereby play a part in legitimizing a system which can only continue if it is allowed to produce these non-useful people. At the same time social political measures function as a mechanism for control: if those people who really are in a bad position can be pacified with social political measues, there is no risk that they might become too revolutionary and start fierce protest. Social political measures soften the worst impacts of a capitalist system, they are a type of human cosmetics. They have the same kind of controlling task, in principle, as the police and army, according to Bjerregaard: social political measures are an alternative to the police and army. But during times of economic recession when there are big cutbacks in social political measures (and worst for minorities), there is a growing need to increase the budgets of police and army, corresponding to (at least) the social cutbacks, because one or the other of the society's apparatus for controlling violence must function. This is exactly the development we see in all capitalist countries now. At the same time minorities, by taking the worst impact of both these cuts *and* other consequences of the "crisis", and being a politically powerless group, help to keep the system going perhaps a little longer than it would otherwise. And by "educating" their children to fulfil this role the schools contribute, too. But they also contribute to controlling the minorities in other ways, namely by teaching them to control themselves according to the norms of the rulers – that is the topic of the last chapter.

Notes to Chapter Eleven

1. The issue has been elaborated in Ekberg's PhD thesis (June 1983).
2. See Keskin, 1978; FIDEF, KOMKAR, KDID: "Informationen über die 'Grauen Wölfe' in der BRD"; TÖK-YD-Verlag: Das wahre Gesicht der Türkei; Türkei Informationen.
3. For literature on the Kurdish question, see Chaliand, 1980; Clason & Baksi, 1979; Committee for the defence of the national democratic rights of the Kurdish people in Turkey: Appeal (no date); Deklaration der Nationaldemokratischen Einheitsfront Kurdistans, KOMKAR 1980; Erdem & Skutnabb-Kangas, 1980; Jänicke, 1980; Muttersprache Kurdisch, KOMKAR, 1980; Türkei Information, FIDEF (no date).
4. A woman in Denmark, for example, who had been repeatedly assaulted by her husband, was taken to the hospital by her brother after one particularly bad assault. Here she was given the choice of returning to her husband (and further ill treatment) or going to stay with her brother (which was what she wanted to) but then being straight away expelled from the country.
5. This point is made, for example, in a written submission made to the Parliamentary Ombudsman in Denmark (30.6.80) by the chairmen of the Pakistani, Turkish, Greek and Yugoslav Associations in Denmark. See Khan, Erdem, Rigas, Özcan & Miljeviĉ, 1980.
6. This is also common for single men in an IP: we may think of barrack villages in many places in Sweden, for example in Gothenberg. There are excellent literary accounts of life in these barracks. Anthropological studies of barrack villages of this type are also beginning to appear – see, for example, Ryall, 1980 on the oil workers in Norway, or Berger & Mohr, 1975 on some of the European barracks.
7. The military political debate in Denmark provides us with a typical example. One MP (Steen Folke) put a question to the Minister of Defence about the American military establishment in Denmark: why had neither the Danish Parliament nor its defence sub-committee even been informed (and it should, of course, have been the Parliament which actually made the decision in this matter) about Denmark's new agreement with NATO concerning fundamental changes in the Danish

attitude to the kinds of war material the Americans were allowed to keep on Danish soil, and to the circumstances under which they could be used? The decision had been taken without the participation and without the knowledge of the Parliament, including the defence sub-committee.

8. See Hammar 1979, 1981, SIV's report: Invandrarna och Folkomröstningen 1980, as well as articles published in a collection of papers entitled "Cultural Identity and Structural Marginalisation of Migrant Workers" presented at a conference of the European Science Foundation in Bochum 10–12.12.80.

9. Here a terminological distinction should be made: when the word "integration" is used in West Germany, it seems to mean what we in Scandinavia would call "assimilation" (learning and acceptance of the language, culture and values of the majority community, so that an individual at the same time distances herself from those of her own group).

10. And now this development has started while this book was in press. *All* the immigrant organizations have come up with a joint plan, "Memorandum zum Muttersprachlichen Unterricht in der Bundesrepublik Deutschland" (see, *Deutsch lernen*, 3, 1983), where they demand mother tongue medium and bilingual classes.

12 Violence and minority education

12.1 Different control mechanisms: physical violence, shame and guilt

By comparison with majorities, minorities in most countries are oppressed both economically and politically (even if there are exceptions). They have the use of a smaller proportion of the country's resources than the majority. The world has enough resources for *everyone* to have what they need for a full life in the material sense. If a society has not enough resources for everybody (or believes or pretends that is has not, like all countries with starving children and huge military budgets), then the existing resources, though insufficient, can be shared equally by all so that everyone has at least enough for bare subsistence. Or it can exclude certain groups within the society from an equal share of most of the resources (material and non-material). This is the way most countries in our world have chosen – and minorities form one of the largest groups left outside.

Before I embark on a discussion of the ways in which minorities are prevented from enjoying their fair share of the world's goods, let me set down some figures:

Total world expenditure on armament today is about 650 milliard dollars per year which amounts to 5–6% of the total world gross national product (Brandt-Report). Finland has the lowest level of defence expenditure in Scandinavia, amounting to 1.5% of its gross national product, while the leading military powers spend from 4–8% and some underdeveloped countries as much as 30%. NATO and the Warsaw pact are responsible between them for 74% of total world expenditure on armament (Lindroos 1980, quoted from Ulfvens, 1980: 13). According to the Swedish disarmament expert, Inga Thorson from the Stockholm International Peace Research Institute (SIPRI), 5% of annual world expenditure on arms would be enough for *all* of the following:

- all the children in the underdeveloped countries could receive the vaccinations needed against all the most common diseases,
- 700 million people could receive reading and writing instruction,
- large parts of the third world could have preventive health care,
- 500 million people could get enough land to live off,
- 300 million children suffering from malnutrition could get extra food,
- 60 million undernourished pregnant women could be helped,
- 100 million new school places could be established,
- everybody in the world could have clean water before 1990 (Andersson, 1980: 23).

In 1982 15.3 million children died according to UN and WHO estimates because of undernourishment, poor sanitary conditions (mostly lack of clean water) and lack of medicine and medical care. This amounts to more than the total population of Finland, Norway and Denmark put together.

A single nuclear submarine costs the same as it does to feed 16 million children for a year.

The resources are there, but they are being misused. When those who control and are mismanaging the world's resources wish to exclude certain groups from their fair share, they need the power to control at least three factors. They need the means:
- to exclude these groups from the use of resources,
- to persuade them that this exclusion is justified and deserved, and their own fault,
- to ensure where they fail to persuade them of the justice of the situation, that the excluded groups are given no chance to do anything about it.

In the past rulers often used physical force to exclude the people from power: those who did not obey were simply physically punished. Even today the culture of physical force is the most common one in many countries. The extent to which physical force is used seems to correlate with the illiteracy rate. It may be a partial explanation to say that everyone understands the language of force, even those who cannot read; but one cannot suppose that there is any causal connection between illiteracy and the use of physical force.

There are many cultures which in the past valued the power of words more than the power of the sword; where injury consisted of verbal insult, the struggle of the people was carried on by songs and spells, and evil was perpetrated or perhaps more often prevented by words and not by any kind of material physical means. Typical examples of the working of such cultures can be found with the Finnish, Same or Indian shamans or the metaphysical struggles in the Kalevala, the Finnish national epic (which contrast with the primitive physical fights common in Old Norse literature); other examples can be found in the Inuit, Amerindian and many African traditions. But all in all the use of physical force has been more widespread, particularly where there has been an imbalance of power between groups.

With the spread of literacy comes an increasing tendency to replace direct physical force by symbolic force: it is easier for those in power to let the people punish themselves than to visit upon every offence direct physical punishment. We can trace a developmental trend away from the use of physical force and towards the use of shame as the means of punishment. When the transgressor was caught doing something that was against the rules devised by those in power, she was made to feel ashamed: her shame was made public and so she was disgraced. The shame culture is ritualized in the use of the pillory, for example, or the punishment stool placed outside churches (or indeed in the corner or seat for naughty children at school or at home): it is plain to everyone who sees that the individual found in these places has sinned. The Islamic notion of IZZAT, family honour, is similarly an example of the ritualized use of shame.

The next step is the development of a culture of guilt: during the process of internalizing the norms of the rulers, the transgressor begins to punish herself before anyone has discovered that she has broken the rules, instead of waiting for physical punishment from outside or the shame of public exposure: the transgressor develops a bad conscience. The culture of guilt is thus even more efficient than the culture of shame, because there is the self-inflicted punishment of guilt for having offended against the proper order of things, whether or not anyone else knows about it.

The school plays its part in this process, in addition to the church. The values, norms and ideology of those in power inculcated and confirmed by the school, to be accepted by all, including minority groups were part of the moral code, the commandments, taught by the school. Schools have been the most important instruments in the process of change from the use of physical force as a means of ordering society to the use of symbolic violence (and in encouraging acceptance of structural violence), what Thomas Mathiesen has called an invisible or hidden discipline (1980).

One of the most important differences between physical violence and symbolic-structural violence is in the degree to which one is aware of whose rules it is you are obeying. If someone punishes you physically, you know very well whose rules you have broken (you are punished by the one who has made the rules, or at any rate by his agent). But if you punish yourself, then you have internalized the rules, and that will normally mean not knowing whether the rules are your own or somebody else's. This is, of course, a very crude way of presenting things, and the great variety of different schools of psychoanalysis makes it clear that I have simplified a complex matter. And in any case, the simple fact of knowing that one is obeying someone else's rules need not in the least mean one is able emotionally or even intellectually to free oneself from their hold. In spite of all this, it can be said, however, that shame and guilt cultures make any struggle against injustice much more difficult, since we may not even necessarily be aware of something as being unjust.

After this introduction let me now discuss the situation of minorities in more detail. I shall discuss the role played by the school in industrialized western countries in the process of the change from the use of physical force to the use of symbolic violence and particularly the part played by the school in excluding minorites from the society of the more privileged and persuading them that this exclusion is well deserved. I have shown in earlier chapters *that* the school helps to keep minority children powerless, educationally, socially, economically and politically – and to perpetuate the powerlessness of their parents. In what follows I shall try to show that the school actually teaches them it is their own fault and that they deserve no better; and it will be clear, too, that the school helps to prevent them fighting this kind of oppression.

Even though here I am speaking only about minorities, I believe it is the case that many other oppressed groups are under very similar attack, and in my view the women's movement is one of the responses to "hidden discipline". Analysis of changes in the way one oppressed group is controlled may conceivably help other groups to recognize their own situation.

12.2 Physical violence as a method: separation from one's own group and punishment for speaking one's own language

I shall discuss two different ways in which physical violence used to be used against minority children: separating them from their parents and their own group, and punishing them for speaking their own language.

First of all the children were separated from their parents and their own group. Schools were centralized in the areas where minorities lived. But even if these were sparsely populated or poor areas, which might have meant centralized schools for majority children, too, one can see the placing of minority children in different kinds of boarding school as a measure consciously aimed at assimilation and this is openly admitted in many of the official documents (for instance for Same in Norway, see Lind Meløy, 1980; Finns in Sweden, Lundemark, 1980; Indians in the U.S.A.; Cahn & Hearne, 1970). We may have in mind here such dissimilar groups as the Same in all the Scandinavian countries, the Torneå Valley Finns (and especially in their case what is called the workhouse system), the Amerindians, Inuit children sent to Denmark, Kurdish children in Turkey, Australian aboriginal children, and so on. By isolating these children from their own groups the authorities prevented them from learning anything (or at least anything significant) about their own culture, history, language and traditions, their own values and characteristic occupations. When the children came home, they often felt strangers to their own culture and ethnic groups because they knew nothing of them. They no longer felt at home.

Of course, it has been the custom, too, for majority children to be sent away to school, but for many of them boarding school education meant no more than a continuation of the social and cultural patterns of the home. Their language, culture and values were part of the educational system, so that this kind of education was for them a constant confirmation of their identity – we need think here only of the English boarding school tradition. In addition they were taught how to be the rulers, not the ruled (Gathorne-Hardy, 1979).

In the second place, minority children were often punished for speaking their own language, even outside the classroom. Many were made to go hungry, or physically punished in a variety of ways for speaking their own language. I have spoken to Torneå Valley Finns who were made to carry heavy logs on their shoulders or wear a stiff collar which prevented them from turning their heads or looking down, all because they had spoken Finnish (and I have heard about the same punishment inflicted on Welsh children – Redfern, 1979). I have Same friends who were beaten or kicked as children for answering questions in Same. Tage Ranängen from Luleå University organized an exhibition of the workhouses in the province of Norrbotten: these were a kind of boarding school which poor children were allowed to attend, and where during the winter they also lived, earning their keep by doing much of the day to day domestic work, so that the whole system ran cheaply. He describes how the children were lined up in the school playground when one of them had spoken a word or two in Finnish to have their ears boxed one by one. Many schools also organized the children to spy on one another, rewarding the child who reported another for speaking the forbidden language, often by giving her extra food. This whole system was such as to lead the children to believe not only that their own language and culture were worthless, since they formed no part of the curriculum, but also that to speak the minority language (and to be part of the minority group) was a shameful thing that they had to get away from as soon as possible. In turn this made them feel ashamed of their own parents, so that they were even more like strangers when they went home.

Examples of this kind of attitude from countries outside Scandinavia are laughably similar (or perhaps one feels more like crying) whatever part of the world they come from:

"For nearly a hundred years the policy of the United States government was to acculturate the Navajo, so that the Navajo could be assimilated into the White society. To effect this assimilation Navajo children were taken from the shelter of the family and sent to boarding school. Almost every child who entered the boarding school spoke only Navajo, and most of the people employed at the boarding schools spoke only English. When a Navajo child spoke the language of his family at school, he was punished." (Platero, 1975: 57).

"Kee was sent to boarding school as a child where – as was the practice – he was punished for speaking Navajo. Since he was only allowed to return home during Christmas and summer, he lost contact with his family. Kee withdrew both from the White and Navajo worlds as he grew older, because he could not comfortably communicate in either language. He became one of the many thousand Navajos who were non-lingual – a man without a language. By the time he was 16, Kee was an alcoholic, uneducated and despondent – without identity. Kee's story is more the rule than the exception." (Platero, 1975: 58).

Physical violence of this kind is still to be found, in very different circumstances. We may find it in countries where the very existence of a minority is not even recognized and their language is forbidden – the Kurds, for example, are called mountain Turks by the Turks, and the Turks say they have "forgotten" their real mother tongue, Turkish, and begun to speak something curious because of their long isolation in the mountains.

"One of the reasons why they began to build boarding schools in 1964 was that they wanted to prevent the children from having contact with their parents. By isolating them in schools far away from their parents for the greater part of the year the authorities hoped to make the children forget their Kurdish. And since the Turkish teachers did not want to work in the primitive Kurdish villages and the government did not trust the Kurdish teachers, it was decided to bring the children to the Turkish teachers rather than the other way about." (Clason & Baksi, 1979: 75).

"I was seven when I started in the first grade in 1962. My sister, who was a year older, started school at the same time. We didn't know a word of Turkish when we started, so one felt totally mute during the first few years. We were not allowed to speak Kurdish during the breaks either but had to play silent games with stones and things like that. The teachers watched us all the time in the playground. Anyone who spoke Kurdish was punished. The teachers hit us on the fingertips or on our heads with a ruler. It hurt terribly. That's why we were always frightened at school and didn't want to go." (Clason & Baksi, 1979: 79).

And the same girl later tells us about the teacher training college she went to after leaving the fifth grade of primary school:

"The really tough indoctrination didn't start until I was at the teacher training college. At primary school only the teachers were nasty, but at the college the older pupils were hostile too, and treated us younger Kurdish girls badly. In the higher grades most of the girls were Turkish and they were always teasing us for not speaking Turkish very well. They called us Kurds with tails. To be a Kurd was the worst thing you could be. It was because we were Kurds that they treated us badly and constantly tried to torment us and make us angry. In the mornings, for example, they took away all our washing bowls so we couldn't wash. . . . All the time the indoctrination went on, and the drift of it was that the Kurds were dirty, bad people. At the boarding schools for young children the process of assimilation is gentler. It is easier to assimilate young children. At the teacher training college they kept up a steady psychological pressure on us. By constant threats of punishments of various kinds they tried to make us behave like frightened robots. We weren't allowed to read newspapers, listen to the radio, or read the books we wanted. They tried to make us deaf and dumb. We were just to be brainwashed into becoming fascist Turkish teachers. They didn't want us to develop at all. With more freedom we would have learnt more, but they were afraid of that. And with the kind of training they had given us we were to go out into the Kurdish villages and teach other Kurdish children to become good Turks." (Clason & Baksi, 1979: 86–87).

"The aim of these schools is assimilation rather than literacy", one of the teachers explained. "The children speak Kurdish, but they are taught in Turkish. Even though at the beginning the children don't understand a single word of what we say, we are obliged to speak Turkish to them. Every morning we have to start the day with these lines from one of Atatürk's speeches: *I am a Turk. I am strong. I never tell a lie. I have respect for my parents, for children, and for old people. I love people. I want to sacrifice myself for my country and my people.* We devote at least an hour every day to the study of Atatürk. We have to tell the children that Atatürk is our dear father, our saviour and beloved protector, even though he killed hundreds of thousands of Kurds. Every Kurdish family can tell you about his atrocities. . . . According to Atatürk's version of history, the Turks were the first people on earth. Without them there would have been no other people on earth. He is the greatest and the best of men. From the age of six we are obliged to fill the children's minds with lies like these. The aim is to brainwash them, since children are more easily assimilated than adults. For the Turkish teachers it's perhaps not so difficult to teach Turkish history, but we Kurdish teachers usually refuse to teach the children Atatürk's special brand of history. And when the educational authorities find out, we are threatened with dismissal, imprisonment, or exile to western Turkey. I am in this situation at the moment. I'm soon to be put on trial for spreading Kurdish propaganda. I've already been exiled and I don't know what's going to happen to me. But even if I have to die, I shall continue to tell the Kurdish children the truth. I refuse to lie to them." (Clason & Baksi, 1979: 70–71).

In other countries, too, where corporal punishment of children is illegal, physical force is nevertheless used upon minority children in separating them from their parents. The following statement was made by a chief welfare officer in Sweden in the mid-1970s, about a Romany boy from

Lovara:
"We want to give these children the best our society can offer them, but their parents tell us they want to keep their children. *We should like to have the chance to take these children away from their families, but we cannot do it.* N., for example, lived for six months with a Swedish family and everything worked perfectly. The boy, who speaks only Swedish, has now gone back to his gipsy parents . . . we thought his behaviour would begin to improve in his foster home and *we tried to persuade the parents to give up their child*, but they refused." (Marta, 1979: 33).

We have not, then, even here seen the last of physically separating children from their parents. . . . I have been involved in several court cases where the immigrant parent has tried to get back her child, taken by force by the Swedish authorities and placed in a Swedish monolingual foster home, where the parent has often been forbidden to speak her own language when visiting the child. But when children are physically separated from their ethnic group and when they are physically punished, they do at least know who their oppressors are. Anyone who, while learning something of the majority language, culture and values, nevertheless refuses to be assimilated, to forget her own language and culture and the values of her own ethnic group, still knows who she is fighting against:

"But in spite of all the problems, the children still like us Kurdish teachers, since we speak the same language as they do. They are afraid of the Turkish teachers. Everyone who hits them they call a Turk because they have heard what their parents have told them about the Turks' use of force against the Kurds. 'But please, Sir, when did you start being a Turk?' they ask if a Kurdish teacher hits them. They have also themselves experienced physical ill-treatment from Turkish soldiers coming into their villages. And since it is the Turkish teachers who beat them for speaking Kurdish in class, they always associate Turkish teachers with physical force and beating. They don't want to go to schools where there are Turkish teachers." (Clason & Baksi, 1979: 74).

"But they didn't succeed. We constantly protested against their oppression of us. After being treated like that, you really hate them." (Clason & Baksi, 1979: 87).

But for many children the process of assimilation is only too effective, and those in power achieve what they set out to achieve:

"After a few years the children no longer want to know their parents. The children are forbidden to speak Kurdish at school. They are taught that the Kurds are dirty and primitive. And when they go home to their villages they tell their parents that now they are Turks and don't want primitive Kurdish parents. They want their parents to start speaking Turkish and being civilized." (Clason & Baksi, 1979: 75–76).

12.3   From physical violence to symbolic and structural violence

In a large part of the industrialized world the use of direct physical violence in the education of minority children is shunned, officially at least. Instead structural and symbolic violence is used. This is at least as effective as direct physical violence in transmitting the same message: "You are worth nothing – your ethnic group is worth nothing – if you want to be accepted you must become like us and give up everything that is yours, you must despise it and be ashamed of it."

Minority children are not usually any longer physically separated from their parents. They are no longer physically punished for speaking their own language. But even so, the children are being separated from their own group in most instructional programmes they participate in. This happens in the assimilation programmes for the children of guest workers in West Germany, where the children are put into German classes with very little help or support. It happens in the submersion programmes in Scandinavia where the only thing of importance is how quickly the children learn Swedish, Danish or Norwegian (in spite of all the fine-sounding words about the importance of their own mother tongue and culture). It happens in the transitional programmes for Chicanos, Spanish-speaking children in the U.S.A., where the children's mother tongue is used as a medium of instruction only for so long as they are unable to follow teaching in English.

This separation from the group takes place in at least two different ways: the children are not taught enough of their own language and culture to be able to appreciate it. And they are made to feel ashamed of their parents and origins. This is not done by means of physical punishment, nor by telling the children their parents are primitive, dirty and uneducated. Instead it is done by the way the school is organized. The school is usually organized so that the minority children's language and culture find no place in it. If their language and culture do have some place in the school, it is usually only as a means by which the transition can be made from instruction in the children's own language to instruction in the majority language. Use of the minority language ensures that the children acquire at least some acquaintance with the different subjects while learning the majority language. The use of the minority language, then, is a way of making the process of assimilation a little less cruel, a little gentler and more "civilized". The children's mother tongue is used merely as a regrettably necessary instrument, which in itself has no value – and this transmits the same message to the children: abandon your language and your culture as soon as you can; your aim is to acquire the majority language (and culture and values).

Since language is also a symbol of the group that speaks it, the status that a language can achieve in society (or has ascribed to it) also reflects (and is perceived as a symbol of) the status of the group that speaks it. An official acceptance of a language gives it status. If the language spoken by minority children has no status at school (their miniature society), if it is not used as a means of instruction, taught as a subject (both to minority and majority children), then the message is being transmitted to the majority children as well, that the minority children's mother tongue is not of the same value as those languages which are used as means of instruction and/or taught as foreign languages in the school. If everything that is judged to be of value at school, everything rewarded with praise and good marks, everything that leads to high status positions (at school and outside) is associated with the majority language, and if all this is accepted as self-evidently the right thing, and if at the same time the minority language is not even accepted at school, then the same goal is achieved that was earlier achieved by the use of physical violence, by separation and punishment: the child is alienated from her own group and begins to feel ashamed of it.

One of the important differences between the results of direct physical violence and those of structural or symbolic violence is that with the latter many minority children (and adults) no longer know whose the message is and who is the enemy. Since the children (and many adults too) have internalized the message, they have developed what Franz Fanon calls a colonized consciousness (1968). Since the children officially have the same opportunities as majority children, especially with an immigrant policy of the Swedish type, and since they have internalized the norms that tell them that they are being given equal opportunities with the majority children, it becomes more difficult for them to see that they are still the victims. But they are nonetheless *being made* scapegoats for the system. They begin to *believe* that they must be inferior, and that their poor performance is their own fault, since the system itself is fair to them. Minority children will begin to explain to themselves that they are simply not as capable as the majority children, and that that is the reason they do not do well in the system.

In earlier times, when physical violence was used, the children could at any rate sometimes succeed in building up among themselves a strong sense of *solidarity* with one another, and could try to survive in this way. The school system today, however, in many different ways stifles this possibility.

It can be done in the name of integration by separating the children from one another. In many cities, with many education authorities and schools, the rule is that in any one class or school there may not be more than 10% of immigrant children (Gladsaxe, Denmark), or 20% (West Berlin), or not more than two immigrant children per class (Tåstrup, Denmark); or the rule may be that "immigrant children should be dispersed as much as possible so that they have to use Swedish/Danish/Norwegian/German as their common means of communication". If there are whole classes of immigrant children, then people begin to protest about dangerous segregation, but no one ever utters a word of protest about the dangerous segregation of the poor Swedish/Danish/Norwegian/German children.

Or let me take an image which seems illuminating to me: about "segregation" and "too much of the children's own language and culture" – all these demands for an end to keeping the children together. The image is of a good gardener and an exotic plant. If I try to transplant, let us say, a bluebell from the woods to my own garden, I try especially to take as much of the root system with me as I can and as much of the soil in which I found the plant, because I know the best thing for the plant is to take with it as much of its own original natural environment as possible (cf. Latin *cultura* – cultivation) so that it will only gradually and not abruptly begin to grow into the soil, the cultivated area in my garden – and so it will grow well in its new place. The good gardener does not say to the plant (as she cuts it off at the roots): "Little plant, of course your roots are very good and your culture is of great value, but *in this country, my garden,* you'll have to forget all about them – here you'll have to grow a bulb not a root."

And then the other side, the shelter (cf. language shelter programmes). If I get a cutting from a neighbour/neighbouring country, I first put it in water until it has rooted well, and then carefully plant it out. And even if I know sunshine is absolutely vital for its growth, I also know that it cannot take too much direct strong sunshine immediately after being planted out. So I put it under glass where it is warm and secure and I might also put it in a fairly shady place out of the direct sunlight until it has taken root properly and has grown strong. The good gardener's special protection of a seedling could not without absurdity be called "indefensible segregation" – this the term for mother tongue classes for minority children used by a group of assimilationists in *Dagens Nyheter*: 3.9.80.

These people conclude their article by saying: "Let us be clear that segregation is and will remain segregation, and will never be integration." They seem to find it difficult to see that the commonsense view has many convincing parallels: shock treatment often kills the patient. What is good in itself and even necessary later on may have disastrous effects if administered too early and too vigorously. *Too* much sun too early (Swedish, Danish or Norwegian) of the blue-yellow, red-white, or red-white-and-blue variety may cause the sprouting seedling to wither and die. On the other hand, once well rooted in the new soil, it will grow excellently under the new sun.

The possibility of solidarity among minority children is gradually being stifled by making the children identify with the majority group and not with their own group (making them want to grow a bulb not a root). Or it may be by making it clear to minority children who have done well or who are accepted, that they are not thought of as belonging to their own minority group ("you don't look like a bluebell at all, you behave almost like one of us"). The children are seldom given an opportunity to experience the fact or demonstrate to the majority children that their knowledge and culture are worth something. And the majority children are themselves seldom taught enough about the minority children to be able to appreciate them properly – rather these minority children are presented to them as somewhat defective

Swedes/Danes/Norwegians/Germans. School and society are gradually and effectively destroying the patterns of solidarity which hold together the family or kinship group or village community that many immigrants brought with them from their homeland. The networks of relationships, with mutual rights and obligations, which once bound them together into larger entities are not recognized in their adopted countries, and of course there is no support given to the valuable features of immigrant society.

Carolyn Swetland describes an immigrant in Norway being accused of lying by the police for calling someone his brother when there was demonstrably no blood relationship between the two of the kind that would allow the use of this term as we define it – and yet this man had the obligations of a brother towards the other. I have many times known sums of money collected in a few days among my Pakistani friends, none of them earning high wages, for the benefit of a widow with young children, or of aged parents whose breadwinner had died, which even in Scandinavia would be enough to live on for several years. And when I have expressed my surprise and asked questions, it has emerged that they think of it as the self-evident duty of the members of their social group to help and defend each other, even at the cost of great sacrifice. I remember, too, discussions I have had with Romany friends, and their astonished contempt for supposedly rich and civilized cultures which are unable to look after old people other than by putting them into "homes" of various kinds. We brutally destroy such patterns of mutual care by the way we organize school and society.

Let me cite a few more examples (see also the examples in sections 2.2.1.2, 2.4 and 2.5):

"Then the headmaster said: 'You have a name which is difficult for us Swedes to pronounce. Couldn't we change it?' 'No,' I thought, 'you can learn it instead.' 'And besides perhaps some nasty person will make fun of your name.' 'Well, I suppose I'd better change it then,' I thought. So I became Anna Varhos . . . Marianne started to tell the others about me: 'This is Anna Varhos.' 'What', I thought, 'Anna? What's she talking about?' Then I remembered I had a new name. That was eighteen months ago and I still have difficulty with it, and I always will. I don't think you can ever forget you're in a foreign country and a different society. No matter how long you live here, you still feel like a foreigner. And they're always calling you a foreigner." (Fisun Varhós, aged 17, from Turkey. 'My name wasn't good enough', *Barnen och Vi*, 1, 1974.5.)

"The Swedish children hadn't been prepared for it either. Just imagine if someone had come into my class and told them about Turkey. I think it would have made things easier for me then. . . . My Swedish friends started laughing at the other Turks. Who I belonged with. Then I started fighting the Swedes. There was never any adult about to intervene and tell the Swedes about Turks and the Turks about Swedes.

You never talk about your problems in class in Sweden. You have to go to the school counsellor for that. So we had to sort out our problems outside the classroom. It was done by fighting. I love my parents and I respect them, but what they are and everything they know count for nothing in Sweden. Like lots of Turkish children here, they know all about farming and farm animals, and some of them have more than one trade; but when is a Turkish child given the task at school of describing the cultivation of vines? So far as I know, never. It's true that in this country's terms our parents are ignorant. My mother is illiterate, and though my father reads and writes Turkish fairly well, he has hardly any Swedish at all, and I don't think he even knows the name of my school. Turkish parents can't give their children any help with homework. And on the other side the school or society in general gives us no help with being Turkish. We find ourselves between two worlds, but don't really belong to either." (Bülent Yilmaz, aged 19, *Arbetet*: 17.2.79.)

"I'm in grade 6 and I find it boring to be in a Norwegian class. I like being with them, but they don't want to talk to me. When I ask them about something, they always say they don't know. They're just unfriendly. Sometimes the teacher asks us to sit together in pairs, and then no one wants to sit with me. Even when the teacher says someone has got to sit with me as well, still no one wants to. If I want to be friends with someone and pat them on the shoulder, they just say 'Oh, shove off'. In gym lessons, no one wants to go with me. It's only the younger boys in grade 4 who talk to us. . . . Sometimes I don't understand anything the teacher's saying. At other times I understand everything, but the teacher only asks the Norwegian children. He doesn't think I know anything. General studies are the worst of all. I don't know anything about Norwegian history and institutions. Even when we're having exams I have to look in the book. Norwegian's a difficult language too. I often don't get anywhere because there's one word I don't understand."

"Once I was fighting with a Norwegian boy, and everyone in the playground stood round and was on his side. No one was on my side. They say things behind my back and tease me. I just hope I can start in a class for foreigners only at Hersleb school in the autumn." (Two Pakistani boys, aged 15, *Klassekampen*, Fremmedarbejderutgave no. 2, 1978, 5.)

"I've only got Turkish friends. We're all being teased, at school and where we live. The Danish children don't want us to join in their games. They don't accept us. Even after two years I haven't got any Danish friends. We can't talk together at all. If I only knew the language properly I think I could make friends. My parents haven't got any Danish friends either. That's pretty common. They can't manage in Danish at all. At work all they've got to do is mind the machine and say nothing. During the day? I don't do anything. I just walk around." (Mustafa, aged 16, *Information*: 29.8.79).

Many children have also described these experiences afterwards, in interviews. There are several small Scandinavian studies which draw upon such experiences. Antti Jalava, a Finnish immigrant author in Sweden, tells in several of his books and short stories about his experiences. The following quotations are from them:

"The longer all this went on, the more urgent and deep the pressure upon me to conform, to assimilate. I began to avoid my brothers and sisters, and in the end distanced myself from my parents as well. I refused to go shopping with my mother, and when we had a Christmas party at school, I simply told my parents they weren't to come. . . . I was scarcely ever at home, and the very few evenings when I did meet my parents and my brothers and sisters, I hardly said more than three or four words to them. Even if I had felt I wanted to talk I wouldn't have been able to do it: by that time my own language was stifled, we could simply no longer talk to each other. While I understood what they said, I couldn't answer, I couldn't put what I thought and what I wanted into words. For their part, they had a very minimal amount of Swedish, but they had succeeded in retaining their feeling for everything Finnish, they met their relations and wrote letters home, they had Finnish friends at work and they went to the sauna. But for me all these things had something downtrodden about them, and even the very thought that I was a Finn induced a reluctant feeling of shame, so that I was ashamed even of shame itself. . . . At school I did worse and worse, I simply couldn't understand the text books, no matter how hard I tried. I began to believe that really I was unusually stupid, and when I was around fourteen, I had the first sensations of self-hatred and death-wish." (Jalava, 1978: 4–5).

(from *Nobody could see that I was a Finn*)
"My parents were welcome, sure enough, but as far as we kids were concerned, matters were altogether different. After all, we were not useful, productive, and on top of everything else we couldn't even speak Swedish. The principal of my new school did not really know what to do with me when I was admitted; she was just as embarrassed and at a loss as I was, and when she escorted me to the elementary third-grade classroom we walked hand in hand. Holding hands was the only language we had in common. There was a vacant seat in the rear of the classroom. The boy I was put next to protested vehemently, but I was ordered to stay put, anyhow. The flush-faced fellow whose bench I had to share was called Osmo. It was a Finnish name and he came from Finland, but even so for some reason he refused to speak a word of Finnish. Later I came to understand why he behaved as he did; and if I had only guessed that his fate would also be mine, I would have taken to my heels and run for my life.
My new classmates were curious: they watched my every movement

closely, they walked in circles around me, they sniffed in my presence, and they felt the muscles on my arms. After that they began to call me Finnbiscuit, and that was my nickname until I learned to speak Swedish as well as Osmo did . . . or, more precisely, until I had adjusted to their ways to the extent of my passing in their eyes for a real Swede.

Adjusting was not, however, at all simple. To what did one have to adjust and how? There was nobody to explain things, there were no interpreters, no Finnish teachers and no kind of teaching of the Swedish language. And I was no chameleon, either, for I only wanted to be myself, out of habit and instinct. When the others wrote in Swedish, I wrote in Finnish. From the time I had learned to spell, it had given me pleasure to put together sentences on paper. But that was something that just couldn't be done. The teacher grabbed my pencil and angrily shook his finger at me. In spite of everything, I continued to fall back on my mother tongue. There was a row at my desk. The teacher tore up my paper and stamped on my words he had thrown on the floor. He scolded me loudly. I pulled a wry face and muttered "Damn fool!" (in Finnish). Osmo pulled at my sleeve and shook his head in warning. But I felt indignant and hurt, and I went into a tantrum. In the principal's office, I got my hair pulled and a Finnish boy from an upper grade was brought in to tell me writing compositions in Finnish was prohibited. I asked him why and he whispered in my ear in his Savoian dialect that he didn't know.

That night I threw a stone through the window of the principal's office. I never again wrote in Finnish. I just sat idly at my desk, silent and bewildered. What the dickens was this all about? Where have I ended up? Has everybody gone crazy? If grandma hears that I've stopped writing Finnish, she'll die.

By the time I was promoted to the junior grade, I had picked up quite a lot of Stockholm slang. The language of my textbooks and teachers, on the other hand, was middle-class Swedish, to me quite incomprehensible and hard even for my classmates to understand, for most of them belonged to the working class and were accustomed to a totally different way of speaking. Their parents, just like my own, knew a lot, but the bourgeois school system despised that kind of knowledge. As time passed, I fell more and more behind my class; school seemed totally meaningless. Somehow I felt as though I didn't exist and the teacher's eyes would always look over my head. I started to daydream and to play hooky. My homesickness was fierce and seared my mind. I went frequently down to the Finnish terminal for Finnish boats, I wept secretly, recollected faces and voices, and in my imagination I was back home. In my sleep, too, I dreamed of familiar faces and voices, of tall pines with trunks a rusty red and the shimmering waters of great Lake Saimaa; and every morning without fail I felt compelled to curse reality and to confront it in a rage or with sobs.

When the idea had eaten itself deeply enough into my soul that it was despicable to be a Finn, I began to feel ashamed of my origins. Since going back was out of the question – and this thought was what had sustained me – there was nothing for me but to surrender. To survive, I had to change my stripes. Thus: to hell with Finland and the Finns! All of a sudden, I was overwhelmed by a desire to shed my skin and smash my face. What could not be accepted had to be denied, hidden, crushed and thrown away. A Swede was what I had to become, and that meant I could not continue to be a Finn. Everything I had held dear and self-evident had to be destroyed. An inner struggle began, a state of crisis of long duration. I had trouble sleeping, I could not look people in the eye, my voice broke down into a whisper, I could no longer trust anybody. My mother tongue was worthless – this I realized at last – on the contrary, it made me the butt of abuse and ridicule. So down with the Finnish language! I spat on myself, gradually committed internal suicide. I rambled by myself through the woods of Årsta and talked to myself aloud in Swedish. I practised pronouncing words to make them sound exactly like the ones that come out of the mouths of Swedes. I resolved to learn Swedish word perfect so nobody could guess who I was or where I came from. They still laughed at my Finnish accent – but after a while, never again!

My tongue was still limber and flexible. At the age of thirteen, I was just about ready. As long as I was a wee bit careful, nobody could tell I was a Finn, neither by my speech nor by my ways. The only thing that betrayed me was my name. But, for some reason, I did not dare to change my name. I kept it.

I spoke Finnish only when it was absolutely unavoidable. 'Why are you always so quiet?' my parents would ask me at mealtime. 'Why don't you talk to us any more?' For an answer they would get an evasive glance. I was incapable of anything else; my tongue had run dry, its power of speech depleted.

When word came from Finland that grandmother was dead, I merely shrugged my shoulders in indifference and went over to see Åke. He was one of my bitterly won-over buddies. I did not want to remember, I would not allow myself to think of grandma, who had existed once upon a time, long ago, when I used to live in another world. But that night I dreamed about grandma: she was out on the pier washing clothes and she called out my name. In the morning I woke up feeling treacherous and filled with longing. I did not go to school but lay in bed all day, staring at the ceiling and remembering, as if in secrecy, what I did not otherwise dare to remember. Then the act continued, that of self-denial, of pretending ever more completely. In short, in order to live in harmony with my surroundings, I had to live in perpetual conflict with myself.

I never told anybody about the old times in Finland, not even by a slip of the tongue. I had cut off part of my life, and this caused me inexplicable distress, which later developed into a sense of alienation. My distress then turned into a longing for sincerity and spontaneity.

In the upper grades, one had to apply oneself to one's studies in earnest and compete for the best marks. Others were way ahead of me in knowledge, so I had to study as hard as I possibly could. But it was no use, no matter how hard I tried – the meaning of words eluded me; I had to read lines over and over again and still I could not understand. My examinations turned out badly; I always got the worst marks. This, again, put me in low spirits and made me think I was stupid. Paradoxically, however, deep down inside me I had a feeling I had a head for books. But words mocked me, refused to open up for me; they gave off no odour and seemed to be totally barren; I recognized words but failed to grasp their sense. The depth and diversity of language were lost; this matched the loss of my mother tongue, my Finnish.

Continuous failure at school forced me to search for something else. Those sliding downhill could always find pot down around the subway stations, or they might seek diversion in pilfering or acts of mischief. For my part, I was attracted to sports. At least, on the athletic field, I had a chance to engage in honest competition; the stop watch ticked away at the same rate for everybody, all you had to do was to run like hell and stay in your own lane. . . . It helped a bit to salve my wounds and restore my self-respect. . . . What it did not give me was a healthy soul, and a healthy soul was my deepest desire, for my mind was in a chaotic state, on the verge of a breakdown. I was troubled by a growing sense of emptiness and alienation. I was conscious of never – hardly ever – using the words 'our country' or 'us Swedes'. It never crossed my mind to speak of 'us Finns' or, with reference to Finland, 'my country'. I was without a people, without ties. Perhaps this is what made me feel empty. Or maybe the reason could be found in the dismal face flitting in the mirror of my soul.

I was sixteen years old when one June day I stood in the sun-drenched schoolyard and looked at my graduation diploma. My ears burned red with shame. Then I let out a hysterical laugh and headed for home. In front of the stairs little Timo was sitting and playing marbles. He had come from Joensuu, Finland, three weeks before, but could already say 'låt pli' (don't touch, my remark). I folded up my diploma to make a paper swallow and lured Timo to accompany me up to the attic. There I lifted him up to the window and I let him fling my swallow into the air. Timo shrieked in delight as the paper swallow spun down toward the ground. As for myself, I was no longer capable of yelling in Finnish – even though, down in my heart, I might have had the desire to do it."
(Jalava, 1980, translated by Paul Sjöblom.)

And so I could go on with quotation after quotation . . .

Another kind of violence not yet discussed is the kind directed especially against children below school age, but also against older children when they are placed in situations where their opportunities for communication are restricted or altogether removed. I am referring here to the practice of placing young children in day nurseries, pre-school classes and schools where they do not understand the language. An adult placed in a situation like this can, in spite of her frustration, understand why it has happened, and perhaps see some end to it; she has more of a chance, too, of making herself understood in non-linguistic ways and she will herself be able to see to it that her most basic needs are satisfied. A young child has much less chance of doing these things (see Nauclér, 1983). To place a young child in institutional care with adults who do not understand her language must be regarded as an act of psychological violence, torture of a kind which is so cruel that it should not be allowed to happen in countries that want to call themselves civilized. The fact that we have laws against the physical ill-treatment of children but not against such psychological ill-treatment tells us something significant about our cultural priorities and blindnesses which bodes no good for us. If someone beats or stabs a child we can go to the police, but where are we to turn for help when a child is being psychologically abused, and when the tormenters themselves have no idea that that is what they are doing? And the scars left by psychological ill-treatment remain longer, I am sure, than those left by physical ill-treatment. I have heard from many psychologists, doctors and psychiatrists of cases of hitherto unknown kinds of serious psychotic illness, forms of mutism and autism, among young immigrant children, psychiatric states they had not met before and which had occurred when children had been placed in foreign-language day nurseries.

Let me end with two more quotations, the first from a Turkish organization in West Germany:

"The neglect of a child's mother tongue at school is a form of national discrimination. The Turkish child must know German in order to make herself understood, at least to some extent, at school; but no German need learn any Turkish. It does not even seem to occur to the teachers that they should learn to pronounce correctly the names of the Turkish children they teach for years on end, even while they are scolding them for their inadequate grasp of German. The Turkish child will, of course, know Turkish (more or less), but knowing Turkish is 'worth nothing', and the child gets no credit for it, no acknowledgement. Teachers think of Turkish children as stupid because they cannot understand complex relationships – there is no one to explain the complexity to them in Turkish. This kind of quite evident, everyday discrimination affects in the first place the Turkish child herself. But the discrimination is also against all those with whom the child continues to communicate in Turkish, especially her parents, whose chance of learning much German is worse than hers. This amounts to discrimination against their country and its people." (FIDEF, 1978: 18).

A second quotation concerns the Navajo Indians of North America:
"Navajo children are taught in a foreign language; they are taught
concepts which are foreign; they are taught values which are foreign;
they are taught lifestyles which are foreign; and they are taught by
human models which are foreign. The intention behind this kind of
schooling is to mould the Navajo child (through speech, action,
thought) to be like members of the predominant Anglo-Saxon
mainstream culture. The apparent assumption seemingly being that
people of other ethnic groups cannot be human unless they can speak
English, and behave according to the values of a capitalist society based
on competition and achievement. The children grow up in these schools
with a sense of: (1) Confusion regarding the values, attitudes, and
behaviour taught at school and the values, attitudes and behaviour
taught at home. (2) Loss of self-identity and pride concerning their
selfhood – their Navajo-ness. (3) Failure in classroom learning activities. (4)
Loss of their own Navajo language development and loss of in-depth
knowledge of their own Navajo culture" (Pfeiffer, 1975: 133).

12.4   Violence as the result

In earlier chapters a good deal has been said about how minority
children perform at school, in linguistic and other tests, and so on. However,
as Christina Bratt Paulston has said in a number of articles, it makes better
sense to evaluate the educational results in terms of parameters which
measure results of social injustice: rates for suicide, crime, alcoholism,
psychiatric difficulty, and unemployment. We know that immigrants,
especially immigrant youths, score high in all these categories. Young
immigrants are over-represented in almost every category that can be used
to measure educational, psychological, economic and social failure.

What is the future going to look like then for that third of Europe's
young people who by the year 2000 will be from immigrant backgrounds? If
this segment of the population has many illiterates, absolute or functional,
many who have not completed their basic education, few with any kind of
occupational training, and very few with higher education? If the
unemployment situation is very bad, even worse than for today's immigrants
(at present, of course, there are many older immigrants who are
considerably better educated than the average native citizen of the host
countries, even if they rarely have the opportunity of using their education)?
If many are struggling with identity problems of various kinds? If most of
them have no chance of finding out what the reasons are for the situation
they find themselves in and of analyzing it? But they are perhaps not willing
to take on the rôle of pariah their parents played? Most of them will make
comparisons with their contemporaries in the majority population –

realizing that they are worse off but not knowing why. And what if even those groups who might perhaps have had some chance of analyzing their situation adequately are now being prevented from developing solidarity, and from having any democratic voice? Let me describe some possible results.

Many individuals who have remained uninfluenced by the school system, either because they have not been to school at all or because they have not understood much of the teaching conducted in a language foreign to them, will no longer belong to the group that has, with the help of the school, internalized the values of those in power. They will not even have *learned* the dominant ideology, let alone have had it impressed upon them by the detailed rehearsal of it at school, as will have happened with most majority children. They will not be socialized into the culture of guilt: a conscience is shaped and sharpened mainly through official institutions which have more and more taken over the ideological formation of children. Many of them will find themselves, too, outside the shame culture, even though the school has done its best to make them feel shame. There will, then, be young immigrants who cannot be controlled with the help of symbolic force, in the shape of guilt and shame.

If, with the school or their own organizations helping them, they had had the opportunity of analyzing their situation, of seeing in whose interest it is that they should be kept on the lowest rung of the social ladder, and of developing a sense of solidarity with each other and with other oppressed groups, they might have had the chance of conducting some organized and constructive struggle to change their situation. Then, through their own organizations, allied with the indigenous working class and its organizations, they might have been able to channel and focus their discontent and frustration and their demand for their just rights. But now even this possibility will have been ruled out to a great extent, partly because of the symbolic violence in schools. They will have no constructive alternative left, as I see it. And when the network of protective mechanisms provided by society, like social welfare, fails any longer to look after them, then other methods of control will become necessary.

And when minority organizations register the fact that little progress can be made even by organized struggle; when they are confronted with the structural violence of our societies; when they for instance realize the rôle of the judiciary in maintaining social control (see both Mathiesen's book on the hidden discipline and Ofstad's introduction, 1980); then we shall reach the final stage: the resort back to physical violence. Minorities who cannot any longer be controlled by simply symbolic force, must be kept under control with the help of physical force. The physical force is used by the official agents of the state's machinery of enforcement, that is the police and the army. This is what we have seen already in for instance Britain and the U.S. But it has started to happen also in Scandinavia – we can think of various minority movements, of the Same hunger strike against the Alta project, as well as of various alternative movements, environmentalist and feminist. We could remember the army in a state of preparedness at Alta and in a number of other places; the incident at Koijärvi; the scene at Byggeren, the children's adventure playground in a part of Copenhagen called Nørrebro, with the most brutal exercise of force on the part of the police in post-war Denmark. We could call to mind the police brutality towards women at the alternative women's conference in Copenhagen, and so on. But aside from these examples of the official use of force, there are in Scandinavia, too, unofficial racist and fascist groups who operate along the same lines, with the indirect approval and even sometimes partial protection of the official machinery of violence.

Instead of the minorities answering with physical violence, too, non-violence following Gandhi's ideology might be used – and has been used by many peace groups, Green groups and women's groups – just think of Greenham Common. But is that a probable alternative for the immigrant and guest worker youth in Europe?

A prerequisite for using methods of non-violence is a careful analysis and a conscience – something many young people from the minorities may not have, partly because of school. Minorities can only answer the violence they are victims of with struggle. This struggle *can* be organized, constructive, democratic. This is not to imply, of course, that these three adjectives are in any way synonymous or that this would be the only kind of struggle I see as necessary, even in Europe. But it is more likely that it will be unorganized, destructive and non-democratic. Violence and aggression without a basis of conscious, reasoned analysis, are the means to no end. Planless, meaningless physical violence where nobody benefits.

If nothing very drastic happens, I see no chance of avoiding a new explosion of physical violence in Europe before the year 2000. We have come full circle in the process of development, back to physical violence – the difference now is that there is no longer a path leading back. If we are not blown to bits first by all the male war idiots in high positions – there are three tons of explosive stored ready on earth for each one of us. Just think if that three tons were bread and roses – and books. . . .

There are alternative views, too. I'll say a few words about a couple of them. This is one of my own (1982c) and I see it as very probable, too. According to Julius Nyerere (1981), president of Tanzania, the industrial countries have 30% of the world's population, but control 80% of the trade and investments, 93% of the industry and almost 100% of the research in the world. More than 1,200 million people live in poverty, 700 million of them in acute poverty (Widgren, 1980). Roughly 450 million suffer from severe malnutrition. More than half of the natural sciences research goes to destructive purposes, like arms production. We have social cutbacks and increases in the military budgets. More Falklands and Lebanons but less milk for schoolchildren and less food for old age pensioners.

In 1950 the world's population was 2.5 billion, 1960, 3.0, 1970 3.6,

1978 4.2, 1979 4.3 and now 4.6 billion (Hufvudstadsbladet.4.7. 82). In 1975
less than half of the world's urban population lived in third world countries,
according to U.N. estimations. In the year 2000 approximately two-thirds of
the urban population is going to live in third world countries – these
countries are going to account for 95% of the world's increase in population
between 1975–2000 (Widgren, 1980: 22–23). Just to take one example:
Nigeria is probably going to have a larger population than the whole of
America. There might be a slight chance for that urban population to
support themselves *there* in 2000 (even if we know that more than 1,000
million *new* job opportunities need to be created before that, according to
ILO 1976) if we rich countries *now* gave back even a tiny part of the capital
we have robbed them of during centuries – and if we gave them a fair chance
after that. But we are not doing this – quite the opposite: we are continuing
to rob them, in several different ways, some of them quite new (see e.g. the
Brandt Report, 1980). That means that most of the people in the urban
slums in the third world in the year 2000 will not be able to survive there.
What are they going to do?

Are they going to starve to death nice and quietly, without disturbing us
too much? After they have exhausted local ways of surviving and tried to
find work in the neighbouring countries, the only chance for survival will be
to emigrate. The U.N. estimates in its latest population prognosis for Europe
that there is going to be a very sharp rise in and pressure for immigration to
Europe from countries outside Europe – it can already be seen in the
statistics. But our borders are already now almost closed to them, and we are
even trying to expel some of those who are already here. But if they cannot
come legally, they are going to come illegally, in larger and larger numbers.
That has already started too, on a much larger scale than most of the publicly
available figures suggest. Are we going to prevent that? With what? With the
help of words, which they don't understand because we don't speak their
languages (and have forced those who did, to forget them)? Or with the help
of arms?

Is it the case that some of "our" arms production is already geared
towards preventing an invasion from the third world? Are both superpowers
partly preparing for that too, while trying to make us believe that their
enemies are somewhere else? How much are we going to let ourselves be
fooled?

In several chapters of this book I have also tried to show "that becoming
bi-something also makes us understand more from inside. The group ruling
us now is *the* group in the world with the least potential to understand other
people from inside. Those who are bi-something are the ones without
power: minorities, women, blacks, working class, those who have been
forced to become bi-something in order to survive. The ones who rule us,
white middle-class males from the majority groups, have never been forced
to look at things from somebody else's perspective. If they are to have the
slightest chance to understand anything, they must have mediators, people

with whom they in some respects can identify because they share the same culture and language, but people who, in addition to that, also understand other cultures, languages and people. The group who could function as mediators are the migrants – if we gave them a chance. But now even the possibility of making people understand by using migrant youth as mediators is systematically destroyed, by preventing those with a potential for understanding from developing that potential." (Skutnabb-Kangas, 1982c).

A third view would be a more optimistic one which I hope I could share – the one held by many of those who see every day the way black youth is organizing, those who speak of the development from resistance to rebellion (see Sivanandan 1982 and literature mentioned in it). I read the interview with the priest in the Finnish congregation in Stockholm, Sweden (Paul Örnberg, Ruotsin Suomalainen 9, 1.3.1983, called "Is self destruction the only solution?") where he says that almost a fifth of the deaths in his congregation are self-inflicted. That is one answer – and the one my people also use. And I read Sivanandan's description which is like mine of Finnish youth but his is of black youth: "The youth know, viscerally, that there will be no work for them, ever, no call for their labour. . . . They are not the unemployed, but the never employed. They have not, like their parents, had jobs and lost them – and so become disciplined into a routine and a culture that preserves the *status quo*. They have not been organized into trade unions and had their politics disciplined by a labour aristocracy. They have not been on the marches of the dis-employed, so valiantly recalled by Labour from the hunger marches of the 1930s. Theirs is a different hunger – a hunger to retain freedom, the life-style, the dignity which they have carved out from the stone of their lives." (p. 49) . . . "He finds solidarity in his group, he has become his own person. But will he enter the pluralist society? Or will he move on, through his growing political consciousness, to a point where, along with his denigrated black British children, he challenges the very structure of this society? Or will he return home to create a revolutionary situation there – as some have already attempted to do in Trinidad? The answers are not clear, but the trend is unmistakable. And given that the 'contagion' of black consciousness grows much faster than white recompense, the auguries for a truly multiracial society in this country are bleak indeed" (p. 64). That seems an optimistic view, as I said. Its precondition is that minority children and young people have an instrument for analysis: a language. Or two.

Bibliography

ÅGREN, GÖSTA 1976, Språk och halvspråk. En duell på Hanaholmen, *Vasabladet* 3.10.1976

AHLFORS, BENGT 1971, *Sånger, dikter*. Söderström & Co Förlags AB, Borgå

AHLGREN, INGER (ed.), 1975, *Språket och skolan*. LiberLäromedel, Lund

The AIR Evaluation of the impact of ESEA Title VII Spanish–English Bilingual Education Programs 1977. The U.S. Office of Education, Office of Planning, Budgeting and Evaluation, Washington, D.C.

ALATIS, JAMES E. (ed.), 1970, *Bilingualism and Language Contact. Anthropological, Linguistic, Psychological and Sociological Aspects*. Report of the 21st Annual Round Table Meeting on Linguistics and Language Studies, Monograph Series on Languages and Linguistics No 23. Washington, D.C.

– (ed.), 1978, *International Dimensions of Bilingual Education*, Georgetown University Round Table on Languages and Linguistics 1978. Georgetown University Press, Washington, D.C.

ALBERT, MARTIN L. & OBLER, LORAINE K. 1978, *The Bilingual Brain. Neuropsychological and Neurolinguistic Aspects of Bilingualism*. Academic Press, New York.

ALBO, XAVIER & QUIROGA, NESTOR HUGO 1975, La Radio como Expresión Libre del Aymara. In TROIKE & MODIANO (eds), 1975, 239–263

ALI, TARIQ 1980, Immigration and Class-struggle in Western Europe. *Immigranten* 2.

ALLARDT, ERIK 1979, Samhörighet och identitet bland finlandssvenskarna. In Finlandssvenska, report published by Svenska Finlands Folkting, Helsingfors, October 1979, *Finlandssvensk år 2000*, 44–48.

ALLARDT, ERIK, MIEMOIS, KARL JOHAN & STARCK, CHRISTIAN 1979, *Multiple and Varying Criteria for Membership in a Linguistic Minority. The Case of the Swedish Speaking Minority in Metropolitan Helsinki*. Research group for comparative sociology, University of Helsinki, Research reports No. 21.

ALLWOOD, JENS 1979, Ickeverbal kommunikation eller konsten att överföra information utan ord. *Invandrare och Minoriteter* 3, 1979, 16–24.

ALTENA, NELLEKE & APPEL, RENÉ 1983, Mother Tongue Teaching and the Acquisition of Dutch by Turkish and Moroccan Immigrant Workers' Children, *Journal of Multilingual and Multicultural Development*, 3:4, 315–322.

ANASTASI, A. & CORDOVA, F. 1953, Some Effects of Bilingualism upon Intelligence Test Performance of Puerto Rican Children in New York City. *Journal of Educational Psychology*, 44, 1–19.

ANDERSON, ALAN B. 1978, *Language Minorities and International Frontiers: the Contemporary Situation. 1 Western Europe*. Paper presented at the 9th World Congress of Sociology, Uppsala, 1978.

ANDERSSON, MARIANNE 1980, Militarismen och kvinnorna. *Fredsposten* 1, 1980 22–24.

ANDERSSON, THEODORE & BOYER, MILDRED 1978, (1970), *Bilingual Schooling in the United States*. National Educational Laboratory Publishers, Inc, Austin, Texas, 2nd ed.

ANDERSSON, THEODORE 1969, *Foreign Languages in the Elementary School: A Struggle Against Mediocrity*. The University of Texas Press, Austin, Texas.

– 1977, Philosophical Perspectives on Bilingual Education. In SPOLSKY & COOPER (eds), 1977, 192–225.

– 1979, *A Guide to Family Reading in Two Languages*. The University of Texas at Austin. Draft.

ANDRESEN, HELGA 1978, *Sex and Language Acquisition: Suggestions of a Categorial Framework for Investigating Sex Specific Differences*. Paper presented at the 9th World Congress of Sociology, Uppsala 1978.

ANGULA, A. N. 1982, SWAPO of Namibia Department of Education and Culture Programme inviting projects.

ANISFELD, ELIZABETH PEAL 1964, *A Comparison of the Cognitive Functioning of Monolinguals and Bilinguals*. Ph.D. Thesis, McGill University.

ANISFELD, ELISABETH & LAMBERT, W. E. 1964, Evaluational Reactions of Bilingual and Monolingual Children to Spoken Languages. *Journal of Abnormal and Social Psychology*, 69, 89–97.

ANISFELD, M. & LAMBERT, W. E. 1961, Social and Psychological Variables in Learning Hebrew. *Journal of Abnormal and Social Psychology*, 63, 524–529.

APPEL, RENÉ 1979, *The Acquisition of Dutch by Turkish and Moroccan children in Two Different School Models*. State University of Utrecht, Holland, manuscript.

– 1980, *Linguistic Problems of Minority Groups in Holland*. Paper presented at the symposium on Linguistic Problems of Minority Groups, Katholieke Hogeschool Tilburg, The Netherlands, 1980.

APPLE, M. W. 1978, Ideology, reproduction and educational reforms. *Comparative Education Review*, 22:3, 367–387.

APPLE, MICHAEL 1979, *Ideology and curriculum*, Routledge and Kegan Paul, Boston.

ARBETET, Gothenburg.

ARGYLE, M. 1975, *Bodily Communication*. Methuen, London.

ARONSSON, KARIN 1977, Tvåspråkighet och kommunikativ kompetens i tidig skolmiljö. In SKUTNABB-KANGAS (ed.) 1977a, 202–211.

– 1978a, Att tala eller inte tala. En deskriptiv analys av tvåspråkiga barns kommunikativa strategier i tidig skolmiljö. In HJELMQUIST (ed.) 1978.

– 1978b, *Language Concepts and Children's Classification Strategies*. Lund University, Dept of Psychology, Dissertation Series.

ARSENIAN, SETH 1937, *Bilingualism and Mental Development. A Study of the Intelligence and the Social Background of Bilingual Children in New York City*. Teachers College, Columbia University.

ARTHUR, G. 1937, The Predictive Value of the Kuhlman-Binet Scale for a Partially Americanized School Population. *Journal of Applied Psychology*, 21, 359–364.

ARWIDSSON, SIRPA 1977, Uppföljning av finska invandrarbarns språkliga och

sociala situationi årskurserna 1–2 på Vallbyskolan, Västerås, 1974–1976. In SKUTNABB-KANGAS, 1977a, 68–83.
AUKIA, PEKKA (ed.) 1972, *Nuorisoaste valinkauhassa*. Kustannusosakeyhtiö Otava, Helsinki.

BACKER, BERIT, BUTTINGSRUD, LIV, HEIBERG, TURID, KRAN, TURID & MATHIESEN, VIGDIS 1981, *Migration research in Norway*. A catalogue of projects and publications. Revised edition 1981, International Peace Research Institute, Oslo.
BAETENS BEARDSMORE, H. 1982, *Bilingualism: Basic Principles*, Multilingual Matters, Clevedon.
BAIN, BRUCE 1975a, Toward an Integration of Piaget and Vygotsky: Bilingual Considerations. *Linguistics*, 160, 5–20.
– 1975b. Commentary: A Canadian Education: Thoughts on Bilingual Education. *Journal of Canadian Studies* 10, 1975, 57–62.
– 1976a, Verbal Regulation of Cognitive Processes: A Replication of Luria's Procedures with Bilingual and Unilingual Infants. *Child Development* 47, 1976, 543–546.
– 1976b, *The Consequence of Unilingualism, Disruptive Bilingualism and Creative Bilingualism for the Development of the Body Schema: A Cross Cultural Study in Canada, Italy and West Germany*. Paper presented at The 1st International Christian University Symposium on Pedolinguistics, Mitaka, Tokyo.
– (ed.) forthcoming, *Sociogenesis of Language and Human Conduct: A Multidisciplinary Book of Readings*. Plenum.
BAIN, BRUCE & YU, AGNES, 1978a, Toward an Integration of Piaget and Vygotsky: A Cross-cultural Replication (France, Germany, Canada) Concerning Cognitive Consequences of Biliguality. In PARADIS (ed.) 1978a, 113–126.
– 1978b, *Language, Cognition, Bilingualsim, the Body Schema: An Outline of a Theory of Perception, and a Cross Cultural Study Involving Immigrant and Indigenous Children in Canada, Italy, West Germany*. University of Alberta, Dept of Educational Psychology, manuscript.
BAKER, K. & DEKANTER, A. 1981, *Effectiveness of Bilingual Education: A Review of the Literature*, Final Draft, U.S. Department of Education, Washington, D.C.
BALKAN, L. 1970, *Les effects du bilingualisme français-anglais sur les aptitudes intellectuelles*. Aimav, Brussels.
BARIK, HENRI C. & SWAIN, MERRILL 1976a, Primary Grade French Immersion in a Unilingual English-Canadian Setting: The Toronto Study through Grade 2. *Canadian Journal of Education*, 39–58.
– 1976b, *A Longitudinal Study of Bilingual and Cognitive Development*. Paper presented at the Annual Conference on the Canadian Educational Researchers Association, Canadian Society for the Study of Education, Université Laval, Quebec, 1976, draft.
BARKE, E. M. 1933, A Study of the Comparative Intelligence of Children in Certain Bilingual and Monoglot Schools in South Wales. *British Journal of Educational Psychology*, 3, 1933, 237–250.
BARNEN OCH VI, Stockholm.
BARTH, FREDRIK 1971, Minoritetsproblem från socialantropologisk synpunkt. In Schwarz (ed.), 1971, 59–78.
BARTON, LEN (ed.), 1982, *Class and Race in Education*, Croom Helm, London.

BENEDIKTSSON, HREINN (ed.) 1970, *The Nordic Languages and Modern Linguistics*. Proceedings of the International Conference of Nordic and General Linguistics in Reykjavík, Vísindafelag Íslendinga. Reykjavík.

BENNEDSEN, DORTE 1980, Problemerne omkring de Fremmedsprogede børn, *Uddannelse*, 5 & 6, 337–343.

BENSE, ELISABETH 1973, *Mentalismus in der Sprachtheorie Noam Chomskys*. Skriptor Verlag, Kronberg/Ts.

BENTON, RICHARD A. 1978, Problems and Prospects for Indigenous Languages and Bilingual Education in New Zealand and Oceania. In SPOLSKY & COOPER (eds) 1978, 126–166.

BEN-ZEEV, SANDRA 1972, *The Influence of Bilingualism on Cognitive Development and Cognitive Strategy*. Ph.D Thesis, University of Chicago.

– 1975, *The effect of Spanish-English Bilingualism in Children from less Privileged Neighborhoods on Cognitive Development and Cognitive Strategy*. Report to National Intitute of Child Health and Human Development.

– 1977a, Mechanisms by which Childhood Bilingualism Affects Understanding of Language and Cognitive Structures. In HORNBY (ed.) 1977, 29–55.

– 1977b, The Influence of Bilingualism on Cognitive Development and Cognitive Strategy. *Child Development*, 48, 1009–1018.

– 1977c, The Effect of Spanish-English Bilingualism in Children from less Priviledged Neighbourhoods on Cognitive Development and Cognitive Strategy. *Working Papers on Bilingualism*, 14, 83–122.

BERGER, JOHN & MOHR, JEAN (with collaboration of Sven Blomberg) 1975, *A Seventh Man. A Book of Images and Words about the Experiences of Migrant Workers in Europe*. Penguin Books, Harmonsworth, Middlesex.

Bericht zur Lage der Ausländer in Berlin, 1978, Herausgeber: Der Regierende Bürgermeister von Berlin. Senatskanzlei, Planungsleitstelle, Berlin.

BERKO, JEAN 1958, The Child's Learning of English Morphology. Word, 14, 150–177.

BERLIN, B. & KAY, P. 1969, *Basic Colour Terms: Their Universality and Evolution*. University of California Press, Berkeley.

BERNSTEIN, BASIL 1960, Language and Social Class: Research Note. *British Journal of Sociology*, 11, 1960, 271–276.

– 1961, Social Class and Linguistic Development: A Theory of Social Learning. In A. H. HALSEY, J. FLOUD & A. ANDERSON (eds) 1961.

– 1972, Social Class, Language and Socialization. In GIGLIOLI (ed.) 1972, 157–178.

– 1973 (1971). *Class, Codes and Control*. Vol 1 *Theoretical Studies towards a Sociology of Language*. Paladin.

– 1977, *Class, Codes and Control*, Vol. 3 Towards a Theory of Educational Transmissions, Routledge and Kegan Paul, London.

BIERWISCH, MANFRED 1970, Semantics. In Lyons (ed.) 1970a, 166–184.

Bilingual Education: Current Perspectives (Center for Applied Linguistics, Arlington, Virginia).

1977, Vol. 1. *Social Science*.

1977, Vol. 2. *Linguistics*.

1977, Vol. 3. *Law*.

1977, Vol. 4. *Education*.

1978, Vol. 5. *Synthesis*.

Bilingual Syntax Measure I 1975, Harcourt Brace Jovanovich, New York.

BILLY, L. 1978, La langue seconde, une nouvelle approche qui met "l'immersion" en question. *Le devoir*, 24.8.1978.

BINSTEAD, H. 1931, Education in the Cook Islands. In JACKSON 1931, 357–392.

BIRDWHISTLE, RAY L. 1970, *Kinesics and Context*. University of Pennsylvania Press.

BJERREGAARD, RITT 1980, Fra stabsarbejde til græsrodsplan – en tale ved OECD:s konference i Paris om socialpolitik i 80'erne. *Information*, 13.11.1980.

BJÖRKLUND, KRISTER 1980, Förteckning över litteratur rörande finlandssvenska samhällsfrågor 1966–1979. *Språkgrupp och mobilitet*, Åbo Akademi, Forsknings-rapporter MOB No 4.

BLAKAR, ROLV MIKKEL 1973, *Språk er makt*. Pax Forlag, Oslo.

– 1975, How the Sex Roles are Represented, Reflected and Conserved in the Norwegian Language. *Acta Sociologica*, 18, 1975, 162–173.

– 1979, Språk som makt og kvinneundertrykking: Språksosiologi som motefag. In KLEIVEN (ed.) 1979, 209–270.

BLAKAR, ROLV MIKKEL & PEDERSEN, TOVE BEATE 1980a, *Sex-bound patterns of control in verbal communication*. Paper presented at the Conference "Language and Power", Bellagio, Italy, 1980.

– 1980b, Control and Self-confidence as Reflected in Sex-bound Patterns in Communication: An Experimental Approach. *Acta Sociologica*, 23:1, 1980, 33–53.

BLAUBURG, MAIJA S. 1978, *Sociolinguistic Change towards Non-sexist Language: An Overview and Analysis of Misunderstandings and Misapplications*. Paper presented at the 9th World Congress of Sociology, Uppsala, 1978.

BLOM, J.-P. & GUMPERZ, J. J. 1972, Social Meanings in Linguistic Structures: Code Switching in Norway. In GUMPERZ & HYMES (ed.) 1972.

BLOOM, BENJAMIN S. 1964. *Stability and Change in Human Characteristics*. Wiley.

BLOOM, BENJAMIN S., HASTINGS, J. THOMAS & MADAUS, GEORGE F. 1971, *Handbook on Formative and Summative Evaluation of Student Learning*. McGraw-Hill Book Company.

BLOOMFIELD, LEONARD 1927. Literate and Illiterate Speech. *American Speech*. 2, 1927, 423–439 (reprinted in HYMES 1964).

– 1933, *Language*. Holt, Reinhard & Winston, New York.

BØ, BENTE PUNTERVOLD 1980, *Fremmedarbeidernes boligsituasjon i Oslo*. Oslo.

BOAS, FRANZ 1911a, Introduction. *Handbook of American Indian Languages*, Part I. Bureau of American Ethnology, Bulletin, 40, 1–83.

– 1911b, *The Mind of Primitive Man*. New York.

BOLINGER, DWIGHT 1975. *Aspects of Language*. Harcourt, Brace and Jovanovich, New York.

BÖÖK-CEDERSTRÖM, LENA, ERIKSSON, KRISTINA, FREDRIKSSON, KERSTIN, 1977, *Invandrare i Sverige* 1965–1974. En bibliografi. Immigrant-Institutet, Borås.

BOOS-NÜNNING, URSULA 1981, Muttersprachliche Klassen für ausländische Kinder: Eine kritische Diskussion des bayerischen "Offenen Modells", *Deutsch lernen*, 2, 1981, 40–70.

BOURDIEU, P. & PASSERON, J. C. 1970, *La Reproduction: éléments pour une théorie du système d'enseignement*, Les Éditions de Minuit, Paris.

BOURNE, JENNY & SIVANANDAN, A. 1980, Cheerleaders and ombudsmen: the sociology of race relations in Britain, *Race and Class*, XXI:4, 1980, 331–352.

BOWLES, SAMUEL & GINTIS, HERBERT 1976, *Schooling in Capitalist America: Educational Reform and the Contradictions of Economic Life*, Routledge and Kegan Paul, London.

BOZARSLAN, MEHMET EMÎN 1980, *Alfabe*, Invandrarförlaget, Borås (1st ed. Istanbul 1968).

Brandt Report 1980, North-South: A Programme for Survival, The Report of the Independent Commission on International Development Issues Under the Chairmanship of Willy Brandt, Pan Books, London.

BRATTEMO, CARL-ERIK & WANDE, ERLING 1980, *Metaforupplevelse hos enspråkiga och tvåspråkiga*. In EJERHED & HENRYSSON (eds) 1981, 114–128.

BRAUN, MAXIMILLIAN 1937, Beobachtungen zur Frage der Mehrsprachigkeit. *Göttingische Gelehrte Anzeigen*, 109, 115–130 (quoted in HAUGEN, Einar, 1968. *Bilingualism. Definitions and Problems*, Harvard University, manuscript).

BRENT-PALMER, CORA 1979, A Sociolinguistic Assessment of the Notion "Immigrant Semilingualism" from a Social Conflict Perspective. *Working Papers on Bilingualism*, 17, 135–180.

BREUER, HELMUT 1975, Theoretische und praktische Aspekte einer Früherfassung und -behandlung verbosensomotorischer Voraussetzungen. In *Zur Frühdiagnose sensomotorischer Voraussetzungen für den Erwerb der Schriftsprache*. Ernst-Moritz-Arndt-Universität, Greifswald.

BREUER, HELMUT & WEUFFEN, MARIA 1975, *Gut vorbereitet auf das Lesen- und Schreibenlernen?* VEB Deutscher Verlag der Wissenschaften, Berlin.

BROMLEY, YU V. & KOZLOV, V. I. 1981, Present-day Ethnic Processes in the Intellectual Culture of the Peoples of the USSR. In GRIGULEVICH & KOZLOV (eds) 1981, 19–38.

BROO, MIKAEL 1980, *Assimilation. Stölden. Solidaritet*. Invandrarrapport, 2, 1980, 5.

BROO, ROGER 1974, Tvåspråkighet och språkgruppsidentitet. In PLATZACK (ed.) 1974, 48–61.

– 1978, Finlandssvenskarna – ett helt vanligt folk. In LAURÉN (ed.) 1978, 7–24.

BROWN, G. L. 1922, Intelligence as Related to Nationality. *Journal of Educational Research*, 5, 1922, 324–327.

BROWN, ROGER 1973, *A First Language. The Early Stages*. George Allen & Unwin Ltd, London.

BROWN, ROGER & GILMAN, ALBERT 1970, The Pronouns of Power and Solidarity. In FISHMAN 1970a, 252–275.

BRUCK, M., RABINOVICH, M. S. & OATES, M. 1973, *The Effects of French Immersion Programs on Children with Language Disabilities – A Preliminary Report*. McGill – Montreal Children's Hospital Learning Center and McGill Psychology Department, November 1973. Duplicated copy.

BRUCK, M., TUCKER, G. R. & JAKIMIK, J. 1977, *Are French Programs Suitable for Working Class Children?* Manuscript.

BRUK, S. I. & GUBOGLO, G. M. N. 1981, The Converging of Nations in the USSR and the Main Trends in the Development of Bilingualism. In GRIGULEVICH & KOZLOV (eds) 1981, 51–89.

BRUNER, JEROME S. 1975, Language as an Instrument of Thought. In DAVIES (ed.) 1975.

BULL, W. E. 1955, Review of Unesco 1953. *International Journal of American Linguistics*, 21, 1955, 288–294.

BURLING, ROBBINS 1959, Language Development of a Garo and English Speaking Child. *Word*, 15, 45–68.

– 1981, Black English, blandspråk and halvspråkighet. In EJERHED & HENRYSSON (eds) 1981, 39–48.

BURT, C. 1958, The Inheritance of Ability. *American Psychologist*, 13 (quoted in BURT 1973b).
– 1973a, The Structure of the Mind. In WISEMAN 1973a, 115–140.
– 1973b, The Evidence for the Concept of Intelligence. In WISEMAN 1973a, 182–204.
BURT, MARINA K., DULAY, HEIDI C. & EDUARDO, HERNÁNDEZ, CHÁVEZ 1975, *Bilingual Syntax Measure* (BSM), New York, The Psychological Corporation.
CAHN, EDGAR S. & HEARNE, DAVID W. (eds) 1970, *Our Brother's Keeper: The Indian in White America*, New Community Press, New York.
CANALE, M., MOUGEON, R. & BENIAK, E. 1978, Acquisition of Some Grammatical Elements in English and French by Monolingual and Bilingual Canadian Students. *Canadian Modern Language Review*, 34:3, 1978, 505–524.
CANALE, M. & SWAIN, MERRILL 1979, *Theoretical Bases of Communicative Approaches to Second Language Teaching and Testing, French as a Second Language*. Ontario Assessment Instrument Pool Project, Preliminary draft.
CÁRDENAS, JOSÉ A. 1977, *The AIR Evaluation of the Impact of ESEA Title VII Spanish/English Bilingual Education Programs: An IDRA Response*. Intercultural Development Research Association, Texas.
CAREY, S. T. (ed.) 1974, *Bilingualism, biculturalism and education*. University of Alberta, Edmonton.
– (ed.) 1978, *Canadian Modern Language Review*, Special Issue.
CAREY, S. T. & CUMMINS, JAMES 1978, *English and French Achievement of Grade 5 Children from English, French and Mixed French-English Home Backgrounds Attending the Edmonton Separate School System English-French Immersion Program*. Report submitted to the Edmonton Separate School System, November 1978.
CARLSSON, EVA & VALÍK, JANNA 1979, *Relationen mellan självvärdering och etnisk värdering hos svenska grundskoleelever – en undersökning i årskurserna 5, 7 och 9 i två rektorsområden i Göteborg*. Invandrarprojektet, Göteborgs skolförvaltning.
CARRINGER, D. C. 1974, Creative Thinking Abilities of Mexican Youth: The Relationship of Bilingualism. *Journal of Cross-Cultural Psychology* 5, 492–504.
CARROW, E. 1971, Comprehension of English and Spanish by Preschool Mexican-American Children, *Modern Language Journal* 55, 299–307.
CASTLES, STEPHEN 1980, The Social Time-Bomb: Education of an Underclass in West Germany. *Race and Class* XXI, 4, 369–387.
CASTLES, STEPHEN & KOSACK, GODULA 1973, *Immigrant Workers and Class Structure in Western Europe*. London, Oxford University Press.
CATANI, MAURIZIO 1982, Changing one's country means changing one's flag. In *Living in two cultures* 1982, 163–239.
CAZDEN, COURTNEY B. 1971, Evaluation of Learning in Preschool Education: Early Language Development. In BLOOM, HASTINGS & MADAUS (eds) 1971, 347–398.
– 1972, The Situation: A Neglected Source of Social Class Differences in Language Use. In PRIDE & HOLMES (eds) 1972, 294–313.
CELCÉ-MURCIA, M. 1975, *Simultaneous Acquisition of English and French in a Two-year-old Child*. Paper presented at TESOL-conference, Los Angeles, 1975.
CERVANTES, ROBERT A. 1979, *An exemplary consafic chingatropic assessment*. The SIR report, Bilingual Education Paper Series, National Dissemination and Assessment Center, California State University, Los Angeles.
CHALIAND, GERARD (ed.) 1980, *People Without a Country. The Kurds and*

Kurdistan. A. R. Ghassemlou, Kendal, M. Nazdar, A. Roosevelt and I. S. Vanly. Zed Press, London.

CHAMPAGNOL, R. 1973, Organisation sémantique et linguistique dans le rappel libre bilingue. *Année Psychologique*, 73, 115–134.

CHILD, I. L. 1943. *Italian or American? The Second Generation in Conflict*. Yale University Press, New Haven.

CHOMSKY, NOAM 1965, *Aspects of the Theory of Syntax*. The M.I.T. Press, Cambridge, Mass.

– 1966 (1957), *Syntactic Structures*. Janua Linguarum, Series Minor nr IV. Mouton & Co, The Hague. 6th printing.

– 1968. *Language and Mind*. Harcourt, Brace & World, New York.

– 1975, *Reflections on Language*. Pantheon Books, Random House, New York.

CHRISTIAN, CHESTER C. Jr. 1977, Minority Language Skills Before Age Three. In MACKEY & ANDERSSON (eds) 1977, 94–108.

CICOUREL, AARON 1982, Living in two cultures: the everyday world of migrant workers. In *Living in two cultures,* 17–65.

Civil Rights Commission Reports on Discrimination 1974, The Linguistic Reporter. A Newsletter in Applied Linguistics, June.

CLARK, H. & CLARK, E. 1977, *Psychology and Language. An Introduction to Psycholinguistics*. Harcourt Brace Jovanovich, New York.

CLASON, ELIN & MAHMUT BAKSI 1979, *Kurdistan. Om förtryck och befrielsekamp*. Arbetarkultur, Stockholm.

CLYNE, MICHAEL 1967, *Transference and Triggering*. Nijhoff.

– 1971, German-English Bilingualism and Linguistic Theory. Dichtung, Sprache und Gesellschaft.

– 1972, *Perspectives on Language Contact, Based on a Study of German in Australia*. The Hawthorn Press, Melbourne.

– (ed.), 1976, *Australia talks. Essays on the Sociology of Australian Immigrant and Aboriginal Languages*. Pacific Linguistics. Series D. No 23.

– 1978, Some Remarks on Foreigner Talk. In DITTMAR, HABERLAND, SKUTNABB-KANGAS & TELEMAN (eds) 1978, 155–170.

COARD, B. 1971, *How the West Indian Child is Made ESN by the British School Systems*. New Beacon Books.

COHEN, ANDREW D. 1974, The Culver City Spanish Immersion Program: The First Two Years. *Modern Language Journal* 58, 95–103.

– 1975, *A Sociolinguistic Approach to Bilingual Education. Experiments in the American Southwest*. Newbury House Publishers, Rowley, Mass.

– 1976, The Case for Partial or Total Immersion Education. In SIMOÉS, A. (ed.) 1976. *The Bilingual Child. Research and Analysis of Existing Educational Themes*. Academic Press, New York, 65–89.

– 1981, Introspecting about second language learning, Paper presented at the Sixth International Congress of Applied Linguistics, Lund, August 9–15, 1981.

COHEN, ANDREW & LAOSA, LUIS M. 1976, Second Language Instruction: Some Research Considerations. *Curriculum Studies* 1976, Vol. 8, No 2, 149–165.

COHEN, ANDREW D., FATHMAN, A. & MERINO, B. 1976, The Redwood City Bilingual Education Project 1971–74: Spanish and English Proficiency, Mathematics and Language Use over Time. *Working Papers on Bilingualism*, 8, 1–29.

– 1979. *Bilingual Education for a Bilingual Community: Some Insights Gained from*

Research. Paper presented at the Interactive Forum, Ethnoperspectives in Bilingual Education Research Project, Eastern Michigan University, 1979.

Committee for the Defence of the National Democratic Rights of the Kurdish People in Turkey (no date), Appeal, Box 1122, 7758 Meersburg, GFD.

CONDON, WILLIAM S. 1977, A Primary Phase in the Organization of Infant Responding Behavior. In SCHAFFER (ed.) 1977, 153–176.

CONDON, WILLIAM S. & SANDER, LOUIS W. 1974, Neonate Movement is Synchronized with Adult Speech: Interactional Participation and Language Acquisition. *Science* 183, 1974, 99–101

COOKE, BENJAMIN G. 1978, Nonverbal Communication among Afro-Americans: An Initial Classification. In LOURIE & CONKLIN (eds) 1978, 116–140.

CORNEJO, R. J. 1974, *A Synthesis of Theories and Research on the Effects of Teaching in First and Second Languages.* Austin, Texas, National Educational Laboratory Publishers.

DECOSTER, W. 1974, Handicapped or Different? Concepts, Problems and Remedies. *Council of Europe Information Bulletin*, 1/1974, 86–89, Documentation Centre for Education in Europe.

CRITCHLEY, M. 1974, Aphasia in Polyglots and Bilinguals. *Brain and Language*, 1. 1974, 15–28.

CUMMINS, JAMES (JIM) 1975, *Sensitivity to Non-Verbal Communication as a Factor in Language Learning.* Paper presented to the 4th International Conference of Applied Linguistics, Stuttgart, 1975.

– 1976a, The Influence of Bilingualism on Cognitive Growth: A Synthesis of Research Findings and Explanatory Hypotheses. *Working Papers on Bilingualism*, 9, 1976, 1–43.

– 1976b, *The Cognitive Development of Bilingual Children.* Centre for the Study of Mental Retardation, The University of Alberta, Manuscript.

– 1977a, Psycholinguistic Evidence. In *Bilingual Education: Current Perspectives.* Vol. 4. *Education*, 78–89.

– 1977b, Cognitive Factors Associated with the Attainment of Intermediate Levels of Bilingual Skills. *Modern Language Journal*, 61, 3–12.

– 1977c, *Metalinguistic Development of Children in Bilingual Education Programs: Data from Irish and Canadian (Ukrainian-English) Programs.* Paper presented to the 4th LACUS Forum, Montreal 1977.

– 1977d, *Educational Implications of Mother Tongue Maintenance in Minority Language Groups.* Paper presented at the Conference on 2nd Language Acquisition College Universitaire St. Jean, The University of Alberta, 1977.

– 1978a. *A Framework for Evaluating Bilingual Education Programs.* Paper presented at the Round Table Discussion "Bilingual Education", 5th International Congress of Applied Linguistics, Montreal 1978.

– 1978b, The Cognitive Development of Children in Immersion Programs. *Canadian Modern Language Review* 34, 1978, 855–883.

– 1978c, Bilingualism and the Development of Metalinguistic Awareness. *Journal of Cross-Cultural Psychology* 9, 131–149.

– 1978d, Educational Implications of Mother Tongue Maintenance in Minority Language Groups. In CAREY 1978.

– 1979a, Blaming the Victim in Minority Education. Paper presented at the Symposium on second generation Finnish immigrants, Hanaholmen, 1979.

– 1979b, *Interpretation of Research Findings on Language of Instruction for*

Immigrant Children: A Critique of Ekstrand, manuscript (forthcoming in CUMMINS & SKUTNABB-KANGAS (eds), Vol. 1).

– 1979c, Cognitive/Academic Language Proficiency, Linguistic Interdependence, The Optimal Age Question and Some Other Matters. *Working Papers on Bilingualism*, 19, 197–205.

– 1979d, *Linguistic Interdependence and the Educational Development of Bilingual Children.* Review of Educational Research, 49, 222–251.

– 1979e. Bilingualism and Educational Developments in Anglophone and Minority Francophone Groups in Canada. *Interchange* 1978–79, 9:4, 40–51.

– 1979f, *Research Findings from French Immersion Programs Across Canada: a Parents Guide.* OISE, Toronto, Manuscript.

– 1980a, Det första språket. Hur tolkas forskningsresultaten om undervisningsspråket för invandrarbarn? En kritik av Lars Henric Ekstrand. *Invandrare och Minoriteter* 1, 1980, 12–18.

– 1980b, The Entry and Exit Fallacy in Bilingual Education. *NABE Journal* IV, 3, 25–60.

– 1980c, Psychological Assessment of Minority Language Students, Logic or Intuition. *Journal of Multilingual and Multicultural Development*, 1:2, 97–111.

– 1980d, The Cross-lingual Dimensions of Language Proficiency: Implications for Bilingual Education and the Optimal Age Question, *TESOL Quarterly* 14.

– 1980e, The Language and Culture Issue in Immigrant Education, *Interchange* 10, 72–88.

– 1980f, *Age on Arrival and Immigrant Second Language Learning: A Reanalysis of the Ramsey and Wright data.* OISE, Toronto, manuscript.

– 1981a, The Role of Primary Language Development in Promoting Educational Success for Language Minority Students, in *Schooling and Language Minority Students* 1981, 3–49.

– 1981b, *Bilingualism and Minority Language Children, Language and Literacy Series*, OISE Press, The Ontario Institute for Studies in Education, Toronto.

– 1983, *Examination of the experiences of educators and researchers in various aspects of the Heritage Language Programs*, A Literature Review, manuscript, Ontario Institute for Studies in Education, January 1983.

CUMMINS, JAMES (JIM) & GULUTSAN, M. 1974, Some Effects of Bilingualism on Cognitive Functioning. In S. CAREY (ed.) 1974.

CUMMINS, JAMES (JIM) & MULCAHY, R. 1979, Orientation to Language in Ukrainian-English Bilingual Children. *Child Development.*

CUMMINS, JAMES (JIM) & ABDOLELL, ALI 1979, Bibliographic Focus: Adjustment of Immigrant Children in Bilingual Situations. *Indian Journal of Applies Lingustics*. 1979.

CUMMINS, JIM & SKUTNABB-KANGAS, TOVE (eds) (forthcoming), Education of Linguistic Minority Children. Vol. 1, *Policy Issues*, Vol. 2, *The Minority Child in School: Case Studies and Community Perspectives*, Multilingual Matters, Clevedon.

CZIKO, G. 1975, *The Effects of Different French Immersion Programs on the Language and Academic Skills of Children from Various Socioeconomic Backgrounds*, M.A. Thesis, McGill University, unpublished.

DAGENS, NYHETER, Stockholm.

DAHLSTEDT, KARL-HAMPUS 1970, The dilemmas of dialectology. In BENEDIKTSSON 1970, 158–184.
- 1971, Den nordiska språkgemenskapen. *Språkvård* 4, 10–16.
- 1975, Den språkliga situationen i Norden. In SKUTNABB-KANGAS 1975e, 19–30.
DARCY, NATALIE T. 1946, The Effect of Bilingualism upon the Measurement of the Intelligence of Children of Pre-school Age. *Journal of Educational Psychology*, 37, 21–44.
- 1953, A Review of the Literature on the Effects of Bilingualism upon the Measurement of Intelligence. *Journal of Genetic Psychology* 82, 21–58.
- 1963, Bilingualism and the Measurement of Intelligence: Review of a Decade of Research. *Journal of Genetic Psychology* 103, 259–282.
DARSIE, M. L. 1926, The Mental Capacity of American-born Japanese Children. *Comparative Psychology Monograms* 3, 1–3.
DAVIES, A. (ed.) 1975, *Problems of Language and Learning*. Heinemann, London.
DAVLETSHIN, T. 1967, *Analysis of Current Developments in the Soviet Union*, 1967 (quoted in LEWIS 1978, 218).
Deklaration der Nationaldemokratischen Einheitsfront Kurdistans (UDG) (Ulusal Demokratik Gücbirligi) 1980, KOMKAR-Publikation 3, 1980, Föderation der Arbeitervereine Kurdistans in der Bundesrepublik Deutschland, Frankfurt/Main.
DEUTSCH, M., KATZ, I. & JENSEN, A. R. (eds) 1968, *Social Class, Race and Psychological Development*, Holt, Rinehart & Winston, New York.
DIEBOLD, RICKARD A. Jr. 1964, Incipient Bilingualism. In Hymes 1964, 495–508.
DILLER, K. C. 1974, "Compound" and "Coordinate" Bilingualism: A Conceptual Artifact, *Word* 26, 254–261.
DITTMAR, NORBERT 1974, *Soziolinguistik. Exemplarische und kritische Darstellung ihrer Theorie, Empirie und Anwendung*. Fischer Athenäum Taschenbücher, Linguistik, Frankfurt/Main.
- 1978, Ordering Adult Learners According to Language Abilities. In DITTMAR, HABERLAND, SKUTNABB-KANGAS & TELEMAN (eds) 1978, 119–154.
DITTMAR, NORBERT, HABERLAND, HARTMUT, SKUTNABB-KANGAS, TOVE & TELEMAN, ULF (eds) 1978, *Papers from the First Scandinavian-German Symposium on the Language of Immigrant Workers and Their Children, Roskilde*, 1978, ROLIG-papir 12, Roskilde Universitetscenter, Lingvistgruppen.
DITTMAR, NORBERT & KÖNIGER, PAUL (eds) 1981, Proceedings of the Second Scandinavian-German Symposium on the Language of Immigrant Workers and Their Children, *Linguistische Arbeite und Berichte*, Heft 16, Freie Universität Berlin.
Dokumentation om indvandrere 1980, Mellemfolkeligt Samvirke, Copenhagen.
DOOB, L. 1957, The Effect of Language on Verbal Expression and Recall, *American Anthropology* 59, 88–100.
DRESSLER, WOLFGANG U., MEID, WOLFGANG, PFEIFFER, OSKAR E. & HEROK, THOMAS (eds) 1978, *Proceedings of the Twelfth International Congress of Linguists, Vienna, August 28–September 2, 1977*. Innsbruck.
DULAY, HEIDI C. & BURT, MARINA K. 1974, You can't learn without goofing. In RICHARDS 1974.
- 1975, see Bilingual Syntax Measure.
- 1980. The Relative Proficiency of Limited English Proficient Students. *NABE Journal* IV, 3, Spring 1980, 1–23.
DURKHEIM, E. 1933, *On the Division of Labour in Society*. Macmillan, London.

DUTCHER, NADINE, 1982, *The Use of First and Second Languages in Primary Education: Selected Case Studies*, World Bank Staff Working Paper No. 504, Washington, D.C.

EAKINS, BARBARA WESTBROOK & EAKINS, R. GENE 1978, *Sex Differences in Human Communication*. Houghton Mifflin Company, Boston.

EBERT, K. H. 1979, *Sprache und Tradition der Kera*. Teil III. *Grammatik*. Marburger Studien zur Afrika- under Asienkunde, Marburg.

EDBERG, LILLEMOR & HOLMEGAARD, MARGARETA 1982, *Invandrareleven i gymnasieskolan* Faktorer som påverkar studiesituationen samt förslag till försöksverksamhet, University of Gothenburg, SPRINS Project 16.

EDWARDS, HENRY P. 1976, Evaluation of the French Immersion Program Offered by the Ottawa Roman Catholic Separate School Board. *Canadian Modern Language Review* 33:2, 137–142.

EDWARDS, HENRY P. & SMYTH, F. 1976, Alternatives to Early Immersion Programs for the Acquisition of French as a Second Language. *Canadian Modern Language Review* 32:5, 524–533.

EHLICH, KONRAD 1980, Fremdsprachlich Handeln: Zur Pragmatik des Zweitspracherwerbs ausländischer Arbeiter. *Deutsch Lernen* 1, 21–37.

EHN, BILLY 1975, *Sötebrödet. En etnologisk skildring av jugoslaver i ett dalsländskt pappersbrukssamhälle*. Tiden, Stockholm.

EJERHED, EVA & HENRYSSON, INGER (eds) 1981, *Tvåspråkighet*, Acta Universitatis Umensis, Umeå Studies in the Humanities 36, Umeå.

VAN EK, J. A. 1972, *Proposal for the Definition of a Threshold-level in Foreign Language Learning by Adults*. Council of Europe, CCC/EEC (72) 22.

– 1975, *The Threshold Level in a European Unit/Credit System for Modern Language Learning by Adults*. Council for Cultural Co-operation, Strasbourg.

– 1976, *The Threshold Level for Modern Language learning in Schools*. Council of Europe, DECS/ETG (76) 19.

EKBERG, JAN 1979, *Invandrarna i Växjö*. Högskolan i Växjö.

– 1980, *Inkomstfördelning mellan invandrare och svenskar via offentlig sektor*. Högskolan Växjö, duplicated copy.

– 1983, Inkomsteffekter av invandring. Högskolan i Växjö, Acta Wexionensia, Serie 2, Economy & Politics 1.

EKSTRAND, LARS HENRIC 1978a, Bara hemspråk dålig lösning för invandrare. *Kommunaktuellt* 14, 27.4.1978.

– 1978b, *Bilingual and Bicultural Adaptation*. Doctoral dissertation, University of Stockholm.

– 1978c, *Fakta och fiktion i invandrardebatten. Exempel på faktorer som har samband med invandrarbarns språkinlärning*. Särtryck och småtryck nr 249, Lärarhögskolan i Malmö.

– 1978d, *Unpopular Views on Popular Beliefs about Immigrant Children*. Paper presented at the symposium "Socio-Personal Adjustment of immigrant children in European and North-American Schools". Munich 1978.

– 1978e, Migrant adaptation – a cross-cultural problem. In FREUDENSTEIN (ed.) 1978.

– 1979a, (title unclear) Förslag och rekommendationer, Malmö, 20.1.1979, duplicated copy, 4 pages.

– 1979b, *Early Bilingualism: Theories and Facts*. In MUNICIO (ed.) 1981a.

– 1983, Inkomsteffekter av invandring (Income effects due to immigration). Acta Wexionensia, ser 2, Economy & Politics 1, Växjö.

EKSTRÖM, LENA 1982, *Invandrarundervisningen och läromedlen*, University of Gothenburg, SPRINS Project 11.

ELERT, CLAES-CHRISTIAN, ELIASSON, STIG, FRIES, SIGURD & URELAND, STURE (eds) 1977, *Dialectology and Sociolinguistics. Essays in honor of Karl-Hampus Dahlstedt*. Acta Universitatis Umensis, Umeå Studies in the Humanities 12, Umeå.

ELIAS- OLIVARES, LUCIA & VALDÉS-FALLIS, GUADALUPE 1978, *Language Diversity in Chicano Speech Communities: Implications for Language Teaching*. Paper presented at the 9th World Congress of Sociology, Uppsala 1978.

ELWERT, W. T. 1960, *Das zweisprachige Individuum: Ein Selbstzeugnis*. Steiner, Wiesbaden.

ENGEL, WALBURGA VON RAFFLER 1965, *Del bilinguismo infantile*. Archivio Glottologico Italiano 50, 175–180.

ENGELBREKTSSON, ULLA-BRITT 1978, *The Force of Tradition, Turkish Migrants at Home and Abroad*. Gothenburg Studies in Social Anthropology, Acta Universitatis Gothoburgensis. Göteborg.

ENGLE, PATRICIA LEE 1975, *The Use of Vernacular Languages in Education. Language Medium in Early School Years for Minority Language Groups*. Papers in Applied Linguistics, Bilingual Education Series 3, Center for Applied Linguistics, Arlington.

ENGSTRÖM, ELISABETH & ANN-MARGRETH MILLESTEN 1977, *Tvåspråkighet och invandrarbarn i för- och grundskola. En kommenterad urvalsbibliografi*. Immigrant-Institutet, Borås.

ENKVIST, NILS ERIK (ed.) 1982, *Impromptu Speech: A Symposium*, Publications of the Research Institute of the Åbo Akademi Foundation No 78, Åbo 1982.

ENSTRÖM, INGEGERD 1982, *Lärarundersökningen*, University of Gothenburg, SPRINS Project 10.

ENSTRÖM, INGEGERD, KÄLLSTRÖM, ROGER & TINGBJÖRN, GUNNAR 1982, *Interim Report on the SPRINS GROUP's Evaluation of Time Schedule Modification Experiments for Immigrant Pupils at the Junior and Intermediate Levels of Compulsory School*, University of Gothenburg, SPRINS Project 8.

ENSTRÖM, INGEGERD & TINGBJÖRN, GUNNAR 1982, *Invandrarkonsulenterna*, University of Gothenburg, SPRINS Project 12.

ERDEM, MAHMUT & SKUTNABB-KANGAS, TOVE 1980, Rätten till eget språk. Kurder i Norden vill ha undervisning i kurdiska. *Audhumla* 4, Nordiska Kultursekretariatet. Copenhagen.

ERVIN, SUSAN & OSGOOD, C. E. 1954, Second Language Learning and Bilingualism. *Journal of Abnormal and Social Psychology*, Supplement 49, 139–146.

ERVIN-TRIPP, SUSAN 1970, An Analysis of the Interaction of Language, Topic and Listener. In FISHMAN 1970a, 192–211.

– 1972, Sociolinguistic Rules of Address. In Price & Holmes 1972, 225–240.

– 1973, *Language Acquisition and Communicative Choice*. Essays by Susan M. Ervin-Tripp, selected and introduced by Anwar S. Dil. Stanford University Press, Stanford, Cal.

ESCOBAR, ALBERTO 1975, La Educación Bilingüe en el Perú. In TROIKE & MODIANO (eds) 1975, 32–42.

European Science Foundation, organizer 1980. *Symposium "Cultural Identity and Structural Marginalization of Migrant Workers"* Bochum, Hamminkeln, 1980.

EVERS, K. 1970, *The Effects of Bilingualism on the Recall of Words Presented Aurally.* Dissertation, University of Minnesota, Dissertation Abstracts 5197 A.

EYSENCK, H. J. 1973 (1967), Intelligence Assessment: A Theoretical and Experimental Approach. In WISEMAN 1973a.

FÆRCH, CLAUS 1979, *Research in Foreign Language Pedagogy – the PIF Project.* Anglica et Americana 7. Dept of English, University of Copenhagen.

FÆRCH, CLAUS, HAASTRUP, KIRSTEN & PHILIPPSON, ROBERT 1983, *Learner Language and Language Learning,* Gyldendal, Copenhagen.

FÆRCH, CLAUS & KASPER, GABRIELE 1980, Processes and Strategies in Foreign Language Learning and Communication. *Interlanguage Studies Bulletin,* 5:1, 47–118.

– 1982, Phatic, metalingual and metacommunicative functions in discource: Gambits and Repairs, in ENKVIST (ed.) 1982, 71–103.

– (eds) 1983, *Strategies in Interlanguage Communication,* Longman, London.

FANON, FRANTZ 1968, *The Wretched of the Earth.* Grove Press, Inc, New York.

FASTBOM, ULRIKA, KOUTONEN-NASIOPOULOS, LEENI & TSALMAS, IRMA 1977, *Identitet och språk.* CD:1, essay, Dept of Psychology, University of Stockholm.

FELIX, SASCHA W. (ed.) 1979, *Second Language Development, Trends and Issues.* Gunter Narr Verlag, Tübingen.

FERGUSON, CHARLES A. 1959, Diglossia. *Word* 15, 1959, 325–340.

– 1968, Language Development. In FISHMAN *et al.,* 1968.

– 1977, Linguistic Theory. In *Bilingual Education: Current Perspectives.* Vol. 2. *Lingustics,* 43–52.

FERGUSON, CHARLES A. & GUMPERZ, JOHN J. (eds) 1960, Lingustic Diversity in South-Asia: Studies in Regional, Social and Functional Variation. *IJAL* 26, 3, Part III, Bloomington, Indiana.

FIDEF, KOMKAR, KDID (publisher, no date) (1980). *Informationen über die "Grauen Wölfe" in der BRD.*

FIDEF 1978 5. Bericht zur Bildungssituation türkischer Kinder in der BRD, dem Kongress zur Bildungssituation türkischer Kinder in der BRD am 11/12 Februar 1978 in Gelsen-Kirchen vom Bundesvorstand den FIDEF vorgelegt.

FILIPOVIĆ, RUDOLF (ed.) 1972, *Active Methods and Modern Aids in the Teaching of Foreign Languages.* Oxford University Press, London.

FISHMAN, JOSHUA A. 1964, Language Maintenance and Language Shift as a Field of Inquiry. *Lingustics* 9, 32–70.

– 1966, *Language Loyalty in the United States. The Maintenance and Perpetuation of Non-English Mother Tongues by American Ethnic and Religious Groups,* Janua Linguarum, Series Maior No XXI, Mouton & Co, The Hague.

– 1968, Sociolinguistic Perspective on the Study of Bilingualism. *Linguistics* 38, 21–50.

– 1970a (1968), *Readings in the Sociology of Language.* Mouton & Co, The Hague, 2nd printing.

– 1970b, *Sociolinguistics. A Brief Introduction.* Newbury House Publishers, Rowley, Mass.

– 1970c, The Politics of Bilingual Education. In ALATIS 1970, 47–58.

– (ed.) 1971a, *Advances in the Sociology of Language.* Vol. I. *Basic Concepts,*

Theories and Problems: Alternative Approaches. Mouton & Co, The Hague.
- 1971b, The Sociology of Language: An Interdisciplinary Social Science Approach to Language in Society. In FISHMAN 1971a, 217–404.
- (ed.) 1972a. *Advances in the Sociology of Language*. Vol. II. *Selected Studies and Applications*. Mouton & Co, The Hague.
- 1972b, The Sociology of Language. In GIGLIOLI 1972a, 45–58.
- 1972c, *Language in Sociocultural Change*. Essays by Joshua A. Fishman, selected and introduced by Anwar S. Dil. Stanford University Press, Stanford, Cal.
- 1972d, *Language and Nationalism: Two Integrative Essays*. Newbury House Publishers, Rowley, Mass.
- 1973, The Sociolinguistics of Nationalism. In WATSON 1973a, 403–414.
- (ed.) 1974, *Advances in Language Planning*. Mouton & Co, The Hague.
- 1976, *Bilingual Education. An International Sociological Perspective*. Newbury House Publishers, Rowley, Mass.
- 1977, The Social Science Perspective. In *Bilingual Education: Current perspectives*. Vol. 1. *Social Science*, 1–52.
- (ed.) 1978, *Advances in the Study of Societal Multilingualism*. Mouton & Co, The Hague.
FISHMAN, JOSHUA A. *et al.* (eds) 1968, *Language Problems of Developing Nations*. Wiley and Sons, New York.
FISHMAN, JOSHUA A. & LOVAS, JOHN 1970, Bilingual Education in Sociolinguistic Perspective. *TESOL Quarterly* 4, 215–222.
FITCH, MICHAEL J. 1966, *Verbal and Performance Test Scores in Bilingual Children*, Ph.D. Thesis, Colorado State College.
Folkmålsstudier XXII 1972, Meddelanden från föreningen för nordisk filologi, Helsingfors.
FORSBERG, KARL-ERIK 1974, Finlandssvenskarna år 1970 – enligt folkräkningen. *Svenskbygden* 5.
Förslag om åtgärder för invandrarbarnen i förskola, grundskola och gymnasieskola, 1975, Utbildningsdepartementet, DsdU 1975:13.
FORUM, National Clearinghouse for Bilingual Education. Rosslyn, Vir.
FOUGSTEDT, GUNNAR 1952, Giftermålen över språkgränsen. *Kalender* 1953, published by Svenska Folkskolans Vänner, Helsingfors.
- 1963, *Finlandssvenskarnas befolkningsfråga. Läget idag och framtidsperspektiv.* Svenska befolkningsförbundets i Finland publikation nr 14. Reprint from Statsvetenskaplig Tidskrift, Lund.
FOUGSTEDT, GUNNAR & HARTMAN, TOR 1956, Social Factors Affecting the Choice of Language by Children of Finnish-Swedish Mixed Marriages in Finland. *Westermarck Society*. Vol. III.
FRANZ, FRITZ, as quoted in RIECK & SENFT 1978.
- 1979, Politische Mitbestimmung für Ausländer – ein Demokratiegebot der Verfassung. *Deutsch Lernen* 3, 60–67.
FREIHOFF, ROLAND & TAKALA, SAULI 1974a, *Kielenkäyttötilanteiden erittelyyn perustuva kielenopetuksen tavoitekuvausjärjestelmä*. Reports from the Language Center No 2, University of Jyväskylä.
- 1974, *A Systematic Description of Language Teaching Objectives*. Reports from the Language Centre No 3, University of Jyväskylä.
FREIRE, PAULO 1972, *Pedagogik för förtryckta*. Gummessons, Stockholm.
- 1974, *Kulturell kamp för frihet*. Gummessons, Stockholm.

Fremmedsprogspædagogik 1980, Katalog over bibliotekets litteratur, Danmarks Pædagogiske Bibliotek, Copenhagen.
FREUDENSTEIN, R. (ed.) 1978, *Teaching the Children of Immigrants*. Brussels, AIMAV, Didier.
FROMKIN, V. & RODMAN, R. 1974, *An Introduction to Language*. Holt, Rinehart and Winston, New York.

GALLOWAY, LINDA 1976, *Bilingual Aphasia: Issues in Bilingual Aphasia. A Case Study and Experimental Evidence for a Theory of the Lexicon*. M.A. Thesis, Dept. of Linguistics, The University of California at Los Angeles.
– 1978, Language Impairment and Recovery in Polyglot Aphasia: A Case Study of a Hepta-Lingual. In PARADIS 1978, 139–148.
GANTSKAYA, O. A. 1981, Ethnos and Family in the USSR, in GRIGULEVICH & KOZLOV (eds) 1981, 90–106.
GARDNER, ROBERT C. 1960, *Motivational Variables in Second-language Acquisition*. Ph.D. Thesis, McGill University, unpublished.
GARDNER, ROBERT C. & LAMBERT, W. E. 1959, Language Aptitude, Intelligence and Second Language Acquisition. *Canadian Journal of Psychology* 13, 266–272.
– 1965, Language Aptitude, Intelligence and Second Language Achievement. *Journal of Educational Psychology* 56, 191–199.
– 1972, *Attitudes and Motivation in Second Language Learning*. Newbury House, Rowley, Mass.
GATBONTON-SEGALOWITZ, E. 1975, *Systematic Variation in Second Language Speech: A Sociolinguistic Study*. Ph.D. Thesis, MGill University.
GATHORNE-HARDY, JONATHAN 1979, *The Public School Phenomenon* 597–1977, Penguin Books, Suffolk.
GAUDINO, VINCENT A., BARIK, HENRI C. & SWAIN, MERRILL K. 1975, *Bilingual Education: French Partial Immersion Classes at the Senior Elementary and Secondary School Levels in Canada*. Paper presented at the 4th International Congress of Applied Linguistics, Stuttgart, 1975.
GEISSLER, H. 1938, *Zweisprachigkeit deutscher Kinder im Ausland*. Kohlhammer, Stuttgart.
GEKOSKI, W. 1970, *Effects of Language Acquisition Contexts on Semantic Processing in Bilinguals*. Proceedings of the Annual Convention of the American Psychological Association 5, 487–488.
GENESEE, FRED 1974. *Bilingual Education: Social Psychological Consequences*. Ph.D. Thesis, Dept of Psychology, McGill University.
– 1976, The Suitability of Immersion Programs for All Children. *Canadian Modern Language Review* 32:5, 494–515.
– 1977, Summary and discussion. In HORNBY (ed.) 1977, 147–164.
– 1978, Individual Differences in Second Language Learning. *Canadian Modern Language Review* 34:3, 490–504.
GENESEE, FRED & HOLOBOW, N. 1978, Children's Reactions to Variations in Second Language Competence. In PARADIS (ed.) 1978a, 185–201.
GENESEE, FRED, SHEINER, E., TUCKER, G. R. & LAMBERT, W. E. 1976, An Experiment in Trilingual Education. *Canadian Modern Language Review*, 32:1, 115–128.
GENESEE, FRED, TUCKER, G. R. & LAMBERT, W. E. 1976. An Experiment in

Trilingual Education: Report 3. *Canadian Modern Language Journal*, 34:3, 621–643 (ed. Carey).

GERVER, D. 1974, The Effects of Noise on the Performance of Simultaneous Interpreters. *Acta Psychologica*, 38, 159–167.

GIGLIOLI, PIER PAOLO (ed.) 1972, *Language and Social Context*. Penguin Modern Sociology Readings, Middlesex, England.

GILBERT, G. (ed.) 1970. *Texas Studies in Bilingualism*, Berlin.

GIRKE, W. & JACHNOW, H. 1974, *Sowjetische Soziolinguistik. Probleme und Genese*. Scriptor Verlag. Kronberg.

GOLDMAN, RONALD 1973, Education and Immigrants. In WATSON 1973a, 343–359.

GOLDMAN-EISLER, FRIEDA 1972, Segmentation of Input in Simultaneous Translation. *Journal of Psycholinguistic Research* 1, 127–139.

GONZÁLES, GUSTAVO 1977. Teaching Bilingual Children. In *Bilingual Education: Current Perspectives*. Vol 2. *Linguistics*, 53–59.

GONZÁLES, J. M. 1975, Coming of Age in Bilingual/Bicultural Education: A Historical Perspective. *Inequality in Education* No. 19, 1975, 5–17.

GOODERHAM, KENT G. 1975, Bilingual Education for Indians and Inuit: The Canadian Experience. In TROIKE & MODIANO (eds) 1975, 43–53.

GRAHAM, V. T. 1925, The Intelligence of Italian and Jewish Children in the Habit Clinic of the Massachusetts Division of Mental Hygiene. *Journal of Abnormal and Social Psychology* 20, 1925, 371–376.

GREEN, ANDY 1982, In Defence of Anti-Racist Teaching, *Multiracial Education*, 10:2, 19–35.

GREENBERG, JOSEPH H. (ed.) 1966 (1963), *Universals of Language*. The M.I.T. Press, Cambridge, Mass, 2nd ed.

GREENBERG, JOSEPH H., OSGOOD, CHARLES E. & JENKINS, JAMES J. 1966, Memorandum Concerning Language Universals. In GREENBERG (ed.) 1966, XV–XXVII.

GREGERSEN, KIRSTEN, BASBØLL, HANS & MEY, JACOB (eds) 1978, *Papers from the Fourth Scandinavian Conference of Linguistics, Hindsgavl, 1978*, Odense University Press.

GRIGULEVICH, I. R. & KOZLOV, S. YA. (eds) 1981a, *Ethnocultural Processes and National Problems in the Modern World*, Progress Publishers, Moscow.

– 1981b, Introduction, in GRIGULEVICH & KOZLOV (eds) 1981a, 4–16.

GRÖNROOS, MARIKA 1972, *Den finlandssvenska språkvården och allmänheten. En språksociologisk studie*. Dept. of Nordic Languages, University of Helsinki.

GUILFORD, J. P. 1966, Intelligence: 1965-model. *American Psychologist* 21, 20–26.

– 1973 (1959), Three Faces of Intellect. In WISEMAN 1973a, 141–160 (reprinted from *American Psychologist* 14, 1959, 469–479).

GULUTSAN, METRO 1976, Third Language Learning. *Canadian Modern Language Review* 32:3, 309–315.

GUMPERZ, JOHN J. 1964, Linguistic and Social Interaction in Two Communities. In GUMPERZ & HYMES (eds) 1964, 137–153.

– 1967, On the Lingistic Markers of Bilingual Communication. *Journal of Social Issues* 23:2, 48–57.

– 1969, How can We Describe and Measure the Behavior of Bilingual Groups? In KELLY (ed.) 1969, 242–249.

– 1971, *Language in Social Groups*. Essays by John J. Gumperz, selected and introduced by Anwar S. Dil. Stanford University Press, Stanford, Cal.

– 1972, Sociolinguistics and Communication in Small Groups. In PRIDE & HOLMES (eds) 1972, 203–334.
– 1979, *The Conversational Analysis of Interethnic Communication*. Paper presented at the SEAMEO Regional Language Centre 14th Regional Seminar, Singapore, 1979.
GUMPERZ, JOHN J. & HYMES, DELL (ed.) 1964, The Ethnography of Communication. *American Anthropologist*, Special Publication, Vol. 6:6, part 2.
– (eds) 1972, *Directions in Sociolinguistics: The Ethnography of Communication*. New York.
GURVICH, I. S. 1981, Present-day Ethnic Processes among the Peoples of Siberia, in GRIGULEVICH & KOZLOV (eds) 1981, 160–176.
HAASTRUP, KIRSTEN & PHILLIPSON, ROBERT 1983, Achievement strategies in learner/native speaker interactions, in FÆRCH & KASPER (eds) 1983, 140–158.
HAASTRUP, NIELS & TELEMAN, ULF 1978, *Svensk, dansk eller skandinavisk? En interviewundersøgelse af svenske laereres sproglige situation ved et dansk universitet*. ROLIG-papir 14, Roskilde Universitetscenter, Lingvistgruppen.
HABERLAND, HARTMUT & SKUTNABB-KANGAS, TOVE 1979, *Political Determinants of Pragmatic and Sociolingustic Choices*. ROLIG-papir 17, Roskilde Universitetscenter, Lingvistgruppen.
HABERMAS, JURGEN 1968, Erkenntnis und Interesse, Suhrkamp, Frankfurt.
HÄKKINEN, SONJA 1974, *Invandrarbarns situation i svenska skolor*. Pedagogiska inst, University of Lund.
HAKUTA, K. 1978, A Report on the Development of Grammatical Morphemes in a Japanese Girl Learning English as a Second Language. In HATCH (ed.) 1978, 132–147.
HALEY, ALEX 1977, *Roots. The Epic Drama of One Man's Search for his Origins*. Pan Books, London.
HALL, ROBERT A. 1952, Bilingualism and Applied Linguistics. *Zeitschrift für Phonetik und Allgemeine. Sprachwissenschaft* 6, 13–30.
HALL, STUART, *et al.* 1978, *Policing the Crisis: Mugging, the State, Law and Order*, The Macmillan Press, London.
HALLIDAY, M. A. K. 1973, *Explorations in the Functions of Language*. Edward Arnold Publishers, London.
HALLIDAY, M. A. K., MCINTOSH, ANGUS & STREVENS, PETER 1970 (1964), The Users and Uses of Language. In FISHMAN 1970a, 139–169 (reprinted from *The Linguistic Sciences and Language Teaching*. Longmans, London, 1964).
HALPERN, G. 1976, An Evaluation of French Learning Alternatives. *Canadian Modern Language Review* 33:2, 162–172.
HAMBERG, EVA M. 1981,Återvandringens långsiktiga effekter, HAMBERG & HAMMAR (eds) 1981, 71–85.
HAMBERG, EVA M. & HAMMAR, TOMAS (eds) 1981, *Invandringen och framtiden*, Publica, Liber Förlag, Stockholm.
HAMERS, J. F. 1973. *Interdependent and Independent States of the Bilingual's Two Languages*. Ph.D. Thesis, McGill University, Montreal.
HAMERS, J. F. & LAMBERT, W. E. 1972, Bilingual Interdependences on Auditory Perception. *Journal of Verbal Learning and Verbal Behavior* 11, 303–310.
HAMMAR, TOMAS 1978, *Migration and Politics. Delimitation and Organization of a Research Field*. ECPR Workshop International Migration and Politics, Grenoble, 1978.
– 1979, *Det första invandrarvalet*. EIFO, Stockholm.

- 1981, Invandringens politiska konsekvenser, in HAMBERG & HAMMAR (eds) 1981, 170–188.
- (ed.) (in preparation) *European Immigration Policy – a comparative study*, Routledge & Kegan Paul, London.
HAMMAR, TOMAS & LINDBY, KERSTIN 1979, *Swedish Immigration Research. Introductory Survey and Annotated Bibliography*. Commission on Immigration Research. Stockholm.
HAMMARBERG, BJÖRN & VIBERG, ÅKE 1977, Felanalys och språktypologi. Orientering om två delstudier i *SSM-projektet*. (=Svenska som målspråk) Report 1, Dept. of Linguistics, Univ. of Stockholm.
HANNERZ, ULF 1981, Sverige som invandrarsamhälle: Några antropologiska frågeställningar, in HAMBERG & HAMMAR (eds) 1981, 120–145.
HANSEGÅRD, NILS ERIK 1962, *Tvåspråkighet eller halvspråkighet?* Radio talk, Röster i Radio/TV.
- 1967, Recent Finnish Loanwords in Jukkasjärvi Lappish, Uppsala, Acta Universitatis Upsaliensis, Studia Uralica et Altaica Upsaliensia.
- 1972 (1968), *Tvåspråkighet eller halvspråkighet?* Aldus series 253, Stockholm, 3rd ed.
- 1975, Tvåspråkighet eller halvspråkighet? *Invandrare och Minoriteter* 3, 1975, 7–13.
- 1977a, Loman och halvspråkigheten. *Invandrare och Minoriteter* 2, 1977, 36–51.
- 1977b, Paneldiskussion om dubbel halvspråkighet. In SKUTNABB-KANGAS 1977a, 212–227.
- 1978. *The Transition of the Jukkasjärvi Lapps from Nomadism to Settled Life and Farming*. Studia Ethnographica Upsaliensia XXXIX.
HANSEN, ERIK & SKYUM-NIELSEN, PEDER (eds) 1979, Sprognormer i Norden, Copenhagen, Akademisk Forlag.
HANSON, GÖTE 1980a, *Jag har inte bett att få komma. En psykologisk betraktelse över hur invandrarbarn har det och kan ha det samt varför.* Diskriminationsutredningen, manuscript.
- 1980b, Modersmålsklasser och övergångsmodeller. *Invandrare och Minoriteter* 3, 1980, 6–8.
- 1980c, Ohederlig forskning om modersmålsklasser – svar till Ekstrand. *Att undervisa* 5, 1980.
- 1980d, Reply to contributions by Ekstrand and others on monolingual classes in schools, written for *Dagens Nyheter* for publication on 3.9.80 (in spite of the promise of publication this reply did not appear, but was printed in *Invandrarbarnen, skolan och språket. Modersmålsklasser kontra sammansatta klasser – är striden verkligen nödvändig?* as part of the debate conducted by the Rädda Barnen organisationen and Kursverksamheten in Uppsala 27.11.80).
- 1980e, Finska modersmålsklasser (FMK) i Södertälje. In *Invandrarbarnen, skolan och språket*. Rädda Barnen (see HANSON 1980d).
- 1982a, *Integration and Participation*, Paper presented at the 5th International School Psychology Colloquium, Stockholm, August 1–6, 1982.
- 1982b, "Finnkampen". *Om finska invandrarbarn i tvåspråkig hemspråksklass*, University of Stockholm, Dept. of Psychology, stencil.
HANSSEN, ESKIL 1979a, Talespråkets normer – mellom ideal og virklighet. In HANSEN & SKYUM-NIELSEN 1979, 83–99.
HARLEY, BIRGIT 1976, Alternative Programs for Teaching French as a Second Language. *Canadian Modern Language Review* 33:2, 134–136.

HASSELMO, NILS 1969, On Diversity in American Swedish, *Svenska landsmål och svenskt folkliv* 92, 53–72.
– 1970, Code-Switching and Modes of Speaking. In GILBERT 1970, 179–210.
– 1972, Språkväxling. In LOMAN 1972, 152–182.
– 1974, *Amerikasvenska. En bok om språkutvecklingen i Svensk-Amerika.* Esselte Studium, Lund.
HATCH, EVELYN R. 1977, Second Language Learning. In *Bilingual Education. Current Perspectives.* Vol. 2 *Linguistics*, 60–86.
HATCH, EVELYN MARCUSSEN (ed.) 1978, *Second Language Acquisition. A Book of Readings.* Newbury House Publishers, Rowley, Mass.
– 1979, *Plenary Lecture at the First Nordic Interlanguage Symposium.* Hanasaari, Finland, 27–31.8.1979.
HAUGEN, EINAR 1953a. *The Norwegian Language in America: A Study in Bilingual Behavior.* University of Philadelphia Press, Philadelphia, 2 volumes.
– 1953b, Nordiske språkproblemer – en opinionsundersökelse. *Nordisk Tidskrift* 29, 1953, 225–249.
– 1964 (1956), *Bilingualism in the Americas: A Bibliography and Research Guide.* University of Alabama Press, 2nd printing.
– 1966a, *Language Conflict and Language Planning. The Case of Modern Norwegian.* Cambridge, Mass.
– 1966b, Semicommunication: The Language Gap in Scandinavia. *Sociological Inquiry* 36:2, 280–297.
– 1968, The Scandinavian Languages as Cultural Artifacts. In FISHMAN *et al.* 1968, 267–284.
– 1970, On the meaning of bilingual competence. In JAKOBSON & KAWAMOTO (eds), 1970, 221–229.
– 1972a. The Stigmata of Bilingualism, In HAUGEN 1972b, 307–324.
– 1972b, *The Ecology of Language*, ed. Anwar S. Dil. Stanford University Press, Stanford.
– 1972c, Language Planning, Theory and Practice, In HAUGEN 1972b.
– 1972d, Bilingualism as a Social and Personal Problem. In FILIPOVIĆ (ed.) 1972, 1–14.
– 1978a, Bilingualism in Retrospect – a Personal View. In ALATIS (ed.) 1978, 35–41.
– 1978b, Bilingualism, Language Contact, and Immigrant Languages in the United States: A Research Report 1956–1970. In FISHMAN (ed.) 1978, 1–111 (originally in *Current Trends in Linguistics*, ed. Thomas A. Sebeok, Vol. 10, 505–591).
– 1978c, Language Norms in Bilingual Communities. In DRESSLER *et al.* (eds) 1978, 283–285.
– 1980. *Skandinavisk som mellomspråk – forskning og fremtid.* Lecture, 24–26.3.1980. Copenhagen, Manuscript.
HAUGEN, EINAR, KANGAS, TOVE, MARGOLIN, DAVID & MARKEY INGER METTE (eds) 1974, *A Bibliography of Scandinavian Languages and Linguistics 1900–1970.* Universitetsforlaget, Oslo.
HAVINGHURST, R. J. & HILKEVITCH, R. H. 1944, The Intelligence of Indian Children as Measured by a Performance Scale, *Journal of Abnormal and Social Psychology* 1944; 39, 419–432.
HEBERT, RAYMOND, BILODEAU, MARCEL, FOIDART, DONALD, LEGER, ROBERT, SAINDON, CLAUDE, SCHAUBROECK, GÉRALD & LAURENCELLE, YVETTE 1976, *Academic Achievement and Language of Instruction among Franco-Manitoban*

Pupils. Collège Universitaire de Saint-Boniface, Centre de Recherches.

HEDMAN, HARDY 1978, *SÖ:s forsknings- och utvecklingsarbete avseende invandrare och språkliga minoriteter*. Skolöverstyrelsen. Byrån för pedagogiskt forsknings- och utvecklingsarbete, Stockholm.

HELANDER, ELINA 1979, Tvåspråkighet hos samer. In *Tvåspråkighet* 1979, 179–185.

HENRYSSON, STEN & BJÖRKQUIST, LARS-MAGNUS 1963, *Standardprovsresultat för tvåspråkiga elever i Norra Sverige*. Report from the Pedagogisk-psykologiska inst, Lärarhögskolan. Stockholm, 6.

HENRYSSON, STEN, LJUNG, BENGT-OLOV 1967, *Tvåspråkigheten i Tornedalen. En studie av standardprovresultat i årskurserna 3 och 6*. Report from the Pedagogisk-psykologiska inst, Lärarhögskolan. Stockholm, 26.

HERAS, I & NELSON, K. 1972, Retention of Semantic, Syntactic and Language Information by Young Bilingual Children. *Psychonomic Science* 29, 391–392.

HERMANN, JESPER, AHLGREN, INGER, ANWARD, JAN & ROSSIPAL, HANS (eds) 1977, *Tendenser i nordisk psyko- og sociolingvistik*, Metodeseminar, University of Copenhagen, Dept. of Applied and Mathematical Linguistics, Copenhagen.

HERNÁNDEZ-CHÁVEZ, EDUARDO 1975, Consideraciones Sociolingüísticas en Materiales para la Educacíon Bilingüe. In TROIKE & MODIANO 1975, 228–238.

– 1978. Language maintenance, bilingual education and philosophies of bilingualism in the United States, in ALATIS (ed.) 1978, 527–550.

HERRELL, ILEANA CÓLLADE & HERRELL, JAMES M. 1980, Affective and Cognitive Aspects of Bilingualism. *NABE Journal* IV, 3, 1980, 81–92.

HEYMAN, ANNA-GRETA 1973, Invandrarbarn. Slutrapport. Stockholms invandrar- nämnd, duplicated copy.

– 1976, *Invandrarbarn*, Extryck, Stockholm.

HILDEBRAND, JOHN F. T. 1974, French Immersion Pilot Program in Fredericton, *Canadian Modern Language Review* 31:2, 181–191.

HILL, JANE 1981, Paper presented at Symposium 2, International language and the vernaculars, Sixth International Congress of Applied Linguistics, Lund, August 9–15, 1981.

HIRSCH, N. D. 1926, A study of natio-racial differences. *Genetic Psychology Monograms* 1, 1926, 231–407.

HJELMQUIST, ERLAND (ed.) 1978, *Kognitiv psykologi i undervisningen*. Almqvist & Wiksell, Stockholm.

HOFFMAN, LASSE 1975, Skolan i ett tvåspråkigt samhälle. In SKUTNABB-KANGAS 1975e, 38–40.

HOFFMAN, MOSES N. H. 1934, *The Measurement of Bilingual Background*. Contributions to Education No 623, Teachers College, Columbia University, New York.

HOLM, WAYNE 1975, The Development of Reading Material: The Rock Point (Navajo) Experience. In TROIKE & MODIANO 1975, 182–192.

HOLMESTAD, EINAR & LADE, ARILD JOSTEIN (eds) 1969, *Lingual Minorities in Europe*. A selection of papers from the European conference of lingual minorities in Oslo. Det norske Samlaget, Oslo.

HOLMSTRAND, LARS 1975, *Presentation av EPÅL,-projektet. Bakgrund problem och uppläggning*. Pedagogiska inst, Lärarhögskolan i Uppsala, Report nr 54.

– 1978a, Den optimala tidpunkten för påbörjandet av undervisning i främmande språk. In GREGERSEN, BASBØLL & MEY 1978, 101–107.

– 1978b, *Effekterna på allmänna färdigheter och attityder i skolan av tidigt påbörjad undervisning i engelska.* En delstudie inom EPÅL-projektet, Pedagogisk forskning i Uppsala nr 2, 1978.

– 1979a, *De långsiktiga effekterna på allmänna färdigheter och attityder i skolan av tidigt påbörjad undervisning i engelska.* En delstudie inom EPÅL-projektet, Pedagogisk forskning i Uppsala nr 10, 1979.

– 1979b, *The Effects on General School Achievement of Early Commencement of English Instruction.* Uppsala Reports on Education No 4, 1979.

– 1980, Effekterna på kunskaper, färdigheter och attityder av tidigt påbörjad undervisning i engelska. En delstudie inom EPÅL-projektet, Pedagogisk forskning i Uppsala nr 18, 1980.

HORN, THOMAS D. (ed.) 1970, *Reading for the Disadvantaged. Problems of Linguistically Different Learners.* Harcourt, Brace & World, New York.

HORNBY, PETER A. (ed.) 1977, *Bilingualism. Psychological, Social and Educational Implications.* Academic Press, Inc, New York.

HORST, CHRISTIAN 1980, Arbejdskraft: vare eller menneske? *Migration og vesteuropæisk kapitalisme.* Akademisk Forlag, Copenhagen.

HOVDHAUGEN, EVEN (ed.) 1975, *Papers from the Second Scandinavian Conference of Linguists.* Lysebu, Dept, of Linguistics, University of Oslo.

– 1976, *Språkminoriteter. Noen eksempler på slike minoriteter og synspunkter på de problemer som språkminoriteter mer generelt har.* Background material for a lecture given at a Nordic research seminar on minorities, Airisto, 1976.

HOYER, A. E. & HOYER, G. 1924, Über die Lallsprache eines Kindes, *Zeitschrift für angewandte Psychologie*, 24, 363–384.

HUANG, J. & HATCH, E. 1978, A Chinese Child's Acquisition of English. In HATCH (ed.) 1978, 118–131.

HUFSTEDLER, SHIRLEY 1980. On bilingual education, civil rights and language minority regulations, *NABE-Journal* 5:1 (Fall), 63–69.

HUFVUDSTADSBLADET, Helsingfors.

HUMMELSTEDT, CHRISTER (ed.) 1973, *Folkmålsstudier* XXIII. Meddelanden från föreningen för nordisk filologi, Svenskans beskrivning 7, Helsingfors.

HUOVINEN, SULO 1977, *Europa: Språkpolitisk översikt* (preliminary version), manuscript.

HYLTENSTAM, KENNETH 1979a, Tröskelnivån i ett språkinlärnings- och språkundervisningsperspektiv. In *Invandrarundervisning. Aspekter på alfabetisering och den första nivån.* Praktisk lingvistik 2, Dept. of Linguistics, Univ. of Lund.

– (ed.) 1979b, *Svenska i invandrarperspektiv*, LiberLäromedel, Lund.

HYMES, DELL (ed.) 1964, Language in Culture and Society. A Reader in Linguistics and Anthropology. Row & Harpers, New York.

– 1974, *Foundations of Sociolinguistics.* University of Pennsylvania Press, Philadelphia.

IANCO-WORRALL, ANITA 1972, Bilingualism and Cognitive Development. *Child Development* 43, 1390–1400.

I-AZAM, FAROOQ, KHAN, WALLAIT, RIGAS, STATHIS, SIDDIQI, NAJMA, SKUTNABB-KANGAS, TOVE & ÖZCAN, MEHMET 1980, Dansk invandrarrapport underblåser fördomar. *Invandrare och Minoriteter* 2, 1980.

IMEDADZE, N. V. 1960, On the Psychological Nature of Early Bilingualism

(translated from K psikhologichoskoy priorode rannego dvuyazyehiya. *Voprosy Psikhologii* 6, 60–68, quoted in CUMMINS 1977c).
– 1967, On the Psychological Nature of Child Speech Formation under Conditions of Exposure to two Languages. *International Journal of Psychology*, 2, 129–132.
INFORMATION, Copenhagen.
Invandrarutredningen
1971 1. *Invandrarnas utbildningssituation. Förslag om grundutbildning i svenska för vuxna invandrare, SOU 1971:51.* Stockholm.
1972 2. *Tolkservice. Nordisk språkkonvention, SOU 1972:83.* Stockholm.
1974 3. *Invandrarna och minoriteterna, SOU 1974: 69.* Stockholm.
1974 4. *Bilagedel, SOU 1974:70.* Stockholm.
INGLEHART, R. F. & WOODWARD, M. 1972, Language Conflicts and Political Community. In GIGLIOLI (ed.) 1972, 358–377.
INGRAM, ELISABETH 1976, *Criteria for Determining Bilingualism*. Paper presented at a Nordic research seminar on minorities, Airisto, 1976.
ISRAEL, JOACHIM 1973, *Sociologi*. Del 2. *Makt, Språk*. Aldus series 402, Stockholm.

JAAKKOLA, MAGDALENA 1969, *Kielten erikoistuminen ja sen seuraukset Ruotsin Tornionlaaksossa.* Research Reports No 137, Inst of Sociology, University of Helsinki.
– 1973, *Språkgränsen. En studie i tvåspråkighetens sociologi.* Aldus series 408, Malmö.
– 1974, Den språkliga variationen i svenska Tornedalen. In LOMAN (ed.) 1974a, 15–42.
– 1976a, Diglossia and Bilingualism among two Minorities in Sweden. *International Journal of the Sociology of Language* 10.
JACKSON, PATRICK M. (ed.) 1931, *Maori and Education, or the Education of Natives in New Zealand and Its Dependencies.* Ferguson and Osborn Limited, Wellington.
JAKOBOVITS, LEON 1968, Dimensionality of Compound-Coordinate Bilingualism. *Language Learning*, Special issue No. 3, 29–49.
JAKOBSON, ROMAN 1941, *Kindersprache, Aphasie und allgemeine Lautgesetze.* Uppsala 1941 (reprinted from Språkvetenskapliga Sällskapets i Uppsala Förhandlingar 1940–42).
JAKOBSON, ROMAN & KAWAMOTO, SHIGEO (eds). 1970, *Studies in General and Oriental Linguistics, Presented to Shiro Hattori on the Occasion of His Sixtieth Birthday.* TEC Company, Tokyo.
JALAVA, ANTTI 1976, *Jag har inte bett att få komma.* Bonniers, Stockholm.
– 1978, Mitt språk är min hud. *Författaren* 3.
– 1980, Ingen kunde märka att jag var finne. In *Finsk i Sverige*. Utbildningsradion, Stockholm, 2–6.
– 1980, Kukaan ei voinut huomata että olin suomalainen. In *Ruotsinsuomalaisuus*. Utbildningsradion, Stockholm, 2–6.
JAMES, C. B. E. 1947, *A Comparative Study of General Performance between Bilingual and Monoglot Children in South Wales.* Ph.D. Thesis, Edinburgh University.
JAMIESON, E. & SANDIFORD, P. 1928, The Mental Capacity of Southern Ontario Indians, *Journal of Educational Psychology*, 19, 313–328.
JÄNICKE, GISBERT 1980, Förord. *Mem och Zin* 1980, 5–11.
JÄRTELIUS, ARNE & MONICA 1978, *Så blev mitt liv i Sverige*. Liber Förlag Stockholm.

JAUHO, SIRKKA & LOIKKANEN, MIRJA 1974, *Finska invandrarbarn i svensk skola. En språkundersökning bland finska invandrarbarn i Göteborg.* Pro gradu dissertation in Nordic languages, University of Tampere.

JENCKS, C. *et al.* 1979, *Who gets ahead?* Basic Books, New York.

JENSEN, A. R. 1973, Intelligence, Learning Ability and Socioeconomics Status. In WISEMAN 1973a, 230–243.

JERNUDD, BJÖRN H. 1976, The Study of Language and Language Problems. In *Språkvitenskapens forhold til samfunnsvitenskapene.* Rapport fra en konferanse. Rådet for humanistisk forskning i Norges almenvitenskapelige forskningsråd, 1976, Oslo, 53–75.

– 1979, *The Language Survey of Sudan. The first Phase: A Questionnaire Survey in Schools.* Acta Universitatis Umensis, Umeå Studies in Humanities 22, Umeå.

JERNUDD, BJÖRN H. & DAS GUPTA, JYOTIRINDRA 1971, Towards a Theory of Language Planning. In RUBIN & JERNUDD (eds) 1971.

JOHANSSON, HENNING & WILKSTRÖM, JOEL 1974, *Definition och mätning av tvåspråkighet – en litteraturgranskning.* Pedagogiska monografier no 15, Umeå.

JONES, W. R. 1952, The Language Handicap in Welsh-speaking Children. *British Journal of Educational Psychology* 22, 114–123

JUNGO, M. 1978, Bibliographie für eine Didaktik der frühen Zweisprachigkeit zugunsten von Unterschichts-, insb. Fremdarbeiterkindern, Institut für Pädagogik, Universität Fribourg.

KAILAS, UUNO 1932, *Runoja.* Werner Söderström Oy, Porvoo.

KÄLLSTRÖM, ROGER, 1982, *Rektorsområdesundersökningen,* University of Gothenburg, SPRINS Project 9.

KANGAS, TOVE – see SKUTNABB-KANGAS, TOVE.

KATZ, IRWIN 1973a, Alternatives to a Personality-Deficit Interpretation of Negro Under-Achievement. In WATSON 1973a, 377–391.

– 1973b, Negro Performance in Interracial Situations. In WATSON 1973a, 256–266.

KATZ, JUDY 1982, Multicultural Education: Games Educators Play. *Multiracial Education* 1982, 10:2, 11–18.

KELLY, L. G. (ed.) 1969, *Description and Measurement of Bilingualism: An International Seminar.* University of Moncton, University of Toronto Press.

KESKIN, HAKKI 1978, *Die Türkei. Vom Osmanischen Reich zum Nationalstaat – Werdegang einer Unterentwicklung,* Verlag Olle & Wolter, Berlin.

KESSLER, CAROLYN 1971, *The Acquisition of Syntax in Bilingual Children.* Georgetown University Press, Washington, D.C.

KEY, MAR" RITCHIE 1977, Nonverbal Communication: A Research Guide and Bibliography, Scarecrow Press.

KEY-ÅBERG, SANDRO 1973. Språket som kommunikationsmedel. *Att undervisa* 1, 1973, 13–15.

KHAN, VERITY SAIFULLAH 1977. *Bilingualism and Linguistic Minorities.* The Runnymede Trust.

– 1980. The "Mother-tongue" of Linguistic Minorities in Multicultural England. *Journal of Multilingual and Multicultural Development.* 1:1, 71–88.

KHAN, WALLAIT, ERDEM, MAHMUT, RIGAS, STATHIS, ÖZCAN, MEHMET & MILJEVIĊ, GEORGE 1980, *Til Folketingets Ombudsman.* Copenhagen, 30.6.1980.

KINTSCH, W & KINTSCH, E. 1969, Interlingual Interference and Memory Processes, *Journal of Verbal Learning and Verbal Behavior* 9, 405–409.

KIRK, S. A., MCCARTHY, J. J. & KIRK, W. D. 1968, *Illinois Test of Psycholinguistic Abilities. Examiner's Manual*. University of Illinois Press, Urbana (revised ed.).

KLASSEKAMPEN, Oslo.

KLEBAK, SØREN & HORST, CHRISTIAN 1978, *Fremmedarbejderbørn/danske børn – lige vilkår? Sundhedstilstand og brug af medicinsk og social profylakse*. Dept. of Social Medicine, University of Copenhagen, publication 8.

– 1979, Intervju av Lene Frøslev, "Fremmedarbejderne er bange for alt der har met det offentlige at gøre", *Information* 3.4.1979.

KLEIN, GILLIAN 1982. *Resources for multicultural education: an introduction*, Longman for Schools Council, London.

KLEIVAN, INGE 1976, Lecture given at the Nordic research seminar on minorities, Airisto, August 1976.

– 1977, Hvorfor kan danskere i Grønland ikke grønlandsk? In SKUTNABB-KANGAS 1977a, 163–176.

KLEIVEN, JO (ed.) 1979, *Språk og samfunn. Bidrag till en norsk sosiolingvistikk*. Pax Forlag, Oslo.

KLOSS, HEINZ 1969, *Research Possibilities on Group Bilingualism: A Report*, International Center for Research on Bilingualism, Quebec, B18.

KNUBB-MANNINEN, GUNNEL 1982, *Språksituationen bland eleverna i de svenskspråkiga grundskolorna*, Reports from the Institute for Educational Research 326/1982, University of Jyväskylä.

KOIRANEN, VILHO 1966, *Suomalaisten siirtolaisten sulautuminen Ruotsissa*. Porvoo.

KOIVISTO V. 1975, Om zigenarspråkets ställning i Finland. In SKUTNABB-KANGAS 1975e, 61–62.

KOIVUKANGAS, OLAVI & TOIVONEN, SIMO 1978, *Suomen siirtolaisuuden ja maassamuuton bibliografia. A Bibliography on Finnish Emigration and Internal Migration*. Migrationsinstitutet, Åbo.

KOLASA, BLAIR JOHN 1954, *The Relationship Between Bilingualism and Performance on a Linguistic Type Intelligence Test*. Ph.D. Thesis, University of Pittsburg.

KOLERS, PAUL 1963, Interlingual Word Associations. *Journal of Verbal Learning and Verbal Behavior*, 2, 291–300.

– 1965, Bilingualism and Bicodalism. *Language and Speech* 8, 122–126.

– 1966, Reading and Talking Bilingually. *American Journal of Psychology* 79, 357–376.

– 1968, Bilingualism and information processing. *Scientific American*. March, 78–86.

KORBØL, AUD 1979, Norsk race relations industry. *Invandrare och Minoriteter* 1–2, 1979, 5–7.

KOSKINEN, IRINA 1974, Svensk interferens i tornedalsfinskan. In LOMAN (ed.) 1974a, 109–121.

KOTSINAS, ULLA 1981, Come and Go: Tense and Aspect in Immigrant Swedish, in DITTMAR & KÖNIGER (eds) 1981, 112–129.

KRAMER, JULIAN Y. 1979, Kontaktmønster blant inderne i Drammen. In TAMBS-LYCHE (ed.) 1979, 22–37.

– 1980, Indiske fremmedarbeidere i Drammen – middelkasse på permisjon. In RINGEN (ed.) 1980, 185–210.

KRASHEN, S. D. 1973, Lateralization, Language Learning, and the Critical Period: Some New Evidence. *Language Learning* 23, 63–74.

– 1975, Additional Dimensions of the Deductive/Inductive Controversy. *Modern Language Journal* 59, 440–441.
KRASHEN, STEPHEN 1981a, Bilingual Education and Second Language Acquisition Theory, in *Schooling and Language Minority Students* 1981, 51–79.
– 1981b, Second Language Acquisition and Second Language Learning, Pergamon Press, London.
KREITOR, NIKOLAJ-KLAUS VON (ed.) 1980a, *Minoritet, kultur, identitet. En antologi.* Invandrarförlaget, Borås.
KÜHN, HEINZ 1979, Memorandum zur Integration der Arbeitsimmigranten in der BRD. Stand und Weiterentwicklung der Integration der ausländischen Arbeitnehmer und Ihrer Familien in der Bundesrepublik Deutschland, *Deutsch Lernen* 3, 82–99.
KÜNG, ANDRES 1974, *Sverige, Sverige, fosterland!* Aldus series 414, Aldus/Bonniers, Stockholm.
KUUSELA, JORMA 1973, *Finnar i Sverige. En studie av assimilation och anpassning.* Essay, Dept. of Sociology, University of Stockholm, No. 4, 1973.

LABOV, WILLIAM 1966, *The Social Stratification of English in New York City.* Urban Language Series no 1, Center for Applied Linguistics, Washington, D.C.
– 1972a (1969), The Logic of Nonstandard English. In GIGLIOLI 1972, 179–215.
– 1972b, Resolution . . . prepared in 1970 and revised following the December 28, 1971 LSA open meeting on "Linguistics and the IQ controversy". *LSA (Linguistic Society of America) Bulletin* No. 52, March 1972, 17–18.
Lagstadgade kulturella minoritetsrättigheter i Sverige 1978, Seminar organised by Rättsfonden 15.4.77 at Lidingö, Rättsfonden, Stockholm.
LAMBERT, WALLACE E. 1955, Measurement of the Linguistic Dominance in Bilinguals. *Journal of Abnormal and Social Psychology* 50, 197–200.
– 1967, A Social Psychology of Bilingualism. *Journal of Social Issues* 23, 1967.
– 1969, Psychological Studies of the Interdependencies of the Bilingual's Two Languages. In PUHVEL (ed.) 1969, 99–126.
– 1972, *Language, Psychology and Culture.* Essays by Wallace E. Lambert, selected and introduced by Anwar S. Dil. Stanford University Press, Stanford, Cal.
– 1974, A Canadian Experiment in the Development of Bilingual Competence. *Canadian Modern Language Review,* 31:2, 108–116.
– 1975, Culture and Language as Factors in Learning and Education. In WOLFGANG (ed.) 1975.
– 1979, *Cognitive, Attitudinal and Social Consequences of Bilingualism.* Paper presented at SEAMEO Regional Language Centre 14th Regional Seminar, Singapore, 1979.
– 1981, *Cognitive Accompaniment of Bilingualism.* Paper prepared for The Third Annual Conference of Psychologists of Upstate New York on Brain and Language, September 26, 1981, Colgate University, Hamilton, New York.
– 1983, Deciding on Language of Instruction: Psychological and Social Considerations, in HUSÉN, T. & OPPER (eds), *Multicultural and Multilingual Education in Immigrant Countries,* Wenner-Gren Symposium, August 1982, Pergamon Press Ltd (in press).
LAMBERT, WALLACE E. & GARDNER, R. C. 1972, *Attitudes and Motivation in Second Language Learning.* Newbury House. Mass.
LAMBERT, WALLACE E., GARDNER, R. C., OLTON, R. & TUNSTALL, K. 1970, A

Study of the Roles of Attitudes and Motivation in Second-language Learning. In FISHMAN 1970a, 473–491.

LAMBERT, WALLACE E., HAVELKA, J. & CROSBY, C. 1958, The Influence of Language Acquisition Context on Bilingualism. *Journal of Abnormal and Social Psychology* 56, 239–244.

LAMBERT, WALLACE E., HAVELKA, J. & GARDNER, R. C. 1959, Linguistic Manifestations of Bilingualism. *American Journal of Psychology* 72, 77–82.

LAMBERT, WALLACE E., IGNATOW, M. & KRAUTHAMMER, M. 1968, Bilingual Organization in Free Recall, *Journal of Verbal Learning and Verbal Behavior* 7, 207–214.

LAMBERT, WALLACE E., JUST, M. & SEGALOWITZ, N. 1970, Some Cognitive Consequences of Following the Curricula of the Early School Grades in a Foreign Language. In ALATIS (ed.) 1970, 229–280.

LAMBERT, WALLACE E. & MACNAMARA, J, 1969, Some Cognitive Consequences of Following a First Grade Curriculum in a Second Language. *Journal of Educational Psychology* 60, 86–96.

LAMBERT, WALLACE E. & PRESTON, M. S. 1965, *The Interdependency of the Bilingual's Two Languages*. Paper presented at the Verbal Behavior Conference, New York City, 1965, quoted in FISHMAN 1968).

LAMBERT, WALLACE E. & RAWLINGS, C. 1969, Bilingual Processing of Mixed-Language Associative Networks. *Journal of Verbal Learning and Verbal Behavior* 8, 604–609.

LAMBERT, WALLACE E. & TAYLOR, D. M. 1982, Language in the Education of Ethnic Minority Immigrants: Issues, Problems and Methods. Paper presented at the conference on The Education of Ethnic Minority Immigrants, December 13–16, 1981, Miami, Florida (in press).

LAMBERT, WALLACE E. & TUCKER, G. RICHARD 1972, *Bilingual Education of Children. The St. Lambert Experiment.* Newbury House Publishers, Rowley, Mass.

LAMBERT, WALLACE E., TUCKER, G. RICHARD & D'ANGLEJAN, ALISON 1973, Cognitive and Attitudinal Consequences of Bilingual Schooling: the St. Lambert Project through Grade Five. *Journal of Educational Psychology* 65:2, 141–159.

LAMY, PAUL 1978, *"Personality" vs. "Territoriality" in Language Status Planning: The Canadian Case.* Paper presented at the 5th International Congress of Applied Linguistics, Montreal, 1978.

LANDÉN, RAGNAR 1971, Inställningen till zigenare vid en större affärsgata i Stockholm. In TRANKELL (ed.) 1971, 131–176.

LANDRY, R. G. 1974, A Comparison of Second Language Learners and Monolinguals on Divergent Thinking Tasks at the Elementary School Level. *Modern Language Journal* 58, 10–15.

LANGLOIS, A. & WEST, T. 1978, *Bilingualism and Adult Aphasia: Research Needs and Clinical Implications.* Paper presented at the 5th International Congress of Applied Linguistics, Montreal, 1978.

Language Planning Newsletter 1975–. East–West Center, Honolulu, Hawaii.

LAR, REDE 1974, *Communication Interference and Bilingual Groups. Bilingual Education.* An occasional paper from The Centre for the Study of Teaching, La Trobe University School of Education, Bundoora, Victoria, Australia.

LARDOT, RAISA 1977, *Ripaskalintu.* Helsinki.

LARSEN, MOGENS BAUMANN 1974, Omkring en testning af den regionale variation i tornedalsområdet. In Loman 1974a, 207–225.

LASONEN, KARI 1978a. *Ruotsin suomalaiset siirtolaisoppilaat.* Osa I. *Teoreettinen viitekehys, Ruotsin suomalaisten siirtolaisoppilaiden kasvatuksen tarkastelua kulttuurin, kielen ja eräiden muiden tekijöiden kannalta.* Research Reports no 65, 1978, Dept. of Education, University of Jyväskylä.

– 1978b, *Ruotsin suomalaiset siirtolaisoppilaat,* Osa II. *Empiirinen tutkimus, Äidinkielellä tapahtuvan opetuksen merkitys Ruotsin suomalaisten siirtolaisoppilaiden koulunkäyntiin peruskoulun ala-asteella.* Research Reports no 66, 1977, Dept of Education, University of Jyväskylä.

LASONEN, KARI & TOUKOMAA, PERTTI 1978, *Linguistic Development and School Achievement among Finnish Immigrant Children in Mother-Tongue Medium Classes in Sweden.* Research Reports no 70, 1978, University of Jyväskylä. Dept of Education.

LAURÉN, CHRISTER (ed.) 1978, *Finlandssvenskan. Fakta och debatt.* Söderström & Co Förlags AB, Borgå.

LAURÉN, KERSTIN 1973, Nationellt främlingsskap och tonårsidentitetsproblem. *Socialmedicinsk Tidsskrift* 6.

LAWTON, DENIS 1970,(1968), *Social Class, Language and Education,* Routledge & Kegan Paul, London.

LEGARRETA-MARCAIDA, DOROTHY 1981, Effective Use of the Primary Language in the Classroom, in *Schooling and Language Minority Students* 1981, 83–116.

LEHMANN, WINFRED P. (ed.) 1975, *Language and Linguistics in the People's Republic of China.* University of Texas Press. Austin & London.

Leitlinien der Landesregierung Nordrhein-Westfalen zur Ausländerpolitik. 1980. Ministerium für Arbeit, Gesundheit und Soziales des Landes NW, Düsseldorf, Sept. 1980.

LENNEBERG, E. H. 1967, *Biological Foundations of Language* (with appendices by Noam Chomsky and Otto Marx). Wiley, New York.

LEOPOLD, WERNER F. 1939–1949, *Speech Development of a Bilingual Child; A Linguist's Record.* Northwestern University Press, Evanston, Ill.

LEPPINEN, ANJA 1980, Mönstret. *Folktidningen Ny Tid* 16.10.1980.

LESSER, G. S., FEIFFER, G. & CLARKE, D. H. 1973, Mental Abilities of Children from Different Social-Class and Cultural Groups. In WISEMAN 1973a, 279–291.

LESTER, O. F. 1929, Performance Tests and Foreign Children. *Journal of Educational Psychology* 20, 1929, 303–309.

LETH-MØLLER, HELLE & PONTOPPIDAN, LONE (eds) *Litteratur om Indvandrere, Annoteret bibliografi 1981, Dokumentation om indvandrere. Bibliografi 1.* Mellemfolkeligt samvirke, Copenhagen.

LEWIS, E. GLYN 1972, *Multilingualism in the Soviet Union.* Mouton, The Hague.

– 1977, Bilingualism and Bilingual Education – The Ancient World to the Rennaissance. In SPOLSKY & COOPER (eds) 1977, 22–93.

– 1978, Bilingual Education and Social Change in the Soviet Union. In SPOLSKY & COOPER (eds) 1978, 203–248.

LEYBA, CHARLES F., MILLER, JAMES P. & ROMERO, MARIANO 1978, *Longitudinal Study Title VII Bilingual Program.* Santa Fe Public Schools, Santa Fe, New Mexico, National Dissemination and Assessment Center, California State University, Los Angeles.

LIEBKIND, KARMELA 1979, *The Social Psychology of Minority Identity. A Case*

Study of Intergroup Identification. Theoretical Refinement and Methodological Experimentation. Research Reports no 2, Dept of Social Psychology, University of Helsinki.

LIEDKE, W. & NELSON, L. 1968, Concept Formation and Bilingualism. *Alberta Journal of Educational Research* 14, 225–232.

LILJESTRÖM, RITA 1979, Invandrarnas barn, skolan och framtiden. In Svensk Invandrarpolitik inför 1980-talet, 15–57.

LIND MELØY, L. 1980, *Internatliv i Finnmark. Skolepolitikk 1900–1940*, Det Norske Samlaget, Oslo.

LINDMAN, RALF & ALHO, LASSE 1971, *Språkfärdighetstest i svenska och finska. Mätning och standardisering på en tvåspråkig population.* Svenska litteratursällskapets i Finland Nämnd för samhällsforskning, Forskningsrapport no 12.

LINDROOS, REIJO 1980, *Aseidenriisunta ja työllisyys* (Nedrustningen och sysselsättningen. En undersökning av upprustningens inverkan på sysselsättningen och möjligheterna att stegvis omvandla vapenproduktion till civil produktion). Freds-och konfliktforskningsinstitutet, Tammerfors.

LINELL, PER 1978, *Människans språk. En orientering om språk, tänkande och kommunikation.* LiberLäromedel, Lund.

LIUNGMAN, CARL G. 1970, *Myten om intelligensen. En bok om intelligens, arv och miljö.* Bokförlaget Prisma, Stockholm.

LOEWE, RICHARD 1888, Die Dialektmischung im magdeburgischen Gebiete. *Jahrbuch des Vereins für niederdeutsche Sprachforschung* XIV, 14–52.

LÖFGREN, HORST & OUVINEN-BIRGERSTAM, PIRJO 1980, *Försök med en tvåspråkig modell för undervisning av invandrarbarn.* Pedagogiska rapporter 22, 1980 Pedagogiska inst, University of Lund.

– 1983, A Bilingual Model for the Teaching of Immigrant Children, *Journal of Multilingual and Multicultural Development*, 3:4, 323–331.

LOMAN, BENGT 1969, Språksociologi. In LOMAN *et al.* 1969, 217–240.

– (ed.), 1972a, *Språk och samhälle. Språksociologiska problem.* Gleerups, Lund.

– 1972b, Om talspråkets varianter. In LOMAN (ed.), 1972a, 45–74.

– (ed), 1974a, *Språk och samhälle 2. Språket i Tornedalen.* Gleerups, Lund.

– 1974b, Inledning. In LOMAN (ed.), 1974a.

– 1974c, Till frågan om tvåspråkighet och halvspråkighet i Tornedalen. In LOMAN (ed.), 1974a, 43–79.

– 1974d, Attityder till tornedalssvenskan. In LOMAN (ed.), 1974a, 189–206.

– 1975, Halvspråkighet eller papegojsvenska? *Invandrare och Minoriteter* 4, 1975, 27–28.

– 1977, Paneldiskussion om dubbel halvspråkighet. In SKUTNABB-KANGAS 1977a, 212–227.

– 1978a, "Man kan inte skrämma folk till tvåspråkighet", *Invandrare och Minoriteter* 3–4, 1978, 35–43.

– 1978b, Siirtolaisuus ja kieli. *Siirtolaisuus* 1, 1–10.

LOMAN, BENGT *et al.* 1968, *Språket i blickpunkten.* Skrifter utgivna av svensklärarföreningen 110.

LOMAN, BENGT & JÖRGENSEN, NILS 1971, *Manual för analys och beskrivning av makrosyntagmer.* Lundastudier i Nordisk språkvetenskap, series c no 1, Lund.

LONDEN, ANNE-MARIE & SKUTNABB-KANGAS, TOVE 1976a, *Minun ja muiden kieli. 1. Kielipelien sääntöjä. 2. Ymmärtääkö juoksupoika konttorityttöä? Auttaako koulu? 3. Från halvspråkighet till kaksikielisyys.* Yleisradio, Kouluradio, Helsinki.

LOONA, SUNIL 1977, *Sosiolingvistikk og tospråklighet.* Migrasjonspedagogisk informasjon nr 7/77, Skolesjefen i Oslo, Undervisningen af fremmedspråklige elever.
– 1980, *Power and Ideology in the Education of Ethnic Minorities in Norway: a Historial Perspective.* Unpublished manuscript, Aug. 1980 (A Norwegian version, Innvandrerbarn i norsk skole, in *Pedagogen*, Oct. 1980, is almost identical).
LOPEZ, M. & YOUNG, R. K. 1974, The Linguistic Interdependence of Bilinguals. *Journal of Experimental Psychology* 102, 981–983
LOPEZ, M., HICKS, R. E. & YOUNG, R. K. 1974, Retroactive inhibition in a bilingual A-B, A-B paradigm. *Journal of Experimental Psychology* 103, 85–90.
LOURIE, MARGARET A. & CONKLIN, NANCY FAIRES (eds) 1978, *A Pluralistic Nation. The Language Issue in the United States.* Newbury House Publishers, Rowley, Mass.
LOZANOV, GEORGI 1978, *Suggestology and Outlines of Suggestopaedia*, Gordon and Breach Science Publishers, Inc., New York.
LUNDEMARK, ERIK 1980, *Arbetsstugorna, Tornedalica* nr 30, I-Tryck, Luleå.
LURIA, A. R. 1973, *The Working Brain.* Penguin, Baltimore, Maryland.
LURIA, A. R. & YUDOVICH, F. 1971, *Speech and the Development of Mental Processes in the Child.* Penguin, Harmondsworth, Middlesex.
LYONS, JOHN (ed.) 1970a, *New Horizons in Linguistics.* Penguin, Harmondsworth, Middlesex.
– 1970b, Introduction. In LYONS (ed.) 1970a, 7–28.

MACKEY, WILLIAM F. 1969, Introduction. How Can Bilingualism Be Described and Measured? In KELLY (ed.) 1970, 1–9.
– 1970, The Description of Bilingualism. In FISHMAN (ed.) 1970a, 554–584.
– 1972, A Typology of Bilingual Education. In FISHMAN, JOSHUA A. (ed.) 1972a, 413–432.
– 1977, The Evaluation of Bilingual Education. In SPOLSKY & COOPER (eds) 1977, 226–281.
– 1978, Foreword. In ANDERSSON & BOYER 1978, 2nd ed, VII–XIII.
MACKEY, WILLIAM F. & ANDERSSON, THEODORE (eds) 1977, *Bilingualism in Early Childhood. Papers from a Conference on Child Language.* Newbury House Publishers, Rowley, Mass.
MACNAMARA, JOHN 1966, *Bilingualism and Primary Education.* Edinburgh.
– 1969, How Can One Measure the Extent of a Person's Bilingual Proficiency? In KELLY (ed.) 1969, 79–97.
– 1970, Bilingualism and Thought. In ALATIS (ed.) 1970, 25–45.
MÄGISTE, EDITH 1979, Utgör flerspråkighet en belastning på vissa hjärnfunktioner? In *Tvåspråkighet* 1979, 91–103.
MALCOLM, I. 1978, The West Australian Aborignal Child and Classroom Interaction: A Sociolinguistic Approach. *Journal of Pragmatics* 3, 305–320.
MALMBERG, BERTIL 1972 (1964) Språket och människan, Aldusserien A 100, Lund.
– 1973, *Förutsättningarna för invandrarbarnens tvåspråkighet.* "De finskspråkiga invandrarbarnens utbildningsmöjligheter i Sverige", Mattby, Finland, 1973.
– 1977, Finns halvspråkighet? *Sydsvenska Dagbladet* 21.11.1977.
MANNIL, RAGNAR 1978, Finlandssvenskarnas situation idag. Ett försök till analys av tendenser och prognoser inför framtiden. *Finlandssvensk odling* no. 3, Svenska Folkskolans Vänner, Helsingfors.

MATHIESEN, THOMAS 1980, *Den dolda disciplineringen. Essäer om politisk kontroll.* Bokförlaget Korpen. Göteborg.

MATUTE-BIANCI, MARIA 1982, *Bilingual education and school failure among Chicanos: rethinking the assumptions*, University of California, Santa Cruz, manuscript.

MAURICE, LOUIS J. & ROY, ROBERT R. 1976, A Measurement of Bilinguality Achieved in Immersion Programs. *Canadian Modern Language Review* 32:5, 575–581.

MAURUD, ØIVIND 1975, *Nabospråksförståelse i Skandinavia. En undersøkelse om gjensidig förståelse av tale- och skriftspråk i Danmark, Norge og Sverige.* Nordisk Utredningsserie 1976:13.

MCCORMACK, P. D. 1974, Bilingual Linguistic Memory: Independence or Interdependence; Two Stores or One. In CAREY (ed.) 1974.

– 1977, Bilingual Linguistic Memory, The Independence–Interdependence Issue Revisited. In HORNBY (ed.) 1977, 57–66.

MCINNIS, C. E. 1976, Three Studies of Experimental French Programs. *Canadian Modern Language Review* 33:2, 151–156.

MCLAUGHLIN, BARRY 1978, *Second-Language Acquisition in Childhood*. Lawrence Erlbaum Associates Publishers, Hillsdale, New Jersey.

MCRAE, KENNETH D. 1978, Bilingual Language Districts in Finland and Canada: Adventures in the Transplanting of an Institution, *Canadian Public Policy*, Vol. 4, 331–351.

– (forthcoming) *Conflict and Compromise in Multilingual Societies*, 3 volumes, Wilfred Laurier University Press.

MEAD, M. 1927, Group Intelligence and Linguistic Disability Among Italian Children. *School and Society* 25, 1927, 465–468.

Mem och Zin 1980, Det kurdiska nationaleposet i tolkning och översättning från engelska av Robert Alftan. Med inledning av Gisbert Jänicke. Samt översättarens radiodramatisering av eposet. Revolt-förlaget, Box 8, 00811 Helsingfors 81.

MEY, JACOB 1978, Reflections of a reformed MCP. In GREGERSEN, BASBØLL & MEY (eds) 1978, 467–470.

– 1981. *Whose language?* (preliminary title). Mouton, The Hague.

MIEMOIS, KARL JOHAN 1980, *Sociologiska synpunkter på tvåspråkighet. Den svenska befolkningen i Finland*, in EJERHED & HENRYSSON (eds) 1981, 262–271.

MIEMOIS, KARL JOHAN & STARCK, CHRISTIAN 1979, *Multiple and Varying Criteria for Membership in a Linguistic Minority. The Case of the Swedish Speaking Minority in Metropolitan Helsinki.* Research group for comparative sociology, University of Helsinki, Research reports No. 21.

Ministry of Health and Social Affairs 1982, Linguistic and Cultural Backing for Immigrant and Minority-Group Children of Pre-School Age, Summary, *SOU* (Statens Offentliga Utredningar) 1982:43, Stockholm.

MITCHELL, A. J. 1937, The Effect of Bilingualism in the Measurement of Intelligence. *Elementary School Journal* 38, 1937, 29–37.

Mitteilungen des Landspressedienstes des Abgeordnetenhauses 18.10.1973, Nordrhein-Westfalen.

MODIANO, NANCY 1966. *Reading Comprehension in the National Language: A Comparative Study of Bilingual and All-Spanish Approaches to Reading Instruction in Selected Indian Schools in the Highlands of Chiapas, Mexico*, Ph.D. Thesis, New York University.

– 1973, *Indian Education in the Chiapas Highlands*. Holt, Rinehart and Winston,

New York.
– 1975, Using Native Instructional Patterns for Teacher Training. In TROIKE &
MODIANO (eds) 1975, 347–355.
MONTELIUS, RAGNAR 1971, Dialektisk materialism och studiet av fördomar mot
invandrare. In TRANKELL (ed.) 1971, 211–231.
MOSSIGE, SVEIN, PETTERSEN, RITA BAST & BLAKAR, ROLV MIKKEL 1979,
Egocentrism and Inefficiency in the Communication of Families Containing
Schizophrenic Members. *Family Process* Vol. 18, 1979, 405–425.
MUKKA, TIMO K. 1964, *Maa on syntinen laulu.* Balladi, Gummerus, Jyväskylä.
MULLARD, CHRIS 1980. *Racism in Society and Schools: History, Policy and Practice,*
University of London Institute of Education, Centre for Multicultural Education,
Occasional Paper No. 1.
– 1981, The Social Context and Meaning of Multicultural Education, *Educational
Analysis* 1981, 3:1, 117–140.
– 1982a, Multiracial Education in Britain: From Assimilation to Cultural Pluralism,
in TIERNEY (ed.) 1982, 120–133.
– 1982b, The Racial Code: its features, rules and change, in BARTON (ed.) 1982.
MUNICIO, INGEGERD (ed.) 1981a, SPLIT-report, Vol. 1, Bilingualism, Models of
Education and Migration Policies, *Commission for Immigration Research Report*
1:1, Stockholm.
– (ed.) 1981b, SPLIT-report, Vol. 2, Family and Position in the Swedish Society,
Commission for Immigration Research Report 1:2, Stockholm.
MUNICIO, INGEGERD & MEISAARI-POLSA, TUIJA 1980, *Språkkunskaper och
levnadsförhållanden – En sekundäranalys av två undersökningar om invandrare i
Sverige 1975–76 (ULF och PRI).* Expertgruppen för invandringsforskning, report
no. 12.
MURRELL, M. 1966. Language Acquisition in a Trilingual Environment: Notes from
a Case Study. *Studia Linguistica* 20, 9–35.
Muttersprache Kurdisch 1980, KOMKAR-Publikation 2, 1980, Frankfurt/Main.

NAGY, GÉZA 1979, *Racist and Xenophobic Tendencies in Swedish Society and
Swedish Schools,* in MUNICIO (ed.) 1981a.
NAHMAD, SALOMON 1975, La Política Educativa en Regiones Interculturales de
México. In TROIKE & MODIANO (eds) 1975, 15–24.
National Indian Brotherhood; *Indian Control of Indian Education* 1972. Ottawa,
Ontario.
NAUCLÉR, KERSTIN 1983, Hemspråket i förskolan, *SPRINS-projektet* 19, University
of Gothenburg.
NELHANS, BERTIL 1975, *Lagstadgad undervisning i svenska för invandrare. En
sociologisk utredning om lagen om rätt til ledighet och lön vid deltagande i
svenskundervisning för invandrare.* Report no 1 from the language teaching
research center, Projekt LUSFI, University of Göteborg.
NEMSER, W. 1971, Approximative Systems of Foreign Language Learners. *IRAL* 9,
115–123.
NEUFELD, GERALD 1977, Language Learning Ability in Adults: A Study on the
Acquisition of Prosodic and Articulatory Features. *Working Papers on
Bilingualism* 12, 45–60.
NICKEL, G. (ed.) 1976, *Proceedings of the Fourth International Congress of Applied
Linguistics,* Vol. 3. Hochschul Verlag, Stuttgart.

NIEKE, WOLFGANG 1981, (Berichterstatter) Bericht über das Kolloquium zu Methodenproblemen bei den international vergleichenden Evaluationen von Modellversuchen zu Erziehung und Unterricht für Kinder von Wanderarbeitnehmern in den Mitgliedsstaaten der Europäischen Gemeinschaft, Durchgeführt von der Kommission der Europäischen Gemeinschaft, 20–21. 11. 1980, Brüssel.

NIEKE, WOLFGANG, BUDDE, HILDEGARD & HENSCHEID, RENATE 1982, *National Report on the German Federal Republic – Report for the project The Role of the Education System in the Process of Marginalization of Members of the Second Generation of Immigrant Workers*, Draft, Center for Multicultural Education, University of London Institute of Education (coordinator Jagdish Gundara).

NIELSEN, HENRIK 1978, Pilotundersøgelse vedrørende invandrerundervisningen på Ishøj Kommunes skolor 1977. *Invandrerrapport II*, Ishøj Kommune.

NIKOLINAKOS, MARIOS 1973, *Politische Ökonomie der Gastarbeiterfrage*, Rowolt Taschenbuchverlag, Hamburg.

– 1982, Research on migrant workers and the crisis of Western Capitalism, in PEURA (ed.) 1983.

NORDIN, KERSTIN 1974, Meningsbyggnaden hos åttondeklassister i Övertorneå. In LOMAN (ed.) 1974a, 140–168.

5. nordiska lingvistkonferensen – see PETTERSSON (ed.) 1979.

NORRGÅRD, DORIS 1978, *Språkgruppsidentifikation och dess styrka. En empirisk undersökning i Pargas*. Svenska litteratursällskapets i Finland Nämnd för samhällsforskning. Forskningsrapport no 30.

NORTHROP, F. S. C. 1946, *The Meeting of East and West: An Inquiry Concerning World Understanding*. The Macmillan Company, New York.

NOTT, C. R. & LAMBERT, W. E. 1968, Free Recall of Bilinguals. *Journal of Verbal Learning and Verbal Behavior*, 7, 1065–1071.

NYERERE, JULIUS 1981, U-landene må hålde sammen og udvikle samarbejdet, velkomsttale ved UNCTAD-konferensens åbning i Arusha, *Kontakt 3*, 1980/81, 43–47.

O'BARR, WILLIAM M. & O'BARR, JEAN F. (eds) 1976, *Language and Politics*. Mouton, The Hague.

ÖBERG, KJELL 1979, Samverkan och/eller konflikt. In *Svensk invandrarpolitik inför 1980-talet*, 1979, 58–81.

OESTREICHER, J. P. 1974, The Early Teaching of a Modern Language, Education and Culture. *Review of the Council for Cultural Cooperation of the Council of Europe* 24, 9–16.

OFSTAD, HARALD 1971, Identitet och minoritet. In SCHWARZ (ed.) 1971.

OKSAAR, ELS 1971, Språkpolitiken och minoriteterna. In SCHWARZ (ed.) 1971, 164–175.

OLLER, JOHN W. Jr. 1979, *Language Tests at School, A Pragmatic Approach*. Longman, London.

OPSAND, OLE-PETTER 1976a, *Språkundervisning, identitet og sosial fungering. Noen problemstillinger vedrörende fremmedspråklige elever i norsk skole*. Paper presented at the Nordic Research seminar on minorities, Airisto.

ORBLIN, HANNA 1980, *Erfarenheter om tidig flerspråkighet enligt metoden en person ett språk. Franska, finska och svenska i kontakt hos en invandrarfamilj i Sverige*, in EJERHED & HENRYSSON (eds) 1981, 280–290.

OSGOOD, CHARLES E. 1966 (1963), Language Universals and Psycholinguistics. In

GREENBERG (ed.) 1966, 299–322.
OSTERRIETH, P. 1974, The Four Belgian Research Projects: Introduction. *Council of Europe Information Bulletin* 1, 1974, 32–54. Documentation Centre for Education in Europe.
OTTOMEYER, KLAUS 1978, *Människan under kapitalismen*. Röda bokförlaget AB, Göteborg.
Oversikt over migrasjonsforskning i Norge 1979. Nyli avsluttete, igangværende og planlagte prosjekter, duplicated copy.
OXMAN, W. G. 1971, *The Effects of Ethnic Identity of Experimenter, Language of Experimental Task, Bilingual vs. Non-Bilingual School Attendance on the Verbal Task Performance of Bilingual Children of Puerto Rican Background*. Ph.D. Thesis, Fordham University, unpublished.

PALMBERG, ROLF 1977, Interlanguage and Interlanguage Studies – A Report, *Kielikeskusuutisia (Language Centre News)* 4, 1–8.
– 1980, *A Select Bibliography of Error Analysis and Interlanguage Studies*. Meddelanden från Stiftelsens för Åbo Akademi Forskningsinstitut no 53.
PARADIS, MICHEL (ed.) 1978a. *Aspects of Bilingualism*. Hornbeam Press Inc, Colombia, S C.
– 1978b, The Stratification of Bilingualism. In PARADIS (ed.) 1978a, 165–176.
– 1979, Bilingualism and Aphasia. In WHITAKER & WHITAKER (eds) 1979.
PATTANAYAK, D. P. 1970, *Language Policy and Programs*. Ministry of Education and Youth Service, Government of India, Publication No 898, Nasik.
– 1976, *Education for the Minority Children*. The Central Institute of Indian Languages, Mysore, manuscript.
PAULSTON, CHRISTINA BRATT 1974, *Questions Concerning Bilingual Education*. Paper presented at the Interamerican Conference on Bilingual Education, 1974.
– 1975a, Ethnic Relations and Bilingual Education: Accounting for Contradictory Data. *Working Papers on Bilingualism* 6, 1–44.
– 1975b, *Implications of Language Learning Theory for Language Planning: Concerns in Bilingual Education*. Papers in Applied Linguistics, Bilingual Education Series 1, Center for Applied Linguistics, Arlington, Vir.
– 1976, *Bilingual Education and its Evaluation: A Reaction Paper*. In Bilingual Education, Current Perspectives, Vol. Linguistics, 1977, 87–151.
– 1977a, Tvåspråkig utbildning i USA 1976. *Invandrare och Minoriteter*.
– 1977b, Theoretical Perspectives on Bilingual Education Programs, *Working Papers on Bilingualism* 13, 130–177.
– 1981, *Recent Developments in Research on Bilingual Education in the United States*, in Ejerhed & Henrysson (eds) 1981, 24–38.
– 1982, *A Critical Review of the Swedish Research and Debate about Bilingualism and Bilingual Education in Sweden from an International Perspective*, A Report to the National Swedish Board of Education.
PAULSTON, CHRISTINA BRATT & PAULSTON, ROLLAND G. 1977, Language and Ethnic Boundaries. In SKUTNABB-KANGAS 1977a.
PAULSTON, ROLLAND G. 1975, *Ethnic Revival and Educational Conflict in Swedish Lapland*. Univ. of Pittsburgh, Manuscript.
– 1976, *Separate Education as an Ethnic Survival Strategy: The Finlandssvenska Case*. Paper presented at the American Anthropological Association Annual Meeting. 1976, Washington, D.C.

PAVLOVITCH, M. 1920, *Le langage enfantin: Acquisition du serbe et du français par un enfant serbe*. Champion, Paris.

PEAL, E. & LAMBERT, W. E. 1962, *The Relation of Bilingualism to Intelligence*. Psychological Monographs 76: 546, 1–23.

PEDERSEN, JESPER BRUUS 1975, *Fremmedarbejdernes Boligforhold i Danmark. Nyt fra Samfundsvidenskaberne*. Forskningsrapport 76–1, Copenhagen.

PENFIELD, W. & ROBERTS, I. 1959, *Speech and Brain Mechanisms*. Princeton University Press, New Jersey.

PETTERSSON, ÅKE 1977, Barnspråk. In PETTERSSON & BADERSTEN 1977, 88–137.

PETTERSSON, ÅKE & BADERSTEN, LENNART (ed.) 1977, *Språk i utveckling*. LiberLäromedel, Lund.

PETTERSSON, THORE (ed.) 1979, Papers from the fifth Scandinavian Conference of Linguists; Almqvist & Wiksell International, Stockholm.

PETTIGREW, THOMAS F. 1964, *A Profile of the Negro American*. The University Series in Psychology, D. Van Nostrand Company Inc, Princeton, New Jersey.

PEURA, MARKKU (ed.) 1983, *Invandrarminoriteter och demokratisk forskning*, Riksförbundet Finska Föreningar, Stockholm.

PFEIFFER BRADLEY, ANITA 1975, Designing a Bilingual Curriculum, in TROIKE & MODIANO (eds), 1975, 132–139.

PHILLIPSON, ROBERT H. L. 1980, Analysis of the PIF Spoken Corpus. *PIF Working Papers* 6. University of Copenhagen.

PHILLIPSON, ROBERT 1983, *Good learning strategies in foreign language, second language and minority mother tongue contexts*, Paper presented at the Second International Conference on Minority Languages, Turku/Åbo, Finland, 6–12.6.1983.

PIAGET, JEAN 1971 (1959), *The Language and Thought of the Child*. Routledge & Kegan Paul, London, 3rd ed.

PIAGET, JEAN & INHELDER, B. 1958, *The Growth of Logical Thinking from Childhood to Adolescence*. New York.

PIENEMANN, MANFRED 1979a, The Second Language Acquisition of Immigrant Children. In FELIX (ed.) 1979, 41–56.

– 1979b, *Überlegungen zur Steuerung des Zweispracherwerbs ausländischer Arbeiterkinder*. Wuppertaler Arbeitspapiere zur Sprachwissenschaft no 1.

DIPIETRO, ROBERT J. 1970, Discovery of Universals in Multilingualism. In ALATIS (ed.) 1970, 13–22.

PINOMAA, MIRJA 1974a, Meningsbyggnaden hos tvåspråkiga tornedalingar. In LOMAN (ed.) 1974a, 122–139

– 1974b, Finsk interferens i tornedalssvenskan. In Loman (ed.) 1974a, 80–108.

PINTNER, R. 1923, Comparison of American and Foreign children on Intelligence Tests, *Journal of Educational Psychology*, 14, 292–295.

PINTNER, R & ARSENIAN, SETH 1937, The Relation of Bilingualism to Verbal Intelligence and School Adjustment. *Journal of Educational Research* 3, 255–263.

PINTNER, R. & KELLER, R. 1922, Intelligence Tests of Foreign Children, *Journal of Educational Psychology*, 13, 214–222.

PIPPING, KNUT 1969, Commentary on Robert Cooper's paper. In KELLY (ed.) 1969, 214–219.

PLATERO, DILLON 1975, Bilingual Education in the Navajo Nation. In TROIKE & MODIANO (eds) 1975, 54–61.

PLATZACK, CHRISTER (ed.) 1974, *Svenskans beskrivning* 8, University of Lund, Inst. for Nordic Languages.

POHL, J. 1965, Bilinguismes. Revue Roumaine de Linguistique 10, 343–349 (quoted in RŪĶE-DRAVIŅA 1967, 14).

POPLACK, SHANA 1978, Syntactic Structure and Social Function of Code-switching. *Centro de Estudios Puertorriqueños, Working Papers* 2. New York.

– 1979. "Sometimes I'll Start a Sentence in Spanish y termino en español": Toward a Typology of Code-Switching. *Centro de Estudios Puertorriqueños, Working Papers* 4.

PRESTON, M. S. & LAMBERT, WALLACE E. 1969, Interlingual Interference in a Bilingual Version of the Stroop Color-word Task. *Journal of Verbal Learning and Verbal Behavior* 8, 299–301.

PRIDE, J. B. 1970, Sociolinguistics. In LYONS (ed.) 1970a, 287–301.

PRIDE, J. B. & HOLMES, JANET 1972, *Sociolinguistics. Selected Readings*. Penguin Modern Linguistics Readings. Middlesex.

PUHVEL, JAAN (ed.) 1969, *Substance and Structure in Language*. University of California Press.

RABEL-HEYMAN, LILI 1978, But How Does a Bilingual Feel? Reflections on Linguistic Attitudes of Immigrant Academics. In PARADIS (ed.) 1978a, 220–228.

Race and Education in Britain 1960–1977, An Overview of the Literature, *Sage Race Relations Abstract 2* (4), November, 1977.

Racial Minorities and Public Housing. PEP (Political and Economic Planning), September 1975, Report no 556.

RADO, MARTHA 1074, *The Implications of Bilingualism. Bilingual Education*. An occasional Paper from The Centre for the Study of Teaching, La Trobe University School of Education, Bundoora, Victoria.

– 1976, *Language Use of Bilingual Adolescent: A Self-appraisal*. In CLYNE, 1976, 187–200.

– 1979, *Student versus Teacher-Centered Bilingual Education: A Neglected Question*. Paper presented at the SEAMEO Regional Language Centre, 14th Regional Seminar, Singapore, 1979.

RAHBEK PEDERSEN, BIRGITTE 1980a, *Invandrerbørnens sociokulturelle baggrund*. Paper presented at the annual meeting of Danish school psychologists 10.9.1980.

– 1980b, *Fremmed – for hvem? Om invandrerbørn i Danmark*. DLH Forsknings-serien 1, Lærerforeningernes materialudvalg, Copenhagen.

RALSTON, L. D. 1978, *"Speaking Well": Bi-dialectalism, Bi-culturalism and Diglossia in a West Indian Community*. Paper prepared for Society for Caribbean Linguistics Meeting 1978 at the University of the West Indies, Cave Hill, Barbados.

Rampton Report – West Indian children in our schools, Interim Report of the Committee of Inquiry into the Education of Children from Ethnic Minority Groups, Her Majesty's Stationery Office, London, June 1981.

RAMSEY, C. A. & WRIGHT, E. N. 1974, Age and Second Language Learning. *Journal of Social Psychology* 94, 115–121.

RAO, T. S. 1964, Development and Use of Directions Test for Measuring Degree of Bilingualism. *Journal of Psychological Researches* 8, 114–119.

RAVEM, R. 1978, Two Norwegian Children's Acquisition of English Syntax. In HATCH (ed.) 1978, 148–154.

RAVEN, J. C. 1965, *Guide to Using the Coloured Progressive Matrices, Sets A. Ab. B.* H. K. Lewis & Co Ltd, London.

RAY, PUNYA SLOKA 1970, Language Standardization. In FISHMAN (ed.) 1970a, 755–765.

REDFERN, EDITH, 1979, personal communication.

REICH, HANS H. 1979, Deutschlehrer für Gastarbeiterkinder: Eine Übersicht über Ausbildungsmöglichkeiten in der Bundesrepublik. *Deutsch Lernen* 3, 3–14.

REKDAL, OLAUG 1975a, *Impulser til kvinneforskningen.* Dept. of Nordic Languages and Literature, University of Oslo, manuscript.

– 1975b, *De spør hva språket er.* Dept. of Nordic Languages and Literature, University of Oslo, manuscript.

– 1977, Kontekstavhengig variasjon i Oslomål. In Hermann, Ahlgren, Anward & Rossipal 1977, 83–89.

– 1979, Språksosiologien og kjønnsrollespråkene & erobringer av språket. In KLEIVEN (ed.) 1979, 107–208.

REKDAL, OLAUG & SKUTNABB-KANGAS, TOVE 1979, Kvinnoperspektiv på språk. In WESTMAN BERG (ed.) 1979, 49–69.

Resolution 1973. De finskspråkiga invandrarbarnens utbildningsmöjligheter i Sverige. Pohjola-Nordens språkpolitiska arbetsgrupp, Helsingfors.

Resolution on Migrants 1980, The NGO-Forum, International Conference for Women, Copenhagen.

RICHARDS, JACK C. (ed.) 1974, *Error Analysis: Perspectives on Second Language Acquisition.* Longman Group Ltd, London.

RIECK, BERT-OLAF & SENFT, INGEBORG 1978, Situation of Foreign Workers in the Federal Republic of German. In DITTMAR, HABERLAND, SKUTNABB-KANGAS & TELEMAN (eds) 1978, 85–98.

RIEGEL, K. 1968, Some theoretical considerations of bilingual duplication. *Psychological Bulletin* 70, 647–670.

RIGG, M. 1928, Some Further Data on the Language Handicap. *Journal of Educational Psychology* 19, 252–256.

RINGBOM, HÅKAN 1962, Tvåspråkigheten som forskningsobjekt. *Finsk Tidskrift* 6.

RINGEN, ANDERS (ed.) 1980, *Migration to and within the Nordic Countries.* Report from the Vth Nordic Conference on Labour Migration Research, Nordic Council of Ministers and Institute of Applied Social Research, Oslo.

RIST, RAY C. 1979, On the Education of Guest-Worker Children in Germany: A Comparative Study of Policies and Programs in Bavaria and Berlin. *School Review* 87, 3, May 1979, 242–268.

RIVERS, WILGA 1969. Commentary on R. M. Jones' paper. In KELLY (ed.) 1969, 35–40.

– 1975, Motivation in Bilingual Programs. In TROIKE & MODIANO (eds) 1975, 112–122.

ROBERTS, MURAT H. 1939, The Problem of the Hybrid Language. *Journal of English and Germanic Philology* 38, 23–41.

RODNEY, WALTER 1973, *How Europe underdeveloped Africa.* Bogle l'ouverture, London.

ROESSEL, ROBERT 1970. They Came Here First. In Alatis (ed.) 1970, 121–127.

ROGERS, CARL R. 1967, The Facilitation of Significant Learning. In SIEGEL (ed.) 1967, 37–54.

RONJAT, JULES 1913. *Le développement du langage observé chez un enfant bilingue.* Paris.

ROSENTHAL, R. & JACOBSON, L. 1968a, *Pygmalion in the Classroom: Teacher Expectation and Pupil's Intellectual Development.* Holt, Rinehard & Winston,

New York.
- 1968b, Self-Fulfilling Prophecies in the Classroom: Teachers' Expectation as
   Unintended Determinants of Pupils' Intellectual Competence. In DEUTSCH, KATZ
   & JENSEN 1968.
Royal Commission on Bilingualism and Bilculturalism 1965, A Preliminary Report.
   Ottawa.
RSKL 1978, *Ruotsin Suomalaisseurojen Keskusliitto*. Resolution, Stockholm, July
   1978.
RUBIN, JOAN 1970, Bilingual Usage in Paraguay. In FISHMAN (ed.) 1970a, 512–530.
- 1972, Evaluation and Language Planning. In FISHMAN (ed.) 1972a, 476–510.
RUBIN, JOAN & JERNUDD, BJÖRN (eds) 1971, *Can Language Be Planned?* The
   East–West Center, Honolulu.
RUBIN, JOAN & SHUY, ROGER (eds) 1973, *Language Planning, Current Issues and
   Research*, Washington, D.C.
RŪĶE-DRAVIŅA, VELTA 1965, The Process of Acquisition of Apical /r/ and Uvular
   /R/ in the Speech of Children. *Linguistics* 17, 56–68.
- 1967, *Mehrsprachigkeit im Vorschulalter*. Travaux de l'institut de phonétique de
   Lund publiés par Bertil Malmberg, Gleerup, Lund.
RUOPPILA, ISTO 1973, *Vieraskielisen varhaiskasvatuksen vaikutuksista lapsen
   kehitykseen*. Reports from the Dept of Psychology no 147, University of
   Jyväskylä.
- 1977, *Lasten kielellisestä kehityksestä, Kieliohjelmaseminaari*. Raportti kielioh-
   jelmakomitean asiantuntijaseminaarista 3–4.9.1977, AFinLA, Ingegerd Nyström, Helsinki, 20–42.
RUOTSIN SUOMALAINEN, Stockholm.
RYALL, ROBERT 1979, Kontaktmønster blant gjestarbeiderne. In TAMBS-LYCHE
   (ed.) 1979, 65–71.
- 1980, Klikkene i den multinationale kortsiktige kontraktarbeidarstikken:
   Redskapene for å overleve i oljeenterprise. In RINGEN (ed.) 1980, 289–306.
RYEN, ELSE (ed.) 1976a, *Språk och kjønn*. Forlaget Novus, Oslo.
- 1976b, Innledning. In RYEN (ed.) 1976a, 9–20.

SAEGERT, J., OBERMEYER, J. & KAZARIAN, S. 1973, Organizational Factors in Free
   Recall of Bilingually Mixed Lists. *Journal of Experimental Psychology* 97,
   397–399.
SAER, D. J. 1922, An Inquiry into the Effect of Bilingualism upon the Intelligence of
   Young Children. *Journal of Experimental Pedagogy* 6, 232–240 and 266–274.
- 1923, The Effects of Bilingualism on Intelligence. *British Journal of Psychology*
   14, 25–38.
SAHLMAN-KARLSSON, SIIRI 1974, *Finska studenter i Umeå. Språkfärdighet och
   skolframgång*. Research Reports from the Dept of Sociology, University of Umeå.
SAHLSTRÖM, ANNA-LISA 1977, *Fem goda år. Historien om vad de räknat med att ta ur
   kvinnorna vid banden*. Skrivor, Vasa.
SAINT-JACQUES, BERNARD 1978, Elicitation of Cultural Stereotypes through the
   Presentation of Voices in Two Languages. In PARADIS (ed.) 1978, 179–184.
SALMINEN, JAAKKO 1977, *Breuer-Weuffenin erottelukokeen standardointi
   Suomessa*. University of Joensuu, manuscript.
Samerna i Sverige. Stöd åt språk och kultur 1975. Betänkande av sameutredningen,
   Statens offentliga utredningar 1975: 99.

Samerna i Sverige. Stöd åt språk och kultur, bilagor 1975. Betänkande av Sameutredningen. Statens offentliga utredningar 1975: 100.

SANCHEZ, GEORGE I. 1932, Scores of Spanish-speaking Children on Repeated Tests. *Pedagogical Seminary and Journal of Genetic Psychology* 40, 223–231.

SANDLUND, TOM 1970, *Språk och gruppidentifikation i Pargas, Lovisa och Gamlakarleby.* Svenska Litteratursällskapets i Finland Nämnd för samhällsforskning, Forskningsrapport no 8, Åbo.

– 1971. *Finlandssvenska attityder. Optimism, resignation och pessimism.* Svenska Litteratursällskapets i Finland Nämnd för samhällsforskning, Forskningsrapport no 13, Åbo.

– 1972, Språkgruppsidentifikation och språkbruk i Finland. In LOMAN 1972a, 113–143.

– 1976, *Social Classes, Ethnic Groups and Capitalist Development – An Outline of a Theory.* Svenska Litteratursällskapet i Finland, Åbo.

SANDLUND, TOM & SUNDÉN, GUNVEIG 1975, *Arbetarna hos Algots i Närpes – infödda, inflyttare och pendlare,* Svenska Litteratursällskapets i Finland Nämnd för samhällsforskning, Forskningsrapporter 21, Åbo.

SANKOFF, DAVID & POPLACK, SHANA 1980, A Formal Grammar for Code-switching. *Centro de Estudios Puertorriqueños, Working Papers* 8. New York.

SAPIR, EDWARD 1921, *Language. An Introduction to the Study of Speech.* Harcourt, Brace & World, Inc, New York.

SAUNDERS, GEORGE 1982, *Bilingual Children: Guidance for the family,* Multilingual Matters 3, Clevedon.

DE SAUSSURE, FERDINAND 1959 (1916), *Course in General Linguistics.* Philosophical Library, New York.

SAVELA, VEIKKO 1974, *Lapsen kulutus- ja koulutuskustannukset,* Siirtolaisuustutkimuksia 6, Työvoimaministeriö, Suunnitteluosasto, Helsinki.

SAVILLE-TROIKE MURIEL 1973, *Bilingual Children: A Resource Document. Papers in Applied Linguistics.* Bilingual Education Series: 2, Center for Applied Linguistics, Arlington, Virginia.

SCB – see Statistiska Centralbyrån.

ŠČERBA, LEV, V. 1926, Sur la notion de mélange des langues. *Jafetičeskij sbornik* IV, 1–19 (quoted in WEINREICH 1967).

– 1945, *Ocerednyje problemy jazykovedenija.* U.S.S.R. Academy of Sciences, Izvestija, Section of Literature and Language IV (5), 173–186 (quoted in Weinreich 1967).

SCHALIN, WILHELM 1975, Verkligheten bakom paragraferna. In SKUTNABB-KANGAS 1975e, 51–58.

SCHMIDT-MACKEY, ILONKA 1977, Language Strategies of the Bilingual Family. In MACKEY & ANDERSON (eds) 1977, 132–146.

SCHMITT, GUIDO 1981, Ausländische Schüler in deutschen Klassen, in Die Unterrichtspraxis. *Beilage zur Lehrerleitung Baden-Württemberg.* 14:3, 17–22.

Schooling and Language Minority Students: A Theoretical Framework, 1981, Office of Bilingual Bicultural Education, Department of Education, Sacramento, California.

SCHUMANN, JOHN H. 1974, The Implications of Pidginization and Creolization of the Study of Adult Second Language Acquisition. *TESOL Quarterly* 8, 145–152.

– 1975, Affective Factors and the Problem of Age in Second Language Acquisition. *Language Learning* 25, 209–235.

SCHWARZ, DAVID (ed.) 1971, *Identitet och minoritet. Teori och praktik i dagens Sverige*. Almqvist & Wiksell, Stockholm.
- 1973, *Invandrar- och minoritetsforskning m m. En bibliografi*. Botkyrkaprojektet, Dept. of Sociology, University of Stockholm.
- 1976, *Invandrar- och minoritetsfrågor, nordisk bibliografi*. Dept. of Sociology, University of Stockholm.
SCOTT, S. 1973. *The Relation of Divergent Thinking to Bilingualism: Cause and Effects*. McGill University (quoted in ALBERT & OBLER 1978).
SEGALOWITZ, NORMAN 1976, Communicative incompetence and the non-fluent bilingual. *Canadian Journal of Behavioural Science*, 8, 122–131.
- 1977, Psychological Perspectives on Bilingual Education. In SPOLSKY & COOPER (eds) 1977, 119–158.
SEGALOWITZ, NORMAN & GATBONTON, ELIZABETH 1977, Studies of the Nonfluent Bilingual. In HORNBY (ed.) 1977, 77–89.
SEGALOWITZ, NORMAN & LAMBERT, WALLACE E. 1969, Semantic Generalization in Bilinguals. *Journal of Verbal Learning and Verbal Behavior* 8, 559–566.
SEIDL, J. C. 1937, *The Effect of Bilingualism on the Measurement of Intelligence*. Ph.D. Thesis, Fordham University, New York.
SELINKER, LARRY 1972, Interlanguage. *IRAL* 10, 219–231.
SENG, MARK W. 1970, The Linguistically Different: Learning Theories and Intellectual Development. In HORN (ed.) 1970, 99–114.
SEVILLA-CASAS, E. *et al.* 1973, *Addenda of Chicanos and Boricuas to Declaration of Chicago*. Paper prepared for the 9th International Congress of Anthropological and Ethnological Sciences (quoted in PAULSTON 1976).
SHAKESPEARE, WILLIAM, *Richard II.*
SHAPSON, STAN & KAUFMAN, DAVID 1976, French Immersion: A Western Perspective. *Canadian Society for the Study of Education*, Yearbook Vol. 3, 1976, 8–26.
SHIBUTANI, T. & KWAN, K. M. 1965, *Ethnic Stratification*, The Macmillan Company.
SHOTWELL, A. A. 1945, Arthur Performance Ratings of Mexican and American High-grade Mental Defectives. *American Journal of Mental Def.* 49, 1945, 445–449.
SIDDIQI, NAJMA 1980, Isolation of Migrant Women: Tradition of Racism? In RINGEN (ed.) 1980, 367–384.
SIEGEL, LAURENCE (ed.) 1967, *Instruction. Some Contemporary Viewpoints*. Chandler Publications in Educational Psychology, San Francisco, Cal.
DA SILVA, GUILEM RODRIGUES 1978, *Jag söker gryningen*. Bo Cavefors Bokförlag, Lund.
SIMON, GERD (ed.) 1979, *Sprachwissenschaft und politisches Engagement. Zur Problem- und Sozialgeschichte einiger sprach-theoretischer, sprachdidaktischer und sprachpflegerischer Ansätze in der Germanistik des 19. und 20. Jahrhunderts*. Beltz Verlag, Weinheim und Basel.
SINCLAIR, J. MCH. & COULTHARD, R. M. 1975, *Towards an Analysis of Discourse*. Oxford University Press, London.
SIV – see Statens Invandrarverk.
SIVANANDAN, A. 1982, A Different Hunger. *Writings on Black Resistance*, Pluto Press, London.
SKINNER, B. F. 1957, *Verbal Behavior*. Appleton–Century–Crofts, New York.
Skolen hvor det er normalt at være anderledes. Om Bjørns internationale skole 1980 Hellerup, duplicated copy.

SKUTNABB, AXEL 1905, Mustalaislähetys. *Armon Sanomat* 1905, 168–170.
SKUTNABB-KANGAS, TOVE 1972a, Om forskningen kring tvåspråkighet och skolframgång. *Folkmålsstudier* XXII, Meddelanden från Föreningen för nordisk filologi, Helsingfors, 83–97.
– 1972b, Forskning, idéer och debatt om tvåspråkighet och barnens skolspråk. In LOMAN 1972, 135–152.
– 1972c, Kaksikielisyyden kuvaamisesta ja mittauksesta. *Virittäjä* 3, 355–356.
– 1973, *Föreläsningar vid Institutionen för nordisk filogi.* University of Helsinki.
– 1975a. *Om tvåspråkighet och skolframgång.* Svenska Litteratursällskapets i Finland Nämnd för samhällsforskning, Forskningsrapport no 20, Åbo.
– 1975b, Vad är halvspråkighet? *Invandrare och Minoriteter* 1, 1975.
– 1975c, Tvåspråkighet eller halvspråkighet – vem utgör normen? In HOVDHAUGEN (ed.) 1975, 346–364.
– 1975d, Modersmål – tvåspråkighet – halvspråkighet. In SKUTNABB-KANGAS (ed.) 1975e, 31–37.
– (ed.) 1975e, *Grannspråk och minoritetsspråk i Norden.* Nordisk utredningsserie 1975:32.
– 1975f, Om tvåspråkighet. In Ahlgren (ed.) 1975, 31–37.
– 1975g, *Om tvåspråkighet och skolframgång hos en grupp yrkesskolelever.* Dept. of Nordic Languages, University of Helsinki, Licentiate thesis, part 1.
– 1975h, Bilingualism, Semilingualism and School Achievement – bilinguisme, semilinguisme et resultats scolaires. *Collection Centre Mondial d'information sur l'education bilingue* 6, Paris.
– 1975i, Review of Språk och samhälle 2, ed. Bengt Loman. *Invandrare och Minoriteter* 2, 1975.
– 1975j, *Tvåspråkighet som mål i invandrarundervisningen.* Lärarhögskolan i Linköping, Fortbildningsavdelningen, Dokumentationsserie, no 1.
– 1975k, Om finnarnas svårigheter i att förstå danska. *Sprog i Norden, Årsskrift for de nordiske sprogncevn,* 68–74.
– 1976a, see S-K & Badersten.
– 1976b, *Två språk i familjen – Kaksi kieltä perheessä.* Folkhälsan, Helsingfors.
– 1976c, Bilingualism, Semilingualism and School Achievement. *Linguistische Berichte* 45, 55–64.
– 1976d, Halvspråkighet: ett medel att få invandrarnas barn till löpande bandet? *Invandrare och Minoriteter* 3–4, 1976.
– 1976e, Are the Finns in Northern Sweden Semilingual? *International Journal of the Sociology of Language* 10, 1977, 144–145.
– (ed.) 1977a, *Papers from the First Scandinavian Conference on Bilingualism,* Dept. of Nordic Languages, Univ. of Helsinki, series B. No 2.
– 1977b, *Kielenopiskelusta vieraana kielenä vai vieraalla kielellä.* Kieliohjelmaseminaari. Raportti kieliohjemakomitean asiantuntijaseminaarista 3–4 10, 1977, toim AFinLA, Ingegerd Nyström, Helsinki, 64–95.
– 1977c, Paneldiskussion om dubbel halvspråkighet. In SKUTNABB-KANGAS 1977a, 212–214.
– 1978a, Vems språk talar du? *Folktidningen Ny Tid,* 1978–79.
– 1978b, Folkräkningen och de tvåspråkiga. *Hufvudstadsbladet,* 16.5.1978.
– 1978c, Något om modersmålsinlärningen. *Invandrarbulletinen,* LO, 3, 16–21.
– 1978d, Något om finlandssvenskarna och tvåspråkigheten. In LAURÉN (ed.) 1978, 107–123.

- 1978e, Semilingualism and the Education of Migrant Children as a Means of Reproducing the Caste of Assembly Line Workers. In DITTMAR, HABERLAND, SKUTNABB-KANGAS & TELEMAN (eds) 1978, 221–252.
- 1979a, *Vad vet vi om den andra generationen? Erfarenheter från förskolan och skolan*, Paper presented at a symposium on Second Generation Finnish Immigrants, Hanaholmen (Finland), 1979.
- 1979b, Invandrarbarnens utbildning – forskning och politik. In *Papers from the Second Nordic Conference on Bilingualism*. Akademilitteratur, Stockholm, 158–178.
- 1979c, *Bilingualism as an Unrealistic Goal in Minority Education*, in MUNICIO (ed.) 1981a.
- 1980a, Forskare som tyckare. *Invandrare och Minoriteter* 3, 9–12.
- 1980b, Tvåspråkighet och svensk språkpolitik, in HAMBERG & HAMMAR (eds) 1981, 146–169.
- 1980c, *Guest Worker or Immigrant – Different Ways of Reproducing an Underclass*. ROLIG-papir 21, Roskilde Universtetscenter, Lingvistgruppen, 4–39.
- 1980d, Tvåspråkighet och skolframgång. In KREITOR (ed.) 1980, 72–92.
- 1980e, Om tvåspråkighet och halvspråkighet – tankar kring Antti och andra invandrarbarn. *Finsk i Sverige – Ruotsinsuomalaisuus*. Utbildningsradion, Stockholm, 7–12.
- 1980f, *Violence as Method and Outcome in the Non-education of Minority Children*, ROLIG-papir 21, Roskilde Universitetscenter, Lingvistgruppen, 40–52.
- 1981a, Lundamodellens slutfacit: värdelös forskningsrapport, *Invandrare och minoriteter* 2, 1981, 14–18.
- 1981b, Löfgren och Ouvinen-Birgerstam undviker att svara på mina frågor, *Invandrare och Minoriteter* 4, 1981, 15–16.
- 1982a, Om metodologier, paradigm och ideologier i minoritetsutbildningsforskningen, in PEURA (ed.), 1983.
- 1982b, Research and its implications for the Swedish setting – an immigrant point of view, in HUSÉN, T. & OPPER (eds) *Multicultural and Multilingual Education in Immigrant Countries*, Wenner-Gren Symposium, Pergamon Press Ltd.
- 1982c, Arguments for teaching and consequences of not teaching minority children through the medium of their mother tongue, or: rise and decline of the "typical" migrant child, in BAETELAAN, PIETER (ed.) *The practice of intercultural education*, The Netherlands (in press).
- 1983a, *All children in the Nordic countries should be bilingual – why aren't they?* Paper presented at the Second International Conference on Minority Languages, Turku/Åbo, Finland, 6–12.6.1983.
- 1983b, Children of guest workers and immigrants – linguistic and educational issues, in EDWARDS, John (ed.) *Bilingualism, Pluralism and Language Planning Policies*, Academic Press, London, Applied Language Studies Series (in press).
SKUTNABB-KANGAS, TOVE & BADERSTEN, LENNART 1977, Tvåspråkighet och språkkontakt. In Pettersson & Badersten (ed.) 1977, 237–247.
SKUTNABB-KANGAS, TOVE & RAHBEK PEDERSEN, BIRGITTE 1981, *Invandrerbørnenes uddannelsessituation i Danmark –hvad ved vi, hvad ved vi ikke, hvad siger udenlandske erfaringer, og hvad skal vi gøre*. Danmarks Lærerhøjskole & Roskilde Universitetscenter.

SKUTNABB-KANGAS, TOVE & REKDAL, OLAUG, 1977a, (edited with a hug) *Vardagsskrift = Arkikirja = Hverdagsskrift til Jan och Jens i anledning det året dom närmade sig 31 og till alle dere andre som tycker om vardagsuppmuntran.* Dept. of Nordic Languages, University of Uppsala.
– 1977b,Varför vardagsskrift? In SKUTNABB-KANGAS & REKDAL, 1977a.
– 1978. Könsroller i språk. Synpunkter på projektets uppläggning. In *Könsroller i språk 2. Uppslag, synpunkter och några resultat.* Rapport nr 61 från Forskningskommittén i Uppsala för modern svenska (FUMS), 77–87.
SKUTNABB-KANGAS, TOVE & TOUKOMAA, PERTTI 1976, *Teaching Migrant Children's Mother Tongue and Learning the Language of the Host Country in the Context of the Socio-cultural Situation of the Migrant Family.* A report prepared for Unesco, Dept of Sociology and Social Psychology, University of Tampere, Research Reports 15. Tampere.
– 1977, Om halvspråkighet: Vi måste skrika högre och forska vidare. *Invandrare och Minoriteter 5,* 1977
– 1979, Semilingualism and Middle Class Bias: A reply to Cora Brent-Palmer, *Working Papers on Bilingualism* 19, 181–196.
SMITH, DAVID, 1977, *Racial Disadvantage in Britain. The PEP Report.* Penguin Books Ltd, Harmondsworth, Middlesex.
SMITH, M. E. 1935, A study of the speech of eight bilingual children of the same family, *Child Development* 6, 19–25.
SÖ 1981, *Compulsory school leavers in 1979 with home languages other than Swedish,* Interim Report 1, Stockholm.
SÖ September 1982, *Redogörelse för tre års försöksverksamhet med jämkade timplaner på grundskolans låg- och mellanstadier för hemspråksundervisning samt förslag till åtgärder,* Skolöverstyrelsen (Swedish National Board of Education), Stockholm.
SÖDERBERGH, RAGNHILD 1978, *Barnets tidiga språkutveckling.* Liber Läromedel, Lund.
SOMBY-SANDVIK, LAILA, 1977, Barnehagevirksomhet i samiske områder. In *Barnehagen og nærmiljøet,* Nærmiljø Barnehage Prosjektet, Rapport no 1, Hamar, 63–72.
SOMMER, B. 1979, *Directions in Aboriginal Bilingual Education in the Northern Territory of Australia.* Paper presented at the SEAMEO Regional Language Centre 14th Regional Seminar, Singapore, 1979.
SOU 1970:44. Språkundersökning bland finländska barn och ungdomar i Sverige. Rapport av finsk-svenska utbildningsrådet, Stockholm.
SOU 1971:51 – see Invandrarutredningen.
SOU 1972:83 – see Invandrarutredningen.
SOU 1974:69 – see Invandrarutredningen.
SOU 1974:70 – see Invandrarutredningen.
SPENDER, DALE 1980, *Man made language,* Routledge & Kegan Paul, Boston.
SPIEGEL, TITEL 1980. "Raus mit dem Volk", Bomben und Hetzparolen – in der Bundesrepublik wächst der Hass gegen die Ausländer. *Der Spiegel* 38, 15.9.1980, 19–26.
SPIESS, U. 1979, Problemwandel in der Ausländerpolitik: Zur Entwicklung der ausländischen Bevölkerung in Berlin (West) 1972–78, *Deutsch Lernen* 2, 43–66.
SPILKA, IRENE 1976, Assessment of Second-Language Performance in Immersion Programs. *Canadian Modern Language Review* 32:5, 543–561.
SPOLSKY, BERNARD 1976, Language Testing: Art or Science. In NICKEL (ed.) 1976,

9–28.

SPOLSKY, BERNARD & COOPER, ROBERT (eds) 1977, *Frontiers of Bilingual Education.* Newbury House Publishers, Rowley, Mass.

– (eds) 1978, *Case Studies in Bilingual Education.* Newbury House Publishers, Rowley, Mass.

Språkskyddskommitténs betänkande 1971. *Kommittébetänkande 1971: B 13.* Helsingfors.

STANLEY, MALCOLM H. 1974, French Immersion Programs: The Experience of the Protestant School Board of Greater Montreal. *Canadian Modern Language Review* 31:2, 152–160.

Statens Invandrarverk, *Dokumentation* 1977–.

Statens Invandrarverk, *Statistik om invandring och invandrare* 1980. Norrköping.

Statistiska Centralbyrån, *Invandrarnas levnadsförhållanden 1975.* Rapport 9, 1978. SO, Stockholm.

Statistiska Centralbyrån, Grundskolan och gymnasieskolan 1981/1982, Elever med annat hemspråk än svenska hösten 1981. U 1982: 17, Stockholm.

– *Pressmeddelanden.*

– *Statistiska meddelanden.*

ST. CLAIR, ROBERT N. & EISEMAN, JAMES 1978, *The politics of teaching English as a foreign language.* Paper presented at the 9th World Congress of Sociology, Uppsala, 1978.

STEDJE, ASTRID & AF TRAMPE, PETER (ed.) 1978, *Tvåspråkighet.* Akademilitteratur. Stockholm.

STERN, H. H. 1976 (1975), Optimal Age: Myth or Reality? *Canadian Modern Language Review* 32:3. 283–294.

STEWARD, WILLIAM A. 1970, A Sociolinguistic Typology for Describing National Multilingualism. In FISHMAN (ed.) 1970a, 531–545.

STOCKFELT-HOATSON, BRITT-INGRID 1978, *Training of Immigrant Children in Pre-school in Norrköping.* Linköping University Dept of Education, Linköping Studies in Education, Dissertations, No 8.

STOLT, BIRGIT 1975a, Om "halvspråkighet" och "språkens känslofunktion". Ett diskussionsinlägg. *Invandrare och Minoriteter* 2, 1975, 5–12.

– 1975b, Halvspråkighet och känslor – en replik. *Invandrare och Minoriteter* 4, 1975, 24–26.

STÖLTING, WILFRIED, 1978, Teaching German to Immigrant Children. In DITTMAR, HABERLAND, SKUTNABB-KANGAS & TELEMAN (eds) 1978, 99–110.

STONE, MAUREEN 1981, The Education of the Black Child in Britain. *The Myth of Multiracial Education*, Fontana Paperbacks.

Svensk invandrarpolitik inför 1980-talet 1979. Rapport från invandrarrådets rådslag den 15–17 juni 1979, Arbetsmarknadsdepartementet, DsA 1979:6, Liber Förlag.

Svenskt i Finland 1973, (ed.) Svenska Finlands Folkting. Helsingfors.

SWAIN, MERRILL 1974, French Immersion Programs across Canada: Research Findings. *Canadian Modern Language Review* 31, 1974, 116–129.

– 1976a, Bibliography: Research on Immersion Education for the Majority Child. *Canadian Modern Language Review* 32, 592–596.

– 1976b, English-Speaking Child + Early French Immersion =Bilingual Child? *Canadian Modern Language Review* 33:2, 180–187.

– 1978, *Immersion Education for the Majority Language Child.* Paper presented at the Round Table Discussion "Bilingual Education", 5th International Congress of Applied Linguistics, Montreal, 1978.

– 1979, *Bilingual education for the English-Canadian.* Paper presented at SEAMEO Regional Language Centre 14th Regional Seminar, Singapore, 1979.

SWAIN, MERRILL & BARIK, HENRI 1978, Bilingual Education in Canada: French and English. In SPOLSKY & COOPER (eds) 1978, 22–71.

SWAIN, MERRILL & BRUCK, MAGGIE 1976, Research Conference on Immersion Education for the Majority Child: Introduction. *Canadian Modern Language Review* 32:5, 490–493.

SWAIN, MERRILL & BURNABY, B. 1976, Personality Characteristics and Second Language Learning in Young Children: A Pilot Study. *Working Papers on Bilingualism* 11, 115–128.

SWAIN, MERRILL & CUMMINS, JAMES 1979, Bilingualism, Cognitive Functioning and Education. *Language Teaching & Linguistics: Abstracts* 12, 4–18.

SWAIN, MERRILL & LAPKIN, SHARON 1981, *Bilingual Education in Ontario: A Decade of Research.* Ministry of Education & Ministry on Colleges and Universities, Toronto.

– 1982, *Evaluating Bilingual Education: A Canadian Case Study,* Multilingual Matters 2, Clevedon.

SWAIN, MERRILL, LAPKIN, S. & BARIK, H. C. 1976, The Cloze Test as a Measure of Second Language Proficiency for Young Children. *Working Papers on Bilingualism,* 11, 32–42.

SWAPO 1982, *Preliminary Perspectives into Emergent Educational System for NAMIBIA,* Department of Education and Culture, Swapo of Namibia, May 1982.

SWEET, ROBERT J. 1974, The Pilot Immersion Program at Allenby Public School Toronto. *Canadian Modern Language Review* 31:2, 161–168.

SWETLAND, CAROLYN 1979 (1977), *The Ghetto of the Soul.* Unesco, Paris.

VON SYDOW, GERT 1980, Finsk elev i svensk skola. *Läkartidningen* 67:16, 1797–1800.

TABOURET-KELLER, A. 1962, L'acquisition du langage parlé chez un petit enfant en milieu bilingue. *Problèmes de psycholinguistique* 8, 205–219.

TAKAČ, MIRKO 1974, *Tvåspråkighet hos invandrarelever – del I. Emotionella och sociala effekter. Pedagogiska angreppssätt.* Report from Invandrarprojektet, Skolpsykologbyrån, Göteborgs skolförvaltning.

– 1978, *Skolelevers attityder till utlänningar och svenskar – en deskriptiv studie av attityder hos grundskoleelever i några invandrartäta områden i Göteborg.* Report from Invandrarprojektet, Skolspykologbyrån, Göteborgs skolförvaltning.

TAMBS-LYCHE, HARALD (ed.) 1979, *Hushold, bolig, og kontaktmønster bland innvandrerne.* Report no. 1 from Fremmedarbeiderprosjektet, Dept. of Social Anthropology, University of Bergen.

TARONE, ELAINE 1979a, *Future Directions in Research on Communication Strategies.* Paper presented at the First Nordic Interlanguage Symposium, Hanaholmen, 1979.

– 1979b, Some thoughts on the Notion of "Communication Strategy". Paper presented at TESOL Summer Institute.

TAVRIS, CAROL & OFFIR, CAROLE 1977, *The Longest War. Sex Differences in Perspective.* Harcourt Brace Jovanovich, Inc, New York.

TELEMAN, ULF 1973, Hur mycket står det i texten? In HUMMELSTEDT (ed.) 1973.

– 1974, *Manual för grammatisk beskrivning av talad och skriven svenska.* Lundastudier i nordisk språkvetenskap. Studentlitteratur, Lund.

- 1977a, Samspråk på grannspråk. In ELERT, ELIASSON, FRIES & URELAND (eds) 1977, 234–243.
- 1977b, De skapliga. En självkritisk berättelse av en samtida lingvist. In SKUTNABB-KANGAS & REKDAL (ed.) 1977a.
- 1979, *Språkrätt. Om skolans språknormer och samhällets*. LiberLäromedel, Lund.
- 1980, Om den dansk-svenska hörförståelsens betingelser. *Nysvenska studier* 59–60, 268–280.

TERENTIEVA, L. N. 1981, Ethnocultural Changes among the Peoples of the Volga, Urals and Far North of Europe, in GRIGULEVICH & KOZLOV (eds), 107–132.

TERRELL, TRACY D. 1981, The Natural Approach in Bilingual Education in Schooling and Language Minority Students 1981, 117–146.

THELANDER, MATS 1974, *Grepp och begrepp i språksociologin. Ord och stil.* Språkvårdssamfundets skrifter, Studentlitteratur, Lund.

THONIS, ELEANOR, W. 1981, Reading Instruction for Language Minority Students, in schooling and Language Minority students 1981, 147–81.

THORNE, BARRIE & HENLEY, NANCY (eds) 1975, *Language and Sex. Difference and Dominance.* Series in Sociolinguistics. Newbury House, Rowley, Mass.

TIERNEY, JOHN (ed.) 1982, *Race, Migration and Schooling*, Holt Saunders, London.

TINGBJÖRN, GUNNAR 1979, *Immigrant Children and Bilingualism*, in MUNICIO (ed.) 1981a, 105–128.
- 1981, Immigrant Children and Bilingualism, In MUNICIO (ed.) 1981a, 105–128.
- 1982a, *Klassrumsstudier*, University of Gothenburg, SPRINS Project 13.
- 1982b, *Sammanställning och förslag*, University of Gothenburg, SPRINS Project 14.

TINGBJÖRN, GUNNAR & ANDERSSON, ANDERS-BÖRJE 1978, The Linguistic Development of Immigrant Children in Sweden, in DITTMAR, HABERLAND, SKUTNABB-KANGAS & TELEMAN (eds) 1978, 259–265.

TÖK/YD (Konfederation der Studenten aus der Türkei im Ausland) (no date), *Das wahre Gesicht der Türkei.* TÖK/YD Verlag Nr 1.

TOMB, J. W. 1925, On the Intuitive Capacity for Children to Understand Spoken Languages. *British Journal of Psychology* 16:52.

TÖRNUDD, KLAUS 1978, *Svenska språkets ställning i Finland.* Holger Schildts förlag, Helsingfors, 3rd rev. ed.

TORRANCE, E. P., GOWAN, J. C., WU, J. M. & ALIOTTI, N. C. 1970, Creative Functioning of Monolingual and Bilingual Children in Singapore. *Journal of Educational Psychology* 61, 72–75.

TOSI, ARTURO 1979, Mother Tongue Teaching for the Children of Migrants. *Language Teaching & Linguistics: Abstracts* 12, 213–231.

TOUKOMAA, PERTTI 1972a, Två invandrarinlägg, Sydsvenska Dagbladet 4.41972.
- 1972b, *Om finska invandrarelevernas utvecklingsförhållanden i den svenska skolan.* University of Uleåborg.
- 1973a, Ruotsin suomalaislasten kielellisestä kehityksestä. *Kasvatus* 1, 40–44.
- 1973b, Korutonta kertomaa. Suomalaisperheet ruotsalaisessa teollisuusyhteiskunnassa. *Tampereen Yliopiston sosiologian ja sosiaalipsykologian laitoksen tutkimuksia 1.*
- 1975a, Om finska invandrarelevs spåkutveckling och skolframgång i den svenska grundskolan. *Invandrare och minoriteter* 2, 1975, 4–6.
- 1975b, Om svårigheten att definiera halvspråkighet. *Invandrare och Minoriteter 3,* 1975, 14.

– 1975c, Siirtolaisoppilaan kielitaito ja koulumenestys. *Työvoimaministeriö, Suunnitteluosasto, Siirtolaisuustutkimuksia* 10.

– 1977a, *Om finska invandrarelevers språkutveckling och skolframgång i den svenska grundskolan.* Expertgruppen för invandringsforskning. Rapport no 2, Stockholm (also published in March 1976 by the Dept. of Education, University of Joensuu.

– 1977b, Vieraskielisen ympäristön vaikutus kognitiiviseen kehitykseen. *Psykologia* 12:1–2, 85–91.

– 1980, Education Through the Medium of the Mother Tongue of Finnish Immigrant Children in Sweden. *Bilingual Education, RELC Antology Series* No 7, Singapore, 136–161.

TOUKOMAA, PERTTI & KUUSELA, JORMA 1978, *Preliminära resultat av undersökningen om socioekologiska samband bakom invandrarbarnens utbildningsituation,* duplicated copy.

TOUKOMAA, PERTTI & LASONEN, KARI 1979, *On the Literacy of Finnish Immigrant Pupils in Sweden.* Research Reports no 86, Dept of Education, University of Jyväskylä.

TOUKOMAA, PERTTI & SEPPO, SIMO 1978, *Vocational Aspirations of Finnish Immigrant Youth in Sweden.* Research Reports no 2, Dept of Social Psychology, University of Helsinki.

TOUKOMAA, PERTTI & SKUTNABB-KANGAS, TOVE 1977, *The Intensive Teaching of the Mother Tongue to Migrant Children at Pre-school Age.* Research Reports no 26, Dept of Sociology and Social Psychology, University of Tampere.

TRANKELL, ARNE (ed.) 1971, *Fem IMFO-studier i invandrar- och minoritetsforskning.* IMFO-gruppen, Stockholm, 1971:3.

– 1973, *Kvarteret FLISAN. Om en kris och dess övervinnande i ett svenskt förortssamhälle.* P. A. Norstedt & Söners förlag, Stockholm.

– 1974, Svenskarnas fördomar mot invandrare. In *Invandrarutredningen* 4. 121–212.

TREISMAN, A. 1965, The Effects of Redundancy and Familiarity on Translation and Repeating Back a Foreign and a Native Language. *British Journal of Psychology*, 56, 369–379.

TRITES, R. & PRICE, M. 1976, *Learning Disabilities Found in Association with French Immersion Programming.* University of Toronto Press, Ottawa.

TROIKE, RUDOLPH C. 1979, *Research Findings Demonstrate the Effectiveness of Bilingual Education.* Paper presented at the NABE Meeting in Seattle, 1979.

TROIKE, RUDOLPH C. & MODIANO, NANCY (eds) 1975, *Proceedings of the First Inter-American Conference on Bilingual Education.* Center for Applied Linguistics, Arlington, Vir.

TSIAKALOS, GEORGIOS 1980, Report on work in progress the group *"Possibilities of developing the language of origin in different immigrant situations"* at the second Scandinavian-German Symposium on the Language of Immigrant Workers and their Children, West Berlin, Sept. 21–27, 1980.

– Forthcoming, in CUMMINS & SKUTNABB-KANGAS (eds).

TUCKER, G. RICHARD, 1974, Methods of Second Language Teaching. *Canadian Modern Language Review* 31:2, 102–107.

– 1976, Summary: Research Conference on Immersion Education for the Majority Child. *Canadian Modern Language Review* 32:5, 585–591.

– 1977, Keynote. The Linguistic Perspective. In *Bilingual Education: Current*

Perspectives. Vol. 2. *Linguistics.* Center for Applied Linguistics, 1–42.

TUCKER, G. RICHARD, HAMAYAN, ELSE & GENESEE, FRED H. 1976, Affective, Cognitive and Social Factors in Second Language Acquisition. *Canadian Modern Language Review* 32:3, 214–226.

TUCKER, G. RICHARD, LAMBERT, W. E. & D'ANGLEJAN, A. 1973, Are French Immersion Programs Suitable for Working Class Children? A Pilot Investigation. *Language Sciences* 25, April 1973, 19–26.

TUCKER, G. RICHARD, OTANES, FE T. & SIBAYAN, BONIFACIO, P. 1970, An Alternate Days Approach to Bilingual Education. In ALATIS (ed.) 1970, 281–299.

TULVIN, E. & COLOTLA, V. 1970, Free Recall of Trilingual Lists. *Cognitive Psychology* 1, 86–98.

Türkei Informationen 1979, Herausgeber FIDEF (Föderation der Arbeitervereine der Türkei in der BRD e.v.) Düsseldorf.

Tvåspråkighet 1979, Papers presented at the Second Nordic Symposium on Bilingualism – see Stedje & af Trampe.

TYLER, LEONA E. 1965, *The Psychology of Human Differences.* Appleton-Century-Crofts. New York, 3rd ed.

ULFVENS, HENRIK 1980, Myten om upprustningen. *Fredsposten* 2, 13–15.

ULLMAN, STEPHEN 1966, Semantic Universals. In GREENBERG (ed.) 1966, 217–263.

UNESCO 1953, *The use of Vernacular Languages in Education.* Paris.

United Nations Institute for Namibia 1981, Toward a Language Policy for Namibia. English as the Official Language: Perspectives and Strategies, *Namibia Studies Series* 4, Lusaka.

VILDOMEC, VEROBOJ 1963, *Multilingualism.* A. W. Sythoff, Leyden.

VITEN, GRO 1982, Vil ikke passifisere elever som forsvarer seg mot rasisme, Intervju med Sunil Loona, *Mot Rasisme* 2, Oslo.

VOLTERRA, V. & TAESCHNER, T. 1975, *The Acquisition and Development of Language of Bilingual Children.* Institute of Psychology, National Council of Research, Rome, December 1975.

VORIH, LILLIAN & ROSIER, PAUL 1978, Rock Point Community School: An Example of a Navajo-English Bilingual Elementary School Program. *TESOL Quarterly* 12:3, 263–269.

VYGOTSKY, LEV SEMENOVICH 1973 (1962), *Thought and Language.* The M.I.T. Press, Cambridge, Mass.

– 1975 (1935), *Multilingualism in children.* Translated by Metro Gulutsan and Irene Arki. Centre for East European and Soviet Studies. University of Alberta (quoted in CUMMINS 1977c).

WAGNER-GOUGH, J. 1978, Excerpts from Comparative Studies in Second Language Learning. In HATCH (ed.) 1978, 155–171.

WALLACE, ANTHONY 1961, Schools in Revolutionary and Conservative Societies. In GRUBER (ed.) 1961.

– 1966, Revitalization Movements. *American Anthropologist*, 59, 1966.

WANDE, ERLING 1977, Halvspråkighetsdebatten fortsätter: Hansegård är ensidig. *Invandrare och Minoriteter* 3–4, 1977, 44–51.

– 1980, Den svenska tvåspråkighetsdebatten under 1970-talet – en argumentationsanalys. In *Rapport från projektet Sverige. Multietniskt samhälle.* Faculty of Humanities, University of Uppsala, Supplement 3:23, 2 pages.

WATSON, PETER (ed.) 1973a, *Psychology and Race.* Penguin Education, Harmondsworth, Middlesex.

– 1973b, Race and Intelligence through the Looking Glass. In WATSON 1973a, 360–376.

– 1973c, Some Mechanics of Racial Etiquette. In WATSON 1973a, 267–285.

WECKMAN, SAGA 1980, *Mustalaisista.* The Conference for Special Education, Communication and Handicap, 4–8.8.1980, Helsinki.

WEIDACHER, ALOIS 1981, Ausländische Arbeiterfamilien. Kinder und Jugendliche. Situationsanalysen und Massnahmen, Verlag Deutsches Jugendinstitut, DJI Dokumentation, München.

WEINREICH, URIEL 1967 (1953). *Languages in Contact. Findings and Problems.* Mouton & Co, The Hague, 5th printing.

Weiterentwicklung der Ausländerpolitik 1980, Beschlüsse der Bundesregierung vom 19. März 1980. *Deutsch Lernen* 1, 65–79.

WEST, MICHAEL 1926, Bilingualism with special reference to Bengal. Calcutta, Bureau of Education, India, Occasional Reports 13.

WESTMAN BERG, KARIN 1979, *Gråt inte – forska!* Kvinnovetenskapliga studier samlade av Karin Westman Berg. Prisma, Stockholm.

WHITAKER, H. & WHITAKER, H. (eds) 1979, *Studies in Neurolinguistics 3.* Academic Press, New York.

WHORF, BENJAMIN LEE 1956, *Language, Thought and Reality: Selected Writings of Benjamin Lee Whorf,* ed. by J. B. Carroll. New York and Cambridge, Mass.

WIDGREN, JONAS 1975, *Migration to Western Europe: The Social Situation of Migrant Workers and Their Families.* UN/SOA/SEM/60/WP 2.

– 1980, *Svensk invandrarpolitik, En faktabok.* LiberLäromedel, Lund.

WIDMARK, GUN 1973, Språkförändring och socialgruppsbyte. In HUMMELSTEDT (ed.) 1973.

WILKINS, D. A. 1972, *Grammatical, Situational and National Syllabuses.* Paper presented at the 3rd International Conference of Applied Linguistics, Copenhagen, 1972.

WILLIS, PAUL 1977, *Learning to labour,* Saxon House, Westmead.

WILTON, FLORENCE 1974, Implications of a Second Language Program: The Coquitlam Experience. *Canadian Modern Language Review,* 31:2, 169–180.

WISEMAN, STEPHEN (ed.) 1973a (1967), *Intelligence and Ability. Selected Readings.* Penguin, Middlesex, 2nd ed.

– 1973b, Introduction. In WISEMAN (ed.) 1973, 9–18.

WISSLER, C. 1901, The Correlation of Mental and Physical Tests. *Psychological Mon. Sup.,* Vol. 3, 29 (quoted in BURT 1973a).

WODE, H. 1978, Developmental sequences in naturalistic L 2 acquisition. In HATCH (ed.) 1978, 101–117.

WOLD, ASTRI HEEN 1978, *Decoding Oral Language.* European Monographs in Social Psychology No 12. Academic Press, London.

WOLFF, H. 1959, Intelligibility and inter-ethnic attitudes. In HYMES (ed.) 1959.

WOLFGANG, A. (ed.) 1975, *Education of Immigrant Students.* Ontario Institute for Studies in Education, Toronto.

Womens Voice 1980, Women's magazine of the Socialist Workers Party, P.O. Box

82, London E2.

WREDE, GUNNEL 1971. *Språkfärdighetens struktur. En undersökning av finska skolbarns kunskaper i svenska.* Licentiate thesis in Psychology, Åbo Akademi.
– 1974, Skolspråket i Tornedalen – några synpunkter baserade på en undersökning av färdigheten i svenska. In LOMAN 1974a, 169–188.

YLETYINEN, RIITTA 1982, Sprachliche und kulturelle Minderheiten in den USA, Schweden und der Bundesrepublik Deutschland. *Ein minderheiten- und bildungspolitischer Vergleich,* Haag + Herchen Verlag, Frankfurt/Main.
YOSHIDA, M. 1978, The Acquisition of English Vocabulary by a Japanese-speaking Child. In HATCH (ed.) 1978, 91–100.
YOSHIOKA, J. G. 1929, A Study of Bilingualism, *Journal of Genetic Psychology* 36, 473–479.

ZHDANKO, T. A. 1981, National State Demarcation and the Ethnic Evolution of the Peoples of Central Asia, in GRIGULEVICH & KOZLOV (eds), 133–159.
ZIRKEL, PERRY ALAN 1972, *An Evaluation of the Effectiveness of Selected Experimental Bilingual Education Programs in Connecticut.* Connecticut Migratory Children's Program, University of Connecticut, Ph.D. Thesis.